CONSTRUCTIONS OF WIDOWHOOD
AND VIRGINITY IN THE MIDDLE AGES

THE NEW MIDDLE AGES

BONNIE WHEELER

Series Editor

The New Middle Ages presents transdisciplinary studies of medieval cultures. It includes both scholarly monographs and essay collections.

PUBLISHED BY ST. MARTIN'S PRESS:

Women in the Medieval Islamic World: Power, Patronage, and Piety
edited by Gavin R. G. Hambly

The Ethics of Nature in the Middle Ages: On Boccaccio's Poetaphysics
by Gregory B. Stone

Presence and Presentation: Women in the Chinese Literati Tradition
by Sherry J. Mou

The Lost Love Letters of Heloise and Abelard:
Perceptions of Dialogue in Twelfth-Century France
by Constant J. Mews

Understanding Scholastic Thought with Foucault
by Philipp W. Rosemann

For Her Good Estate: Elizabeth de Burgh (1295–1360)
by Frances Underhill

Constructions of Widowhood and Virginity in the Middle Ages
edited by Cindy L. Carlson and Angela Jane Weisl

CONSTRUCTIONS OF WIDOWHOOD AND VIRGINITY IN THE MIDDLE AGES

Edited by

Cindy L. Carlson and Angela Jane Weisl

St. Martin's Press
New York

ISBN 0-312-21136-8

Library of Congress Cataloging-in-Publication Data
Constructions of widowhood and virginity in the Middle Ages/edited
    by Cindy L. Carlson & Angela Jane Weisl.
        p.   cm.
    Includes bibliographical references (p.) and index.
    ISBN 0–312–21136–8
    1. Literature, Medieval—History and criticism.   2. Women and
literature—Europe—History—To 1500.   3. Virginity in literature.
4. Chastity in literature.   5. Widows in literature.   I. Carlson,
Cindy L., 1953-.   II. Weisl, Angela Jane, 1963-.
PN682.W6C66   1999
809'.93352042—dc21   99–27418
                                                                                                    CIP

Internal design and typesetting by Letra Libre

First edition: November 1999
10   9   8   7   6   5   4   3   2   1

CONTENTS

ACKNOWLEDGMENTS

A ll books are the products of more than their authors; edited collections are more so. And while it is less conventional for the editors of these collections to give thanks to the many people outside the table of contents who have provided help, support, and encouragement, we feel it necessary to express our gratitude to those without whom this work would never have been produced.

To the English Departments at Metropolitan State College and Seton Hall University who saw the value of this project and provided help in the guise of small stipends, course releases, and excused absences from meetings, we give no small thanks, with some additional to Acting Dean Jo Renee Formicola at Seton Hall who provided a necessary course reduction. Many colleagues have provided invaluable advice and suggestions about this project and its processes, and they, too, have been essential to the result. Special notice must go to Mary Balkun, Chrysanthy Grieco, and Kate McCoy for their willingness to listen and for providing a necessary cheering section.

Our research assistants—Justin Romano, who did vital legwork at the library, Robert Dakis, Melissa Filosa, and especially Marie Polito who provided endless and exceptional technological support—deserve boundless thanks. Their help in the preparation of this manuscript went far above and beyond what they expected when they signed on for this project. Thanks, too, must go to the staff of the Center for Academic Technology at Seton Hall, particularly to Paul Fisher and Brad Stoudt, who solved major computer problems with good humor.

We are indebted to Bonnie Wheeler, editor of the New Middle Ages series for her primary interest in this project, and to the editorial staff at St. Martin's Press, Michael Flamini, Elizabeth Paukstis, Mara Nelson, and Rick Delaney, whose understanding and assistance were legion.

Our contributors, who provided revisions at short notice, changed citation systems midstream, and generally met all our requests with good humor, must also receive our public thanks. It is their work that makes this volume what it is.

Finally, too, our great appreciation must be for our families who listened to ideas and complaints, never wavering in their support for this project. To them, we are profoundly grateful.

SERIES EDITOR'S FOREWORD

The *New Middle Ages* contributes to lively transdisciplinary conversations in medieval cultural studies through its scholarly monographs and essay collections. This series provides focused research in a contemporary idiom about specific but diverse practices, expressions, and ideologies in the Middle Ages; it aims especially to recuperate the histories of medieval women. *Constructions of Widowhood and Virginity in the Middle Ages,* edited by Cindy L. Carlson and Angela Jane Weisl, is the eleventh volume in this series. The scholars who have collaborated in this project have culled their perceptions from a range of often highly conventional historical, religious, and (mostly) literary texts as they focus on issues of freedom and constraint experienced by virgins and widows primarily in the later Middle Ages. Furthermore the chapters collectively interrogate the problematics of virginity and widowhood as social constructions that both serve and subvert the reigning order that was deeply invested in controlling female bodies. "I am myn owene womman, wel at ese," asserted Chaucer's widowed Criseyde as she recoiled against the possibility of a new love. She might, like some of the women mentioned in this volume, usefully have heeded her own words.

—*Bonnie Wheeler*
Southern Methodist University

INTRODUCTION

CONSTRUCTIONS OF
WIDOWHOOD AND VIRGINITY

Cindy L. Carlson and Angela Jane Weisl

> *Although virgins, because of their perfect integrity and inviolate purity, will look upon the face of God most closely, yet the life a widow leads is more difficult, since it is easy not to desire that of which you are ignorant and easy to turn your back upon what you have never desired. Chastity is most praiseworthy when it is sensible of the right it has sacrificed and knows what it has experienced. The condition of the virgin may be regarded as one of greater felicity, but that of the widow is one of greater difficulty; the former has always possessed the good, the latter has had to find it on her own. In the former it is grace that is crowned, in the latter, virtue. For some things there are which come to us from the divine bounty, and others we have of our own efforts. Those which are bestowed upon us by the Lord are governed by his generosity; those which are achieved by man are won at the cost of personal endeavor.*

> —*Tertullian,* To His Wife[1]

Examining the female population of the emerging Christian world, Tertullian assured his community that "the most perfect sanctity is that of the virgin, since it has nothing in common with fornication."[2] Because fornication was evil and virginity sacred, it was easy to argue against a first marriage; even more so, then, was it possible to argue against a second. Widows, Tertullian believed, would have "no problem" on Judgment Day: "at the first sound of the angel's trumpet they will leap forth lightly, easily able to endure any distress or persecution, with none of the heaving baggage of marriage in their wombs or at their breasts."[3] Chastity had degrees; virgins occupied the highest rung, yet widowhood was doubly virtuous.

Virgins were blessed because they had no experience of sex at all, thus achieving the first degree of chastity; "the third degree, that is, not to re-wed after the death of one's spouse, besides the merit of self-control also has the merit of resignation to God's will."[4] Widows and virgins, linked through abstinence, acquired special access to the divine.

Tertullian was by no means unique in ascribing special status to these two groups of women; Augustine considered chastity to be a gift from God, a grace bestowed on both widows and virgins, while Clement, Jerome, Ambrose, and others also expressed similar sentiments about chastity—that it is a gift not to be taken lightly, sentiments they expressed to both widows and virgins in extended treatises.[5] Orders of Widows were established within the Church, giving women almost clerical power,[6] while virgins were said to ennoble families and bring sanctity upon entire communities; they were often treated as intermediaries between the people and God and were even thought to hold the powers of prophecy.[7] Asceticism, then, provided women in the patristic era with greater freedom than their married counterparts; indeed, most Church Fathers believed that women "who renounced the sexual life were elevated above their natural abject condition to the degree that they almost constituted a 'third sex,' so much did they differ from females in the thrall of Eve's birth pains and submission to husbands."[8] Because marriage placed women in an inferior role, legally and socially, "sexual functioning in itself made women subordinate."[9] Virginity and widowhood, at least in part, reversed that subordination by freeing women from the carnality of the world. While virginity remained the ideal, widows, at least, could be encouraged not to return to the "vileness of marriage," joining their virginal counterparts in rejecting their "sexual roles as allayers of male lust and as bearers of men's children"; as a result, the rejection of sexuality became "the essential point in raising women to personhood, to individuality."[10] That the two groups occupied similar idealized and perfected spaces is perhaps best articulated by John Chrysostom, in *Against Remarriage,* when he says, "the widow starts off inferior only to the virgin; but at the last, she equals and joins her."[11]

What this elevated status actually meant for widows and virgins of the early Christian age was not codified; while widowhood was not strictly an office of the church, within the Christian community widows were expected to seek a perfected lifestyle and serve a mission to the younger women in the community, either to urge them to remain virgins or to encourage them to practice chaste marriage and not remarry after their husbands' deaths; some widows regarded their position as an opportunity for greater devotional and ascetic efforts. Importantly, one of the "most frequently attested and important functions of the more dedicated widows became the supervision of the 'more princely order'" of virgins; indeed,

Ambrose felt that virginity was strengthened by the example of widows.[12] Holy widows were essentially virgins manqué. Virgins, however, were held to stricter standards of behavior; if widows gained a kind of community status and mobility through their active choice to remain chaste, virgins were seen as being in need of protection to prevent them from the temptations of the world. The widow's fortitude was measured by her will; having rejected the carnal world, she was able to live within it. By having rejected sexuality before experiencing it, the virgin was less able to defend herself against seduction. As a result of this conception, virgins were expected to remain in seclusion, either in anchorholds or in their parents' houses, fasting, praying, and holding holy vigils, observing meekness, poverty, obedience, humility, and patience.[13] Practically, this means an almost total withdrawal from the community; virgins were expected to be seen only at worship; they were supposed to have as little company as possible (apart from the virtuous widows who guided them, family members, and spiritual counselors); they were supposed to follow a regime of prayer, study, and physical work, enhanced by deprivation and frequent fasting.[14] In the early Church, virginal practice was accorded enormous status, investing virgins with theoretical (if not actual or meaningful) power. Some virgins, however, chose more public means of enacting their chastity, leading to Ignatius' recognition of the "virgins who are called *widows,*" because they joined the Order of Widows to become more active agents of the Church.[15]

This early history of ascetic women reveals a preoccupation that continues throughout the medieval period; women's integral nature was "indissolubly linked to the body, backed by traditional philosophic thinking as by apostolic teaching, and this association was advanced as their historical destiny following Eve's sin."[16] Because woman had tempted man, and temptation is the responsibility of the tempter, not the innocent who gives into seduction, women were considered bodily, carnal, and dangerous. Only through sufficient piety could she transcend women's vile status; only through a rejection of the world of sexuality and bodily function could she achieve virtue. Since virtue was constructed as masculine ("vir" [man] being said to be the root of the word "virtue"; the properties of virtue were thus the properties of masculinity), women had the potential to achieve virtue only through a "rejecting of her original abject nature."[17] Doing so set these women apart from the rest of their sex, in the eyes of the Church Fathers; as a reward for their piety, they gained the potential to reject the feminine body that enslaved them and attain "that self-same angelic nature as a reward, the self-same sex as men."[18]

In the later Middle Ages, this conception was both continued and refined; women occupied three primary positions: virgin, wife, and widow, each determined by the state of her affairs and the state of her body. Each status had its permutations; virgins were both potentially wives (or at least ex-virgins) and potentially perpetually chaste; wives themselves could be chaste or procreative, but they also lived with the possibility of widow-hood; widows were often chaste and thus aligned with virgins, or else they awaited remarriage and the return to the wifely state. The understanding of these states drew from the Church Fathers but also altered them; as Jocelyn Wogan-Browne notes in an examination of the *Ancrene Wisse* and its contemporary religious texts for women, a "review of virginity's long history of representation and social practice might well conclude that the literature of female chastity is the literature of textual oppression and misogyny, of the containment of women and their absence from history."[19] While the silencing of women through isolation is indeed a part of the history of virgins, the uncorrupted body also allows virgins (both literary and real; the saints and martyrs are matched in their verbal vigor by the female mystics who record their own experiences for posterity) to articulate themselves in ways that women inside the sexual economy of marriage cannot. Widows, too, while often portrayed negatively, also occupy power-ful roles, both narrative and real; the possibility open to them is effectively expressed by Chaucer's Criseyde, who, when considering entering into sexual relations with Troilus, notes:

> I am myn owene womman, wel at ese—
> I thank it God—as after myn estat,
> Right yong, and stonde unteyd in lusty leese,
> Withouten jalousie or swich debat:
> Shal noon housbounde seyn to me "Chek mat!"
> For either they ben ful of jalousie,
> Or maisterfull, or loven novelrie.[20]

While Criseyde's conception of widowhood is not religious nor especially pious, she reveals the actual freedom widows experienced by rejecting the world of men; it is her reentry into the sexual economy that silences and eventually destroys her. This choice is often confronted by textual (and no doubt real) widows; the lure of the world often loses out to the safety and sanctity of the convent. Widows who remain in the world, however, are able to exercise powers and mobility not available to wives, creating female networks of support and protection (often for other widows and virgins), serving as literary patrons and exempla, and even writing their own works. The rejection of the bodily thus permitted widows and virgins certain kinds of choice and certain kinds of autonomy; their exile from the sexual community, real or figurative, accompanied by their special access to the divine, created spaces for self-articulation.

This female power, albeit limited, created anxiety for male authors; a great deal was invested in protecting widows and virgins, yet this protection manifested itself as an obsessive concern with the preservation of bodily virtue. Virgins and widows who failed in their chastity were chastised; if the Church Fathers told stories of fallen virgins—usually deflowered through the agency of evil clerics—to warn virgins of what lay in wait for them in the world outside, later medieval writers used these stories to call into question the entire office of virginity. Virgins were threatened by temptation in stories that cast them as guilty temptresses; their enticing female bodies—which they strove to reject—became sites of danger; merely being seen by men, regardless of the virgin's desire or intent, could lead to rape and defilement, a loss of status and total abjection. The reemergence of the Widow of Ephesus story as paradigm in later literature also served to call the virtue of widowhood (as well as of widows) into question. The loss of purity was dangerous for the individual widow and virgin but doubly so for the institutionalized states of widowhood and virginity themselves.[21] Whatever these states constituted in real life for later medieval women, they remained important definers and differentiators for medieval authors; within most literary texts, women still were identified, described, and defined through their relationship to these sexually-defined roles.

In examining the construction of widowhood and virginity as modes that define, confine, and invite women to re-create their identities by their own words and actions, this collection centers on texts that explore the limits of these statuses and their availability to exploitation. By choosing "construction" as our governing image for the exploration of widows and virgins as they exist in medieval texts, we signal our intention to consider the ways that virginity and widowhood are constructed as social concepts through the creation of these texts by authors and readers. Virgin and widow mean beyond themselves, beyond their physical or textual identities; they serve social functions, both as arbiters of virtue and potential sites of vice. Often the texts considered in this collection seem to show a widow or virgin inhabiting a given status; the texts do not acknowledge that the text itself helps to create that status. Ideals of widowhood and virginity are thus created by the stories of widows and virgins themselves; just as the widows and virgins of the early Church acted to define these roles as they played them out, so, too, do definitions within these texts serve to create ideas of the institutions as well as the members of these groups that they portray. At the same time, women who are virgins and widows do not simply inhabit a ready-made role. They create maneuvering room by defying convention as well as by working visibly within conventional limits. Their enduring or temporary freedom from the *coverture* of marriage puts them at risk but opens up new avenues for expression. Their enduring or temporary freedom from openly expressed sexuality does not remove them from the sexual realm but may allow them to express a different sort of physicality. Widows and virgins occupy contested social space and embody that contested space within the confines of the texts they inhabit and create. As such, the texts examined here reveal an oscillation between orthodoxy and transgression, between clearly defined social roles that partially empower and partially confine and roles that subvert authorized avenues of power as well as bodily containment. Within the same work, a virgin can be both the inviolate, perfected servant of God and a self-articulating opposition to the male hierarchy that defines the former position; a widow can be chaste and virtuous while undermining the masculine authority that establishes that role by creating an alternative secular and sacred history.

The women in these texts create their identity through action, endurance, and visibility. Widows provide charity and friendship, virgin martyrs endure torture for the faith; both place their bodies into postures of ritual visibility that have meaning for their audience of readers and on lookers. Even when the widow or virgin seems "placed" into visibility or acted upon ritually, these texts show her activity in constructing how she will be seen, how she will be put into social circulation as a bearer of meaning.

While some texts considered in this collection were written under the aegis of women's sponsorship and primary readership, most are the work of men. As texts are put into some kind of social circulation, their readers include, to some extent, women. Even texts that one might expect to show a kind of "orthodoxy" with regard to the status of widows and virgins reveal that the proper widow and the proper virgin are never fully disposable figures bearing a stable social meaning. Instead, women's chastity and good works, exemplary lives, and martyrdom reveal that chastity is an ambivalent concept and that good works create networks of womanly connection and action. Widows and virgins function doubly; defined by men and male authority, they reject men and male authority through their rejection of sex. Because chastity is a male-defined virtue, constructed by the male founders of the early Church, these women occupy an orthodox space with specifically created expectations; however, this space itself encodes its own problematics; by rejecting marriage and the male superiority that it authorizes, widows and virgins gain access to transgressive subjectivity, mobility, and language. Their lives become examples of certain degrees of freedom as well as restriction. Even tales of virgin martyrs show a body that acts at least as much as it is acted upon.

In Lynn Staley and David Aers' examination of certain fourteenth-century English writings, they conclude that mere suffering or femininity cannot be "canonized for its utterly nonresistant endurance, an endurance that thus refuses to offer any direct and prophetic challenge to the revered structures of worldly power." Instead, these writers realize that "the feminine" may be linked to "knowledge" and a call to holiness may be a call to "consciousness," even a politicized consciousness.[22] If we consider that widows and virgins are to be characterized only by their chastity, which is itself to be defined negatively as an abstention from heterosexual relations, then we have safely limited these women to static images of endurance. They endure their chastity as they endure their relative powerlessness. Even if they endure as martyrs to the faith, they endure as suffering bodies rather than as bearers of consciousness and conscience.

As they are chaste, their silence may be too easily assumed. As Howard Bloch has noted, "the reproach against women is a form of reproach against language itself," perhaps especially the torrent of language that the married man might endure from his wife. The virgin might appear as a woman who does not speak and is not spoken about. The widow, if not a garrulous antitype, might assume the posture of a woman whose silence has been regained. And yet these women speak. They speak their devotion to Christianity verbally and with the triumphant display of the body, suffering but not defeated. They speak of their dynastic plans. They speak in courts of law in order to restore justice. The silence that is restored along with justice is a new silence of the virgin's own making. They speak of devotional and relational practices that may flourish aside from those prescribed by those apparently more active and authoritative.

These women are visible and create the images of their visibility. The Virgin Mary in English cycle drama speaks, both orally and with her body, to demonstrate her virginity and to embody a humility appropriate to believers, even powerful male believers. In medieval French lyric, she appears as a sovereign willing and able to be personal with her believers as well as to intercede for them in heaven. While the Virgin may be acted upon, these texts make clear that it is her chosen humility that might make her available not only to the acts of others but also to their imitation. She may even appear as the agent or protector of a belief threatened by the Jews who reject the Christian faith. In this guise, her body or her name may justify or create the conditions necessary to the rejection, abjection, even the murder of Jews. While this collection seeks to consider virginity in favor of the Virgin, Mary nonetheless informs all discussions of virginity; she is its model and its ideal, the measure against which all human virgins are tested and ultimately fail.

The virgin saint, martyred in the body for her pure belief, is also able to create a visibility in the text. Through the body, she enacts her faith by her acceptance of the suffering that threatens the martyr's body. Yet, that body remains inviolate as long as it remains visible. Whatever else may be ripped and torn, the text does not narrate her loss of virginity (it does not take place "off stage," either. The violence against her serves as a metaphor for her potential violation without having it literally enacted.). Her integrity, contested at the level of spirit and body, becomes a powerful image of the social integrity Christian believers (wished they) had. This sacrifice of a body that remains whole may be the act of the virgin saint, but this act may also be endured by her as another puts her body to the test of purity. If the body remains visibly virginal, the contested space in those texts concerning the deaths of virgins may be the will of the virgin. To what extent may she be seen to choose the death that may accompany her preserved virginity? The variety of answers supplied by these texts indicate just how unstable those answers might be.

Widowed queens with the ability to command the creating of memorial texts are able to make themselves textually visible as charitable, chaste, and powerful. They have little difficulty in presenting themselves as acting rather than being acted upon. If widows in romance remind the reader of misogynistic stereotypes of the sexually rapacious and conniving widow, even the romances grant widows the ability to create charitable friendships that benefit other female protagonists. When widows "author" or authorize the text, the text may recount rituals in which the widow displays her charity or her power even as she memorializes herself for having such attributes. She appears to create a textually powerful version of herself out of the materials of her life, using, too, the cultural materials that belong to widows in order to do so.

The contested space of widowhood and virginity appears in the ways the texts create a widow or virgin, exalting and at times undermining her. The potential for willed action the (partially) free or unprotected widow or virgin may have appears as a recognized and worrisome capacity that these essays begin to explore. While widowhood and virginity signify fixed bodily states, widows and virgins themselves are far more slippery. Other factors—queenship, potential sainthood, authorship, genre—establish their identities, shaping some of the ways these women are received; each individual example uses her chastity differently, both to make use of and to resist social convention. If virginity is a kind of masculinization—or, better, a desexualization—as Augustine believed, and widowhood is like virginity in sharing the special status that chastity imparts, then widows and virgins, at least textually, gain a mobility rarely seen among women in the literature of the Middle Ages.

In its opening section, entitled "Widows and Virgins," this collection examines widows and virgins together. A careful look at the historical conception of widows and virgins has revealed obvious connections between them; however, these points of contact go beyond the rejection of sexuality and the concomitant access to spirituality that their bodily states entail. Chaste widowhood was good; virginity was better. The body told the story, but the body was guided by the will; intent was vital to true chastity. But these clerical definitions merely show the orthodox understanding of the links between widowhood and virginity, between widows and virgins. The ways these connections were used, literally and literarily, provide both an understanding of the transgressive and available empowerment that a rejection of sex provided and a window into the problematics of occupying these positions.

In "Helpful Widows, Virgins in Distress: Women's Friendship in French Romance of the Thirteenth and Fourteenth Centuries," Anna Roberts examines some of the challenges to social structures that widows and virgins in romance create. Beginning with the exceptional status of the unmarried woman outside the economic cycles of exchange, Roberts considers the gendered concepts of widowhood and virginity in male-determined society, community, and family. Roberts extends the terms "widow" and "virgin" to encompass women who are bereft of the social network of male-dominated society that subordinates and supports them. Virginity was an episode in a woman's life, a state of vulnerability, and a state of autonomy impossible under other circumstances; in this state, women created alternate networks of support.

That widowhood describes a specifically female position is born out in language; the word *veuve* has no male equivalent (*veuf* is not attested until the sixteenth century); widowhood had a social, rather than private, meaning, connoting a woman without social standing, economic means, or legal representation. However, it also constituted an emancipation in the choice not to remarry. This combination of isolation and vulnerability, on the one hand, and autonomy on the other, was also inhabited, in literature if not in life, by runaway virgins and abandoned married women. Thus, Roberts creates the term "social widowhood" to constitute all women who are noncirculating, who act independently from men and often in opposition to them.

What replaced the social support system these "social widows" fell out of is a network of solidarity between women. In romance, women receiving help are virgins or women abandoned by their families; the women providing that support are widows or women who act independently from their husbands and male relatives. This female hospitality, which echoed real, historical female networks, was often ended by male intervention. While many medieval treatises on friendship denied that state to women, citing their inferiority, others entertained the possibility of female friendship, understanding it as a spiritual union mediated by God. Because of their special religious status, widows and virgins were ideal partakers in friendly, supportive acts. In romances, widows and virgins were typical heroic figures, as the prerequisite of romance heroism is vulnerability and exposure; as a result, these female networks in their multiple forms rival the importance of battle and other virile activities in constructing romance values.

The importance of widowhood and virginity is paramount in Christine de Pizan's *Livre de la Cité des Dames,* the late-medieval work celebrating women and revising the derision they often receive in patriarchal readings. In "The Widow as Virgin: Desexualized Narrative in Christine de Pizan's *Livre de la Cité des Dames,*" Angela Jane Weisl examines Christine's construction of her own female, authoritative voice from her identity as a widow and the perfect virginity of her namesake, St. Christine. Christine begins the work alone and despairing; she has read Matheolus on women and is dismayed by her imperfect womanhood, despite her own experiential knowledge of women's virtue. Three allegorical ladies make an "annunciation" to Christine, aligning her with Mary, the most perfect virgin of all; instead of giving birth to the Word made Flesh, Christine produces her book, the Word made Text. Her authority to speak comes not solely from the philosophical, exegetical tradition of Matheolus and his cohort but also from a particularly female combination of authority tempered by experience; Christine writes from what she has read and what she knows. That her authority also originates in her separation from the sexual economy of marriage is revealed in the parallels to Mary mentioned above— only a pure vessel can channel the word of God (in the voices of the three ladies). However, the text also establishes another model for female authority, further desexualizing Christine's narrative.

St. Christine, virgin and martyr, is a double text; like all martyrs, she is an authoritative textual body, readable in its perfection despite its concomitant dismemberment. And St. Christine is gloriously dismembered. However, she is also authoritative in her speech; preaching the Word of God, she converts all who understand her as truth. The symbol for her speaking, the tongue that the judge twice tries to tear from her mouth, suggests the efficacy of women's speech. When, in a fury at her continued recital of the true word, the judge insists that her tongue wasn't cut short enough the first time, and orders the torturers to get the rest of it, he clearly misses the point. St. Christine spits the root of her tongue into his face, blinding him, demonstrating that he was blind already, unable to see the truth of women's speech, as a route to the true path. In being named for St. Christine, and in seeing her authorial role as being to tell the saint's story and praise her, Christine de Pizan allies herself with the saint in a tra-

dition of effective female speech. This power comes through the desexualized body of virgin and widow, which, in its separation from the tradition
that disenfranchises and castigates women, is given special access to God's
word, to revealed truth.

The problematics of being both widow and virgin are revealed in
Monika Otter's "Closed Doors: An Epithalamium for Queen Edith,
Widow and Virgin." Written for Queen Edith herself, the *Vita Aedwardi
Regis* reveals thematic and symbolic associations between the queen's
chastity, her fertility, her power, and the prosperity of the land. While
Queen Edith is barren, resulting in the suffering of the land and the loss
of her power, the poet of the *Vita* attempts to salvage Edith as a chaste
and powerful queen through some of the same strategies seen in the earlier *Encomium Emmae Reginae*. Putting forward new roles, including suffering, threatened widowhood, and alliance with Mary, the poet attempts
extravagant praise and celebration while always remaining on the verge of
failure, showing glimpses of defeat.

Edith, Edward the Confessor's widow, is the text's patron and addressee;
although the story is about her male relations and the events surrounding
the Battle of Hastings, she is woven into the narrative, particularly in the
"epithalamium" on the dedication of the Abbey Church at Wilton, Edith's
most important religious foundation.

The poem's author attempts to solve the problem of Edith's childlessness by hinting that her marriage to Edward was a chaste one for religious
reasons; since he can't talk about the marriage's failure to produce an heir,
he supplies metonymic substitutions: for Edward, saintliness; for Edith, an
act of monastic foundation that recasts her as a figure in a sacred narrative,
drawing on liturgical, Marian, and even Christological material. In the
"epithalamium," the poet calls up Marian themes of virgin motherhood,
the Virgin as a type of the Church, Christ as the Church's bridegroom, and
the assurance to virgins that they take part in Mary's spiritual motherhood.
This motherhood, at least in religious terms, provides a consolation; it is a
better maternity than the physical one the virgin eschews. As such, the
foundation becomes a kind of substitute for the children Edith didn't have,
a spiritual family replacing those whose absence the text's attempts to conceal instead reveal. By supplying alternative maternity, the author recalls
the very physical notions of womb and conception, motherhood and
childbirth, and the lack thereof. Edith's need to be a surrogate mother suggests her inability to be a real one.

"The Varieties of Virginity," the collection's second section, shifts to an
exploration of the rhetoric of virginity and its multiple functions in both
religious and secular literature. While virginity in the previous articles
was linked to Mary's celestial power, here it is inextricably connected

with violence and violation. The virgin's body is both inviolate and violable; this paradox can both destroy and elevate her. And both the destruction and the elevation can serve in contradictory ways; the virgin's death is both a punishment for her dangerous and finally inescapable female nature, and a glorious, canonizing martyrdom. The power she is given through her perfected body is both authorized and transgressive.

In "Performing Virginity: Sex and Violence in the Katherine Group," Sarah Salih examines the extreme violence in the virgin martyr legends that focus on the display and dismemberment of the virgin body. Female sanctity demanded protracted suffering; the experience of that suffering encapsulated the virgin's meaning. Salih considers the question of why nakedness was so featured in a group of texts designed for anchoritic women, concluding that sanctity was achieved through the body because of the medieval idea that women's piety was based in women's experience of themselves as corporeal. Chastity enclosed the body and corrected its grotesqueness; it repaired inchoate flesh, making it whole and holy. Virginity in the Katherine Group is a gender unto itself, separate from other versions of the feminine; it requires continual performance, allowing the body to be read through concrete signs of itself. Necessarily unstable, gender demanded repeated acts of performance.

This sense of virginity as a separate gender plays out in both medieval and contemporary theory; St. Ambrose believed that a woman who served Christ in the world became a man, and even the word "virgin," made up of the parts "vir" and "ago," suggested a woman acting as a man. As a result the feminine body, antithetical to virginity through its association with sexuality, became a contested space. Virginity was performed through spectacle; St. Katherine, St. Margaret, and St. Juliana all appear invulnerable, making themselves a dangerous spectacle from which onlookers flinch. The control of the performance that these martyrs exerted came from a shifting of the focus from body to voice; just as the saint faces the dismembering of her body, she also speaks her truth. Her body's resistance to violation enacts her words in a different—and living—text.

The need to perform virginity, Salih argues, comes in part from the actual difficulty of reading the body as virginal; the hymen functioned more as a metaphor, a cultural fantasy, than a real test of bodily intactness. Virginity thus was read from behavior; the veiling and enclosure of the anchorite were signs from which the inviolate body was inferred. As final proof, the virgins in the Katherine Group essentially seek out their own martyrdoms; in suffering and resisting torture, the virgin body is revealed to be unfeminine, unashamed, impenetrable, and miraculously self-healing.

The *Wohunge* Group, unlike the Katherine Group, casts virgins in a more erotic light, as the lovers of Christ; in "The Paradox of Virginity within the Anchoritic Tradition: The Masculine Gaze and the Feminine Body in the *Wohunge* Group," Susannah Mary Chewning examines the shifting gender of wooer and wooed within these texts, showing a fluid sexual identity of readers and speakers. Despite the model of Mary, who was able to renounce her earthly body through the rejection of human sexuality and birth, even chaste women could not be more than their bodies; they were constantly reminded of their fallen status, considered temptresses to men and identified by their innate sexual nature. The devotional literature written for women worked in this context, using the language of love, the language of the body, to describe ritual devotion.

This use of secular love terms, however, accompanied a gender slippage caused by mysticism; male mystics were feminized by their erotic love of God, surrendering their identities in a love relationship with Christ. If women mystics had the same experience, Chewning asks, what subjectivity/identity do they surrender, and where do they get it? In the process of wooing Christ, the female speaker of the *Wohunge* Group becomes male.

Indeed, the education available through convents and anchorholds endowed women with the subjectivity to lose through their love of Christ, providing access to transcendence. Because Mary was so often the focus of her devotion and love, she became masculinized; the Virgin was the virgin's desired other, partner, or wife. In its desiring, then, the woman's gaze becomes masculine, leading to further gender slippage. This gender complication is a defining quality in the *Wohunge* Group; while the medieval definitions of "woman" were a product of the masculine gaze that fixed women as bodily objects, unable to transcend the physical world, the mystical, eroticized devotion portrayed for the anchoresses allowed them a masculine subjectivity to subordinate to their beloved, alternately Mary and Christ.

This power and subjectivity accorded to virgins in the *Wohunge* Group is shaded by the vulnerability to rape that they face in many saints' lives. Kathleen Coyne Kelly, in "Useful Virgins in Medieval Hagiography," looks at multiple examples of narratives in which divine intervention saves virginity. This shows the essential value of virginity as a sign of the docility and utility of female bodies in hagiography, as well as demonstrating how this narrative form privileges meaning over events and the general over the specific in order to produce "useful" virgins. This utility, Kelly argues, comes from the metonymic representation of the virgin body as church, its sealed, closed, intact state serving as the first line of defense for the institution behind it. The violation of the consecrated body is a violation of the church; therefore, the rape of that body must be suppressed in hagiography. As a result, the virgin body may be violently dismembered but not raped; virginity must outlast the virgin.

Kelly focuses her discussion on menaced virgins of late antiquity—Agatha, Agnes, Euphemia, and Lucy from the *Legenda Aurea*. Examining sources such as Eusebius, Jerome, Ambrose, and Augustine, Kelly reveals the virgin martyr as social document, useful for the readers of her text. Rape is not a useful narrative in a semiotic system in which the virgin functions as a metonym for the Church. While real Christian women were raped in late antiquity, their salvation in hagiographic material allows them to take on figurative meaning. Dismemberment and death are less complicated than rape; they prevent further traffic with the virgin body and end the danger of violation. Therefore, they leave the represented church intact; the abstract virginity of assigned meaning is more valuable than the specific, fleshly body, just as the soul supersedes the corporeal on earth.

Virginity need not function solely in a monastic or anchoritic context, however; while Kelly's hagiographic examples lived outside of religious orders, their stories functioned within the religious establishment. In secular material, the virgin body can take on roles beyond those presented by Salih, Chewning, and Kelly. As Sandra Pierson Prior demonstrates in "Virginity and Sacrifice in Chaucer's 'Physician's Tale,'" this tale has much to tell about problems and inconsistencies that characterize the medieval Christian valorization of virginity. Three understandings of that state combine in this tale: the traditional Christian ideal of virginity as sinlessness, a monastic ideal in which perpetual virginity is an end in itself; a classical view in which the virgin protects patriarchal society and patrilineal descent, encoding her own loss as she moves from chaste daughter to faithful wife; and a burdensome remnant of the cultic, sacrificial tradition that values virginity for the sake of offering up and killing the perfect victim. The story of Jeptha's daughter, which serves as a type scene for the tragic events of the tale, reveals the virgin's place in patriarchal culture and her potential role as a sacrificial victim. This is a different mode than Christian sacrifice and is essentially pagan; Virginia and Jeptha's daughter differ from their Christian counterparts, Christ and Isaac; as women they are less valuable and, more crucially, they actually die. Until the final scene, Virginia is a nonperson; she has no voice, little character, and a name that is merely a patronymic—she is an expendable form of her father. Virginia is cut off, juggling sacrifice and honor: the more precious the victim, the greater the guilt; the more worthy the victim, the greater the satisfaction of the community's need. Virginity both valorizes Virginia and makes her an expendable piece of Virginius' household; as a result, the ritualistic sacrifice of her is a way of containing and channeling a community's violent tendencies. After a brief explosion of violence at the end of the tale, order is restored. Chaucer shows the ways that society needs sacrifice to atone for evil; virgins are intact, pure victims. However, in revealing this less authorized aspect of virginity, Chaucer raises important questions about why his culture valued virgin innocence so greatly.

Kathleen M. Hobbs continues the discussion of violence and virginity in Chaucer in "Blood and Rosaries: Virginity, Violence and Desire in Chaucer's 'Prioress's Tale.'" In the Middle Ages, the Virgin birth, Hobbs points out, emphasized Christian unity and separation from the Jews, substituting for the Davidic line that was more important in the early Church. Mary was cast as the "slayer of all heresies," carrying with her the threat of physical violence as a penalty for failing to accept Christian doctrine. Within the Church, Mary was distinguished from all other women; she didn't menstruate or have pain in childbirth, separating her from Eve's curse; her bodily ascension allowed her to end her life on earth without leaving a corpse. Her "marked difference" (her rejection of essential female bodily experience) made her the standard against which all women, even chaste nuns, were measured and found wanting, but this difference also helped separate Christianity and Judaism. Her inviolate body allowed the Church to perceive itself as timeless, whole, and inviolate, the wellspring of absolute truth.

Mary's direct opposition to the Jewish community proves ironic in the essential connection between women—even holy ones—and Jews, both in medieval society and in the world of the tale. The Church's ambivalent attitude towards holy women—exalting and debasing them at the same time—matched its attitude toward Judaism. While the Church accepted the history of revelation and its beginnings in the Jewish tradition, it also debased contemporary Jews. Its attitude towards women was much the same; holy women were defended and defamed at the same time. The Prioress isn't spared being bound to the sins of Eve; she sees her speech as inadequate to her prayer and prays for the voice of the disembodied virgin to take over for the purposes of her prayer. While she is holy enough to identify with the mother of God, she was too sinful to achieve a heavenly ideal. Despite the virgin ideal, the Prioress is stuck in an inescapable body.

The Prioress both affirms and denies her gender, identifying with Mary and the little clergeon; yet her portrait in the General Prologue shows a kind of hyperfemininity, an embracing of her gender as virginity, at the same time as she rejects it through virginity. Indeed the women in the tale, Mary and the Widow, are women without husbands, selflessly devoted to their children. As such, they are divorced from femininity and sexuality, like the Prioress herself. The Prioress also allies herself with the little clergeon, masculinizing herself in order to achieve the ideal of perfect chastity. This is a process of desexualization; the clergeon is not a virile man but a seven-year-old child, perfect in his innocence. The illiterate, hymn-singing boy is the perfect representation of the eternal virginity into which the Prioress transforms herself. Just as Mary is simultaneously virginal and procreative, the clergeon is simultaneously dead (bodily) and living (spiritually).

This innocence and perfection exist in sharp contrast to the "filth" of the Jewish community, whose violence against the child ends in the privy where the citizens dispose of his body. The resulting destruction of the entire community by multiple tortures, enacted on the Jews as the enemy of the perfect Church symbolized by Mary, also recalls the spectacle of violence performed on the female bodies of the virgin martyrs. In order to lay its claim to timeless truth, the Church must be figured by Mary, slayer of heresies, and destroy its "dirty" physical specimens—sexualized women and the Jews.

Cindy L. Carlson, in "Like a Virgin: Mary and her Doubters in the N-Town Cycle" demonstrates the deep connection between Mary's virginal body and the social body of which she was an anomalous part. Mary's continuing virginity through conception and childbirth provides a model for that society to recover its purity and wholeness. The visibility of her pregnancy and motherhood and the invisibility of her virginity present a radical challenge to the constitution of the chaste female body; her vindication through her humility is a social model for women and men, especially those exercising princely judgment and judicial power as they create themselves as virtuous believers enacting God's will.

Accepting Mary's unnatural miracle becomes a sign of inclusion in the portion of redeemed humanity; rejection is the sign of a doubter and ultimately, of factionalism and destruction. In the cycle dramas, Mary's virginity is tested and proven; her miraculous childbirth with its painless delivery convinces Joseph and the midwives. And if it does not, an attempt to examine her virginity causes the hands of the doubters to shrivel up. The test damages the integrity of the doubter, not the virginal status of the new mother. The unity of Mary's virginity and childbirth, then, join humanity in a peace far beyond what human rulers can impose, a unification that leaves out only the Jews because they refuse to believe in Christian prophecy. In their acceptance of God's overwhelming power, the community and Mary are made one. In these dramas, the trials of virginity imposed upon Mary serve to encourage the audience to see themselves as a part of the integral body of Christian believers; like Joseph, they must learn to accept the Virgin miracle humbly. The socializing body of Mary contains all believers, yet it also creates hierarchies that establish a social order. Doubt confirms belief; those who question truth only serve to establish the integrity of those whose faith is unwavering and who are ordained to protect the social body that defines them. Thus the body of Mary, both ordained and subversive, becomes the measure of one's place in both the secular world of law and court and the sacred world, present and to come.

The final section, "Constructing Widowhood," turns to a consideration of women who choose their absence, who elect a rejection of the world after tasting its fruits. Like the virgin, the widow occupies a space that is variously defined. The ideal of the chaste widow, a "virtual virgin" who is to be commended for her fortitude in rejecting the fruits of the world that she has tasted, stands only a rung below the virgin on the ladder of salvation; however, her knowledge of the world makes her a problematic figure, and the ideal often appears in contrast to the figure of the lustful widow who uses her freedom as a license to vice. Widowhood's empowerment, considered in the first group of articles and again here, created extreme anxiety about its misuse. Yet widows could also be positive models for ideals of mourning; given special access to God and to death at once allowed them to provide spaces in which to construct what Leslie Abend Callahan calls a "pedagogy of grief."

Rebecca Hayward, in "Between the Living and the Dead: Widows as Heroines of Medieval Romance," examines the two prevailing stereotypes of widows: the misogynistic idea developed from the satirical tradition whose best known example is the Widow of Ephesus, and the Christian idea of chaste widowhood and exclusive ownership. The romance heroine who is also a widow is a problematic figure, caught between the romance necessity for possession by the hero and her own ideals of chastity. Through the genre that defines her, the widow heroine always treads a fine line, running the risk of sliding into the misogynistic mode, as antithetical to romance conventions as chastity. This discourse can destabilize romance itself, the idealized narrative, and the generic boundaries of the text.

Hayward examines Jocasta in the *Roman de Thèbes*, Laudine in *Yvain*, and Criseyde. Both Jocasta and Laudine are caught between private desire and public duty; Jocasta must find a protector for Thebes, while Laudine needs a defender for her spring. While Jocasta's actions are ultimately viewed as a tragic mistake, her behavior is considered much like that of other widows. The author has nothing invested in making her look good, so her choice to marry Oedipus quickly descends into scandal. Chrétien de Troyes is more committed to romance as a genre and thus to constructing Laudine as a widow heroine; therefore, Lunette functions as a mediator between Laudine's roles as wife and widow, effectively absorbing desires that would subject Laudine to misogynistic stereotypes. She shapes both Yvain's and Laudine's desires for each other; she brings them together at the beginning, and she brings them back together at the end of the romance. Through her, Laudine is successfully transformed from a chaste, grieving widow to a remarrying one.

Criseyde, or Criseyda in Boccaccio's *Filostrato,* receives very different presentations in the two most famous romances about her; while Boccaccio freely associates Criseyda with the misogynistic stereotype of the lustful widow, tempered by romance, Chaucer works harder to spare Criseyde, as long as her actions fulfill the desires of the poem's hero. In Boccaccio's poem, the fact that Criseyda is persuadable once (by Pandaro and Troilus) suggests that she will be again; even in the end, her untrustworthiness is demonstrated when she lies to Diomede. The secrecy and transgression of her affair are both erotic and scandalous. Once she ceases to function primarily to satisfy the hero, she is bad.

Chaucer presents a more complex picture; the poem begins by making use of romance elements, but Crisyede's failure to return to Troy and her affair with Diomende destabilize romance within the narrative. While the facile misogyny we see in Boccaccio is not present here, by taking on the roles expected of her, Criseyde reveals the expectations of women in romance. Unable to represent herself, because her own representations are in conflict with social and narrative necessity, she must be mutable, adaptable. She falls into misogyny when she is no longer fulfilling Troilus' desires, which, Hayward argues, is the poem's foremost goal. Chaucer has no way to portray Criseyde outside the categories of chastity and lustfulness; if Criseyde can't be a heroine, *Troilus and Crisyede* can't be a romance. Therefore, the widow heroine serves a more central function in the poem than her marginalization suggests; her compliance with the narrative structures undermines her ability to function positively, and as the text slides into misogyny, she brings it down with her.

These contradictory stereotypes of widows also inform Leslie Abend Callahan's "The Widow's Tears: The Pedagogy of Grief in Medieval France and the Image of the Grieving Widow." Because the widow herself did not encode one specific meaning, her display of grief was a polyvalent sign as well. An examination of widow's grief reveals tensions between widows' secular concerns and their religious duties. Medieval discourse on tears was an attempt to control the conduct of women, even in the pens of women writers. The tradition of commentary set models for grief, particularly negative examples, constructing a body of literature that Callahan calls "the pedagogy of grief." While tears could provide a release for emotion and constitute devotion to the deceased spouse, this material also asked, "is it not selfish, 'unchristian,' to mourn someone who has gone on to an eternal life?"

In its approach, chaste widowhood was ideal; chaste widows had special powers of prayer and were considered to inhabit a kind of "second virginity"; Jerome and Ambrose wrote treatises assisting widows in avoiding the temptation to remarry. When absolutely necessary, they recommended chaste marriages of convenience. This attempt to coerce women into behavioral norms, established by the Church Fathers, provided society with an outlet of social control over women's lives. These treatises counseled moderation; excessive grief was part of the misogynistic Widow of Ephesus topos, which led to facile consolation by a new lover. Yet women were forced into a double bind; insufficient grief was considered a feigned response as well. Tears were a multivalent symbol, a sign of grief but also a potential invitation to other men. Even women writers, Christine de Pizan and Anne de Beaujeu, suggest the exercise of restraint in mourning.

Therefore, the widows' tears in the examples that Callahan considers, coupled with their sexual transgressions, can be read as a sign of resistance against the values constructed and controlled by men, while the moderate tears that Christine and Anne advocate can be read as a gesture of compliance. Just as the widow herself occupied a complex and shifting symbolic (and literal) position in the medieval world, so, too, did her grief, the outward show of the mourning that made and thus defined her, function both to uphold and challenge the values of that society.

The constructions of widowhood and virginity presented in this collection show, finally, how the female body is a blank page on which multiple meanings can be inscribed. If wifehood and the world of sexual exchange write their own familiar pictures, those meanings written on the body that separates itself from that world, either "before" or "after," are more diverse and various. While two models of behavior for widows governed literary understanding—the misogynistic Widow of Ephesus and the model of chastity—literary widows seem to resist falling neatly into those patterns; widowhood can mean suffering and isolation; it can mean significant power, both authoritative and financial; it can mean an opportunity to become a patron of other women, religious and secular; it can mean a combination of those things. Virginity, too, reveals multiple understandings; as a position, it is both powerfully rhetorical and physically threatened. Even Mary, the greatest virgin of them all, resists a single meaning, taking on diverse functions from the suffering mother to the Queen of Heaven, a symbol of the Church, the community of believers, women's spirituality, and divine right. From the conflicts between orthodox understandings of the female body and anxiety about its possibilities to transgress and undermine that orthodoxy, and from the ways that the confinement of widows and virgins contrasts with the power they are given and take upon themselves come not a unity but a diversity; the unifying feature of that diversity is the way that it springs from a body that, in rejecting sexuality, becomes a contested space. In a world defined by men, women become virtuous by rejecting the thing—their sexuality—that men use to define them; however, by rejecting their womanliness, they are no longer bound by the definitions of the abject feminine body. While medieval authority sought to supplant the defined feminine with other definitions that both praised and limited these women without sex, the very complex nature of their rejection created spaces for transgression. Women who are not women are not men; because it is difficult to say what they are, they emerge in multiple ways that reveal both the desire for and the impossibility of fixing them. Without the clear identity and role that marriage provides, the widow and virgin become mysteries. Their bodies—the seat of their resistance—tell many stories.

Notes

1. Tertullian, "Ad Uxorem" ("To His Wife"), *Treatises on Marriage and Remarriage,* trans. William P. Le Saint, Ancient Christian Writers No. 13 (Westminster, VA: The Newman Press, 1951), p. 21.
2. Tertullian, "De Exortatione Castitatis" ("An Exhortation to Chastity"), *Treatises on Marriage and Remarriage,* trans. William P. Le Saint. Ancient Christian Writers No. 13 (Westminster, VA: The Newman Press, 1951), p. 57.
3. Tertullian, "Ad Uxorem," p. 17.
4. Tertullian, "De Exortatione Castitatis," p. 43.
5. For an extended discussion of the Church Fathers on chastity, see Gillian Cloke, *"This Female Man of God": Women and Spiritual Power in the Patristic Age, AD 350 – 450* (London: Routledge, 1995), pp. 39–40ff.
6. For a discussion of the origin, role, and development of the Orders of Widows, see Cloke and Bonnie Bowman Thurston, *The Widows: A Women's Ministry in the Early Church* (Minneapolis: Fortress Press, 1989).
7. Cloke, pp. 68–70.
8. Elizabeth A. Clark, *Women in the Early Church* (Wilmington, DE: Michael Glazer, 1983), p. 17.
9. Clark, p. 17.
10. Clark, p. 18.
11. John Chrysostom, *Against Remarriage* 2, qtd. in Cloke, p. 99.
12. Ambrose, *On Widows* 1, qtd. in Cloke, p. 96. Cloke also notes that Jerome felt that widowed mothers provided "guarantees of chastity" for their virgin daughters who might otherwise choose marriage without this prominent example of chastity (p. 98).
13. Specifically articulated by John Chrysostom in *On Virginity* 63:1, these rules became de rigeur for the de facto "order of virgins." Cloke examines both Chrysostom's idealized virginity alongside contemporary narratives of holy virgins (p. 63ff).
14. Cloke, p. 63.
15. Ignatius, *Smyrneans* 13.1; qtd. In Thurston, p. 54.
16. Cloke, p. 212.
17. Cloke, p. 212.
18. Cloke, p. 212.

19. Jocelyn Wogan-Browne, "Chaste bodies: frames and experiences," *Framing Medieval Bodies,* ed. Sarah Kay and Miri Rubin (Manchester: Manchester University Press, 1994), p. 24.

20. Geoffrey Chaucer, *Troilus and Criseyde,* II ll. 750–55, *The Riverside Chaucer,* ed. Larry D. Benson (Boston: Houghton Mifflin, 1987).

21. While Cloke discusses the patristic attitude towards fallen virgins on pp. 71–77, the change in emphasis in the later period is revealed through several articles in this collection; see for example, Roberts, Callahan, and Hayward.

22. David Aers and Lynn Staley, *The Powers of the Holy: Religion, Politics, and Gender in Late Medieval English Culture* (University Park, Pennsylvania: Penn State University Press, 1996), p. 263.

PART I

WIDOWS AND VIRGINS

CHAPTER 1

HELPFUL WIDOWS, VIRGINS IN DISTRESS: WOMEN'S FRIENDSHIP IN FRENCH ROMANCE OF THE THIRTEENTH AND FOURTEENTH CENTURIES

Anna Roberts

Widows and virgins challenge the social structures in the French romances of the thirteenth and fourteenth centuries by existing in a state of autonomy impossible within marriage.

Virgin and Widow as Social Constructs

In French, the word *veuve* ("widow," from Latin *vidua*, "deprived of") is not known to have a parallel masculine form (*veuf*, widower) until the sixteenth century.[1] This straightforward fact of the history of language may serve as a point of departure in the discussion of the condition of women in medieval France. Widowhood was a gendered concept; so was virginity. Both categories were determined by the place women occupied in the male-dominated society, community, and family. The exceptional status of unmarried women is reflected in fiction as well as in codices and compilations of custom law. Specific legal practices, different from those applied to married women, governed the lives of widows and virgins. Special rights benefited or compensated widows in the economy of the village (such as the right to glean after a harvest) and town (the not infrequent economic presence of widows who continued in their deceased husbands'

businesses, while the confraternities and other statutes specifically banned
women from all but the least profitable professions; women creditors were
almost exclusively widows).[2] The temporary exception from the sexual-
economic cycle of exchange, an exception that widows and virgins enjoyed or suffered, is expressed in the rich tradition of proverbs, prejudices,
and romances. For, in turn, women's place and their interests determined
legal and literary fictions—if one regards literature as some legal historians
view the law, that is as "a tool, a technique in the service of the society, not
of the society as it exists, but as it wants to be."[3]

In my study, I argue that the terms "widow" and "virgin" can be usefully
extended to encompass other women who are bereft of the social network
of male-dominated family that subordinates as well as supports them. In that
sense, widowhood as well as virginity can be viewed as an episode in a
woman's life (framed by her belonging to such a family structure) or as a
state of vulnerability (proverbially attested as such), yet simultaneously as a
state of autonomy (impossible under other circumstances). I argue that in
this circumstance of vulnerable autonomy, women turn—willingly or per-
force—to allies other than the patriarchal family, creating alternative networks of support. This is why my study on friendships among women finds
its proper place in a collection devoted to widows and virgins.

I approach this study from my limited perspective of an expert on
French romance. However, I feel it is fruitful to follow similar studies devoted to English literature, in providing historical grounding to the study
of texts and to mention examples of real women while analyzing fictional
ones. I do it somewhat obliquely, by referring to the work of historians on
the poor; other examples of the phenomena to which I refer can be found.
Thus, my discussion is oriented toward three subjects: the meanings of
widowhood and virginity; archival documentation on solidarity networks
between women; and finally, the medieval theory of friendship and fictional representation of women's friendships.

I have proposed that the terms "widow" and "virgin" can be extended to
cover all women who are removed from the male-dominated social structures
of support and coercion. The social meaning of the word "widow" favors this
proposition. As the historical separation of the terms widow and widower in
French implies, *veuve* describes during the French Middle Ages a woman who
finds herself in a condition without equivalent in the case of a man who has
lost his spouse. The meaning of widowhood is social rather than private or affective. It does not pertain to the situation of a woman who found herself
without her lover and companion but to one without legal representation,
economic means, and social standing. Privately, affectively, men and women
are equal in their loss, whether they suffer or benefit from it. A man who lost
his spouse still controls the economic means of his well-being, conserves his

legal rights and social standing, and may continue to represent himself in social and legal circumstances. On the other hand, a woman who loses her
spouse also loses all or some of the means of support, as well as the legal and
social representation provided by her husband and his family. While the widower is now free to remarry, the widow is also free from the subordination of
marriage and (prior to marriage, during her maidenhood) of the patriarchal
family. She is, in this sense, emancipated as well as bereft, and may choose not
to remarry if her social and economic circumstances are favorable enough.

The best illustration of the social dimension of widowhood that I can
give is *a contrario* and comes from a later age. In her ballads, perhaps the
most original poetic achievement of her period, Christine de Pizan infuses
the idea of marriage with the tradition of courtly love.[4] Both the texts that
describe her happy marriage and those that show the poignant difference
between her past married happiness and present widowed misery adapt in
an unprecedented manner the vocabulary and themes of passionate love
relationship to marriage, heretofore (and indeed for many centuries to
come) considered incompatible with love. Among the better known, "Les
douceurs du mariage" (the sweetness of marriage) describes the pleasures
of the wedding night in such terms that only the direct and insistent references to "mariage" (l.1), "mari" [husband] (l.3), and even "menage" (here
in the sense of cohabitation, holding house together; but the most common meaning is "household"; l.9) prevent us from reaching the conclusion
that this is a night of courtly love's test, in which the lover must demonstrate his true love by obeying the lady's every wish. The quoted references
seem almost insufficient to anchor the meaning of the poem in the realm
of matrimonial bliss; the refrain, "le Doux m'aime bien" [the Sweet loves
me well] (ll. 8, 16, 28), seems incongruous in such context.

The innovative poet who bent the courtly love tradition to the description of marriage also used it to describe widowhood; and it is in the
group of poems that can be described as "widow's laments" that I trace the
hegemony of the social over the affective sphere in fictional depictions of
widowhood. Equally well known as the "Douceurs du mariage," the "Solitude" also borrows from the convention of courtly passion. The haunting
repetition of the diminutive of the adjective "lonely" ("seulete sui" [I am
alone]) opens every verse, bringing forth the image of a vulnerable, too
young or too old, fragile, isolated woman. If the first verse opens boldly:
"Seulete sui et seulete vueil estre" [I am alone and I want to be alone] (l.1),
it is followed by a litany of lack and passive dispossession, dominated by
negative expressions ("sanz compaignon" [without companion] l. 3, "plus
que nulle" [more than none] l. 6, "riens n'est qui tant messie" [there is no
thing that displeases as much] l. 12). Passive form is chosen where an active expression is possible: "m'a . . . laissiee" [left me] (l.2), "[sui] delaissiee"

[I am abandoned] l. 18, "[sui] abaissiee" [I am abased] l. 19, "[sui] menaciee" [I am threatened]—not "I feel lonely," "I flee," "I fear;" "or est ma
douleur comenciee" [now my pain has begun]—not "I suffer." The active
form is reserved for the refrain, where it is the choice of the verb—*de-
mourer* [to remain]—that expresses the passive bent: "Seulete sui, sanz ami
demouree" [I am alone, remaining with no friend] (ll. 7, 21, 25).[5] The device of the refrain (where the passive meaning is conveyed by the semantic of the verb instead of passive syntax) is repeated in line 9 ("[sui]
muciee" [I am hidden]), and line 14 ("[sui] enserree" [I am enclosed]). The
verb ("sui" [I am]) is always omitted, so that these inactions are no different from the states, the latter almost exclusively related by participles: "dolente et courrouciee" [pained and angered] l. 4, "mesaisiee" [upset] l. 5,
"esgaree" [lost] l. 6, "dolente ou apaisiee" [pained or quieted] l. 11, l. 19,
"esplouree" [in tears] l. 20, "teinte" [darkened] l. 24. The semantically and
syntactically active verb "voise" [I go] in line 16 emphasizes the futility of
all action, since it is used as the symmetrical equivalent of "siee" [I sit]:
"Seulete sui, ou je voise ou je siee" [I am alone whether I walk or sit]. Similarly, positive adverbs are used to express emptiness: "Seulete sui partout et
en tout estre" [I am alone *everywhere* and in *all* being] l. 15; "Seulete sui plus
qu'autre riens terrestre" [I am alone *more than any* earthly thing] l. 17; "sou-
vent toute esploree" [*often* all in tears] l. 20; "de tout dueil menaciee"
[threatened by *all* mourning] l. 23. At the opening of the second strophe,
the traditional *loci* of amorous encounter—the door and the window—are
empty spaces: "Seulete sui a uis ou a fenestre" [I am alone at the door or
the window] (l. 8).

This poem, translating the numbing pain of bereavement with such im-
mediacy, could not be more obvious in figuring the social dimension of
widowhood. As I have shown, passivity is the poem's trope. Yet passivity
was hardly Christine's choice. On the contrary, this twenty-five-year-old
widow of a promising but not wealthy court secretary carved a career for
herself and her son by remaining at court as a poet. Her choice of active
rather than passive life may well have been influenced by the very extent
of the immediate household that depended on her: three young children,
her niece, and her mother.[6] Considering these facts of Christine's life and
poetic practice, in the accumulation of passivity figures in "Solitude" we
may see more than the expression of grief. In my view, the idea of social
precariousness or overt discrimination is also vividly present. The subject
of the poem characterizes herself as an undesirable presence: "riens n'est
qui tant messiee" [no thing displeases as much] l. 12, and especially "Seulete
sui, de chascun delaissiee, / Seulete sui, durement abaissiee" [I am alone,
forsaken by every one, / I am alone, harshly abased] (ll. 18–19) must be
read in this sense, and as such they change the meaning of the refrain in

the third strophe from "mon douz ami" [my sweet friend], that is the lover, in the first strophe (l. 2), to "friends" in the sense of social network: ("Seulete sui, sanz ami demouree" [I am alone, I remained with no friend] l. 21). In the *envoi* that follows immediately, the subject addresses the patron: "Princes, or est ma douleur commenciee" [my suffering has now begun] (l. 22); this can be read as a plea for economic survival—a personal address to procure funds is traditionally the visible motivation in ballads. The social dimension of solitude in this poem is complementary with Christine's social understanding of friendship, expressly articulated in such writings as the "Dits moraux à son fils" [Moral Precepts to Her Son]. There it is quite explicitly the common wisdom, not philosophical debate on *amicitia vera* that underlies her notion of friendship: "Aimes qui te tient pour ami / Et te gard' de ton ennemi: / Nul ne peut avoir trop d'amis, / Il n'est nuls petits ennemis" [Love whoever has you for a friend / And beware of your enemy: / No one can have too many friends, / There are no small enemies] (ll. 13–16, strophe 4).

Even in a poem such as "Solitude," which focuses in an almost incantatory style on private emotions, the alienation from social structures of support is made visible. The very idea of solitude is here twofold: "ami" [friend] is both the "douz ami" of the courtly love relationship and the "ami," a friend of the social network. As I intended to show, the idea of social isolation, "social widowhood," is present even in Christine de Pizan's innovative, unprecedented poems, which use the ideology of courtly love in the description of marriage and widowhood. *A fortiori,* in the configurations of widowhood of the earlier period, unaffected by the courtly love rhetoric, the share of social meanings must have been the greater.

To recapitulate: if the concept of widowhood is primarily social, not personal or affective, then women who are not widows—who remain married—when abandoned by their families are like widows in the most important sense: they lack legal representation and economic support. The second point of my demonstration lies in collapsing the meanings of "widow" and "virgin." Orphaned or emancipated ("runaway") virgins—the last case is frequent in the heroic paradigm of the French romance—are like widows because their sexuality is no longer a jealously guarded commodity, to be traded off for political alliances or economic favors. Moreover, the virgins who are part of their family are temporarily excepted from sexual and economic exchange by their very virginity. This aspect is clear in the semantism of the word *virgin;* even modern French preserves the qualifier *virgin* in the sense of "noncirculating" in a number of expressions, of which *page vierge,* "blank page," and *terre vierge,* "uncultivated terrain," are the most ubiquitous. I take this essential meaning, amplified in the typical romance scenario by the dramatic isolation of the virgin-heroine, as the defining feature of virginity. Thus, I consider virgins and widows equivalent in the extended sense of "noncirculating women." To describe the phenomenon of noncirculation, exception—for better or for worse—from the male-dominated social structures, I would like to propose the phrase "social widowhood." This phrase would apply to women who act independently from and frequently in opposition to men (kin or potential, institutionalized charity givers). Whether married or not, these women approximate the social isolation of widows and virgins, both in their autonomy and in their vulnerability. Like widows or virgins, they fell out of the social circulation accomplished through the exchange of sexual and reproductive favors for protection and subsistence in marriage, prostitution, and other contexts.

What support structures replace the patriarchal family and community in the situation of "social widowhood"? I argue that the most frequent one, in fiction as well as in the archives, is the network of solidarity between women, in its diverse forms. In the romances, the women receiving help are most often virgins or married women abandoned by their families. The help-givers are most frequently widows or married women acting independently of their husbands. While some characters giving or benefiting from help are neither widows nor virgins, almost all women (whether they receive, dispense, or refuse help) act independently from men—they are, in my term, "social widows." The case that best shows the existence of gender solidarity in the absence of kinship network is the "calumniated woman" story, in which an exiled woman, usually a virgin or abandoned wife, receives hospitality and support from a widow or a married woman (in exchange for money or services, or out of charity). In most cases, female hospitality is ended by the intervention of a male character (lecherous villain, stingy husband returning from a business trip, etc.). The appearance of female protectors can be considered a natural narrative second choice in the absence of family protectors. Indeed, this mechanism strongly imposes itself in the analysis of the narrative tradition of the "calumniated wife" and the "heroine's rejection of incest."

Since the representation of women's friendship is heavily dependent on narrative necessity, one might argue that it constitutes merely a literary device. This is why I insist on demonstrating the parallelism between the fictional and the documented social behavior. In that discussion, I take advantage of the current work of those medieval historians who have recently focused on female solidarity networks emerging in the absence of family solidarity. While not all the romance patterns duplicate the relationships attested to by the historical sources, and while the fiction emphasizes (and draws narrative momentum from) the differences in social standing between charity givers and recipients, both fiction and documents point to a pattern of social networking that is not exclusively class- and kin-, but also—perhaps predominantly—gender-based. However, before entering the discussion of literary and historical examples of friendship between women, we must first address the question of its absence in the theoretical debate.

Theory and Fiction of Friendship in Thirteenth and Fourteenth-Century France

The thirteenth and fourteenth centuries provide a particularly appropriate time frame for the study of friendship among women in the French tradition because they comprise the period of heightened interest in the theory of friendship, after the circulation of Platonic theories and before the merger of Latin and vernacular traditions in France; that is, after the twelfth-century Renaissance and before Laurent de Premierfait's 1416 translation of Cicero's *Laelius de amicitia,* which marks the proto-Renaissance era of which Montaigne, in his famous essay on friendship, is a tributary (*Essais* 1, 27).[7] As Reginald Hyatte reminds us, the thirteenth century is marked by the appearance of many treatises on friendship, especially in Latin. He proposes a distinction between the first half marked by Cicero, Seneca's *Letters to Lucilius,* biblical and Greek examples, and the second half dominated by Aristotle's *Nicomachean Ethics.*[8] A sizable portion of this activity is by French authors. As Hyatte notes, Andreas Capellanus's sources in *De amore, de arte honeste amandi et de reprobatione inhonesti amoris* (ca. 1185) include *Laelius,* specifically on the impossibility of love between spouses. Part of Vincent de Beauvais's *Speculum majus,* the *Speculum doctrinale* contains twelve chapters on friendship (book 5, 82–93; Hyatte 204). This part of the *Speculum* is influenced by the late twelfth- and thirteenth-century translations of the *Nicomachean Ethics* (first, anonymously, part of book 8; then, Robert Grosseteste, ca. 1246–1247, the whole 10 books).[9] Similarly, Albertus Magnus in the 1250s, and Thomas Aquinas in the 1270s, have comprehensively glossed the *Ethics.*

Vernacular French compilations include the well-known *Livres du tresor* by Brunetto Latini (1260s). *Ethics* corresponds to the first half of the second book of this French language adaptation based, as Hyatte points out, on "Hermannus Alemannus' Latin rendition of an Arabic [Averroes's] version of an anonymous Greek summary of the *Nicomachean Ethics*" (Hyatte 207–208). The second half of the second book, based on Latin compendia (Guillaume Perrault's *Summa aurea de virtutibus,* Guillaume de Conches's *Moralium dogma philosophorum,* Albertano da Brescia's *Ars loquendi et tacendi,* Martin of Dumium's *De quattuor virtutibus cardinalibus,* Isidore of Seville's *Sententiae*), also contains five chapters on friendship, "which cite Cicero,

Proverbs, Seneca, Jerome, Ambrose, Boethius, Sallust, Lucan, and the legendary lives of Aristotle and Merlin" (Hyatte 207). There also exist a number of lesser known, mostly derivative works that comment on the subject of friendship. Among these are for instance Alard de Cambrai's *Livre de philosophie et de moralité* (ed. Jean-Charles Payen. Bibliothéque française et romane. Series B: Editions critiques des textes 9. Paris: Klincksieck, 1970) or Jehan le Bel's *Li Ars d'amours de vertu et de boneurté* (ed. Jules Petit. Academie Royale de Belgique. 2 vols. Bruxelles: V. Devaux, 1867–1869).

The philosophical definition of friendship is economical—or, as Derrida (1994) would prefer it, political. Aristotelian and Ciceronian reflection on perfect friendship is focused on the intrinsic value of friendship.[10] This value can appear only in certain conditions that eliminate the variables devalued as degrading or interfering: utility, pleasure, profit. Thus, true friendship—*amicitia vera*—is a friendship among disinterested equals, *inter pares.* Medieval moral treatises, which are primarily interested in friendship among men, and which entertain the question of female friendship mostly as it applies to men, deny women the possibility of friendship on the logical assumption that women as social subordinates cannot aspire to *amicitia inter pares.* Yet, it is important to note that this tradition, derivative of Aristotle's *Nicomachean Ethics* and Cicero's *Laelius de amicitia,* is not the only one present in the Middle Ages. A tradition that does entertain a possibility of feminine friendship is that of spiritual friendship, mediated by God who is its source and object. This Christian blend of *amicitia vera* was most notably developed by Aelred of Rievaulx (*De Spirituali amicitia,* twelfth century), but was present in Augustinian thought and earlier (see Hyatte 43–86 for an outline of the evolution of the concept of spiritual friendship). However, the mysticism of spiritual friendship has not weakened, but rather marginally coexisted with the Aristotelian/Ciceronian tradition. This would account for the fact that the theoretical paradigm excluding women from friendship persists in moral treatises throughout the Middle Ages and into the Renaissance.

We must be reminded that outside of the realm of philosophical speculation, the negative paradigm was not the only one available nor, perhaps, the predominant one. The biblical tradition provides examples of noble friendship among women and between women and men, and so do the narrative traditions of the vernacular romance. These traditions of women's friendship, however, remained genre-specific. There exists in the thirteenth and fourteenth centuries a clear division along the gender and genre lines: while the moral treatises, both vernacular and Latin, define friendship in terms of gender (limiting the true friendship to relationships between men), the romance tradition provides abundant examples of not only masculine but also feminine friendships—most notably friendships between women, which are the focus of my study. In understanding this polarization, it is useful to go beyond facile explanation: different genres have opposite objectives predicated on their purpose, readership, and traditions (philosophy as examining the male world for the masculine audience imbued with Latin traditions; fiction as more inclusive, perhaps subversive, vernacular). Apart from being obviously inaccurate in its premises, such an answer would obscure certain interesting mechanisms that become apparent when the theoretical definition of women's friendship is explored in some detail.

Ulrich Langer has recently noted the paradox of the exclusively male friendship: a gender-exclusive affective space that produces and acts out the feminine anti-economy of love. In order to illustrate this paradox, Langer pertinently quotes the definition of the anti-economy of feminine desire by Irigaray:

> Thus what they [women] desire is just nothing and, at the same time, all. Always more and always something else than that "one"—of sex, for instance—which you give them, which you imply they want. This is often interpreted, and feared, as some kind of insatiable hunger, a voracity which will engulf you entirely; while what's actually at stake here is really a different economy, an economy which derails the linearity of a project, undermines the object-goal of a desire, explodes the polarization on a single pleasure, disconcerts the fidelity to a single discourse.[11]

Langer pursues, pointing out that Irigaray's "refusal of an economy of love"

> is nonetheless also characteristic of the discourse of friendship that, as we have seen, is so markedly dominated by male examples. Cicero emphasizes the absence of hope of gain in relationships of true friendship: "for as we are kind and generous, not so that we may demand repayment—for we do not give favors with interest, but they are by nature given to generosity—so we believe that friendship is desirable, not because we are influenced by hope of gain, but because its entire profit is in the love itself" (*De amicitia* 488 [9.31]). . . . We find, then, in friendship theory the opposition between an economic model of investment and return, and a love of the "person" detached from usefulness to the lover, or an enjoyment of the love itself, as a virtuous activity. . . . The resistance to an economic model underlying the relationship of love is prefigured in the friendship with another for his own sake (Langer 140–141).

The resistance to the economic model that characterizes the feminine desire constructs a gender-exclusive space of masculine friendship where that model can be acted out safely without the fear of castration, of losing oneself in the presence of an "other" of a different and socially subordinate gender.

This is not the only paradox of perfect friendship. As Langer also points out, perfection is incompatible with the economy of lack that fuels narration. We are presented with a second contradiction: "the incompatibility of ethical (lack of) motivation and literary motivation in the representation of perfect friendships" (Langer 27). The appreciation of this paradox is essential to any study of fictive friendships, because it explains why the theoretical *amicitia vera* cannot be encountered in the fictional space. Thus, the perfect male friends, medieval Castor and Pollux or *Ami and Amile* are presented in the linear (goal-bound) economy of narration in all the instances of desire and need necessary to depict the all-inclusive nature of their friendship. The narrative motivation, the "necessity of lack" contaminates the fictional representation of *amicitia vera*.

The acknowledgment of this paradox is indispensable to the approach I adopt in my study. I argue that it eliminates the need for distinction between *amicitia vera,* benevolence, charity, and interested friendship. Since the fictional friendship must by definition be motivated by lack, and therefore interested, the theoretically posited distinctions between unmotivated *amicitia vera* and motivated "vulgar" friendships are erased. These philosophical distinctions are void in the realm of fiction—a hypothesis consistent with the previously observed genre differentiation in the representation of friendship. Therefore, for the purpose of this study, I will use indistinctly such terms as solidarity, networking, friendship, charity, and benevolence.

Thus my line of inquiry authorizes, and indeed imposes as indispensable, the search for covert and overt motivation in the acts of friendship. The categories of social stratification (wealth, allegiance, kinship, or other vehicles of social worth) are as positively relevant to the fictional representation of friendship as they are negatively relevant to the theory of perfect friendship. In many cases, great narrative importance is assigned to worth, valuation, and suitability in the acts of friendship. Since most acts of friendship among women occur when the heroine is bereft of the social framework (family, etc.) normally ensuring her well-being, the social context of friendship is complicated by the fluctuating status of the heroine. While the suffering, abandoned heroine's "overt" status is undervalued with respect to her birth, or "covert" status by the characters in the romance, the reader's valuation and the conclusions of the narrative are based on her "covert" social worth. Social status, as much as gender, is an important variable in the practice of friendship among women as represented in the medieval texts. Since this study only summarily addresses the complex issues accompanying the fictional representation of the society, I will use the imprecise yet common terminology in referring to the social status as "class."

Women's Networks: Historical Documentation

Historically documented patterns of women's interaction include primarily wills and accounts of monasteries, hospitals, shelters, and other charitable institutions, which were frequently run by and for women. Groundbreaking research on the poor in medieval France led by Michel Mollat in the 1970s[12] was followed by such works as Nicole Gonthier's study of Lyons or Marie-Thérèse Lacroix's study of the St. Nicolas hospice in Tours, revealing interesting patterns of women's giving and support.[13] For instance, some shelters or hospices were run by a small group of nuns and lay keepers, not only providing help to the predominantly female poor and sick but also providing means of support and respectable social status to the unmarried women employed there. The wills and accounts of many of these institutions show that they were self-sufficient—that is they were largely funded by the dowries brought in by the unmarried women upon entry and wills left by these women at death. These institutions also tended to attract more bequests from the women's families than from unrelated donors (Lacroix, *L'Hôpital Saint-Nicolas du Bruille,* 1977). We may observe that this situation attests to the importance of the institutions to these families, as well as to the fundraising leverage and skills of the women—leverage and skills superior to those of the bishops or other heads of the ecclesiastical or secular hierarchy who typically supervised and may have been expected to fund these communities. Interestingly, we can also see that in some foundations started by rich men for poor women there evolved forms of self-governance, transforming men-managed institutions into women's solidarity networks *de facto* if not *de jure.* Such evidence is available from the more abundantly documented charitable institutions of the city states of Italy. For instance, Richard Texler's study of the Orbatello, a Florentine shelter for widows and their dependents funded by a rich merchant in the second half of the fourteenth century, shows that the long-time inhabitants of the shelter successfully manipulated and disregarded the rules of the shelter (including the prohibitions concerning race, gender, and marital status of the inhabitants) in order to accommodate their own family and solidarity networks.[14] Texler argues that these women were able to maintain a balanced community, and produce generations of socially acceptable, endowed, marriageable girls for nearly a century, until a major intervention of the city impeded women's *de facto* self-governance.

Studies such as these show important patterns of networking between women in the charitable institutions, but they are far from presenting a full picture of women's networks. Specifically, the institutionalized charities run by and for the minorities are much less well documented—such is the case of Jewish hospices, among others.

For instance, the Jewish hospice in Aix-en-Provence, whose short presence and disappearance in the 1450s is documented only by the bills of sale of the adjacent real estate, stands in contrast to other hospitals in Aix, much better documented, partly because they are larger.[15] Similarly, the charitable institutions in rural areas are far less well documented than are the urban institutions.[16]

Apart from the underrepresentation of charities run by and for the nondominant groups (be they defined by ethnicity or economy), the most important absence in the historical documents is that of noninstitutional charity. While the extent of unorganized almsgiving and aid to the poor is impossible to estimate, many specialists assume that the value of unrecorded alms was comparable to if not greater than the value recorded in bequests and accounts. The urban legends of beggars supporting extended families or networks of clients by reselling bread and redistributing money from alms correlate with many historical (as well as fictional) sources that show that alms distribution was monitored by individual givers, as well as by charitable institutions. The latter can be expected to have been particularly vigilant, since the unorganized alms diminished the flow of resources that the institutional charities hoped to tap. Considering these stakes, we might argue whether attempts at regulation of mendacity resulted from any factual abuse by recipients.[17] In any case, professional begging could be a means of support, even if it was not a lucrative trade. It is a matter of consensus among historians that unrecorded charity was as important to the poor as institutionalized charity.

Some historians have found ways to access information on noninstitutional charity. For instance, Sharon Farmer determined through the study of miracle rolls that female neighbors or acquaintances provided services such as lodging, board, sick care, reference to the wealthier members of the community, to women seeking miracles in thirteenth and fourteenth century Ile-de-France.[18] While some of the needy women were married, they did not receive support from their husbands or families; they therefore fall into the category of "social widowhood" proposed earlier. There are also traces of female networking in the domain which we do not normally consider that of charity, namely credit. Recent research documents that in some geographical areas women, especially widows, were significantly involved in credit and investment during the Middle Ages.[19] While it is supposed that such women might have maintained a female clientele, definitive case studies are still unavailable. Although considered immoral by the church, for-profit moneylending was effectively a resource to the poor, to whom the availability of high-interest, short-term subsistence loans often meant the difference between starvation and survival.[20]

Types of Women's Solidarity in the Romance

While records of unorganized and unauthorized help to the needy, especially those concerning women, are scarce and difficult to access, romance fictions often represent noninstitutional networks between women. Indeed, widowhood or maidenhood are quasi-prerequisites of participating in female solidarity networks. The romance heroine being by definition without means, she also falls into the category of deprived or "socially widowed" women. Among these fictions, the richest in references to women's solidarity are those that include the motif of calumniated wife, forsaken maiden or widow, or virgin rejecting incest. In all these three circumstances, women are banished from or abandon their family or (usually aristocratic) marriage, most frequently because their husbands were killed, intend to kill them, or because their fathers are incestuous. In some romances, the repudiated wife or maiden finds a male champion who helps, shelters, and represents her in armed combat. However, especially in the heroine's rejection of incest stories, the helpers are predominantly female, and males often intervene to disrupt the tranquillity of the shelter through attempted rape, or to end the charitable women's involvement with the poor, which they view as *economically undesirable*. The benefactresses, however, often value the needy women's skills, and while no transactions are recorded at the time of charitable action other than the payment of rent and reimbursement of expenses, the interactions between the needy and charitable women are frequently presented as mutually desirable. In some specific cases, the charitable women are also rewarded at the end of the story, when the heroine returns to her privileged social and marital position and recompenses those who supported her in her poverty.

Characteristically, even the romances in which the isolated woman finds a male protector allow interactions between women (indeed, the protector need not be masculine; thus, in the widely popular twelfth-century *Roman d'Alexandre,* Porus leaving for war entrusts his daughter to Candace, a neighboring queen). Three types of women's solidarity occur there most frequently: emotional support, midwifery, and nursing or other help in caring for the infant. A representative case of emotional support occurs for instance in *Alixandre l'Orphélin,*[21] where the mother of the hero flees after her husband was killed by the jealous king Marc of Cornwall. She arrives in the castle of her father, Magence. Her father is dead but has ordered the knight in charge of the castle to receive her; the knight is a close kin of her father, his wife is the heroine's first cousin. When the knight grants her refuge from the pursuers, the narrative focus shifts to an extended description of the reception by the knight's wife, "who was very happy on account of her coming and sorry for her ill luck. And they start to shed many tears from their eyes; one and the other, when they saw and recognized each other, embraced each other closely and many times" (*Alixandre l'Orphélin* p. 2, ll. 3–10). Here, the knight and his wife offer two distinct, complementary, gendered types of support.

Another instance of gender-marked interaction occurs in a surprisingly large subgroup of romances with female heroes, where the heroine is exiled right before or after parturition. She is therefore either forced to give birth in the wilderness (*Floriant et Florete, Parise la duchesse, Galiens li restorés, Charles de Venise,* among others), or travel during her lying-in period (the "heroine rejecting incest" cycle, including *Belle Hélène de Constantinople,* Philippe de Beaumanoir's *Manekine* and the *Roman du comte d'Anjou*). The "birth in the wilderness" episodes sometimes refer to the unfortunate absence of women (as in the thirteenth-century *Parise la duchesse:* "O God! she has no woman to whom she could talk!" [l. 801], a comment out of character in this knightly fiction composed in the traditionally epic form of assonanced *laisses*).[22] In other texts, as in *Floriant et Florete,* a few women are present in the suit of the young widow. While they are in the minority (four, compared to ten men), they are mentioned with respect to the care of the parturient mother and child: bathing, clothing, and feeding.[23] The ten men, while enumerated, are granted no comparable narrative presence; their function is expressed by labeling (squires, etc.), while the women are characterized by their actions.

Parturition was clearly a defining moment in the relationship between the woman and her social framework, and the romances show dramatic scenarios contrasting with the proper social conduct. Under normal circumstances, new mothers were confined to bed, or at least denied entry to church, during a period rightly considered dangerous to their health; the parturient women were also considered dangerous to the community (and still are so in the folkloric unconscious). The proper social conduct in this context may well be illustrated by texts of laudatory nature. For instance, Ramon Muntaner's *Chronicle* intends to portray the lord in a favorable light as a husband prohibiting to divulge bad news and waiting with an important expedition until his wife's lying-in period elapses.[24] The romance fictions, on the other hand, rehearse the scandal of the improper conduct. In the early fourteenth-century *Roman du comte d'Anjou,* the new mother is a vagrant—in the double sense of Latin *vagari,* 1) "wandering" away from her social framework and her geographical and familial origins; and 2) "vague," an ambivalent sign (she travels incognito and her social worth fluctuates, depending on the subjective assessment of each fictional character she encounters).[25] The meaning of this ambiguous figure is not determined by its content but rather by the gender of the interpreter. The fictional woman reacts with sympathy to the ambiguous sign: a bourgeoise, "when she sees [the child] of such a young age, she sees clearly that the mother should still lay, if she had her right. Pity moves her and she prays courteously that [the mother] tell her if this child is borne of her and why she has not finished all the established days of lying-in" (ll. 4464–4471). On his part, the fictional man, the chief almsgiver, reacts to the equivocal sign with suspicion, disbelief, and presupposition of fault (much as modern congressmen discussing welfare) "and asks of the little child if it's hers. 'Certainly, yes, sir'—What? says he, How dare you say this? The child is not even three weeks old, and you conduct yourself in this manner? If it were yours, you should be in bed, and you shouldn't be able to get up yet" (ll. 4654–4660).

While, as in the above example, the helpful women frequently act in a gender-distinctive fashion, an extreme (and isolated) example is that of female networking across religious and political divide in *Aye d'Avignon*. Detained by the Muslim king Ganor, Aye is imprisoned in a fortified tower and served by three queens of the land who "sweetly, by love and devotion, show her the law of Tervagant and Mahomet."[26] In this striking example, gender seems to be the operating category, overriding the distinctions of race, politics and faith, which normally rule the fictional encounters with the "Other."

On the other hand, women's solidarity crossing class divides is a stock motif in the romance—although, as documents show, in reality women's networks were largely class-confined, even in charitable institutions providing services to the poor.[27] Among the most frequently encountered motifs of female solidarity is that of the aristocratic heroine in exile taking shelter with a poor widow or other social subordinate. A measure of realism is provided by the fact that, at the time, the aristocratic heroine travels incognito, on foot, without retinue and often without money. In Adenet le Roi's *Berte aus grands pieds,* Jean Renart's *Escoufle,* in *Aye d'Avignon* and in the "heroine rejecting incest" cycle, the pursued heroine finds shelter among women. In *Aye,* the heroine finds a ruined and impoverished monastery, where the ascetic marchioness Audegont lives with fifteen ladies. In this liminary location, "this ruined place, this desert, with bears, lions, pigs and wilderness" (ll. 928–929), the marchioness addresses thus the solitary fugitive: "Friend, have you escaped or run from home, or were you taken from a lord or has he abandoned you? Whatever you have done, do not hide it from me, and do not fear any living men, for you are here entirely secure" (ll. 930–935). The refugee then states her lineage, and further reception is established on the principle of close kinship. However, the initial welcome is as unconditional as it is insightful in guessing why a woman seeks refuge (abuse, *raptus,* abandonment), as well as in anticipating the typical cause for the interruption of female solidarity in the economy of romance—masculine intervention.

This episode combines two motifs present in other texts: reception by the hermit (in *Berte,* the hermit refuses to let the young woman in for fear of temptation, but he directs her to another shelter), and reception by destitute women (once in *Escoufle,* twice in the *Roman du comte d'Anjou*).[28] In *Escoufle* and *Anjou,* the heroines are explicit about their choice: since they travel unaccompanied by men, staying in a large house would expose them to loss of reputation; the implication seems to be forced prostitution (*Escoufle* ll. 4941–4956, *Anjou* ll. 1220–1221).[29] Prior to reception, the poor charity givers (widows in all three cases) dwell on the "inadequacy topos": the bed offered is hard, the food too common for the fugitive whom they recognize as socially superior. The heroine responds by assurances that not the amenities but the social context of a poor widow's home is essential: the shelter is selected as part of strategy to avoid loss of reputation (or rape).

A poor widow's house provides a social frame to women unaccompanied by men or retinue. Aélis, the heroine of *Escoufle,* is a notable exception, as she seeks rather than avoids adventure; however, throughout the narrative, our attention is drawn to her economic power. Money can provide a social frame as effectively, and more, than a poor widow's house. The widow's house is a basic protection against the threat of rape that looms on the narrative horizon, but it is not a permanent one. In order to remain safe, the women never go out unless to receive alms, and are not seen except by their hostess. Once they are seen by the outsiders, neither the poor widow's house nor the castle offers sufficient protection. The status of women invariably changes: they either leave, move to a hospital, or marry. In *Anjou,* approached by a young bourgeois and asked to procure the young fugitive, the widow warns the heroine and her nurse who flee at once. In *Berte,* the king (Berte's estranged husband) nearly rapes the heroine, believing her to be a shepherdess. The shelter provides a sort of narrative *plateau,* allowing the author to turn his attention to the male counterpart of the heroine. The disruption of the security of the shelter forces the heroine to reenter the narrative circulation of the sexual-economic kind.

While the poor widow is paid for her services, a similar motif—taking shelter in a castle, manor, or bourgeois house—involves a different type of exchange: here, the needy women often work at embroidery. The textile production, so skillfully analyzed in recent criticism in its relationship to the text (by Burns, Durling, and Joplin, among others), can serve many narrative purposes, from a token of moral righteousness (*Anjou*) to the premise of a complex plot involving three amorous and marital pairs in *Escoufle*.[30] Whatever the ultimate narrative function, in the episodes of women's friendship in *Berte, Escoufle,* and *Anjou,* the skill at embroidery justifies the protection of the heroine by wealthier women. In *Berte* and

Anjou, the fugitive becomes part of a family already comprising parents and daughters, following a charitable decision made by the father. The utility of the skilled protégé to these women is differently emphasized in the two texts. In *Berte,* this utility justifies the constancy of the women's kindness; in *Anjou,* it justifies the shift from hostility to kindness. Here, when the husband finds the heroine and her nurse in the forest, his wife suspects the younger is the husband's mistress, and refuses to take them into the castle. They are lodged in a small house outside and lead an exemplary life; their workmanship becomes well known. The wife eventually invites them to live in the castle and teach embroidery to her daughters.

The Economy of the Charitable Interaction in the Romance: Class or Gender?

The economies of these two relationships—that between the heroine and the poor widow, and that between the heroine and the rich mother and wife—differ. The poor widows receive the fugitives and assist them in the purchase of embroidering supplies (*Anjou*). They collect rent (*Anjou, Escoufle*) and money to purchase provisions (*Escoufle*). At the end of the narration, the poor widows who lodged the fugitive are not among the charitable women rewarded by the heroine restored to her social status. As Planche observed for the *Roman du comte d'Anjou,* the economy of these fictions requires adapting the gift to the needs and estate of the recipient: the charity of the romance is far from blind.[31] The impoverished heroes are subject to careful scrutiny on the part of the charity givers; this scrutiny first determines that they are "honest poor" and not otherwise marginal (passive sexual behavior validation for women; inability to work validation for men) and secondly classifies them not as poor but impoverished. Planche summarizes the kindness to strangers operating in *Anjou* as "paternalistic"; the poor are "catagorized before being helped and given information necessary to their survival." In representing the charitable women's actions as those of "both a secrest police agent and a public welfare Bureau" (Planche, "Surveillance policiére" 277), that is in evaluating the poor and dispensing help adequate to circumstances (that is, to the social standing of the recipient), the text exhibits "the precepts of a morality categorized by caste" (Planche, "Surveillance policiére" 282).

It may be observed that the conclusion of the romance presents a picture of female friendship as strongly marked by caste distinctions as Planche suggests. At the close of the romance, the reward goes only to the bourgeoisie and to the female administrator of the hospital in which the heroine resides when she meets her husband—to each of those, according to her needs, which are predicated on their respective social standing.

The poor widows are not in a position to offer charity; they are reimbursed immediately, and they are granted no further rewards. We may also add to Planche's remarks that not only the monetary gift but the "gift" of narrative presence, the "staying power" of a charity giver reflects her social status. The socially inferior benefactress has only an episodic role in the narration and does not enjoy the epiphany in the conclusion. Thus, both the charity givers and recipients participate in caste distinctions that divide gender along the poverty line. The appropriateness to the social standing of the recipient does not only structure the giving but also the rewards. Neither are the generous adoptive mothers (the heroine's husband's vassals in *Anjou* and *Berte*) directly recompensed by the heroine. While the exchange between nurture and skill in embroidery supposes a measure of equality, when the adoptive families turn out to be vassals of the heroine's husband, the latter recompenses them by placing them in his retinue. The alliances that have previously established a "feminine economy" of exchange (skills versus protection) are thus reclaimed by the dominant allegiance systems.

Nonetheless, it is important to emphasize that Planche's reading of class as organizing principle of charity in *Anjou* reveals a covert, not an overt structure. Overtly, the text posits gender, not class, as the operating principle of women's friendship. The bourgeoisie of Etampes who helped the parturient mother and child in the absence of her husband explains the functioning of her charity in these terms: "For a woman shall pity another woman when she sees her poor and suffering" (Jehan Maillart, *Le Roman du comte d'Anjou*, ll. 5545–5546). A similar (although not expressly articulated) social rule seems to govern the presentation of the aristocratic heroine at the beginning of the romance: among her attributes is listed generosity towards "orphaned maidens, widows, poor girls, when they contracted marriage" (Jehan Maillart, *Le Roman du comte d'Anjou*, ll.129–131).

Planche's class-bound reading also erases another overtly expressed, gendered condition of charity: in the society of men, the consequences of charity are not always positive for the charity giver. The bourgeoisie of Etampes fears that her husband will "beat and insult her" (Jehan Maillart, *Le Roman du comte d'Anjou*, ll. 5575). This double fear is later repeated when the benefactress helps the heroine's husband in turn—the fear of verbal abuse is expressed identically on both occasions. The husband, who sees charity as depletion of resources, reacts with passion: "quit! says he, do I go through such pains to earn in order to spend on this? I know full well how to defend myself! You've found a good reason! She will leave my house tomorrow" (Jehan Maillart, *Le Roman du comte d'Anjou*, ll. 4510–4514). The structure of the romance justifies the generosity of the wife (and, by corollary, condemns the husband), since the heroine richly rewards her benefactress in the end.

In order to further emphasize the overt, gender-based structure of charity to women, I would like to briefly mention the illumination program in the *Roman du comte d'Anjou* (described by the editor, TKTK–TK). Among its twenty-some illustrations, we find all but one of the acts of charity between women (the second episode of reception by a poor widow is absent). There is a visible emphasis on the relationships between women: the scenes represent women consoling each other (the nurse consoling the young countess of Anjou), suffering together (two fugitives in the forest), receiving shelter and care (arrival at the first widow's house; the countess's, then the count's encounter with the charitable bourgeoisie of Etampes; joyful reception by the mistress of Hôtel Dieu), bidding farewell (departure from the first widow's house), hiring the poor woman's services (the knight and his wife bidding the women to come to the castle), assisting in the happy ending (the mistress of Hôtel Dieu at the reunion of the spouses), receiving rewards (bourgeoisie and mistress of Hôtel Dieu receiving gold cups from the countess). Thus, out of the 28 miniatures that originally illustrated the BN 4531 manuscript of the *Roman du comte d'Anjou,* fully one-third depict women's friendships; in the entire program, almost as many female as male figures are represented.

Conclusion

Women's friendship is devalued and excluded by the dominant medieval theories of friendship. Even as these theories developed, the possibility of friendship among women was more strongly denied. Yet, as suggested by Ulrich Langer, the perfect friendship among men effectively duplicates the "anti-economy" of women's bonds. As a corollary, we may suppose that the need for differentiation—the necessity of obscuring the link between perfect friendship and women's "anti-economy" of love—may have served as a powerful motive of the exclusion of women's friendship from the philosophical discussion. It further accentuates the division between the philosophical and moral treatises and the romance genre, in which examples of women's friendship abound.

Langer's second and perhaps ultimately more convincing paradox is the observation that the fiction and theory of friendship cannot be ruled by the same model (supposing that we reduce the theory of friendship to its dominant Aristotelian/Ciceronian variant). While the theory excludes motivation, the economy of fiction requires it. Thus, the functioning of the narration necessarily calls for such definition of friendship as would include the variables (economy, pleasure, interest) devalued in the theory of friendship. This necessity of narrative motivation justifies my adopting of a vocabulary of friendship that does not recognize the philosophical distinction between charity, "vulgar" friendship, and *amicitia vera* in the study of the romance texts.

Taking as a point of departure a "broad spectrum," inclusive definition, and terminology of friendship among women, I show the context of this motif in the romance. First, I focus on the figures linked by the bond of friendship. Based on the semantic functioning of the words "widow" and "virgin" in the French language, I use them not in their primary, modern sense—emotional or physiological markers—but rather as they apply to a woman's social position. I argue that it is useful to extend these labels beyond widows and virgins in the literal sense, and therefore I consider in this chapter other women who, like widow and virgins, are not secured by the male-dominated social networks (marriage, family, community). I propose the term "social widowhood" as an inclusive label for all cases.

These feminine figures, "widows and virgins," are characterized both by autonomy and by vulnerability. The vulnerability is a narrative prerequisite of heroism, and it allows the depiction of autonomous female figures acting independently from men both in receiving and in giving help. As a result, women's networks are presented in the romance in an array of configurations, prominently featuring such motivations as proper aristocratic behavior (charity), proper women's behavior (gender solidarity), and exchange of money or skills for shelter. Friendships between women are defined by such variables as class, economic interest, and health. In all, my research shows (even in the modest sample offered here) that during the medieval French "golden age" of romance, the motif of women's friendship was prominently and diversely featured.

However, I argue that the fictional friendships between women were not merely a stock device and fruit of the literary tradition but rather that they were congruent with the social experience of the contemporary audience, an experience in which "social widowhood" was complementary with women's solidarity networks. The story of women's friendship, while a severely limited (episodic) motif heavily dependent on narrative economy—abandoned heroines find in other women natural adjuvants—is also carried out by the historical documents. Therefore, I argue for a much greater impact of women's friendship fictions than could be surmised from reading the romances in the context of literary tradition alone, without reference to historical sources, and a greater impact than can be surmised from reading the romances in the context of the contemporary philosophical and moral treatises.

Widows and virgins, typical heroic figures of the romance (in the sense that the prerequisite of heroism is vulnerability and exposure), appear therefore paradoxically less precarious, and perhaps more interesting as positive (rather than pathetic) models. Moreover, the assumption of readers' interest in women's networking—an interest enhanced by the coherence between fictional representation and social practice, as opposed to mere narrative functionality—adds emphasis to these parts of the romance that present the multiform world of relationships between women, from emotional help to midwifery, caring for children and the sick, employment, and cohabitation. This emphasis may rival the importance accorded to battle and other virile scenes. The archaeology of female reception of medieval texts, so aptly proposed by Krueger, can be usefully extended to this case, where fictional widows and virgins play roles performed by their real-life counterparts.[32]

The final observation again participates in the series of paradoxes revealed by the parallel reading of theory and fiction of friendship. The romances frequently show the conflicts of loyalty featured by the moralists, where women's acts of friendship willingly and knowingly undermine men's sovereignty. However, rather than menacing, these gender solidarities are cast as positive and are justified by the conclusion of the romance. They are presented as acts of Christian charity, and also as small infractions preventing greater evils of forced prostitution or incest. Such interpretation would be coherent with the social functioning of these fictions which appear as moral exempla as well as romances—"heroine's rejection of incest" type appears in Marian miracles, as well as in two important collections of *exempla*: Jean Gobi's *Scala coeli* (1322–1330) and Heunannus Bononiensis *Viaticum narrationum*. It is also found in historiography (in fact, *Vita Offae primi* is generally regarded as the first medieval occurrence), in *roman d'aventures*, and in the late epic. Thus, the romances paint a very positive picture of the social acceptability of women's friendship—indeed, a picture opposite to the one drawn by the majority of moral and philosophical treatises.

Notes

1. I would like to thank Angela Jane Weisl and Cindy Carlson, whose editing and comments significantly influenced my contribution.
2. See William C. Jordan, *Women and Credit in Pre-Industrial and Developing Societies.* (Philadelphia: University of Pennsylvania Press, 1993).
3. André Tunc, quoted by Gérard Giordanengo, *Le Droit féodal dans les pays de droit écrit: l'exemple de la Provence et du Dauphiné, XIIe-début du XIVe siécle* (Rome: Ecole Française de Rome, 1988), p. XI. All translations are mine unless otherwise indicated.
4. Christine de Pizan, *Oeuvres poétiques complétes de Christine de Pizan,* ed. Maurice Roy, 3 vols., Société des Anciens Textes Français (Paris: Firmin Didot, 1886–1896). The emphasis in the English translations is mine.

5. Literally, the refrain reads: "I am alone, without friend remained;" however, "am remained," possible in French, is impossible in English. To match the rhythm and sense, I translate the French past participle with English present.

6. Charity Cannon Willard, *Christine de Pizan, Her Life and Works* (New York: Persea, 1984).

7. Michel de Montaigne, *Essais,* ed. Albert Thibaudet, Bibiothéque de la Pléiade 14 (Paris: Gallimard, 1950).

8. Reginald Hyatte, *The Arts of Friendship: The Idealization of Friendship in Medieval and Early Renaissance Literature* (Leiden and New York: E. J. Brill, 1994), p. 203.

9. Hyatte, *Arts of Friendship,* p. 16, quoting Auguste Pelzer, "Les versions latines des ouvrages de morale conservés sous le nom d'Aristote en usage au XIIIe siécle." *Revue néo-scolastique de philosophie* 23 (1921): 333–335; and Hyatte Appendix B.

10. Jacques Derrida, *Politiques de l'amitié, suivi de L'Oreille de Heidegger,* La philosophie en effet (Paris: Galilée, 1994).

11. Luce Irigaray, *Ce sexe qui n'en est pas un* (Paris: Minuit, 1977), quoted in Ulrich Langer, *Perfect Friendship: Studies in Literature and Moral Philosophy from Bocaccio to Corneille* (Geneva: Droz, 1994), p. 140.

12. Michel Mollat, *Les Pauvres au moyen âge. Etude sociale* (Paris: Hachette, 1978), and Jean-Louis Goglin, *Les misérables dans l'Occident médiéval* (Paris: Seuil, 1976).

13. Marie-Thérèse Lacroix, *L'Hôpital Saint-Nicolas du Bruille (Saint-André) à Tournai de sa fondation à sa mutation en cloître (~1230–1611),* 2 vols. (Louvain: Université Catholique de Louvain, 1977).

14. Richard C. Texler, *The Women of Renaissance Florence: Power and Dependence in Renaissance Florence,* vol. 2 (Binghamton: Medieval and Renaissance Texts and Studies, 1993).

15. Jean Pourriére, *Les hôpitaux d'Aix-en-Provence au Moyen Age, 13e, 14e et 15e siécles* (Aix-en-Provence: Paul Roubaud, 1969).

16. Marie-Thérèse Lorcin, "Ripailles de funérailles aux 14e et 15e siécles, ou les pauvres seront-ils invités au repas d'enterrement?" In *Mélanges Fournival* (St. Etienne, 1979), pp. 239–251; Monique Bourin and Robert Durand, *Vivre au village au moyen âge: Les solidarités paysannes du 11e au 13e siécles* (Paris: Messidor, 1984).

17. Nicole Gonthier discusses this issue in *Lyon et ses pauvres au moyen âge (1350 – 1500)* (Lyon: L'Hermés, 1978).

18. Sharon Farmer, "Down and Out—and Female—In Thirteenth-Century Paris," Presentation at the Twenty-ninth International Congress on Medieval Studies at Kalamazoo, MI, 1994.

19. William C. Jordan, *Women and Credit.*

20. William C. Jordan, *Women and Credit.*

21. In the fourteenth-century prose *Prophecies of Merlin.* I am using a fifteenth century prose version, *Les prophécies Merlin,* ed. L. A. Paton. (New York: PMLA, 1926–1927).

22. *Fierabras; Parise la duchesse,* Les Anciens poétes de la France (Nedeln: Kraus Reprint Ltd., 1966).
23. *Floriant et Florete,* ed. Harry F. Williams, Language and Literature 23 (Ann Arbor: University of Michigan Press, 1947), ll. 542–548.
24. Ramon Muntanez, *From the Chronicle of Muntanez,* trans. Lady Goodenough. (London: The Hakluyt Society #50, 1921), in Jeremy du Quesnay Adams, *Patterns of Medieval Society* (Englewood Cliffs, NJ: Prentice-Hall, 1969).
25. Jehan Maillart, *Le Roman du comte d'Anjou,* ed. Mario Roques (Paris: Champion, 1931).
26. *Aye d'Avignon: Chanson de geste,* ed. F. Guessard and P. Meyer, Anciens poétes de la France 6 (Paris: F. Vieweg, 1861, l. 1852).
27. Historians seem to agree that charitable institutions are always prone to shifting their financial focus inwards; cf. among others Texler, *The Women of Renaissance Florence,* Lorcin, "Ripailles de funérailles," Lacroix, *L'Hôpital Saint-Nicolas du Bruille.*
28. Adenet le Roi, *Berte aus grans pies,* Textes littérraires français 305 (Geneva: Droz, 1982).
29. Jehan Renart, *L'Escoufle: Roman d'aventure,* ed. Franklin Sweetser (Paris: Droz, 1974).
30. E. Jane Burns, *Bodytalk: When Women Speak in Old French Literature* (Philadelphia: The University of Pennsylvania Press, 1993); Nancy Vine Durling, "Chaste Pairs: *Justa Victoria* and the French Wager Tale Tradition," *Romance Languages Annual* 4 (1992): 47–50; Patricia Klindienst Joplin, "The Voice of the Shuttle is Ours," *Stanford Literature Review* 1 (1984): 25–53.
31. Alice Planche, "Surveillance policiére et auto-surveillance des pauvres. Le témoignage du *Roman du comte d'Anjou* (1316)," in Danielle Buschinger, ed., *Actes du colloque des 5 et 6 mai 1978, Littérature et société au moyen âge* (Paris: Champion, 1978).
32. Roberta Krueger, *Women Readers and the Ideology of Gender in Old French Verse Romance,* Cambridge Studies in French 43 (Cambridge: Cambridge University Press, 1993).

CHAPTER 2

THE WIDOW AS VIRGIN: DESEXUALIZED NARRATIVE IN CHRISTINE DE PIZAN'S *LIVRE DE LA CITÉ DES DAMES*

Angela Jane Weisl

> *Christine de Pizan constructs her own female, authoritative voice from her identity as a widow and the perfect virginity of her namesake, St. Christine; this voice allows her to speak the "truth" denied women within the sexual economy of marriage.*

Christine de Pizan, often lauded as the first woman to make her living as a writer, is also frequently remembered for her striking metaphorical sex change in the *Mutacion de Fortune*. Anxious and alone after the death of her husband, Christine imagines herself cast out to sea in a boat she cannot control. After striking a rock and capsizing the ship, Christine awakens and says, "Je m'esveillay et fu le cas / Tel qu'incontinent et sanz doubte / Transmuee me senti toute" [I woke up immediately / There is no doubting it—/ I was changed all over]:

> Estoit muee et enforcie
> Et ma voix forment engrossie
> Et corps plus dur et plus isnel
> Mais choit de mon doy fu l'anel
> Qu'Ymenetis donné m'avoit . . .
> . . . . . .

Fort et hardi cuer me trouvay,
Dont,'esbahi, mais j'espouvay
Que vray homme fus devenu . . .

[My appearance was altered and made stronger,
My voice became deeper,
My body, harder and more agile.
But the ring that Hymen had given me
Fell from my finger.
. . . . .
I found within myself a strong and hardy spirit,
Which amazed me,
And proved that I
Had become a real man.][1]

This well-known passage, repeated in *L'Avision Christine*,[2] seems an odd strategy for the author of the best-known medieval defense of women, the *Livre de la Cité des Dames*. Indeed, at the beginning of the *Cité*, Christine reallies herself with women, drawing on another sense of herself from Ballad XI, "Seulete suy et seluete vueil estre" [I am a woman alone, and I wish to be a woman alone].[3] Christine begins the *Cité "seule"* in her study, echoing the line from her ballad; that sense of solitude, shown even in her transformation scene by the loss of her wedding ring, perhaps goes further towards constructing Christine's authorial identity than her sex-change does. It is Christine's widowhood that forces her to become a writer; it is her solitude and separation from the world of sexual relations (although not gender relations) that give her the means and the authority to write. While this cross-gendered sense of herself as social person and author seemed fitting to Christine in the *Mutacion* and *L'Avision,* her choice not to reuse it in the *Cité des Dames* suggests that as she undertakes her most overt and programmatic defense of her sex, she rejects this strategy as too masculinizing for her purpose. As a result, Christine does not fall into being an essentially masculine authority, a kind of male impersonator; she creates an entirely new female authority, one that draws on both the traditionally feminine provinces of experience and body and the masculine arena of textual exegesis. That Christine is again female at the beginning of the *Cité* is manifested both in her cause and in her empathy for the women slandered in Matheolus' text: "une grant desplaisance et tristesce de couragie en desprisant moy meismes dt tout le sexe fiminin, si comme ce ce fust monstre en nature" (620) [A great unhappiness and sadness welled up in my heart, for I detested myself and the entire feminine sex, as though we were monstrosities in nature] (I.1.1) she says, aligning herself with the oppressed group.[4] Christine even demands of God, "Helas! Dieux,

pourquoy ne me faiz tu naistre au monde en masculin sexe, a celle fin que
mes inclinacions fussent toutes a te mieulx servir et que je ne errasse en
riens et fusse de si grant parfeccion comme homme masle ce dit estre?"
[why did you not let me be born in the world as a man, so that I would
not stray in anything and would be perfect as a man is said to be?]
(621)(I.1.2).The sense of inferiority that her femaleness imparts here is un-
dercut as she says, "ci comme celle qui par ma foulour me tenoye tres mal-
contente de ce qu'en corps femenin m'ot fait Dieux estre au monde" (621)
[in my folly, I considered myself most unfortunate because God had made
me inhabit a female body in this world] (I.1.2).

   This denunciation might well have set the stage for another sex-change.
However, had Christine perceived herself in a masculine mode, even
metaphorically, as she does in the *Mutacion* and *L'Avision Christine* (written
in the same year as the *Cité*), she would have been unlikely to make her
womanhood such an essential part of this text. Indeed, her womanhood is
the catalyst for the *Cité des Dames*. Instead of being transmuted into a man
by Dame Fortune, this time Christine is disabused of her folly by the appearance of three female allegorical figures—Reason, Rectitude, and Justice—who come to show her the error of her ways. Instead of remaining
an imperfect woman, Christine becomes allied with the most perfect
woman of all, Mary, through this metaphorical annunciation.This female
trinity comes to Christine, informing her that "Ainsi, belle fille, t'est
[donné] la prerogative entre les femmes de faire et bastir la Cité des
Dames" (630) [the prerogative among women has been bestowed on you
to establish and build the City of Ladies] (I.1.4).That the same phrase is
used by Justice to describe Mary, "et a ycelle sera l'onneru et la prerogative entre les autres femmes comme les plus excellentes" (637) [Hers will
be the honor and prerogative among all other women] (I.1.6), is no coin-
cidence; Christine further connects herself with Mary by answering to the
ladies, "voycy vostre chambrerciere preste d'obeir. Or commandez, je
obeyrey, et soit fait de moy selonc voz paroles" (639) [Behold your hand-
maiden, ready to serve. Command, and I will obey, and may it be unto me
according to your words] (I.1.7), a direct translation of Mary's *Ecce ancilla
Domini fiat mihi secundum verbum tuum.*[5] V.A. Kolve notes that Christine distinguishes herself from Mary by having God's light fall upon her lap, "the
place of ordinary conception and parturition," instead of her eye and ear,
calling her to "conceive a true (or truer) word, but as a widow."[6] This difference is important, but Christine nonetheless becomes, like Mary, a vessel of the word of God. If Gabriel's annunciation to Mary brings forth the
Word made Flesh, the annunciation to Christine brings forth the Word
made Text. By speaking in Mary's words, Christine has "authorized herself
as an author."[7]

By superimposing her widowed self on the Virgin Queen, Christine creates a new female authority; she opposes prohibitions against women's speech with the salutory power of God's word. Medieval women, after all, were divided into three categories: virgins, wives, and widows, all defined by different relationships to sexuality. Virgins, by voluntary renunciation, and widows, by a fortuitous act that deprived them of their husbands, occupy much higher rungs on the ladder of authority. Virginity, the highest state, freed the mind of lust, allowing pure, unsullied thought; widowhood, the halfway point, was attracted upward by potential future purity, made possible by an event that freed the mind from carnal desires.[8] The obligations upon widows create a context for them similar to that of the cloistered virgins; widows were obliged to observe strictly religious fasts, prayer, and acts of charity. When the husband's and father's custody was missing, "Christ himself claimed the newly liberated woman, body and soul."[9] Dame Reason exhorts Christine: "Comment, belle filled, qu'est ton scens devenu? As tu doncques oublié que le fin or s'esprouve en las fournaise, qui ne se change ne muet de sa vertu, ains plus affine, de tant plus est martellé et demené en diverse façons?" (623) [Fair daughter, have you lost all sense? Have you forgotten that when fine gold is tested in the furnace, it does not change or vary in strength but becomes purer the more it is hammered and handled in different ways?] (1.2.2); it is Christine's widowhood that has tested her in the furnace (her oft documented loss of her husband, need to care for her mother and children, and her financial travails), from which she has emerged as purer, finer gold.

As brides of Christ, either in first or second marriages, virgins and widows gained an authority lost to married women. Despite the medieval sense that women "talked too much and badly," the efficacy of the virgin martyr's words and deeds is shown repeatedly in hagiographic literature. Desexualizing their femininity by rejecting the act that defines it as other and different, virgins and widows occupied a distinct space, often freed from the castigation married (and marriageable) women suffered. In her attempt to "create a new and singular voice in the very heart of the codified literary tradition,"[10] Christine must find a position that allows her to be a self-defined, self-controlled, self-articulating figure. In creating a kind of female literary utopia that only women can inhabit, Christine "invokes the language and examples of women."[11] Since "the feminine voice is in constant tension with its phallic inscription in a masculine order precisely because the feminine voice cannot speak itself," Christine finds a voice that, rejecting its definition as feminine (and therefore negative) by rejecting sexuality, speaks outside of the phallic mode.[12] To suggest, as Lynne Huffer does, that in the *Cité des Dames,* Christine is the male figure of the *Mutacion de Fortune,* is to miss the distinct qualities of the new voice she creates.

Christine uses totems traditionally associated with masculine authority—education, writing, classical and biblical material, dream visions, latinate syntax—but she uses them in a new context, combining them with their feminine counterparts to create a new kind of authority. In her language, her use of experience, and her text/body relationships, she brings qualities traditionally in tension into harmony. Christine's authorial position is marginalized because of her sex; however, from that margin, Christine "takes a master discourse and makes it speak of her own concerns, explicitly commenting on her own process of rewriting her tradition."[13] While female authority, as Maureen Quilligan contends, is a "non-scripted, prophetic mode, grounded in a realm of discourse that is made to stand as far outside the textual as anything within a text can get,"[14] Christine's own authority is essentially literary; indeed, Reason, Rectitude, and Justice often remind her of her own earlier writings, making her own corpus a part of the tradition of learning to which they often refer.

The latinate syntax of Christine's French is often cited as an example of her rejection of femininity, a manifestation of her "true" masculine identity. To read her style in this way is to miss the importance of Christine's choice of the vernacular. Christine makes use of the authoritative language in which her predecessors (most notably Matheolus and Boccaccio for this argument) wrote; however, she feminizes it by placing its structures into her mother tongue. This locution reveals the femininity of the vernacular; as a poetic device, the feminized, vulnerable self-definition of its first writers, the troubadours and the *jarcha* poets, echoes this sense of a *written* language separate from the authoritative Latin of the Church Fathers. Regardless of who was actually doing the writing, it is impossible to miss the primacy of women's voices in the development of the romance lyric tradition (the *jarchas,* the trobairiz, etc.). Vernacular language itself is essentially a literary representation of the woman's voice—of the position of inferiority and vulnerability essential to the woman's position, whether a man or a woman writes the words, a way of preserving what had previously been considered unworthy of record. Thus the female voice becomes a mode of expression that challenges the classical, clerical voice, a voice that speaks the personal and the popular. In its early examples, writing in the vernacular, lyric voice, metaphorically or metonymically, was to authenticate the feminine, because in its profound opposition to masculine literary language, it was a female voice.[15]

While Christine writes two hundred years later than the trobairiz, her romances and lyric poems are different enough from the language of the *Cité* to suggest her awareness of the "feminine" qualities of the vernacular. This being the case, Christine's masculinization of French in the *Cité des Dames* serves not so much to masculinize her as it does to desexualize her books' language. By rejecting the linguistic structures of lyric and romance, Christine rejects the most sexual of literatures. And in doing so, she authorizes her text; her language rejects the inferiority of the female position inherent in the vernacular material that precedes her while maintaining its femaleness. Her syntax, then, makes her French a kind of widowed or virgin body, female but not feminine, a woman renouncing the sexuality that seeks to define and silence her and claiming authority as a result.

Just as her language rejects easy gender definition, Christine's interpretive program also mediates between traditionally masculine and feminine poles. In the process of making a cause of the feminine condition, as Daniel Poirion notes, Christine's "personal experience became a system and a style." Christine's writing cannot be separated from its writer: she "is our first *author*, and that author is a woman."[16] If her style is a desexualized version of the mother tongue, her system is equally distinct from those that precede it. The separation of experience and authority, so famously delineated in the Wife of Bath's exclamation, "Experience tho noon auctoritee / were in this world is right ynough for me / to speak of wo that is in marriage,"[17] is challenged by Christine's insistence on combining the two. Rather than suggesting that authority is not women's province and should be left alone, Christine, at the beginning of the *Cité*, insists that female experience must authorize authority itself. Despondent after reading Matheolus' criticisms, Christine is ready to disavow the truth of her first-hand knowledge of women until Reason shows her the error of her ways. At first, Christine mistrusts her experience; setting it against male philosophy, she is ready to reject what she knows empirically in favor of traditionally lauded scholars. Looking at herself and her friends, Christine begins:

> examiner moy meismes et mes meurs comme femme naturelle, et semblablement discoutoye des autres femmes que j'ay hantees: tant princepes, grandes dames, moyennes et petites a grant foison, dui de leurs graces m'ont dit de leurs privetés et estroittes penssees, sçavoir mon a jugier en conscience et sans faveur ce ce puet estre vray ce que tant de notables hommes, et uns et autres, en tesmongnent. Mais nonobstant que pour chose que je y peusse congnoistre, / tant longuement y sceusse viser ne espluchier, je ne apperceusse ne congneusse telz jugemens estre vrays encontre les naturelz meurs et condiciouns feminines (ll. 618–619).

> [to examine my character and conduct as a natural woman and, similarly, I considered other women whose company I frequently kept, princesses, great ladies, women of the middle and lower classes, who had graciously told me their most private and intimate thoughts, hoping that I could judge impartially and in good conscience whether the testimony of so many notable men could be true. To the best of my knowledge, no matter how long I con-

fronted or dissected the problem, I could not see or realize how their claims could be true when compared to the natural behavior and character of women.] (I.1.1.)

Unwilling to trust what she sees, Christine argues against women until she is saved from her misapprehensions by the descent of the three ladies, who make clear that Christine's experience (and the reader's—especially the female reader's) must provide the test against which authority is measured. Since male writers often employ rhetorical devices that conceal and delude, Reason points out, one must read carefully, for "c'est chose clere prouvee par l'experience que la contraire est vray du mal qu'ilz proposent et dient . . . a la grant charge et couple des femmes" (625–626) [it is evident and proved by experience that the contrary of the evil which they posit and claim to be found . . . through the fault of women is true] (I.2.2). Christine must be instructed—or at least reminded—how to read; however, her background makes her the ideal writer for the task at hand. As Maureen Quilligan notes, Christine "occupies a position which is defined by the special authority conferred upon her by a transversal of the conventional categories—she is both an ignorant woman and a learned (because self taught) author."[18] Her learning allows her to understand and challenge the authorities who oppose her, but she also reads "*as a woman,* using her own experience as a yardstick against which to measure the authority, truth, and male-authored books."[19]

Essential as her style and system are to understanding her program for the *Cité des Dames,* the relationship of text and body that her language and reading program produce is even more vital. A frequent criticism of Christine's work suggests that throughout the *Cité,* one is "aware of a denial or flight away from the body" that serves both to defend and deny her femininity.[20] (This denial, however, is not a hypocritical refusal to be what she defends; she is not speaking like a man in the cause of women, as Lynne Huffer suggests in the comment above.) By making the female body of her text female-inscribed for a primarily female audience, Christine creates a City of Lady Readers, a community like that of the Amazons that resists being an "other" by refusing contact with the universal phallic. The text as virgin (with its widow author) exists unpenetrated by the masculine "pen as penis"[21] and as a result rejects masculine readings of itself and of women. Christine's versions of traditional stories resist masculine inscription; they redress the misreadings of their past as Christine liberates them into their "true" feminine context. The Amazons, the model for the female culture that Christine creates and thus one of the earliest examples in the *Cité,* present a rather different picture than they do in classical (and indeed, other medieval) works; rather than being man-killing monsters, they create a rational, peaceful, and courageous society and decide not to be subject to men. (I.16.1). Heroes like Hercules, Christine reports, feared the Amazons because of their prowess, and they fought with Hector in the Trojan War. This rewriting of the Amazon story is only one example of the revisions Christine makes; her Semiramus is a fine leader who only follows the customs of her time, instead of being an incestuous harpie; Medea is a clever sorceress who is grossly mistreated by Jason, not the evil murderer of her own children. Any look through the first two books of *La Livre de la Cité des Dames* reveals numerous reworkings of classical stories into a feminine context.

Over and over again, Christine suggests that masculine history has misread and miswritten women's stories; only the reading and writing of women can tell the correct versions. Christine's distancing of herself from the body allows her to write the body in a kind of proto-*écriture feminine;* taking away that which defines women as "other" in relation to men allows her to define them in an entirely female and thus desexualized context.[22] As a result, Christine offers a different model of the woman as text. While woman is still "written by Nature to be 'read' as a mythopoetic text," as Judith Kellog points out, the allegorical ladies (and by extension Christine) signify the substance of the text, resulting in the "identification of a universal female creative principle" that turns the woman from the sign, the other, into the inscribed text. She becomes the "fundamental principle that generates poetic creation"; she is the creator and the text. Instead of the writer and the work being two separate entities, the model of the phallus inscribing the text is replaced by "a model where creator and text are inseparable, for the subject of the text becomes the reconstruction of the creator herself."[23] Just as the woman functions as both experience and authority, she is both author and text, reader and read.

The text as reconstruction of the creator is made manifest in the story of Christine's namesake, St. Christine. The author and saint become double narrators through their similarities; the voice of the widow and the voice of the virgin stand in each other's place as each produces textual authority both through and as a result of their desexualized bodies, misread by men but understood by those who seek truth. The woman's words spoken by St. Christine are mirrors of the stories told by Christine de Pizan in her book; they both supply the message that the voice of God speaks through female vessels. The pagan judges cannot silence St. Christine, just as Matheolus and Company finally cannot prevent Christine herself from telling her truth. While three angels come from Christ to baptize and name St. Christine, making her a feminine mirror of God the son, the three allegorical ladies authorize Christine de Pizan's writing, speaking the word of God through her. Both become religious figures, as St. Christine becomes a feminine Christ and Christine allies herself with Mary.

St. Christine's efficacy as a symbolic text, however, supersedes Christine de Pizan's in the physicality of her experience; while Christine may function as a metaphorical text at the beginning, read by woman's detractors, as a martyr whose dismemberment becomes a visual and verbal spectacle, St. Christine serves textually as she speaks. While she produces one narrative with her voice, another is being produced on her body. The martyrology focuses on the physical body, but a body of a special kind, one that remains inviolate, despite being ceaselessly violated. Margaret Miles contends that "martyrs used their nakedness as a symbolic rejection, not only of sexuality, but also of secular society's identification of the female body with male desire, its relegation of the female body to spectacle and object";[24] by remaining whole despite her constant violation, St. Christine rejects the world that attempts to destroy her, becoming instead a symbol of resistance to a wicked and lawless society.[25] Throughout her story, St. Christine rejects the masculine authorities who attempt to define her as evil and to silence her. A relentless speaker, St. Christine takes on her father and several judges, challenging them with the truth of her words. When her father attempts to stop her worship of Christ, "elle disoit plainement qu'il estoit decei d'aourer ces faulx ymages" (1002) [she openly declared that he was deceived to worship these false image] (III.10.1) and calls him "Tirant, que je ne doy appeller pere, ains annemy de ma beneurté" (1003) [Tyrant who should not be called my father but rather enemy of my happiness] (III.10.1) making him sound like the male authorities who make Christine de Pizan despair at the beginning of the work. Her speech is pure and true; she will not allow her father to kiss her, saying "Ne touches a ma bouche, car je vueil offrir offrande nette a Dieu celestre" (1002) [Do not touch my mouth, for I wish to offer a pure offering to the celestial God] (III.10.1). She rejects penetration at the source of her speech; by preventing its sexualization, she retains its efficacy. Her voice as text is an unsullied offering, the virgin body untainted by sexual contact. As a result, many are converted, and many other *women* are compelled to speak out on her behalf, crying to Urban, "Cruel felon, plus que beste sauvage, commes puet avoir conceu en cuer de homme tant de cruelté contre pucelle tant belle et si tendre" (1005) [cruel felon, crueler than a savage beast, how could a man's heart conceive such a monstrous cruelty against such a beautiful and tender maiden?] (III.10.1). Other women understand her truth and are thus compelled to speak.

St. Christine also remains undeceived by male speech; both her father and the judge attempt to trick her into worshipping Jupiter, but she sees through their rhetoric and remains steadfast in her praise of Christ. Her body remains equally resistant to male violation; the judges devise various and sundry vile tortures for Christine, but because of her continued worship: "et la vierge delivera saine et entirer" (1004) [God delivers the virgin, healthy and whole] (III.10.1). St. Christine resists being crushed and burnt, maintaining her whole body and her holy speech. Throughout the story, body and text combine; many are converted by "les *parolles* et *signes* de la vierge" (1006) [the *words* and *signs* of this virgin] (III.10.1, emphasis mine). Indeed, St. Christine is a kind of word made flesh; baptized by Christ with the feminine version of his own name, Christine begins to take on his qualities as well: walking on water, raising the dead, and vanquishing the devil in the Temple. She is also the Word made Text; as a final punishment, Dyon attempts to silence her by cutting out her tongue.

St. Christine speaks even better once her tongue is removed; the judge insists on cutting the rest of it off, but St. Christine

> Et celle cracha le couppon de sa langue au visaige du tirant et luy se creva l'ueil. Et luy dist aussi sainement que oncaues main, "Tirant, que te vault avoir couppee ma lanuge adfine que elle ne beneysse Dieu, quant mon esperit a tousjours le beneystrat et le tien demourera perpetual en maleysson? Et pource que to ne congnois ma parolle, c'est bien raison que ma lanuge t'ait aveuglé." (1009)

> [spat the cut-off piece of her tongue into the tyrant's face, putting out one of his eyes. She then said to him as clearly as ever, "Tyrant, what does it profit you to have my tongue cut out so that it cannot bless God, when my soul will bless Him forever while yours languishes forever in eternal damnation? And because you did not heed my words, my tongue has blinded you, with good reason"] (III.10.1).

Dyon attempts to violate St. Christine by silencing her, a male "operation" on the female text, seeking to destroy it. Here, though, the female text (St. Christine's speech, literally her tongue) is impervious to male destruction because it is the word of God: truth, justice, and the Christian way. As a model for Christine herself, St. Christine exemplifies the power of female speech, the word of God emanating from the virginal body. Although men attempt to violate and destroy her, she remains constant because the words she speaks are true and the body that speaks them is pure. Her tongue—female speech, authorized by God—remains mobile in the face of those who would silence her. The Judge, another model for the antifeminist authorities Christine is challenging, is literally blinded by the truth because he is metaphorically blind already; he trusts his own tradition (here paganism) instead of what he sees enacted before him. Like Matheolus and his cohort, the woman before him, in all her truth and perfection, cannot sway the judge from his misconceptions; as a reader, he does not use his experience to test authority.

Just as St. Christine is God's prophet, so is Christine St. Christine's prophet. When Christine writes, "Si voir que je m'esjoys / de avoir cause de enexer et mettre ta sainte legende en mes escriptures, qulle pour ta reverence ay recordee assez au long" (1010) [Behold my joy at being able to make use of your holy legend and to include it in my writings, which I have recorded here at such length out of reverence for you] (III.10.2), she establishes a tradition of women's speech—and of women's bodies as their speech—that replaces the masculine tradition against which she has been working. Christine's invocation, as Quilligan notes, "turns hagiography into prophecy,"[26] forging a living linguistic tradition that focuses not on the body as text but on the words as text.

This feminine textual tradition provides a continuity of veracity and power, but it is also exclusive; the City of Ladies itself is a kind of inviolate body. The virgins and martyrs of Book III, who form its walls, towers, and roofs, surround the city and keep trouble out. In a manner that mirrors the inviolability of their own bodies, these virgins create a physical barrier around the city; because they are authorized by God, like St. Christine and Christine herself, they are protected from criticism and reproach. Christine's problematic message to wives at the end of the work, which has led critics to claim that she merely re-creates the misogynistic structures of her time,[27] implies that while all women have access to this truth, only widows and virgins are able to speak it. Certainly, as Kolve asserts, "in Christine's city, the virgin is invoked not as an impossible standard by which other women fail, but as a rebuke to misogyny," but she also has access to a privileged voice within it.[28]

This voice, and Christine's own, speaks as an authority that is feminine but not sexualized; by presenting this authority through herself (a widow) and her namesake St. Christine (a virgin), Christine de Pizan creates a female authority that encompasses author, text, and reader; by rejecting sexuality, the text/body nexus becomes a female text that speaks itself. By allying widows and virgins, by creating parallels between herself, St. Christine, and Mary, and by desexualizing language through mixing the feminine vernacular with masculine Latin structures, Christine negotiates female authority in a world that takes it away; she creates a kind of authority that is judged by experience and is not found wanting. The masculine authority that throws Christine into despair at the beginning of the work by attempting to supersede experience is overthrown by an authority whose discourse is truth. Through it, the textual body becomes prophecy; Christine's truth is joined to St. Christine's in its efficacy and ability to convert those who, rejecting blindness, seek the true way.

Notes

1. Christine de Pizan, *Le Livre de la Mutacion de Fortune,* ed. Susan Solente. 4 vols. (Paris: Picard, 1959–66), vol. I, pp. 51–53.; the translation is from Diane Bornstein, *Ideals for Women in the Works of Christine de Pizan.* (Detroit: Wayne State University Press, 1981) pp. 13–14.

2. See Christine de Pizan, *L'Avision Christine: Introduction and Text,* ed. Sister M. L. Towner (Washington: Catholic University of America Press, 1932), p. 181; Christine returns to her sex-change metaphor in the same year that she writes the *Cité des Dames;* however, in the latter, she does not represent a transmutation into a man.

3. Christine de Pizan, "Ballade XI" in *Centes Ballades,* in *Oevres Poetiques de Christine de Pizan,* ed. Maurice Roy, 3 vols. (Paris, 1986–1996). The English translation is my own.

4. Christine de Pizan, *La Livre de la Cité des Dames,* ed. Maureen C. Curnow (Ph.D. diss., Vanderbilt University, 1975), p. 620; translations are from Christine de Pizan, *The Book of the City of Ladies,* ed. and trans. Earl Jeffrey Richards (New York: Persea, 1982), p. 5. All further references to the *Cité des Dames* will be cited in the text.

5. Luke 1:38 (Vulgate).

6. V. A. Kolve, "The Annunciation to Christine: Authorial Empowerment in the *Book of the City of Ladies,*" in *Iconography at the Crossroads,* ed. Brendan Cassidy, Index of Christian Art (Princeton: Princeton University Press, 1993), p. 187.

7. Kolve, "Annunciation," p. 187.

8. Carla Cassagrande, "The Protected Woman," trans. Clarissa Botsford. In *A History of Women in the West,* vol. II: *Silences of the Middle Ages,* ed. Christiane Klapisch-Zuber (Cambridge, MA: Harvard University Press, 1992), pp. 80–81.

9. Cassagrande, "Protected Woman," p. 91.

10. Daniele Régnier-Bohler, "Literary and Mystical Voices," trans. Arthur Goldhammer. In *A History of Women in the West,* vol. II: *Silences of the Middle Ages,* ed. Christiane Klapisch-Zuber (Cambridge, MA: Harvard University Press, 1992), p. 437.

11. Régnier-Bohler, "Literary and Mystical Voices," p. 439.

12. Lynne Huffer, "Christine de Pizan: Speaking like a Woman/Speaking like a Man," in *New Images of Medieval Women: Essays Towards a Cultural Anthropology,* ed. Edelgard F. DuBruck, Medieval Studies, vol. I (Lewiston, NY: Edwin Mellen Press, 1989), p. 70. It is Lynne Huffer's contention that Christine remasculinizes herself in the *Cité,* much as she does in *L'Avision-Christine* and *La Mutacion de Fortune,* becoming a masculine voice speaking for women, countering the masculine authorities who speak against women at the beginning of the work. However, the striking absence of an overt transmutation suggests that Christine works in a different mode in the *Cité.*

13. Maureen Quilligan, "Allegory and the Textual Body: Authorial Empowerment in the *Book of the City of Ladies*," *Romanic Review* 79:1 (1988): 223; Quilligan's book-length study, *The Allegory of Female Authority: Christine de Pizan's* Book of the City of Ladies (Ithaca: Cornell University Press, 1991), particularly chapter 4, "Rewriting the Body: the Politics of Martyrdom," builds this argument further. While I take the direct quotation from Quilligan's article, both works were influential on my thinking.

14. Quilligan, "Allegory," p. 229.

15. In the Prologue to Marie de France's *Lais*, she rejects the Latin of Priscian, the ancients, and male writers, choosing instead to translate/compose lais from the Breton tradition in French, her vernacular. This choice opposes her vernacular works to the masculine philosophical, authoritative tradition, which she accuses of obscurity and "glossing." Marie de France, *Lais*, ed. Jean Rychner (Paris: Champion, 1983), pp. 1–3. The lyric tradition in Provençal that precedes her shows an anxiety about the vernacular, as the poets establish it as a literary language through their works. While the troubadours do not write in women's voices, as the vulnerable lovers of more powerful ladies, the poets place themselves in a feminized, inferior position. That this body of work may be influenced by earlier vernacular works, such as the *jarchas* (short Spanish poems in female voices, attached to longer Hebrew and Arabic works), suggests that regardless of the sex of the author, the vernacular as a poetic language began as a representation of the feminine, either literally, metaphorically, or metonymically.

16. Daniel Poirion, *Literature Française: Le Moyen Age, 1300 – 1480* (Paris: Presses Universitaires, 1971), p. 206, qtd. in Chairty Cannon Willard, Christine de Pizan: Her Life and Works (New York: Persea, 1984), p. 223.

17. Geoffrey Chaucer, "The Wife of Bath's Prologue," in *The Riverside Chaucer*, 3rd ed., ed. Larry D. Benson (Boston: Houghton Mifflin, 1987), frag. III, ll. 1–2.

18. Maureen Quilligan, "The Name of the Author: Self-Representation in Christine de Pizan's *Livre de la Cité des Dames*," *Exemplaria* 4.1(1992): 206.

19. Meale, p. 57.

20. Huffer, "Christine de Pizan," p. 62.

21. Sandra Gilbert and Susan Gubar, *The Madwoman in the Attic: The Woman Writer and the Nineteenth Century Literary Imagination* (New Haven: Yale University Press, 1979), pp. 3–4. Gilbert and Gubar begin their study of female creativity in the nineteenth century by asking, "Is the pen a metaphorical penis?" (3); it takes them only a paragraph to conclude that "male sexuality . . . is not just analogically but actually the essence of literary power. The poet's pen is in some sense (even more than figuratively) a penis" (4).

22. Gay Zoldesy, in an unpublished essay entitled "L'Ecriture Feminine," proposed that Christine writes the body, using distinctly feminine physical/emotional experience to perceive and express her material.

23. Judith L. Kellog, "*Le Livre de la Cité des Dames:* Feminist Myth and Community," *Essays in Arts and Sciences* 18 (1989): p. 9.
24. Margaret R. Miles, *Carnal Knowing: Female Nakedness and Religious Meaning in the Christian West* (New York: Vintage, 1989), p. 54.
25. Miles, *Carnal Knowing,* p. 57.
26. Quilligan, "Allegory," p. 240.
27. There are many examples of critics who read Christine's program as essentially conservative; one of the most notable is Sheila Delaney, "'Mothers to Think Back Through,' Who Are They? The Ambiguous Example of Christine de Pizan," in *Medieval Texts and Contemporary Readers,* ed. Laurie A. Finke and Martin B. Schichtman (Ithaca: Cornell University Press, 1987), pp. 177–197.
28. Kolve, "Annunciation," 188.

CHAPTER 3

CLOSED DOORS: AN EPITHALAMIUM
FOR QUEEN EDITH, WIDOW AND VIRGIN

Monika Otter

The Vita Aedwardi Regis *reveals thematic and symbolic associations between Queen Edith's chastity, fertility, power, and the prosperity of the land; thus, the poet salvages Edith as a chaste and powerful queen, despite her barrenness.*

In her essay "The Body Politic and the Queen's Adulterous Body," Peggy McCracken demonstrates a close thematic and symbolic association in twelfth-century romance between the queen's chastity, the queen's fertility, the queen's power, and the prosperity of the land.[1] The late eleventh century *Vita Ædwardi Regis*,[2] the earliest life of King Edward the Confessor, shows a very similar nexus at work, not in romance but in a narrative of real, contemporary events, a narrative that is, moreover, written for Edward's widow, Queen Edith herself. The anonymous author's problem is almost the exact opposite of what McCracken describes. The romance writers are involved in a sort of damage control, keeping the adulterous queen (most often Guinevere) childless to limit her power and to limit the political harm inflicted by her wayward body. In the *Vita Ædwardi*, the queen's barrenness is the given, the *fait accompli;* the land has suffered, and the queen has lost her power because of it. The poet is working backwards from there, as it were, to salvage what he can of her dignity as a chaste and powerful queen. His goal clearly is to console her: not only is she widowed, but she has lost her entire family as well, and she may well fear for her status, perhaps even her safety, under the brand-new Norman regime that has overthrown and killed her brother Harold.

As the anonymous author offers Edith new roles, new identificatory patterns that may help her at a difficult juncture of her life, he draws, quite naturally, on the hagiographic conventions used in lives of and advice literature for aristocratic widows; and, perhaps a little more surprisingly, on the rhetoric of virginity as well.[3] This may point to one of his major rhetorical problems in this panegyrical text: Edith does not comfortably fit into any of the three "estates" open to a medieval woman, all defined in terms of her marital status. As a wife and queen, her marriage was difficult both politically and personally; and she failed in her most important queenly duty, namely to produce an heir. As widow, her status is problematic. Even though she is treated well by the new regime, being the widow of a former king whose lineage is defunct (not to mention the sister of the most recent king who was overthrown and denounced as a usurper) hardly conveys the kind of secure authority, prestige, and dignity a royal dowager might otherwise enjoy. Moreover, these failures are all complexly linked, and they are linked precisely in the person of the Queen for whose consolation the book is written. Her precarious state as widow can be construed as a direct consequence of her barrenness as a wife: had Edith produced a male heir, there might have been no contested succession, and hence, presumably, no Norman Conquest. The *Vita Ædwardi* of course never quite articulates this idea. But it is there as a disturbing undercurrent, threatening the book's overt rhetorical agenda, namely to nudge Edith retroactively into the last remaining "estate" open to her—that of chaste virgin.

The other consequence of this hidden subtext is to blur the distinction between Edith's personal story and the story of her realm, to literalize the equation (largely metaphoric in the contexts McCracken describes) between the queen's body and the prosperity of the land. Edith's childlessness is not only described as a personal or dynastic failure, but is closely linked to the catastrophe that has befallen the entire nation. Therefore, the book's rhetoric—panegyric, consolatory, and vaguely accusatory—also applies indirectly to England. The nation, too, is bereaved, widowed, barren; and it, too, is exhorted to return to virginal purity. In some places Edith is almost explicitly equated with the realm; more consistently, the link is made through the muted but pervasive themes of lineage and progeny, which concern both the queen and the country. Yet there is something uncomfortable about the book's rhetorical strategy; as one might expect, consolation and royal panegyric do not mix well, and the added element of reproach is no help. The Anonymous's rhetoric for both queen and country is always on the verge of failure, always letting us glimpse defeat in extravagant praise and celebration.

The *Vita Ædwardi Regis* is an immensely interesting historical work, if only for one circumstance: according to its own account of its composition, its writing straddles the Norman Conquest. It was (or appears to have been) begun shortly before, perhaps in 1065, and finished quite shortly after, most likely in 1067, but certainly before 1075, the year Queen Edith died.[4] The author is not known, though suggestions have been made.[5] It is, to my knowledge, the only work about 1066 composed virtually during 1066, or at any rate the only one that makes an issue of this contemporaneity. In this self-consciousness, in the self-reflexive fussing over what to write and how to write it, lies the book's chief literary and historical interest. The *Vita* has always been appreciated, despite its biases and errors, as a very early source on the reign and death of King Edward.[6] But apart from narrating the events, the author is in constant dialogue with his muse, discussing what to say and how to say it, deploring the difficulties arising from his extraordinary historical situation. Far from interfering with the book's source value, this continuous metanarrative is invaluable as a record of what it felt like to be writing history at that time, and perhaps what it generally feels like to be writing contemporary history while enmeshed and embroiled in the middle of it.

It is not surprising that the author is nervous, for his task is not exactly enviable. The status of his patroness has changed, from Edward's queen and sister of some of the realm's most powerful earls, to (briefly) the king's sister, to lonely widow nervous about how she might be treated by the new king.[7] If, as the author says, he began before the Conquest to write a laudatory history of Edith's family for her edification, he now has to weigh carefully how to continue. The main subjects of his panegyric—Edith's father Godwin and her brothers Harold and Tostig—are not only dead but have died losers and failures. King Edward, as the muse says almost explicitly, is now a safer subject both for the author and for Edith (88–91). Yet that, too, is not without its pitfalls. It cannot have been a secret that the marriage was not a loving one, that Edward hesitated long before marrying Edith, and that Edith continued to identify and be identified more with her natal family than with her husband.[8] The panegyrist has to deal with the awkward events of 1051, when Godwin and his sons were banished on accusations of treason, Edith was made to retire temporarily to a convent, and Edward apparently considered a divorce.[9] All this makes it hard to laud Edward—but equally hard not to laud him—without embarrassing Edith. In the first part of the book, the lack of enthusiasm for Edward on the part of both writer and patron is palpable.

The panegyrist's most intractable difficulty, however, is Edith's childlessness. He solves this problem—followed by all later hagiographers—by hinting that the marriage was chaste by mutual agreement, for religious reasons. Yet, characteristically, he can neither address that problem outright nor leave it alone. He never directly mentions that Edward and Edith had no children, or even states explicitly that they had agreed on a chaste marriage.[10] Essentially, the author tries to avoid the matter altogether. But as if refusing to be repressed, the theme of progeny surfaces everywhere, becoming the central metaphor of the book, in ways that go well beyond the fortunes of one particular couple or lineage. We are concerned with the future of the entire nation, from the opening vision by Brihtwald, in which St. Peter announces Edward's lifelong celibacy but declines to answer the question of Edward's successor; from the praise of Earl Godwin as the well from whence spring the four rivers of paradise, to Edward's famous deathbed vision of the Green Tree: the tree's trunk is severed, and as long as it remains so, he is told in his vision, the English nation will not prosper (116–119). Edith's fate is intimately linked to that of England.

The accident of the book's having been written when it was is of course very neat—perhaps too neat. Its authenticity has therefore been questioned, or else interpreters have tried to explain the book's built-in account of its own genesis as a literary fiction created after the Norman Conquest.[11] The *Vita Ædwardi*'s precise textual history is not our present concern; the readings proposed here are consistent with a number of theories. The book's own account of its composition is, however, of great relevance, and merits a quick summary. The Anonymous begins, in classical style, with an extensive dialogue with his muse. He names Queen Edith, Edward's widow, as his patron; and Book I, as Barlow says, is really not so much a life of Edward as an encomium of Edith through her family.[12] This explains the poem's lavish praise of the Godwin family, even the widely unpopular Tostig; Edward is a major figure but not necessarily the main focus in Book I. This first part is a prosimetrum, alternating sections of rhymed prose with highly crafted, difficult, metrically ambitious poems; it is clear that the encomiast spared no effort to produce a dazzling, prestigious work. Book I ends with Edward's death, which at that point is only mentioned rather than fully narrated.

Then, there appears to be a break, after which the poet addresses the muse again, in a despairing lament.[13] Everybody is dead: in Barlow's translation, "Amid the many graves, hurt by the death / Of lords, what, Clio, are you writing now?" (85). The muse reassures him that there is still plenty for him to write about—in fact, an even better topic: the saintliness of King Edward. The poet accepts that suggestion with moderate enthusiasm: "Pareo suadenti, nimium sed corde dolenti / tot tantisque miser orphanus a dominis" [I yield to counsel, but with broken heart, / Sad and bereaved of all those famous lords] (90–91). Book I is now implicitly redefined on the Einhard-Suetonius model as the "gesta" or "deeds" of Edward, and

Book II will deal with his character and his piety—all in prose, from here on. It also contains Edward's prophecies regarding disasters to come and a discussion of their fulfillment. This is the closest the *Vita* ever comes to saying what happened in 1066.[14] Indeed, it is not much of an exaggeration to say that the hagiography of Edward—introduced as an afterthought on the muse's part—is a substitute, a way for the narrative to avoid what would happen next in chronological order. Book II seems determined to act just as one would expect of a saint's life. It, too, avoids speaking directly of the Norman Conquest; and it ends with a few miracles at Edward's shrine, as *vitae* of recent saints often do—just enough to provide a hook from which to hang a "miracula" sequel at a later time.[15]

Here, then, is a book contemporary with the Norman Conquest— even, arguably, about the Norman Conquest—that manages not to mention Hastings, William, or the Normans. It is also a book about a royal succession crisis that manages not to mention its central cause, the failure of the king and queen to produce an heir. Yet in the act of being tactful or cautious, it manages to draw attention to what it is avoiding; by writing around rather than about the big contemporary calamity at its center, it becomes a historical record of a different sort.[16] It is interesting not so much for its account of events as for its fretfulness about what it cannot say, its constant attempts to change the subject. One of the Anonymous's main strategies of evasion is metonymic substitution: instead of the Norman Conquest, the book talks about Edward's claim to sainthood. Instead of Edith and her apparent barrenness, it talks, as we shall see, about a building. Whenever a painful matter needs to be addressed, the narrator shifts to a different though related, adjacent subject, through which he can avoid— but also indirectly address—the matter thus supplanted. But apart from avoiding or circumnavigating the tough issues, he also talks about his doing so. He portrays himself as failing, or almost failing, in his poetic endeavor. His attempt to sing a praise song in the style of classical epic has been rudely interrupted, rendered pointless by contemporary events, and he just barely manages to finish his book with some dignity. It does not particularly matter how faithful this account is to the actual genesis of the book; the conceit works because it parallels, depicts, and discusses the disruption of the events of 1066 on a different level.

Although Edith, Edward the Confessor's widow, is the patron and addressee of the work, her role in the narrated events is marginal; this is primarily the story of her male relatives—her father Godwin, and her brothers Harold and Tostig—and secondarily that of her husband, Edward. Nonetheless, she is given a strong, almost physical presence in the book in other, barely acknowledged ways. As a woman in general and a queen in particular, she is charged in her real role in history (apart from such incidental things as being pious or being a good wife and daughter) to bear children. The queen's fertility, a taboo subject in this book, is not addressed directly. But the poet nonetheless manages to put it center stage, and in such a way that its motivic correspondences with other parts of the book place it inside a web of allusions to progeny, fertility, the country's prosperity, the country's future. In other words, even though he purports not to do so, he does place Edith quite centrally into the discourse about the nation's debacle. In a book meant to flatter and console the widowed, childless queen, the poet artfully and half-surreptitiously weaves her figure into the narrative through a series of metonymical substitutions, at the heart of which is an odd, poignant and suggestive "epithalamium" on the dedication of the Abbey Church of Wilton, Edith's most important religious foundation. These rhetorical tropes link Edith, on the one hand, to the realm of England; on the other hand, they connect her to things not of this world, as if to lift the otherwise dispiriting account onto a higher plane: Edith is associated with the Wilton church, the Bride of the Song of Songs, the Virgin Mary. But laudatory though these associations may be, they are risky, since they all tend to slip back into the very trains of thought they are designed to steer away from: Edith's failure to become a mother, the failure of the Anglo-Saxon royal lineage, the Norman Conquest.

These problematic metonymies also place her at the center of a third, metapoetic discourse that talks about the work itself. The poet's overt objective is to use sacred imagery to provide consolation and to elevate Edith onto a quasi-saintly plane by using liturgical, Marian, and even Christological allusions. But at the same time, he cannot get away from very physical notions: wombs and conception, motherhood and childbirth—or the lack thereof. His constant view of Edith as a corporeal being, more precisely a reproductive being, interferes with the other role offers, the other, spiritual kind of imagery he attempts in order to flatter and console her. Since his failure to achieve consolation is also one of his themes, Edith and her failure to give birth, and his own failure to divert attention from this are central images of his poetic debacle also. The rhetorical acrobatics of the "epithalamium" in particular thus threaten to derail, but they also curiously reinforce, the strange, contorted consolatory rhetoric of this strange, despairing book.

The idiosyncratic poem celebrating Wilton is placed at the heart of the book; it is the last poem before the death of Edward and the end of Book I. This "epithalamium," or "wedding song," as the poet calls it, is fascinating not only in itself but also in its ramifications and echoes throughout the book. It merits a careful analysis, with attention to the many rhetorical traditions it draws on and blends, with bizarre but paradoxically powerful results.

Having described first Edward's building of Westminster Abbey
(67–71), then Edith's rival project at Wilton (70–73), the Anonymous addresses a song to "this new bride of God":

Inclita mater, aue, prolem paritura beatam,
quam dum concipies, nulla maculabere culpa,
in cuius partu nullum patiere dolorem,
nec numero rara   merebis de genitura,
intereatue tuo quisquam de uentre creatus;   5
sed iungere tuo   per federa casta marito,
eterno sociata deo complexibus almis;
cuius fusa tua sata celica germen in aluo
uiuificante suo   reddunt de flamine sancto;
nec partu maris letabere siue puellę,   10
sed centum prolis cunis circumdata mille;
non quorum fletu tribulentur uiscera matris,
sed quibus angelicas   clare modulantibus odas
uel pulsu citharę   toto resonabis in orbe.
Tum pro defectu non sollicitabere lactis,   15
nempe dator uitę   diues genitor deus ipse
de cęlis escas   pluet, hos ut in ęthere pascas;
Nec te de numero tedet, uexantue labores,
sed magis exoptas tot iugiter his super addi.
Tempore nec tardo tardam profers genituram,   20
decursis longo tot mensibus ordine pigris.
Cotidie potius celebras natalia multa,
certe cara tuo,   quia sic fecunda, marito.
Sed nec tot natis   habitacula tot uariabis,
nec cogere pati   caros a te segregari;   25
sed magis in lata   fulchris renitentibus aula
te coram melius   discumbet leta iuuentus,
quam speciosa tuę   reseras hęc claustra tabernę.
· · · ··

[Hail, peerless mother, blessed babes to bear,
Conceived immaculate from any sin,
And at whose bringing-forth you'll feel no pangs.
Nor will you grieve at scanty progeny,
Nor will one fashioned in your womb expire;   5
But you will make chaste marriage vows, and lie
In the sweet arms of everlasting God;
Whose heavenly seed, in your womb cast, returns
A crop from his life-giving Holy Ghost.
Nor will you joy in man child or in girl: 10
But surrounded by a hundred thousand cots,

With babes not rending mother's heart with tears,
But singing clear angelic odes or with
The harp, you will resound throughout the world.
Nor will you fear for lack of milk, for life's   15
Rich giver, Father God himself, will rain
Manna from heav'n, that you may feed them there.
Nor do the numbers tire or labours vex:
You long, indeed, for ever-growing brood.
Nor in slow time do you produce slow birth   20
By ordered lapse of those long, lazy months:
Loved by your spouse for your fecundity,
Each day you celebrate the many births.
Nor will you take a new abode for each,
Nor need t'endure your darling's banishment: 25
But rather let the happy children rest
In the great shining pillared hall with you
Than ope the lovely doorways of your inn.] (72–75)

(The remaining seventeen lines of the poem are a paraphrase of Psalm 83, "How amiable are your tabernacles.")

Barlow identifies no sources for this remarkable poem, and it is indeed woven primarily of well-known, ubiquitous images and ideas, if in a somewhat unusual combination. But its main inspiration is presumably Augustine's "De sancta virginitate," or perhaps Ælfric's Anglo-Saxon adaptation of it, the homily "Nativitas Sanctae Mariae Virginis."[17] This text is a convenient choice, since it combines several themes that suit the Anonymous's purpose: the Mariological themes of motherhood and virginity, the Virgin as a type of the Church, Christ as the Church's (and Mary's) bridegroom; an assurance to virgins that they partake in Mary's spiritual motherhood; and a discussion of the choices open to Christian women: virginity, marriage and procreation, and chaste widowhood. Nominally, of course, the Anonymous's poem is addressed to the new abbey church. But it takes no special interpretive skill to see that it is also addressed metonymically to the church's founder, Edith herself, consoling her for her childlessness by suggesting that the surrogate motherhood she has chosen by building a nunnery is much preferable to biological motherhood. Perhaps it is also consoling her, after the Conquest, that all is not lost; there is something of hers that has endured and will continue to flourish and procreate.[18] All this, of course, is achieved by substitution—without ever mentioning Edith's childlessness, or the Norman Conquest.

If any encouragement is needed for such a metonymic reading, there is plenty to be found. The poet introduces this song as an "epithalamium typicum," that is, an allegorical one. In the first place, he no doubt means to acknowledge that a wedding song can be applied to a church only in an "improper," tropological way of speaking; but the implications of *typicum* surely extend further. The liturgy and theology of the dedication of churches is fond of pointing to the metonymical ambiguities of the word *church:* it designates a place as well as a community of people, a local congregation as well as a huge, transregional institution, a building of bricks, wood or stone as well as a living organism, the "body of Christ" composed of all individual believers. Cesarius of Arles's influential sermons on the feast, sometimes transmitted together with the liturgical texts, explicitly instruct the faithful in allegorical readings of this sort ("construitur autem [ecclesia] hystoricę, typologicae [sic], anagogicę"), and even begin by explaining to the faithful what a metonymy is.[19] One major source for language about churches or the Church, the Song of Songs, is also a *locus classicus* for explaining the nature of allegory. Many commentaries on the Song of Songs, or on Psalm 44, the other major epithalamium in the Bible, begin by doing so.[20] The Bride of the songs is variously said to be the Church, the individual soul, or the Virgin Mary; since all these readings can coexist in a single exegetical text, there is a sense of general substitutability throughout.[21]

The poem's imagery is clever and complex, and it radiates out into the rest of the work. The Augustinian source (or the tradition it belongs to) accounts for the Marian language that suffuses the poem, not in quotations but allusions and echoes, for instance in the suggested conception through the Holy Spirit (ll. 9–10), or the reference to guiltless conception ("quam dum concipies, nulla maculabere culpa," l. 2). These Marian echoes are an important part of the poem's project, but they are also a main reason why the project comes so close to failing. The Anonymous's basic conceit, however, is to combine two well-established *topoi,* both possibly prompted by but not really contained in Augustine's tract: addressing an epithalamium to a church on its dedication, and congratulating a founder, or most often a foundress, of a monastery on her spiritual progeny.

Augustine's "De sancta virginitate," evidently addressed to a religious community of virgins,[22] offers in its first third or so a meditation on two role models for women vowing themselves to virginity: the Virgin and the Church, who often stand for each other in the Scriptures. Both are the *sponsa* of Christ the Bridegroom; both are virgins and mothers, the Church in a spiritual sense, Mary both physically and spiritually: "in utraque virginitas fecunditatem non impedit: in utraque fecunditas virginitatem not adimit" [in both, virginity does not impede fertility; in both, fertility does not destroy virginity].[23] All Christian virgins partake in Mary's motherhood, becoming through her spiritually mothers of Christ; they should therefore not grieve over foregoing physical motherhood, since spiritual motherhood is superior.[24]

In connection with the consecration of a church dedicated to the Virgin Mary, the bridal language of the sermon might well trigger the idea of an epithalamium for a church. Epithalamic language is suggested in the liturgy for the consecration of churches, though it is not elaborated.[25] Sermons and hymns go a bit further: several well-known and widely transmitted medieval hymns on the dedication of churches employ epithalamic imagery; some even call themselves "epithalamia," though they do not exploit that association to any great degree.[26] A literary, nonliturgical instance from the immediate surroundings of our text is Goscelin's *Vita S. Edithae:* besides addressing a cute "epithalamium" to Edith as a two-year-old infant oblate marrying the infant Christ, Goscelin also refers to the entire *Vita* as an epithalamium for Lanfranc's rebuilding of Christ Church cathedral.[27] The bridal imagery in such texts is mediated through the exegetical tradition of the biblical epithalamia, Psalm 44 and the Song of Songs, which interpret the bride and groom as the Church and Christ.[28] We have already noted the general substitutability encouraged by this line of biblical exegesis: the virginal bride can be the Church, a church, an individual soul, or, of course, the Virgin Mary.

To be used in this Christian context, the epithalamium, the often raucous, bawdy classical wedding song must be tamed, and for this the Christian poets can draw on a tradition of paradoxical epithalamia going back to patristic literature and beyond. The "ascetic epithalamium," as Virginia Tufte calls it, takes up the conventions of the classical epithalamium, negating or reinterpreting them one by one to suit the new Christian purpose, either to celebrate a Christian wedding or to encourage and congratulate someone on forgoing marriage altogether.[29] Paulinus of Nola addresses such an epithalamium to Iulianus and Ia, a Christian couple. He warns them against celebrating their Christian wedding in the noisy, ostentatious pagan manner. No festive crowd is to throng the streets or to accompany them to their bedchamber ("absit ab his thalamis vani lascivia vulgi. . . . Nulla per ornates insultet turba plateas. . . . Ne sit Christicolam fanatice turba per urbem"). The house is not to be decorated with leaves and foliage. There are to be no exotic fragrances, no lavish meal, no expensive jewelry or clothing. The wedding night is to be modest and pious, the greatest pattern of marriage being that of Mary and the Lord.[30] The biblical epithalamia in Psalm 44 and the Song of Songs, having long been reinterpreted allegorically, are highly suitable and much used sources for such poems. It is just the Anonymous's luck that his ascetic epithalamium threatens to shade into what Tufte has called the "anti-epithalamium," an epithalamium that serves, either by ironic use or by ominous reversal of all the descriptive conventions, as a harbinger of death, infertility, and destruction.[31]

On the surface, however, all is fecundity, joy and birth in this poem. The church as Virgin Bride is also a prodigiously fertile mother. It is of course standard to refer to the Mother Church, meaning the whole institution;[32] but Augustine's "De sancta virginitate" offers an especially detailed elaboration of the theme, including the rather disturbing idea that the Church gives birth to the members of Christ's body, while Mary gives birth to the head.[33] Whereas Augustine means Ecclesia, the Church as a worldwide institution, one also finds maternal references to a particular church. Suger refers to the abbey church of St. Denis as "mater ecclesia," which has "most tenderly fostered us from mother's milk to old age."[34] The same idea is spun into a charming conceit by the monk Purchard in his "Gesta Witigowonis" (ca. 1000), a dialogue with his "mother" Reichenau about her successive "husbands," his "fathers," the abbots of Reichenau.[35] Closer in time and geography to our example, the charters for Westminster Abbey by William the Conqueror and several of his successors refer to Westminster as the royal mausoleum, "in cujus materno utero corpus domini et praedecessoris mei [that is, Edward] requiescit" [in whose maternal womb rests the body of my lord and predecessor].[36]

While all these examples relate to males and male monasteries, both the *mater ecclesia* topos and the virgin-bride topos are especially suitable for a convent church. Augustine specifically associates both ideas with religious women: Ecclesia is the mother of all the members of Christ's body, but particularly of female virgins. Denying married women even the distinction of potentially giving birth to holy virgins, Augustine asserts that physical motherhood counts for nothing in that respect. All children are born virgins; what makes some of them choose virginity as a vocation has nothing to do with their biological parents. The Church is the true spiritual mother of those vowed to virginity.[37] Cyprian, too, stresses the special link between the virgin Church and her virgin offspring: virginal progeny are doubly pleasing to Mother Church since they mirror and, paradoxically, add to her own virginity: "Gaudet per illas adque in illis largiter floret Ecclesiae Matris gloriosa fecunditas, quantoque plus copiosa virginitas numero suo addit, gaudium Matris augescit" [The Church rejoices in them (the virgins,) and in them flourishes greatly the Mother Church's glorious fecundity. And the more virginity is added to her numbers, the more the mother's joy increases].[38] There is thus a rich tradition for the Anonymous's choice of an "epithalamium" to celebrate Wilton.

The Anonymous's trick is to layer his epithalamic apostrophe to Wilton loosely and transparently over another indirect address: the praise of and consolation for Edith as the convent's patron and surrogate mother. It is easy to see how Augustine's tract might have suggested this idea: even though it does not encourage virgins to see themselves as mothers of other Christians, it does speak of the Church in this way, and it also consoles childless women by pointing to their spiritual maternity. The combination of both ideas, the monastic founder as spiritual mother, is a hagiographic commonplace in medieval literature on holy widows. It is offered as encouragement to women making a major change in their lives—such as retreating to the convent they founded, or preparing for a life of saintly widowhood "in the world" after their husbands died;[39] it is sometimes offered, as it is here, as a consolation for women who had no biological children, or who left children behind "in the world." Empress Kunigunde and Emperor Henry II, another childless ruling couple of the eleventh century, are lauded for their pious foundations, a deliberate choice of spiritual progeny over biological children: "propter regnum celorum se castrantes, nec prolem terrene fecunditatis expectantes, celibem a Deo generationem recupient, a quorum ore laus Dei numquam deficit" [castrating themselves for the Heavenly Kingdom, not expecting progeny of earthly fertility, they ask of God a chaste issue, in whose mouths the praise of God will never fail].[40] Marcswidis of Schildesche, a tenth-century founder of a nunnery, is explicitly said in her later *vita* (ca. 1200) to have been given the grace of spiritual motherhood in compensation for her sterility.[41] Other widows, such as Paulina of Paulinzella, or Amalberga, Begge, Waudru, and Rictrud, a group of saintly women from the area that is now Belgium, whose *vitae* date from the eleventh century, did have biological children but turned their attention to their spiritual "children" later in life.[42]

A related tactic the Anonymous borrows from the literature on saintly widows, also suggested in "De sancta virginitate," is the topos of overlapping, blurring family relationships. Augustine uses the well-known passage from Matthew 12, in which Jesus asks "Who is my mother, and who are my brothers?" to privilege spiritual family ties over biological ones: even for Mary, physical motherhood was less of a blessing than her spiritual relationship with her son. Mary became Christ's sister as well as mother; all Christ's sisters through her also become His mothers.[43] Such games with family roles are something of a monastic topos in general, of obvious interest to those foregoing secular family lives and finding new familial relationships in the cloister.[44] In the case of the aristocratic widow who retired to a nunnery (especially if it was the nunnery she had founded) the topos, and the foundress's surrogate motherhood, might extend to the practical realities of her new life. These older nuns—or lay sisters, if they did not take vows—are often described in hagiographic writing as mothers to all the younger nuns.[45] The resulting jumble of all family relationships, biological and spiritual and across generations, is often enthusiastically elaborated. The older nun is sister and mother to her fellow nuns; the abbess, often actually her biological daughter or niece, is her mother and daughter as well as her sister, and so forth. Goscelin of St. Bertin exploits these mixed roles in his life of St. Edith of Wilton, whose mother, Wulftryth, also retired to the abbey where her daughter was a nun.[46] Peter the Venerable, Abbot of Cluny, plays the family game with great abandon in his moving eulogy of his mother, who died in 1136 after a long widowhood in the convent of Marcigny.[47] The eulogy, written as a letter, is addressed in the first place to his biological brothers, who are, however, his sons also, since he is a priest and abbot. Secondarily, it is addressed to the nuns of Marcigny, his spiritual sisters and daughters. (He does not call them "mothers," presumably because of his own high rank, but the monk Goscelin, for instance, speaks of the nuns of Wilton as "matres."[48]) Peter's mother, in her later years as a nun, had been sister and mother to the other nuns; and mother, sister, and daughter to her son Peter, the abbot of Cluny.

The Anonymous, most likely a monk himself, adapts this commonplace to Edith's secular context.[49] Edith is described in playful and/or pious role mixtures throughout, in part to gloss over the strains between her husband and her father's family and her lackluster marriage; in part, surely, to offer yet another consolation for her failure to be a mother. (Particularly poignant is the phrase, "certe cara tuo, quia sic fecunda, marito" [loved by your spouse for your fecundity], (l. 23). Edith is Edward's daughter, wife, and mother, for instance when she grooms the reluctant Edward and takes charge of his wardrobe: "In quo non tam uidebatur illi uxor esse quam filia, non tam coniux quam mater pia" [In this she seemed more like a daughter than a wife, not so much a spouse as a good mother] (24–25). Surrogate motherhood is also suggested when the Anonymous praises her maternal care for any children attached to the royal household (24–25).[50] As in the monastic setting, the topos is meant to be friendly and consolatory, comforting people who were denied more standard family ties. And at least as a secondary effect, the fluidity of all the relationships, especially the blurring of "wife" and "daughter," may have helped Edith make the vital shift from Godwin's daughter and Harold's sister, now an undesirable association, to Edward's queen. William the Conqueror had some interest in keeping Edward's image untarnished, and to treat his widow generously, since his own claim to the throne rested in Edward.[51] Yet the topos is on shaky ground here; it threatens to backfire, exposing the anomalies—Edith's preference for her family of origin over her husband, the coldness in their marital relations, and above all, their childlessness—in the very act of making them look positive and cheerful.

Insofar as the poem is addressed to Edith, then, its purpose is apparently to offer her two pious role models: that of the saintly widow, who dedicates her energies and resources to her religious foundations; and that of the holy virgin finding ample compensation for her childlessness in her spiritual motherhood. Augustine makes much of the notion that Mary must have made a vow of virginity at some time prior to the Annunciation: only freely chosen virginity counts.[52] It is quite possible that this is one of the features that made the Anonymous turn to this particular text: he does not say, but insinuates throughout the book, what later became an integral part of Edward's hagiography: that the couple had vowed to remain "pure" and not to consummate their marriage. William of Malmesbury, despite his skepticism about this story, reports that Edith swore on her deathbed that she had always remained a virgin.[53]

The indirect reference to the Virgin Mary is the capstone of all the poem's identificatory offers to Edith: an identification that, among other things, allows her to look back to her former position as queen. The idea of Mary as queen and the queen as Mary appears to have been common in late Anglo-Saxon England. Mary's queenship, as Clayton shows, became a prominent concern in the literature and iconography of the Feast of the Assumption. The identification of the queen and the Virgin works both ways: artists and writers honor Mary by giving her the attributes of an earthly queen; the queen's status is enhanced by her association with Mary. The Virgin Mary was seen as a special patron of reformed monasticism, with many abbeys and cathedrals having or acquiring at least a secondary dedication to her. So was the queen, whose role as protector of nunneries—in symmetry with the king's patronage of male houses—is explicitly laid down in the *Regularis Concordia*.[54] Wilton was dedicated to the Virgin Mary, and Queen Edith was its earthly patron.[55]

The Marian inflection of the poem's chief themes—virginity and surrogate motherhood—is modeled in its Augustinian source, and the connection is natural and unforced. Mary is a type of the Church; Mary, as well as the Church, is the virginal Bride of the Song of Songs; Mary is, of course, the true Virgin Mother.[56] Mary is also, as Augustine emphasizes, the ultimate example of mixed family roles: she is her son's sister, daughter, and spouse as well as mother, "vergine madre, figlia del tuo figlio," as Dante famously put it.[57]

Thus, quite logically, the series of equivalencies between church, bride, mother, virgin, and Mary extends to Edith: if Wilton is Mary, then Edith, too, must be Mary. Edith's Marian associations in the *Vita Ædwardi* are always subtle but quite unmistakable. We are told that Edith liked to sit modestly at Edward's feet, as his obedient daughter, until he would raise up his daughter-wife-mother to sit beside him (64), recalling the assumption of the Virgin and her elevation to the throne of Christ. In his sermon on that feast, Ælfric paints an extended picture of the scene:

. . . hu miccle swiðor wenst þu þæt he nu todæg þæt heofonlice werod togeanes his agenre meder sendan wolde, þæt hi mid ormætum leohte and
unasecgendlicum lofsangum hi to þam þrymsetle gelæddon þe hire
gegearcod wæs fram frymðe middangearedes.
. . . Soðlice eac we gelyfað þæt Drihten sylf hire togeanes come, and
wynsumlice mid gefean to him on his þrymsetle hi gesette . . .

[How much rather thinkest thou [Christ] would now to-day send the heavenly host to meet his own mother, that they with light immense, and unut-
terable hymns might lead her to the throne which was prepared for her from
the beginning of the world? . . . Verily we also believe that the Lord himself
came to meet her, and benignly with delight placed her by him on his
throne.][58]

On his deathbed, Edward commends Edith (calling her his "daughter")
"cum omni regno" [with the entire realm] to Harold's safekeeping. Not
only does this suggest a strong identification of Edith and England, it also
is reminiscent of Christ on the Cross giving his mother/daughter/spouse
into the care of the disciple whom he loved (122).[59] This episode, too, is
used in Ælfric's assumption homily (and its Latin source), where it is linked
with Mary's and John's virginity and with Mary's queenship: Jesus loved
John so much "þæt he him þone deorwurðan maðm, ealles middangeardes
cwene, betæcan wolde" [that he would commit to him that most precious
treasure, the queen of the whole world].[60] After the most awkward
episode, Edith's banishment from the court in connection with her family's disgrace, the poet has Edward take her back in outright Song of Songs,
epithalamic language: "fugatis ymbrium siue tempestatum condensibus
nubis, reducitur regina, eiusdem ducis filia, ad thalamum regis" [just as after
the thick clouds of rain-storms or tempests have been driven away, clear
sky and the jovial splendor of the sun are restored, so after all the kingdom's turmoil had abated, the queen, that earl's daughter, was brought back
to the king's bedchamber] (44–45). The allusion is to Song of Songs 2:10:
"et dilectus meus loquitur mihi / surge propera amica mea formosa mea
et ueni / iam enim hiemps transit imber abiit et recessit / flores ap-
paruerunt in terra tempus putationis aduenit / vox turturis auditur in terra
nostra" [my beloved speaks and says to me: "Arise, my love, my fair one,
and come away; for now the winter is passed, the rain is over and gone; the
time of singing has come, and the voice of the turtle-dove is heard in our
land"]; and more generally to the epithalamic Psalm 44, where a king's
daughter is brought to a king's "thalamus."

If this intermittently casts Edward as Christ, that is evidently intended.
He is, after all, also announced in visions before his birth; and there may
even be vague hints at his rising again.[61] If Edward is the biblical groom,

then that approximates him to Christ, just as it makes Edith the Church or the Virgin. Granted, this Christological and nuptial sentiment does not last long. In the poem that follows, Edward is rather insultingly made to play Saul to Godwin's David; for Godwin, in the poet's judgment, had generously refrained from a coup d'etat when he could easily have succeeded, just as David could have slain Saul when Saul entered the cave—to defecate, as the poet quite gratuitously specifies (46–47). The project is not, apparently, to turn Edward into a messianic figure, or to turn Edith into the Blessed Virgin, but to create sporadic echoes that help us make the association with Mary, Christ, and salvation history.

The Virgin Mary echoes also help explain in part what must surely be the most striking, and perhaps the most off-putting, idea in the Wilton epithalamium: that of the nonbirth of the "children." It refers, of course, to the church, or even the dormitory of the convent, which, unlike a real, human mother, can shelter its babies in a womblike enclosure even after "birth." Insofar as it refers to Edith, it is simply part of the "lucky you" rhetorical figure that makes up most of the poem: you are blessed because you have numerous offspring; because you are spared the practical anxieties of motherhood, such as housing or feeding your babies, or worrying during your pregnancy whether this is the male heir you are under so much pressure to produce; because you are spared the noise, dirt, and inconvenience that comes with real children; because you are spared the pain of childbirth, which is of course one of the curses laid on Eve after the fall; and because, indeed, you are spared the pain of separation from your infants.[62]

This, too, taps into Marian language. Edith/Wilton is reversing the curse of Eve. She remains a virgin, conceives without guilt, sin, or "defilement" by a man. Like Mary, she remains a virgin despite "motherhood." The phrase, "reseras haec claustra tabernae," "shut the gates of the inn," or in Barlow's rendition, "nor ope the lovely doorways of your inn," recalls Ezekiel's vision of the closed door, which had been interpreted as a Marian allegory from St. Ambrose onwards:

> Then he brought me back to the outer gate of the sanctuary, which faces east; and it was shut. The Lord said to me: this gate shall remain shut; it shall not be opened, and no one shall enter by it; for the Lord, the God of Israel, has entered by it; therefore it shall remain shut. Only the prince, because he is a prince, may sit in it to eat food before the Lord; he shall enter by way of the vestibule of the gate, and shall go out by the same way.[63]

This became one of the classic scriptures to cite in support of Mary's virginity "in partu" and "post partum," highlighting Mary's special status as the one who conceived and gave birth without "opening her womb."[64]

Despite the cleverness of this allusion, readers may be forgiven for feeling that it is not entirely successful. "Closing the door" (as opposed to "the door that shall remain closed") is an unfortunate phrase in this context. Mary is supposed to open the door; Eve was the one who shut it. "Paradisi porta per Evam cunctis clausa est, et per Mariam virginem iterum patefacta est, alleluia," says an antiphon for the Feast of the Assumption.[65] Rather than appearing miraculous or fruitful, the "closed door" takes on an ominous significance, more an image of denied possibilities than of a mysterious birth. In part simply because Edith is not actually Mary and does not in fact bring forth the savior (indeed, one may be reminded that she failed to produce an heir, who would have been something of a savior) there is something faintly disturbing about the image. Mary, after all, does give birth; the whole point of the Ezekiel allegory is that Christ is born of a human mother, though in ways that mysteriously leave her womb "closed." Wilton/Edith does not give birth, and there is something oddly frustrated, retentive, even physically uncomfortable about that twist to the image. Not having to let go, or, from the children's perspective, never having to leave the womb, may be comforting, but in a slightly monstrous way, one that, far from Mary's miraculous fecundity, seems very barren indeed.

In its overt praise of fertility and paradoxical stress on frustration, the poem does not stand isolated within the book. The progeny theme throughout the book is always potentially happy, celebratory, but always frustrated or in danger of being frustrated. The "epithalamium" is answered, not much later, in the opening poem of Book II. The Wilton eulogy marks a turning point; after it, Book I turns reluctantly to the falling out between Harold and Tostig, then swiftly draws to a close. Book II begins with a poignant lament on the failure of the Godwin lineage. The Battle of Stamford Bridge as well as Hastings, alluded to rather than narrated, have taken place in the interim; the muse and her poet now find themselves "surrounded by so many graves" (or "by so much darkness").[66] The poet complains bitterly to the muse: is this the great matter she had reserved for him to write about? He expected to sing the praises of Godwin and his Four Rivers of Paradise; now that picture of harmony has turned into "a Theban song," as the brothers have turned against each other—Thebes, with its history of fratricidal civil war, being the classic example of dysfunctional families and dysfunctional nations. The whole theme of "happy progeny" has fallen apart under the panegyrist's hands, has turned into a monstrous parody of itself:

> Vsque sub extremum   deuoti codicis unguem
> rebamur sanctam   dicere progeniem;

nunc, ut prisca canunt, feṭe telluris in aluo
dentibus insertis prodiit horrida stirps,
nata neci subite; grauis et—proh!—portio dira
nobis inuisa!—proh dolor!—id tamen est.

[We thought
To the last page of this devoted book
To tell of blessed progeny. But now,
As ancients sang, teeth put in fertile earth's
Recess produce a horrid people, born
To sudden death, a heavy and dire lot,
A curse to us; and yet, alas, 'tis so!] (84–85)

Of course the poet makes no direct connection back to the epithalamium—there is no tactful way he could do so; but since they stand so
close together, one is struck by the correspondences between the two
poems. Both concern numerous, even prodigious offspring, brought
forth miraculously; yet the second poem, with its allusion to the monstrous seed from the tale of the Argonauts, has completely inverted the
happy maternity ward of the first. The "heavenly seed" sown in the
Church's womb ("fusa . . . sata celica . . . in aluo") has become the
macabre seed of teeth sown in the earth's "womb" ("telluris in aluo /
dentibus insertis").[67]

This does not altogether come as a surprise, since, as we have seen, there
are troubling hints in the epithalamium itself. And indeed the theme of
progeny, wherever it surfaces, is set up to be doomed from the start. Disquieting notes are struck from the very beginning, in the prophetic style
the book usually favors for hinting at unpleasantness that it has to avoid in
the actual narrative. On the occasion of Edith's and Edward's marriage,
there is a poem—the epithalamium proper, if you will—lauding those
"quibus hac historia famulamur" [whom we serve in this history], that is,
Godwin's family (not Edward, or even really Edith, although it is their
marriage). In gloriously mixed metaphors, Godwin is both the fountain
from whence spring the Four Rivers of Paradise, and the trunk of a family tree. Godwin's issue, which includes Edith, "gemma . . . in medio regni"
[gem-like on the kingdom's breast] is, however, fatally split. The passage is
rather obscure:

Aera conscendit pars hec herendo supernis,
spemque sui generis nido fouet arbore alṭe.
Illa profunda petit tranans inimica uoratrix,
dampna suẹ stirpis faciens truncumque parentem
pendit ab ore tenens, dum certo tempore uitẹ

flatus uiuificans animal de non animata
matre creat; studet inde suis resoluta rapinis.

[The one part mounts the skies, to heaven twined,
And tends its race's hope in tree-top nest.
The other, gulping monster, seeks the depths,
Attacks its root and mouths the parent trunk,
And holds, until, as doomed, the breath of life
Creates a creature from a lifeless dam.] (26–27)

In its particulars, as Barlow points out, the passage resists interpretation. It is hard to determine exactly which of Godwin's children are meant by the "four rivers" or by the "tranans inimica uoratrix."[68] But the general imagery makes immediate sense. Something is gnawing at the very lineage, the very foundation of this family, to produce a perverse birth, an abomination born of a dead mother. By extension, since the Godwin family is here said to be "irrigating" the entire realm, by gnawing the stem the monster—in a somewhat mixed metaphor—also threatens to cut off the water supply for the entire realm of England.

The tree and stem part of this memorable catachresis gives us a direct link to the famous Green Tree prophecy, which, despairingly, becomes the focal point of Book II. Edward on his deathbed reports that he has just had a vision in which he was told that the people of England must brace themselves for a major disaster, in punishment for their sins. These afflictions, he was told, would last a long time; they would end only "tunc . . . si arbor uiridis a medio sui succidatur corpore, et pars abscisa trium iugerum spatio a suo deportetur stipite, cum per se et absque humana manu uel quouis amminiculo suo connectetur trunco, ceperitque denuo uirescere et fructificare ex coalescentis suci amore pristino" [at that time when a green tree, if cut down in the middle of its trunk, and the part cut off carried the space of three furlongs from the stock, shall be joined again to its trunk, by itself and without the hand of man or any sort of stake, and begin once more to push leaves and bear fruit from the old love of its uniting sap] (118–119). Despite optimistic reinterpretations in later renditions of this famous passage, in its context the prophecy is thoroughly gloomy: far from holding out hope for a future reflowering, the image is meant to be an impossible condition, familiar from folksongs and tales.[69] The poet leaves us in no doubt about that: the vision vouchsafed to the king is a "reuelatio impossibilitatis. . . . Neque enim arborem abscisam per se mouere, uel semel suci sui gratia destitutam, solide trunco suo incorporari et uirescere et fructificare apud homines est possibile" [a vision of something impossible. . . . For with men it is impossible for a felled tree to move of itself, or, once deprived of the service of its sap, to join itself firmly to its trunk and push leaves and bear fruit] (120–121). The only faint hope discernible here lies in the implied, not stated, second half of the biblical quotation, "with men it is impossible": "but with God all things are possible."[70] That, however, is not said, and it is a faint and remote consolation, especially since the poet adds that God, looking at his depraved people now, would find little motivation to intervene and help (120–123).

But the Green Tree is not just any impossible condition; it is specifically a dynastic one. Later interpreters unerringly read the tree as a family tree, a "stirps" (as when, a generation later, the prophecy is retroactively applied to the son born to Henry I; or two generations after that, to Henry II, who through his maternal ancestry continues the pre-Conquest English line).[71] The Anonymous does not explicitly read the prophecy in this way, but "lineage" cannot be far from his thoughts. This is, after all, the deathbed prophecy of a king dying without issue. The tree prophecy inevitably throws a pall over the scene that immediately follows it, in which Edward tries—vainly, of course—to institute an heir by entrusting his queen and realm to Harold. Though the Anonymous cannot or will not address the catastrophe of Harold's brief reign directly, he has spoken about it in prophecies and images.

The (family) tree trunk that comes back to life, the sprig that flourishes against the odds, is of course also a Marian image: Isaiah's shoot from the root of Jesse ("et egredietur virga de radice Iesse et flos de radice eius ascendet")[72] had long been taken to refer to the Virgin Mary.[72] But this is where the Marian imagery definitively falls apart. This root does not flourish, and its failure to thrive has the effect of retroactively undermining the entire panegyric topos of Edith's chaste motherhood. The passing on of the realm, which echoes the commendation under the Cross, is futile—we already know how it is going to end; its failure is already in the past at the time of writing. Edith is indeed emblematic of the realm here: introduced early as the "gem on the realm's breast," she is now virtually equated with it.[73] Honorific though that may be, her barrenness thus also becomes emblematic of the calamity that has befallen the land.

This is not the way the panegyric should have turned out. But of course the Anonymous is not explicit about any of these bitter thoughts. Like all that is painful, disastrous, or possibly offensive, the line of associations that keeps returning to Edith's barrenness and implicitly blaming her for the national disaster is curiously repressed, coming out only—but perhaps more vigorously—in form of lament and prophecy, indirect hint rather than narration. The Anonymous has tried to associate Edith metonymically with both her nation and, through her Abbey Church, with the Bride of the Song of Songs and the Blessed Virgin. Not only should this work nicely as both panegyric and consolation, it could also help in lifting the sorry narrative of contemporary events from its desperate earthly state, to sacralize it and the English nation, and to give the calamities meaning within salvation history. The author and the muse say as much when they decide on a hagiography of the king as a way out of the bogged-down history. The entire book is opened by a prophecy that makes explicit the sacralization of the realm. Before Edward is born, Bishop Brihtwald sees "the blessed Peter, the first of the Apostles, consecrate the image of a seemly man as king, assign him the life of a bachelor, and set the years of his reign by a fixed reckoning of his life. And when the king, even at this juncture, asked him who of the generations to come would reign in the kingdom, Peter answered, 'The kingdom of the English belongs to God [Regnum Anglorum est dei]; and after you He has already provided a king according to His own will'" (15).

There is no real coherence to these sacred gestures; Edward, as we have seen, bears the features of Christ only intermittently, appearing weak, ineffectual, sometimes even silly in between. Perhaps there need not be any coherence for the gestures to work. But they do not quite work; the sacralization of English history is only partially successful, and it may be symptomatic after all that the sacred history motif remains diffuse. Likewise, the panegyric of Edith as virgin mother rings hollow. Instead of becoming an image of virginal fecundity—precisely through her identification with the realm, and with the Abbey Church—Edith becomes an emblem of failure, of sterility, of barred future prospects, of "closed doors."

While this cannot have been intended in quite this way, there is a logic to the book's rhetorical problems. As the poet says in his conversation with the muse, the national catastrophe interrupts and frustrates his enterprise; the national failure, so to speak, coincides with his own literary failure, which he just barely manages to avoid by diverting the narrative into a decidedly hagiographic direction. He saves his book by avoidance, substitution, indirection: when you cannot talk about the Norman Conquest, write—as the muse suggests—about Edward's sanctity instead; when you cannot talk about the queen's sterility, talk about her by way of talking about a church. At the same time, the substitutions do permit some sort of muffled, distorted articulation of the displaced subjects. Since the Anonymous directly addresses his problems and authorial decisions, his book is also about writing under duress, about things you cannot say and how to say them anyway. The "retentive," "frustrated" image of Edith's nonbirth is paradoxically once again a perfect embodiment of the spirit of the work: its suppressed despair, its forced optimism, its compulsion to return to subjects it would rather leave alone, its scurrying for some sort of comfort or safety.

Edith, meanwhile, is left with somewhat cold comfort. She may take pride and consolation in the book's overt agenda of lauding her and her family, in the roles of "pious widow" and "virgin mother" it offers her, and in its sheer rhetorical polish and display. But she is also saddled with a stubborn subtext, in which her apotheosis, like that of the country, has fallen short, and she is naggingly reminded of her role of bearing children—in which she has conspicuously failed.

Notes

1. Peggy McCracken, "The Body Politic and the Queen's Adulterous Body in French Romance," in *Feminist Approaches to the Body in Medieval Literature,* ed. Linda Lomperis and Sarah Stanbury (Philadelphia: University of Pennsylvania Press, 1993), pp. 38–64. The other element of McCracken's argument, namely the Queen's adultery, is not addressed in the *Vita Ædwardi;* but interestingly William of Malmesbury reports that there were rumors about it: *De Gestis Regum Anglorum,* ed. William Stubbs, Rolls Series 90 (London: Eyre and Spottiswoode, 1887), 1:239. See also Pauline Stafford, *Queens, Concubines and Dowagers: The King's Wife in the Early Middle Ages* (London: Batsford, 1983), p. 82.

2. Frank Barlow, ed. and trans., *The Life of King Edward Who Rests at Westminster,* 2nd ed., Oxford Medieval Texts (Oxford: Clarendon, 1992). Parenthetical references in the text will refer to this edition and facing-page translation; Barlow's introduction and editorial matter will be referred to in the notes as "Barlow."

3. Not so surprising in view of the later tradition—not stated but strongly suggested in this work—that Edith's and Edward's marriage was not consummated and both remained virgins by choice (see below at nn. 10 and 53). Moreover, religious language on widowhood and virginity is closely related, both widows and virgins being exhorted to a marriage with Christ in language borrowed from the Song of Songs. See, for instance, Peter Damian's advice for and encomium of Empress Agnes (PL 145:812–820).

4. The exact dating of the work is problematic. I am here following Barlow's opinion (pp. xxix-xxxiii); but see n. 11 below.

5. Barlow makes a strong, attractive case for Goscelin of St. Bertin as a possible contender but acknowledges that such an attribution cannot be proven (pp. xliv-lix; Appendix C, pp. 133–149). Pauline Stafford posits a kind of "mediated authorship" for Edith, suggesting that her role in planning and shaping this commissioned work was so strong that we are at just one remove from her own ideas, and that she consciously encouraged the rhetorical identification of queen and country in an attempt to consolidate her shaky position ("The Portrayal of Royal Women in England, Mid-Tenth to Mid-Twelfth Centuries," in *Medieval Queenship,* ed. John Carmi Parsons

(Stroud, Gloucestershire: Alan Sutton, 1993), pp. 165–167; cf. Barlow, p. lxi). For reasons that my discussion of the work's rhetoric will make clear, I am inclined to think that her involvement did not extend to micro-managing the work's linguistic and rhetorical choices. But my readings do not preclude Stafford's thesis; indeed, it would be most intriguing to think of Edith as the quasi-author behind the rhetoric I am about to describe.

6. On the *Vita's* source value, see Barlow, pp. lix–lxxviii.

7. Kenneth E. Cutler, "Edith, Queen of England, 1045 – 1066," *Mediaeval Studies* 35 (1973), 225–226.

8. Cutler, "Edith," p. 231.

9. *Vita Ædwardi*, pp. 36–37. Cf. Barlow, p. lxxiv; Stafford, *Queens, Dowagers,* p. 82.

10. The later lives of Edward are not reticent on that point; neither are the *vitas* of Emperor Henry II and his wife Kunigunde, which are often compared with this text (for instance Marc Bloch, "La vie de S. Éduard le Confesseur par Osbert de Clare," *Analecta Bollandiana* 41 [1923], 74–75; "Vitae Heinrici et Cunegundis imperatorum," ed. G. Waitz, *MGH SS* 4:805, 810, 816–818, 821–822. Cf. Michel Parisse, "Des veuves au monastère," in *Veuves et veuvage dans le haut Moyen Age,* ed. Michel Parisse (Paris: Picard, 1993), pp. 260, 265 n. 50; and Barlow, pp. lxxiii–lxxvii. William of Malmesbury knew the tradition of Edith's and Edward's chaste marriage but was highly skeptical, especially of the alleged religious motivation (*Gesta Regum* 1:239).

11. Marc Bloch's contention that the whole work is an early twelfth-century "forgery" ("Vie de Saint Édouard," pp. 17–44) is no longer widely accepted, having been refuted by R. W. Southern, "The First Life of Edward the Confessor," *English Historical Review* 58 (1943), 385–400; Eleanor K. Heningham, "The Genuineness of the *Vita Aeduuardi Regis,*" *Speculum* 21 (1946), 419–456; and Barlow, pp. xxix–xxxiii. There are, however, still serious disagreements. Barlow is inclined to take the book's own account—composition in two distinct stages, interrupted by the events of 1066—pretty much at face value; Eleanor K. Heningham, "The Literary Unity, the Date, and the Purpose of Lady Edith's Book:'The Life of King Edward Who Rests in Westminster,'" *Albion* 7 (1975), 24–40, argues that the whole must postdate the Norman Conquest. Barlow's argument that "A book written in praise of the house of Godwin is more likely to have started before 1066 than after" (p. xxxi n. 69) seems persuasive: "A book which is written in praise of Edith's family, probably with reference to the succession to the throne, lauds Godwin, Harold, and Tostig, is hostile to Robert of Jumièges, Edward's Norman archbishop, and which criticizes Edward whenever he acts contrary to the interests of his wife's kin . . . could not have been written long after Edward's death. Such a book would have been unwise—indeed quite pointless—after William I had gained secure possession of the throne" (p. xxx). Barlow also points out that early in Book I, especially in the opening poem, Edward is spoken of as if still alive, which would suggest that the book was started before January 1066. On

the other hand, Heningham is right that the book's rhetorical purpose seems of a piece, with much in Book I that appears to hint at the disasters to come; it seems reasonable to assume, if not a post–Conquest date for the entire work, at least a revision of earlier, already extant parts at the time the project was resumed shortly after the Norman Conquest.

12. Barlow, pp. xxi–xxii.
13. Heningham points out that the division into two "books" is editorial and has no manuscript support ("Literary Unity," p. 27 and n. 17). But a major break is nonetheless indicated: the poet, for the first time since the beginning, abandons the chronology of the narrative, readdresses the Muse, declares the purpose of the work lost, and implies that an unspecified interval has elapsed, during which unspecified terrible things have happened; the Muse also counsels a redirection of the work and a new beginning. I am therefore accepting Barlow's editorially imposed division into Books I and II.
14. This has to be said with the serious reservation that there is a major lacuna in the unique manuscript, which could in theory have contained anything. Yet Barlow's detective work from sources dependent on the *Vita Ædwardi* has given us a good idea of what most likely was in the lost portions. The most direct mention of the Norman Conquest in those related textual traditions is a paragraph of lament over England, in connection with Edward's vision of the Seven Sleepers of Ephesus:

   And what shall I say about England? What shall I tell generations to come? Woe is to you England, you who once shone bright with holy, angelic progeny, but now with anxious expectation groan exceedingly for your sins. You have lost your native king and suffered defeat, with much spilling of blood of many of your men, in a war against the foreigner. Pitiably your sons have been slain within you. Your counselors and princes are bound in chains, killed, or disinherited. (108–111)

   Even this does not narrate the Norman Conquest as an event in the chronological sequence or mention any names or specifics. For further discussion of the textual problems surrounding the Seven Sleepers, see Frank Barlow, "The *Vita Ædwardi* (Book II); The Seven Sleepers: Some Further Evidence and Reflections," *Speculum* 40 (1965), 391.
15. Barlow, p. xlii.
16. I discuss these issues more fully in my forthcoming essay, "Ten-sixty-six: The Moment of Transition in Two Narratives About the Norman Conquest."
17. Augustine, "De sancta virginitate," PL 40:395–428; Ælfric, "Nativitas Sanctae Mariae Virginis," in *Angelsächsische Homilien und Heiligenleben,* ed. Bruno Assmann, Bibliothek der angelsächsischen Prosa (Kassel: Wigand, 1889), pp. 24–48. On both texts and their relationship, see Mary Clayton, *The Cult of the Virgin Mary in Anglo-Saxon England* (Cambridge: Cambridge University Press, 1990), pp. 247–248, and Mary Clayton, "Ælfric and the Nativity of the Blessed Virgin Mary," *Anglia* 104 (1986): 286–315. Ælfric's

homily is a free adaptation of Augustine's tract, with added material; in some respects it seems closer to the Anonymous's poem. But the poet's dependence on any sources is loose; it would be hard to demonstrate which text, if either, he had in front of him.

18. This would obviously depend on one's dating of that portion of the book. But see n. 11 above.

19. Quoted from what appears to be an abridgment of the full set of three church dedication sermons in *The Benedictional of Archbishop Robert,* ed. H. A. Wilson, Henry Bradshaw Society 24 (London: Harrison, 1902), p. 72. This is a liturgical source close to our text in time, place, and possibly even personal connections: made in England in the tenth century, it appears to have been taken to Normandy in the mid-eleventh; "Archbishop Robert" might just be Robert of Jumièges, or else Robert Archbishop of Rouen, Queen Emma's brother, that is, King Edward's uncle (pp. xiv–xvi). The full version of Cesarius's sermons can be found in PL 39:2166–2172 (Sermons CCXXIX-CCXXI). Similar explanations of the metonymy "ecclesia" are found elsewhere, for instance in (Pseudo-) Remigius of Auxerre, "Tractatus de dedicatione ecclesiae," [ca. 900], PL 131:846–847; also, briefly in William Durandus's encyclopedic compilation *Rationale divinorum officiorum: The Symbolism of Churches and Church Ornaments,* trans. and introd. John Mason and Benjamin Webb (Leeds: Green, 1843), p. 117.

20. For instance Honorius Augustodunensis, "Expositio in Cantica Canticorum," PL 172:347–353, which is discussed in E. Ann Matter, *The Voice of My Beloved: The Song of Songs in Western Medieval Christianity* (Philadelphia: University of Pennsylvania Press, 1990), pp. 58–76. See also Augustine's commentary on Psalm 44 in his *Enarrationes in Psalmos, Aurelii Augustini Opera* 10.1, ed. D. Eligius Dekkers and Johannes Fraipont, Corpus Christianorum, Series Latina, 38 (Turnhout: Brepols, 1956), pp. 493–517.

21. An impressive and convenient demonstration of this substitutability is Hrabanus Maurus's "Allegoriae in Universam Sacram Scripturam," an alphabetical glossary of all manner of things mentioned in the Bible, with their allegorical meaning(s). A small sample: "*Tabernaculum* [tent or "dwelling place"] est patria coelestis, ut in Psalmis, 'Domine, quis habitabit in tabernaculo tuo?' . . . *Tabernaculum,* humanitas Christi, ut in Psalmis 'In sole posuit tabernaculum suum,' id est, in virgine posuit humanitatem suam. *Tabernaculum,* virgo Maria . . . *Tabernaculum,* sancta Ecclesia . . . *Tabernaculum,* corpus nostrum . . . *Tabernaculum,* mens nostra . . . *Tabernaculum,* caro impii, ut in Job, 'Affligetur relictus in tabernaculo suo' . . . *Tabernaculum,* sancti angeli . . . Per *tabernacula* antiqui sancti . . . Per *tabernacula,* gentiles . . . Per *tabernacula* crimina cujuslibet reprobi . . . (PL 112:1062). On the "allegorical fluidity" between signifier and signified—for example, the Virgin Mary and Ecclesia—see Matter, *Voice,* p. 156.

22. See caput XLVI, col. 425.

23. Augustine, "De sancta virginitate," p. 397; my translation.

24. Augustine, "De sancta virginitate," pp. 395–402.

25. The liturgy and the readings for the feast draw primarily on the Apocalypse, the Psalms, and the story of Jacob's ladder in Genesis 18. Generally present in most early sources is the *postcommunio* "Deus qui ecclesiam tuam sponsam vocare dignatus es . . . ," for example, *The Leofric Missal, as Used in the Cathedral of Exeter . . . A.D. 1050 – 1072*, ed. F. E. Warren (Oxford: Clarendon, 1883), pp. 18, 264; *The Missal of Robert of Jumièges*, ed. H. A. Wilson, Henry Bradshaw Society 11 (London: Harrison, 1896), p. 239; *The Leofric Collectar (Harley Ms. 2961)*, ed. E. S. Dewick, vol. 1, Henry Bradshaw Society 45 (London: Harrison, 1914) also contains a *capitulum* from Apoc. 21:2–3: "Vidi sanctam hierusalem nouam descendentem de cęlo a deo paratam. sicut sponsam ornatam uiro suo" (pp. 349, 352). The *Sarum Missal*'s opening *ad processionem*, "Salue festa dies toto uenerabilis euo qua sponso sponsa iungitur ecclesia" (*The Sarum Missal*, ed. J. Wickham Legg [Oxford: Clarendon, 1916], p. 202) is not found in the earlier sources.

26. For example, *Analecta Hymnica Medii Aevi*, eds. G. M. Dreves, C. Blume and H. Bannister (Leipzig: Reisland, 1886–1922), 7:226; 51:102; 53:2247.

27. A. Wilmart, ed., "La légende de Ste Édith en prose et vers par le moine Goscelin," *Analecta Bollandiana* 56 (1938), 46–47, 35–36. Osbert of Clare's 1138 redaction of the *Vita Ædwardi* uses some epithalamic language in describing the dedication of Westminster Abbey; the *Vita Ædwardi* itself may have contained a similar passage in the section that is now lost (Bloch, "Vie," p. 104; Barlow, pp. 110–111, 114–115; see n. 13 above, and Barlow, p. 114 n. 289).

28. Although the specific language, as Herde notes, is derived more often from New Testament loci such as 2 Cor. 11:2, Ephes. 5:32, 37, and Apoc. 21:2. Rosemarie Herde, "Das Hohelied in der lateinischen Literatur des Mittelalters bis zum 12. Jahrhundert," *Studi medievali* 3d ser., 8 (1967), 962. On the allegorical reading of the Song of Songs as Church and Virgin Mary, see Matter, *Voice*, pp. 86–111, 151–170; Ann W. Astell, *The Song of Songs in the Middle Ages* (Ithaca: Cornell University Press, 1990), pp. 42–72.

29. Virginia Tufte, *The Poetry of Marriage: The Epithalamium in Europe and Its Development in England*, University of Southern California Studies in Comparative Literature (Los Angeles: Tinnon-Brown, 1970), pp. 77–79. See also E. Faye Wilson, "Pastoral and Epithalamium in Latin Literature," *Speculum* 23 (1948), 35–57.

30. PL 61:633–638. Cf. Sebastian Tromp S. J., "Ecclesia sponsa virgo mater," *Gregorianum* 18 (1937), 28–29.

31. Tufte, *Poetry of Marriage*, pp. 38–39.

32. Joseph C. Plumpe, *Mater Ecclesia: An Inquiry Into the Concept of the Church as Mother in Early Christianity* (Washington, D. C.: The Catholic University of America Press, 1943); Tromp, "Ecclesia sponsa virgo mater," pp. 17–20.

33. Augustine, "De sancta virginitate," p. 397.

34. Erwin Panofsky, ed. and trans., *Abbot Suger on the Abbey Church of St.-Denis and its Art Treasures* (Princeton: Princeton University Press, 1946), pp. 40–41, 98–99.

35. MGH Poet. Lat. 5:260–279.
36. J. Armitage Robinson, ed. *The History of Westminster Abbey by John Flete* (Cambridge: Cambridge University Press, 1909), p. 54; my translation. The authenticity of these charters is doubtful, but even so they are probably no later than the mid-twelfth century (Robinson, *History of Westminster Abbey,* pp. 15–17).
37. Augustine, "De sancta virginitate," p. 401.
38. "De Habitu Virginum," *S. Thasci Caecilii Cypriani Opera Omnia,* ed. Guilelmus Hartel, Corpus Scriptorum Ecclesiasticorum Latinorum 3 (Vindobonae: Gerold, 1868), 1:189; quoted by Plumpe, *Mater Ecclesia,* p. 82; my translation.
39. Stafford, "Queens, Concubines," pp. 178–180. Patrick Corbet suggests that the aristocratic widow's retreat to an "Eigenkloster"-like foundation becomes less common after ca. 1000, when more women found it advantageous and feasible to "remain in the world": "Pro anima senioris sui: La pastorale ottonienne du veuvage," in *Veuves et veuvage dans le haut Moyen Age,* ed. Michel Parisse (Paris: Picard, 1993), pp. 233–257.
40. "Vita Sanctae Cunegundis," MGH SS 4: 822; my translation.
41. "Fundatio Monasterii Schildecensis," MGH SS 15:1046–1047. See Michel Parisse, "Des veuves au monastère," in *Veuves et veuvage dans le haut Moyen Age,* ed. Michel Parisse (Paris: Picard, 1993), p. 259 and n. 21, 22, 50.
42. Parisse, "Veuves," pp. 258, 272.
43. Augustine, "De sancta virginitate," pp. 397–398.
44. Clarissa W. Atkinson, *The Oldest Vocation: Christian Motherhood in the Middle Ages* (Ithaca: Cornell University Press, 1991), pp. 65, 94, and passim.
45. Parisse, "Veuves," pp. 268–269.
46. Wilmart, "Légende de Ste Édith," pp. 42–43, 58–60.
47. Peter the Venerable, "Letter 53: Item ad germanos suos eiusdem matris epitaphium," in *The Letters of Peter the Venerable,* ed. Giles Constable, 2 vols. (Cambridge: Harvard University Press, 1967), 1:153–173. See also Parisse, "Veuves," pp. 272–273.
48. Wilmart, "Légende de Ste Édith," pp. 36–37.
49. For secular resonances of the monastic theme, see Atkinson, *Oldest Vocation,* pp. 130–131.
50. Cf. Barlow, p. lxvi.
51. Cutler, "Edith," pp. 225–226. On relations between Edith and William the Conqueror, see also Heningham, "Literary Unity," p. 25 n.7; Barlow, p. xvi; on differing accounts in the early sources, see Catherine Morton and Hope Muntz, eds., *The Carmen de Hastingae Proelio of Guy Bishop of Amiens* (Oxford: Clarendon, 1972), pp. xxi, xlviii, 58 n.4.
52. Augustine, "De sancta virginitate," p. 398.
53. See nn. 3 and 11 above.
54. Clayton, *Cult,* pp. 164–165; Thomas Symons, *Regularis Concordia* (London: Nelson, 1953), pp. 3, 7.
55. Clayton, *Cult,* pp. 130–131.

56. Cf. Tromp, "Ecclesia," pp. 21–22.

57. Augustine, "De sancta virginitate," pp. 398–399. For a reflection on the psychological needs served by this idea, see Julia Kristeva, "Stabat Mater," trans. Arthur Goldhammer, in *The Female Body in Western Culture: Contemporary Perspectives*, ed. Susan Rubin Suleiman (Cambridge, MA: Harvard University Press, 1986), p. 105.

58. Ælfric, "De Assumptione Beatae Mariae, "in *Homilies of the Anglo-Saxon Church, Part I: The Sermones Catholici, or Homilies of Ælfric*, ed. and trans. Benjamin Thorpe (London: Ælfric Society, 1864), 1:442–443. Ælfric is here expanding his source, the pseudo-Jerome (really Paschasius Radbertus) "Cogitis me," in a concrete, visual way (Paschasius Radbertus, "De Assumptione Mariae Virginis," ed. Albert Ripberger, Corpus Christianorum Continuatio Mediaevalis 56c [Turnhout, 1985], p. 130; on this text, see also Matter, *Voice*, pp. 151–155). English art is precocious in Western art in devising iconographies for the dormition and assumption of the Virgin; but the familiar iconography of Christ crowning his mother seated beside him does not occur until the twelfth century (Clayton, *Cult*, pp. 154–155; Robert Deshman, "Christus rex et magi reges: Kingship and Christology in Ottonian and Anglo-Saxon Art," *Frühmittelalterliche Studien* 10 (1976), 397–398; George Zarnecki, "The Coronation of the Virgin on a Capital from Reading Abbey," *Journal of the Warburg and Courtauld Institutes* 13 (1950), 1–12). However, Clayton shows that the image was well developed in religious literature. Besides liturgical antiphons and the Ælfric homily, she cites an eleventh-century poem from Abingdon (*Cult*, pp. 107–108).

59. John 20: 26–27.

60. Ælfric, "De Assumptione," pp. 438–439; Thorpe's translation; cf. Paschasius Radbertus, pp. 116–117. "De Assumptione" is followed in the collection of Ælfric's homilies by a sermon on the feast of St. Bartholomew for August 25 (*Homilies of the Anglo-Saxon Church*, pp. 454–477). Wilton was dedicated to the Virgin Mary and St. Bartholomew (Clayton, *Cult*, pp. 130–131). If the Anonymous had access to a volume of Ælfric's homilies and was thumbing through it in search of material to use in a poem on Wilton, he might well have hit upon the Assumption homily.

61. The strongest hints to this effect comes in the textually problematic passage on the Seven Sleepers (see n. 14 above), where a possible resurrection (of sorts) seems to be alluded to. (See Otter, "Ten-Sixty-Six" [forthcoming].) On Christological views of kingship in the high Middle Ages see, generally, Ernst H. Kantorowicz, *The King's Two Bodies: A Study in Medieval Political Theology* (Princeton: Princeton University Press, 1957), pp. 42–86; on the iconography of Christ the King in Anglo-Saxon England, see Deshman, "Christus rex et magi reges," and Deshman, "Benedictus Monarcha et Monachus: Early Medieval Ruler Theology and the Anglo-Saxon Reform," *Frühmittelalterliche Studien* 22 (1988), pp. 204–240.

62. A similar catalogue of the pains of motherhood and the corresponding blessings of sterility, spoken by St. Marcswidis, appears in the "Fundatio

Monasterii Schildecensis" 1047. Cf. also a poem by Venantius Fortunatus, addressed to the queen-turned-nun Radegund and her younger friend and surrogate daughter Agnes, which uses the same sentiment. It is rather less strained in this context: the poet quite naturally congratulates the two women on being able to stay together in religious life and in the world to come. Of course he is also redefining Radegund's maternity, retroactively making her a "virgin mother":

Hanc tibi non uterus natam, sed gratia fecit;
non caro, sed Christus hanc in amore dedit.
quae sit in aeternum tecum, tibi contulit auctor,
perpetuam prolem dat sine fine pater.
felix posteritas quae nullo deficit aevo
quae cum matre simul non moritura manet

[Not your womb brought forth this child, but God's grace;
Not flesh, but Christ gave her to you in love.
Her Maker grants you that she may stay with you forever;
The father grants eternal offspring without end.
Happy the progeny that will not decline with age,
Which will remain with the mother and never die.]

(Venantius Fortunatus, *Opera Poetica*, MGH Auct. Antiqu. 5:1:259; my translation.)

63. Ezekiel 44:1–3.
64. Gail McMurray Gibson, "'Porta haec clausa erit': Comedy, Conception, and Ezekiel's Closed Door in the *Ludus Coventriae* Play of Joseph's Return," *Journal of Medieval and Renaissance Studies* 8 (1976), 137–156; Robert Favreau, "Le thème épigraphique de la porte," *Cahiers de civilisation médiévale* 34 (1991), 277. See also Charles T. Wood, "The Doctor's Dilemma: Sin, Salvation, and the Menstrual Cycle in Medieval Thought," *Speculum* 56 (1981), 710–727. For Anglo-Saxon instances of the Ezekiel theme, see Clayton, "Cult," pp. 197–198, 199–200.
65. Gregory the Great, "Liber Responsalis," PL 78:799. Cf. Ælfric, "De Assumptione," 446–447.
66. If "graves"("sepultis") were the right reading, it would make a very nice counterpoint to the mother "surrounded by a hundred thousand cots" of the epithalamium. But the manuscript reads "tenebris," not "sepultis"; while Barlow's emendation is highly attractive, and has some support in the poem's structure ("assonance and alliteration"), it still remains a bold and doubtful editorial intervention, especially since the manuscript reading does make sense and produces no serious difficulties of rhyme or meter.
67. The source, according to Barlow, is probably Ovid's *Metamorphoses* (Book VII). If the Anonymous was drawing on Ælfric's "Nativitas" homily, then

the Ovidian reminiscence could have been triggered by Ælfric's passage—not paralleled in Augustine's "De sancta virginitate"—on another sort of "monstrous seed." Ælfric is answering those who ask why God allows children to be born from adulterous relationships:

Ic acsiȝe þone man nu anes þinges:
ȝif hwa forstelð hwæte and þæt forstolne sæwð
hwæt ah þæt corn ȝeweald þæt hit wearp se sædere
mid unclænre handa on ða clænan moldan,
oððe hwi sceolde seo eorðe hyre wæstmas ofteon
þam unscyldi₃um sæde for ðam scyldi an sædere . . . ?

[I ask that person now one question:
If anyone steals wheat and sows what he has stolen,
Is it the grain's fault that it was thrown by the sower
With unclean hand on the clean soil,
Or why should the earth withhold her fertility
From the guiltless seed because of the guilty sower?]

(Ælfric, "Nativitas," lines 310–315; my translation. Cf. Clayton, "Ælfric," p. 309)

68. As Barlow explains, if the four rivers are taken to represent the four sons mentioned by name in the book, then it is hard to decide how we are to divide them up into high-flyers and gulping monsters. If, on the other hand, the gulping monster alludes to Swegn, the family black sheep—not otherwise mentioned in this book—then he would have to be one of the four, leaving us to decide which of the others is not included. It is possible, though, that no such precision is intended. It could even be that the poet is distinguishing not among different Godwin sons but between the higher and lower impulses in all of them, or more specifically in Harold and Tostig, whom he admires but whose fratricidal quarrel he regards as one of the root causes of the country's catastrophe.

69. Stith Thompson, *Motif Index of Folk Literature,* rev. ed. (Copenhagen: Rosenkilde and Bagger, 1956), vol. 3, nos. H.1000–1049 ("Impossible or absurd tasks") and nos. F.970–971 ("Extraordinary behavior of trees or plants").

70. Matthew 19:26.

71. On the later interpretations of the Green Tree, see Bloch, "Vie," pp. 35–38; Heningham, "Genuineness," pp. 422–424; Barlow, pp. 131–132.

72. Isaiah 11:1; cf. Clayton, "Cult," pp. 55, 171, 175.

73. Stafford, "Portrayal," p. 165.

PART II

THE VARIETIES OF VIRGINITY

CHAPTER 4

PERFORMING VIRGINITY:
SEX AND VIOLENCE IN
THE *KATHERINE* GROUP

Sarah Salih

> *Sanctity, in the virgin martyr legends, was achieved through the body because women's piety was based in women's corporeal experiences; thus virginity, in the* Katherine Group, *is a gender unto itself, requiring continual performance.*

Him bigon to gremien, ant o grome gredde: "Strupeð hire steortnaket and heoueð hire on heh up, swa þet ha hongi to mede of hire hokeres, ant ontendeð hire bodi wið bearninde teaperes."

Þe driueles unduhtie swa duden sone, þet te hude snawhwit swartede as hit snercte, ant bearst on to bleinin as hit aras oueral; ant hire leofliche lich reschte of þe leie, swa þet alle remden þet on hire softe siden sehen þet rewðe.

[He began to be angry, and furiously cried, "Strip her stark naked and raise her up high, so she may hang as payment for her insults, and burn her body with lighted tapers."

The wretched menials did so at once, so that the snowwhite skin blackened as it was scorched, and broke into blisters as it swelled all over, and her beautiful body crackled in the flame, so that there was an outcry from all those who saw the pitiful injury to her soft sides.][1]

Scenes of extreme violence mark out the genre of the virgin martyr legend. This example, taken from "Seinte Margarete," is entirely typical. The virginal heroine defies her tormentors, is stripped, and put through an ever more ingenious catalogue of tortures: whips, rods, metal spikes, wheels, boiling oil. The narrative stresses the presence of a crowd of spectators and emphasizes in detail the effects of violence on the body. The saints' legends of the Katherine Group seem obsessed with torture; again and again the virgin's body is displayed and dismembered.[2] When the virgin is not being tortured, she may be threatened with torture, or she may proclaim her own readiness to suffer it.[3] Suffering torture is what she does best. The instrument of torture—Katherine's wheel, or the dragon that swallows Margaret—may become the saint's identifying emblem, as if the experience of suffering encapsulates her meaning. Sometimes, by way of variation, other people are tortured, such as the Empress in *Seinte Katerine,* and all three legends include mass martyrdoms of converts. Why should female sanctity demand such protracted suffering? And why should the example of public nakedness be appropriate to the anchoritic readership of the manuscripts of the Katherine Group, women who, far from practicing public exposure, "hare ahne wah wriheð wið euch monnes sihðe" [are concealed by their own wall from any man's sight]?[4]

A possible explanation for the prevalence of torture scenes in these narratives can be found in the thesis that women's piety in the medieval period is based in women's experience of themselves as corporeal, meaning that their sanctity must necessarily be achieved through the body. Elizabeth Robertson, for example, in her work on the Katherine Group argues that "the female saints must overcome their inherent feminine weakness through the twin processes of physical identification with Christ's suffering and the endurance of extreme physical torture."[5] In citing women's religious experience in their bodily experience, Robertson is in good company. Caroline Bynum's influential study of female mysticism, *Holy Feast and Holy Fast,* claims that:

> The goal of religious women was thus to realise the opportunity of physicality. They strove not to eradicate body but to merge their own humiliating and painful flesh with that flesh whose agony, espoused by choice, was salvation. Luxuriating in Christ's physicality, they found there the lifting up—the redemption—of their own.[6]

Karma Lochrie changes the terms but continues the analysis: "Women's position as flesh carries over into medieval ideas about the female body and character as pervious, excessive, and susceptible. . . . By occupying and exploiting her position as flesh, the woman writer has recourse to a power derived from the taboo which defines her and which she breaks with her speech."[7]

We seem to be in the presence of a consensus. These writers vary in their theoretical standpoints and in the texts on which they choose to focus, but they share the central thesis that women's piety, and perhaps all of women's experience, is governed by the dualistic association of women with the body or flesh, and men with the spirit. The female body is characterized as "pervious, excessive and susceptible," and these qualities are reevaluated through specifically feminine forms of piety. Women's only option is to accept their identification with the flesh and thus confirm the patriarchal categorization that makes them bodily others, nature to men's culture. Robertson herself is aware of the potential difficulties of this position: "It can be argued that medieval women gained power by accepting medieval categories of male and female and then manipulating them to their own advantage. Perhaps these women would finally have been more powerful had they abandoned these categories altogether."[8] Perhaps, however, "medieval categories of male and female" are less absolute and more context-specific than this account suggests. Lochrie acknowledges that pious women need not necessarily choose to privilege the flesh. In her view, this strategy stands in opposition to the ideology of chastity, which works by containing the flesh: "Integrity, viewed as a repairing of the natural but dangerous accessibility of the female body, becomes the spiritual and moral standard for religious women in the Middle Ages. The natural grotesqueness of the woman's body is thus corrected through moral and physical enclosure."[9] Women's piety, then, need not mean redemption of the flesh: it could mean a redefinition of the body through chastity. The chaste body, enclosed and corrected of its grotesqueness, is the body that I intend to discuss in this essay. If chastity does succeed in repairing such dangerous, inchoate flesh, what is the result? What possibilities are open to the woman whose body is perceived as neither accessible nor pervious? Surely such an achievement would require that both terms, "woman" and "body," be redefined. I believe that an analysis of the virgin martyrs of the Katherine Group will help to answer these questions. These martyrs are women who, through the practice of virginity, successfully redefine their bodies and identities as not feminine but virgin.

Judith Butler's concept of "performative gender" provides a theoretical basis for my enquiry. My account of Butler's theory is necessarily partial and is limited to those aspects of her thought that aid the analysis of medieval virgin martyr legends. Her central contention is that the body is not self-evident but is discursively produced: "But the 'body' itself is a construction, as are the myriad 'bodies' that constitute the domain of gendered subjects. Bodies cannot be said to have a signifiable existence prior to the mark of their gender; the question then emerges: To what extent does the body come into being in and through the mark(s) of gender?"[10] A body is a negotiable sign, not a prediscursive thing. This is not to say that bodies do not actually exist: rather, the perception of bodies must occur within a preexisting, culture-specific discourse. In the case of twentieth century Western societies, that preexisting discourse is what Butler terms the "heterosexual matrix" or "heterosexual hegemony," which demands a binary distinction of sexes into male and female. "Sex," then, can no longer be understood as the ahistorical, absolute bodily difference on which "gender" is culturally imposed. Because the body is read through the signs of gender, gender can be said to precede sex. Gender (and therefore sex also) is constituted performatively; it is not what you are, but what you do, "the repeated stylisation of the body, a set of repeated acts."[11] It is therefore a continual process rather than a fixed state. If gender identity requires repeated acts, it must be theoretically possible to stop repeating these acts, and to "do" your gender differently. Gender identity is necessarily unstable. If gender is not based on sex, then it need not be binary:

> Even if the sexes appear to be unproblematically binary in their morphology and constitution . . . there is no reason to assume that genders ought also to remain as two. The presumption of a binary gender system implicitly retains the belief in a mimetic relation of gender to sex whereby gender mirrors sex or is otherwise restricted by it.[12]

This theory should not be understood as referring to merely abstract possibilities. Henrietta Moore points out that anthropologists have documented numerous examples of societies that operate multiple-gender systems, allowing at least some individuals effectively to select their gender.[13] To be significant at all, a gender must be "culturally intelligible:" "'Intelligible' genders are those which in some sense institute and maintain relations of coherence and continuity among sex, gender, sexual practice, and desire."[14]

I would suggest that "virginity" in the Katherine Group represents, in Butler's terms, a successful rearticulation of the heterosexual hegemony, and that it can be understood as a distinct gender. Butler's engagement is with the late twentieth-century present, but she asks rhetorically, "Does sex have a history?"[15] My intention is to elucidate a fragment of that history. I am not the first critic to believe that Butler's insight into the fluidity of gender is particularly relevant to the medieval period. Miri Rubin refers to Butler to argue that the medieval world "possessed very fluid notions of sexuality and of bodily contours. Thus gender will be revealed as a complex system, not grounded in biology."[16] The "one-sex model" identified in Thomas Laqueur's *Making Sex* as being dominant in medieval medical thought in fact bears a striking resemblance to Butler's understanding of performative gender. Laqueur argues that "to be a man or a woman was to hold a social rank, a place in society, to assume a cultural role, not to be organically one or the other of two incommensurable sexes."[17] As in Butler, gender must be "done," with the necessary risk that if it is not done correctly, gender identity—and even bodily anatomy—are subject to alteration. "Male" and "female" are not discrete essences but points on a continuum, creating the possibility of intermediate genders.

The patristic accounts of virtuous women documented by Peter Brown, Jo Ann McNamara, and Elizabeth Castelli confirm that religious as well as medical discourse can understand gender as a cultural rather than a bodily state.[18] Virginity is a circumstance that has the potential to unsettle the boundaries of sexual difference. The most familiar expression of this tradition is perhaps St. Ambrose's, "While a woman serves for birth and children, she is different from man as body is from soul. But when she wants to serve Christ more than the world, then she shall cease to be woman and be called a man."[19] Being a woman, then, is inseparable from being a wife and mother. It is social role and sexual activity, not genital anatomy, that determine gender. Anatomically female persons who do not marry are not part of the cultural category of "woman." As virgins, moreover, they are not to be identified with the body, as women are. The very rigidity of gender *roles* paradoxically ensures a fluidity of gender *identity*. The bearing of children is so fundamental to the construction of "woman" that virgin women need to be recategorized. A woman who is a man is less of an anomaly than a woman who is childless. Likewise, religious virtue is so strongly marked as masculine that persons displaying it must themselves be masculine. As Castelli points out, this produces a deeply paradoxical situation:

> "Becoming male" marks for these thinkers the transcendence of gendered differences, but it does so only by reinscribing the traditional gender hierarchies of male over female, masculine over feminine; the possibility that women can "become male" paradoxically however also reveals the tenuousness and malleability of the naturalized categories of male and female.[20]

Positing "virgin" as a distinct gender identity offers an escape from this paradox. The virgin martyrs' distinctive qualities—their eloquence, determination, and strength—can then be categorized as neither masculine nor feminine but proper to virgins while retaining a sense of the malleability of gender categories.

Jocelyn Wogan-Browne doubts the relevance of early Christian models of virginity to the Katherine Group, arguing that "in the high middle ages, although the idea of the virgin as a *vir-ago*, a woman acting like a man, survives, virginity is (re-)sexualised and feminised."[21] Certainly the legends of the Katherine Group do not suggest that their heroines act like men, but I would argue that this need not mean that they can be adequately described as "feminine." Nor would I choose the word "androgynous." Androgyny signifies a combination of masculine and feminine, thus reinforcing these gender categories. If persons who present some sort of challenge to binary gender are described as combining the two genders, "masculinity" and "femininity" are therefore retained as basic categories. Although the virgin martyrs display qualities that are conventionally associated with both males and females, these become redefined as virginal qualities. The virgins should not be understood as a mixture of male and female but as a separate category altogether. The rejection of heterosexual relationships, a standard element of the virgin martyr legend, allows the binary opposition of male and female required by the heterosexual hegemony to be broken down, and a third gender, "virgin," to be produced. Virginity constitutes a "culturally consistent gender," in which the virgin's desire is directed towards God and her body is whole and impenetrable.

If virginity is a gender in Butler's terms, it cannot be self-evident but must be constituted performatively and read onto the body. The Katherine Group legends, like Butler, understand the body as negotiable: its meanings can always be contested. Margaret, stripped naked, hung up and beaten with rods so "þet tet blod bearst ut ant strac adun of hire bodi as streem deð of welle" [that the blood burst out and ran down her body like a stream from a spring],[22] prays: "Lauerd, loke to me ant haue merci of me; softe me mi sar swa ant salue mine wunden þet hit ne seme nowher, ne suteli o mi samblant, þet Ich derf drehe" [Lord, protect me and have mercy on me; lighten my suffering and heal my wounds so it may not appear, or show on my face, that I feel any pain].[23] She prays, that is, not for rescue from her tormentors, or invulnerability to her pain, but for the appearance of that invulnerability. Robertson finds this passage "odd in its assumption that a woman would be most concerned with her appearance," and thus further evidence for the text's reductively stereotypical view of women.[24] I would suggest that Margaret prays for the appearance of invulnerability not out of feminine vanity, but because she understands the importance of spectacle. Her model is surely Perpetua, pinning up her hair in mid-martyrdom because loosened hair would inappropriately signify mourning.[25] If Margaret were to show pain, she would allow her persecutor, Olibrius, to dictate the terms of the spectacle, displaying his power and her vulnerability. To appear invulnerable is to engage in a contest of signification. Having been put on display, Margaret turns the situation to her own advantage, making herself a dangerous spectacle from which the onlookers flinch.[26]

The spectacle of Margaret's torn and bleeding flesh is ambiguous, and so must be read. It is therefore necessary for the torture scenes to take place in front of an audience, whom Margaret engages in a debate about the meaning of her body:

> Alle þe bear weren, wepmen ba ant wummen, remden of reowæ ant meanden bes meiden, ant summe of ham seiden: "Margarete, Margarete, meide swa muche wurð def þu wel waldest, wa is us bet we seoa bi softe leofliche lich toluken se ladliche!" . . .
> "O," quoð ha, "wrecches, unweoten bute wit, weila, hwet wene ȝe? ȝef mi lich is toloken, mi sawle schal resten wið þe rihtwise; sorhe ant licomes sar is sawulene heale."

[All those who were there, both men and women, wept for compassion and pitied this maiden, and some of them said: "Margaret, Margaret, maiden who might be worth so much if you wanted to be, we are sorry to see your soft, lovely body so cruelly torn to pieces!" . . .
"Oh!" she said, "wretches, you senseless fools, what do you expect? if my body is torn apart, my soul will be at peace among the righteous; through sorrow and bodily pain, souls are saved."][27]

This exchange, like Margaret's prayer, makes the point that the meaning of the body is contested. The onlookers make the mistake of seeing Margaret as a victim, of focusing on her beauty and her blood. They see her, in fact, as typically female, having a body "pervious, excessive and susceptible." They demand that she live out a female identity, suggesting that she must marry in order to realize her "worth." Despite their sympathy for Margaret, their understanding of the display of her body is close to that of Olibrius.

The onlookers' mistake, and Margaret's rebuke to them, should warn us to be careful how we read the torture scenes. To argue, as some critics do, that the torture should be understood as sexual assault is perhaps to make the same mistake as the spectators in "Seinte Margarete," accepting the torturers' reading of the violence rather than the virgins'. In *Seinte Iuliene,* Eleusius, Juliana's suitor and persecutor, conflates his sexual desire for Juliana with his desire to harm her. Looking at Juliana, "him þuhte in his þonc þet ne bede he i þe worlt nanes cunnes blisse bute hire bodi ane, to wealden hire wið wil efter þet he walde" [he thought that he could desire no joy in the world unless it be her body, to do with as he wanted].[28] His desire is for power and control over her body, whether it is to be exercised by sexual or violent means. At this point Eleusius still hopes to marry Juliana; thwarted by her resistance, he turns to violence instead. Catherine Innes-Parker argues that "The torture of Juliana is clearly presented as a sexual attack, symbolic of the rape which Eleusius desires but can not attain. The public exhibition of her naked body and her exposure to the gaze of the onlookers and the reader becomes a kind of symbolic 'gang rape.'"[29] Eleusius might well regard the torture as a substitute for sex; Juliana, however, does not. She clearly does not consider herself to have been raped, symbolically or otherwise; she continues to glory in her chastity, defying her tormentors, praying aloud and confidently referring to herself as "meiden."[30] To read all the acts of violence as attempted or symbolic rape is to underestimate the thoroughness of the legends' critique of heterosexual relations. The saints resist not violent rape but legitimate and suitable marriages. The legends write all male desire, even in its most romantic and socially sanctioned forms, as violence.[31]

Juliana shows no consciousness that her torments could be read as symbolic rape; nor does she regard her public nakedness as sexual objectification. The torturers presumably order the saints stripped in order to humiliate them; the martyrs, without exception, are serenely indifferent to their being so displayed. They seem to be utterly devoid of sexual shame. In distinguishing between nakedness and sexuality, they part company with many modern commentators. Thomas Heffernan, for example, moves unproblematically from nakedness to sexual allure: "Juliana's father in a savage voice ordered her stripped stark naked . . . before her male captors. Because it emphasized the young woman embattled, the narrative highlights the allure of her sexuality."[32] Nakedness, however, does not necessarily signify sexuality. In these legends there are indications that, at least in the eyes of the heroines, it does not. Their indifference to being naked in public can be explained within their religious context. Margaret Miles has shown that in Christian discourse nakedness is a complex signifier. The early Christian martyrs, the historical prototypes for the fictional figures of Katherine, Margaret, and Juliana, turned their nakedness in the arena to their own purposes: "these women used their nakedness as a symbolic rejection, not only of sexuality, but also of secular society's identification of the female body with male desire, its relegation of the female naked body to spectacle and object."[33] By being unashamed of their nakedness, the virgins of the Katherine Group deny that they are sexually desirable females. Their bodies may be spectacles, but they are spectacles on the virgins' own terms. The martyrs take control of the spectacle of their naked bodies, subverting the meanings intended by their persecutors. Olibrius, Eleusius, and Maxentius think to shame the martyrs as women by displaying them naked; they fail to understand that virgins, who have rejected sexual activity, have therefore no reason to be ashamed of their nakedness. Their pursuit of virginity reverses the effects of the Fall: like the prelapsarian Adam and Eve, they are naked and not ashamed.[34]

If, then, the torture of naked virgins is intended to be pornographic, as Kathryn Gravdal suggests, or to represent "the violent imposition of sexual difference" in Gayle Margherita's formulation, it is remarkably unsuc-cessful.[35] Gravdal suggests that rape in courtly literature, a category in which she seems to include violence in hagiographic literature, "ceaselessly repeats the moment in which an act of violence makes sexual difference into subordination."[36] This seems wholly inapplicable to the violence in the Katherine Group. Sexual subordination is not imposed but successfully resisted, and sexual difference is destabilized rather than confirmed. In the torture scenes, the narrative typically moves away from the sight of the naked virgin to merge itself with her voice. *Seinte Iuliene* describes how Ju-liana is hung by the hair and beaten; instead of lingering on this scene, however, it reports Juliana's long and eloquent prayer, in which she com-pares herself with Abraham. The focus is on Juliana as speaking subject, not on her torn body. It is her prayer, rather than the beating, that moves the narrative onwards: Eleusius, maddened by her undaunted faith, orders her to be drenched in molten brass.[37]

Gravdal argues that violence in the virgin martyr legend is essentially pornographic:

> The authors do not hesitate to indulge in descriptions of the nubile attrac-tiveness of thirteen-year-old virgins; their smooth, tender flesh as they are stripped bare in public before a crowd. . . . Hagiography affords a sanctioned space in which eroticism can flourish, and in which male voyeurism be-comes licit.[38]

I do not think this is the case in the Katherine Group. If the legends in-tended to encourage a pornographic, voyeuristic reading of the violence, they would surely present a more clearly sexed vision of the virgins' bod-ies. As it is, the representation of these bodies is deliberately vague. Eleu-sius, gazing at the clothed Juliana, borrows the diction of the romance to admire "hire lufsome leor, lilies ilicnesse ant rudi ase rose, ant under hire nebscheft al se freoliche ischapet" [her lovely complexion, lilywhite and rosered, and below her face everything so shapely].[39] When Juliana is stripped, we might expect to see more clearly exactly *what* is "se freoliche ischapet"; this is perhaps Eleusius' intention. At this point, however, the narrative chooses to avert its gaze. It sees a "beare bodi" and "freoliche flesch," it sees blood and wounds; what it does not see is anything that might suggest a specifically female object of desire.[40] In the many scenes of naked tortured virgins in the three legends, the narrative manages never to see female hips, genitalia, or, perhaps most significantly, breasts.

Heffernan finds the torture of the breasts to be a significant feature of the virgin martyr legend: "In the overwhelming majority of scenes of physical abuse in the lives of virgin saints, the focus of torture is the symbol of

woman's sexuality and maternity, the breasts."[41] He perhaps overstates his
case. It may be true of some examples of the genre, such as the legends of
Agnes and Agatha, but Katherine, Margaret, and Juliana seem not to have
breasts that can be tortured. The Katherine Group legends deliberately resist
sexualizing violence in this way. The virgins' lack of breasts, moreover, serves
to distinguish them from women. Juliana's father, Africanus, threatens his
daughter, "þu schalt . . . swa beon ibeaten wið bittere besmen, þet tu wani
þet tu were wummon of wummone bosum to wraðer heale eauer iboren i
þe world" [you shall . . . be so beaten with biting birches that you will regret
that you were ever born a woman of a woman's bosom to suffer misfortune
in this world].[42] "Bosum" here is used synecdochically to signify the body of
a childbearing woman; a bosom is perceived to be the proper attribute of
such a person. Breasts are indeed the "symbol of women's sexuality and maternity": in these texts, they function as markers of femininity. The queen in
Seinte Katerine, a married woman, also has breasts, which are the objects of
her husband's sadistic attentions when she declares herself converted by
Katherine's example: "Sone se he understot wel þet he ne sturede hire nawt,
het on hat heorte unhendeliche neomen hire ant bute dom ananriht
þurhdriuen her tittes wið irnene neiles and rende ham up hetterliche wið
þe breoste roten" [When he understood that he could not move her, in his
anger he commanded that she be roughly seized, and immediately, without
trial, iron nails should be driven through her nipples, violently tearing them
up with the roots of the breasts].[43] It cannot, then, be simple modesty, a reluctance to name such parts, that accounts for the absence of breasts in the
descriptions of the naked virgins. *Seinte Katerine* effectively shows us the
queen's tortured breasts three times; first Maxentius threatens to have her
breasts tortured, then, in the passage quoted, he orders it done, and finally his
order is carried out.[44] This, I think, can fairly be described as pornographic,
sexualized violence. It is a torture enacted on the specifically female body of
a rebellious wife, on the orders of her husband. If breasts signify femaleness,
it is femaleness that is under attack. This does constitute the "violent imposition of sexual difference"; it is inflicted, however, on a person whose position as a wife already marks her as a sexual, subordinate female. The tortures
of the virgin heroines are never sexualized in this manner; the texts refuse to
mark their naked bodies as female.

The scenes of the stripping and torturing of the virgins can be understood as a dramatization of the difficulty of reading the body correctly. They
rehearse various perceptions of bodies. Clothed, the virgins can be perceived as female objects of desire because of the social positions they occupy. Juliana and Katherine, young and wealthy heiresses—Katherine,
indeed, is a reigning queen—are perceived as eligible for marriage, and
therefore desirable. Fifteen-year-old Margaret, tending sheep, appears to

Olibrius as a figure from a pastourelle, a genre, as Gravdal reminds us, in which knights can assault shepherdesses with impunity: "As he wende a dei his wei, seh þis seli meiden Margarete as ha wes ant wiste upo þe feld hire fostermodres schep, þe schimede ant schan al of wlite ant of westume" [One day as he rode out he caught sight of Margaret, this innocent maiden, as she was tending her fostermother's sheep out in the fields, and was dazzled by the beauty of her face and figure].[45] The word "meiden," the standard term for the virgins, is itself ambiguous; it can mean either "young girl" or "virgin" (not gender-specific). The persecutors understand the virgins to be "meidens" in the first sense: marriageable young women. By ordering them publicly stripped, they intend to humiliate and expose them as women. Once they are stripped, however, the virgins cease to be objects of desire: their demeanor under torture reveals them to be virgins in the more radical sense: persons unsexed by their choice of absolute chastity.

When Eleusius orders Juliana to be covered with molten brass, the narrative's gaze on her body registers a shift in viewpoint. Eleusius has learnt nothing from Juliana's indifference to being beaten: "Þa Eleusius seh þet ha þus feng on to festnin hire seoluen i soðe bileaue, þohte he walde don hire anan ut of dahene, ant bed biliue bringen forð brunewallinde bres, ant healden hit se walhat hehe up on hire heaued þet hit urne endelong hire leofliche lich adun to hire helen" [When Eleusius saw how she fortified herself with true faith, he thought he would at once end her days, and he ordered that molten brass be quickly brought forth, and that it be poured, boiling hot, over her head, so that it ran all the way down her lovely body to her heels].[46] This passage shows Eleusius's reading of Juliana's body. He again looks on her with desire, conflating sex and violence; his perception of her beauty is inseparable from his desire to harm that beauty. He perceives Juliana as both vulnerable and desirable, a passive body on which he can work his will. This penetrable, eroticized female body is the paradigmatic female body of the period, that which Lochrie characterizes as "pervious, excessive and susceptible."

The narrative then writes Juliana's body differently:

Ah þe worldes wealdent þet wiste Sein Iuhan, his ewangeliste, unhurt i þe ueat of wallinde eoli þer he wes idon in, þet ase hal com up þrof as he wes hal meiden, þe ilke liues lauerd wiste him unwemmet his brud of þe bres þet wes wallinde; swa þet ne þuhte hit hire buten ase wlech weater al þet ha felde.

[But the ruler of the world, who kept his evangelist, St John, unhurt in the vat of boiling oil in which he had been placed, so that he came out of it whole, just as he was a whole maiden; that same lord of life kept his woman untouched by the boiling brass, so that she thought it was only warm water that she felt].[47]

This miracle allows Juliana to contest Eleusius's reading of her body. Lethal molten metal is reread as the life-giving water of baptism, and the female body is reread as a virginal body. Sex and violence are still intimately connected: the virgin, "hal" and sexually impenetrable, is also "hal," immune to violence. The virgin body reveals itself to be impermeable, "iseilet" [sealed], in Margaret's phrase.[48] Binary gender is an irrelevance to the virgin; the same word, "meiden," refers to both Juliana and St. John. If women's bodies are fleshly and penetrable, this torture shows that Juliana does not have a woman's body. Dismemberment, in these texts, is the fate of nonvirgins. *Hali Meiðhad* warns us, "for hwa se swa falleð of meiðhades menske þet wedlakes heuel bedd nawt ham ne ihente, se ferliche ha driueð dun to þe eorðe þet al. ham is tolimet, lið ba ant lire" [for if anyone falls from the honour of virginity so that the mattress of wedlock does not catch them, they rush down so fast towards the ground that they are torn all to pieces, limb from limb].[49] Eleusius, likewise, is finally dismembered, "wilde deor limmel toluken ham ant tolimeden eauereuch lið from þe lire" [the wild animals chewed them up, and tore every limb from the flesh].[50] The immunity of Juliana and her fellow martyrs to violent dismemberment proves their virginity; they emerge from every form of violence "whole, as whole maidens."

The scenes of torture, by revealing the martyrs' virginity, their difference from women, can also be said to bring it into being. As a Butlerian gender, virginity must be produced in embodied performance. Virginity is never an unambiguous bodily state. Clarissa Atkinson describes different ways of understanding virginity:

> At one extreme, virginity is understood as a physical state. The virgin is a person who has never experienced sexual intercourse: if the virgin is female, her hymen is unbroken. At the other extreme, virginity is defined as a moral or spiritual state—as purity, or humility, or that quality of spirit belonging to those whose primary relationship is with God.[51]

The purely physical definition of virginity, however, is always problematic. It requires that someone read the body as virgin and judge the hymen unbroken; a practice that, according to St. Ambrose, might well destroy virginity in the moment of confirming it.[52] Wogan-Browne points out that "since the hymen is composed of inner folds of flesh, few women are born with an imperforate one. Its cultural construction as imperforate is driven by the demand for blood as evidence of technical intactness."[53] To read a body as virgin, then, is not an easy task. Wogan-Browne demonstrates the medieval belief in the material, imperforate hymen, but there is often a strange insecurity about its representations. St. Augustine writes that in Eden, humanity existed in a state of bodily perfection. Sex would have occurred under the control of reason, without lust, for purely reproductive purposes and without compromising virginity: "the male seed could have been dispatched into the womb, with no loss of the wife's integrity, just as the menstrual flux can now be produced from the womb of a virgin without loss of maidenhead. For the seed could be injected through the same passage by which the flux is ejected."[54] Now you see it, now you don't. Augustine's knowledge that the hymen is not imperforate, that a "passage" exists, does not seem to affect his belief in "integrity" and "maidenhead." In this quotation the status of the hymen is uncertain; is it broken by the "passage" and if so, can its "integrity" be other than metaphorical? Can it actually be seen, or must its presence be inferred? Augustine seems almost to acknowledge that the imperforate hymen is a cultural fantasy.

Hali Meiðhad's representation of the imperforate hymen shows a similar instability. "Meiðhad is þet tresor þet, beo hit eanes forloren, ne bið hit neauer ifunden. Meiðhad is þe blostme þet, beo ha fulliche eanes forcoruen, ne spruteð ha eft neauer (ah þah ha falewi sumchere mid misliche þonkes ha mei eft grenin neauer þe leatere)" [Virginity is the treasure which, if it is once lost, will never be found again. Virginity is the blossom which, if it is once completely cut off, will never grow again (but though it may wither sometimes through indecent thoughts, it can grow green again nevertheless)].[55] The description of the irreplaceability of virginity does suggest the fantasy of the imperforate hymen, which, once broken, cannot be mended, just as a cut flower cannot be replanted. This hymen, however, seems to be a highly metaphorical object: a treasure, or a flower, but not a membrane. It is invoked as a physical reality in order to be treated as metaphor; this is a bodily part that can wither or grow green again through thought. Atkinson's analysis, that virginity can be seen as physical, or spiritual, or both, does not quite cover this situation. In Hali Meiðhad and the associated texts there is no simple physical dimension; rather, the physical, in this case the hymen, is an effect produced by the spiritual.

Medieval medical texts also acknowledge the difficulty of reading a body as virginal. Esther Lastique and Helen Lemay report that descriptions of virginity tests are uncommon in medieval medical treatises but cite some examples: "Gilbert said that if a woman is covered with a piece of cloth and fumigated with the best coal, if she is a virgin she does not perceive its odour through her mouth and nose; if she smells it, she is not a virgin."[56] The virgin body, then, is so firmly sealed that even smells cannot penetrate it. It is unclear whether such tests were actually performed. If they were, they can hardly have been reliable: it would be extremely easy for any woman undergoing the test to cheat. Gilbert, perhaps recognizing this drawback, adds, "the signs of virginity are modesty, a faultless gait and speech, approaching men with eyes cast to the side."[57] Virginity, then, should be read from a woman's behavior rather than her body. Any physician applying the fumigation test would presumably be guided in his judgment by his impression of the woman's demeanor; her virginity would therefore be constituted in her modesty. She would be a virgin because she was modest, rather than vice versa. An unbroken hymen (or an inability to smell coal) cannot in itself signify virginity: rather, an intact body is inferred through those signs that Butler names as "the marks of gender," the bodily stylizations of dress and demeanor: the modest gait and the downcast eyes. Medieval culture used various practices to signify virginity and bodily intactness. Nuns and anchoresses, professional virgins, were veiled and enclosed, this twofold enclosure functioning as an embodied statement of virginity from which the intact body could be inferred. The practice of enclosure, then, can be said to produce the intact, virginal body, a body that in Butler's terms comes into being through the marks of gender.

In the Katherine Group legends, it is not veiling and enclosure but stripping and torture that produce the virginal body and the virgin identity. Before the torture scenes, some doubt is possible about the virgins' commitment to the chaste life. Juliana refuses to marry Eleusius unless he has himself appointed high reeve; the narrative presents this as the action of a committed virgin trying to avoid marriage, but Eleusius seems to understand it as a chivalric task by which he must prove his worthiness. It is only the torture that reveals the real reason why Eleusius must be high reeve: it is this position that gives him the authority to have his reluctant fiancée tortured. All three virgins make a conscious choice to seek torture and martyrdom. Margaret chooses martyrdom as her career long before she ever meets Olibrius:

Þus ha wes ant wiste, meokest alre milde, wið oðre meidnes o þe feld hire fostermodres hahte; ant herde on euich half hire hu me droh to deaðe Cristes icorene for rihte bileaue; ant ȝirnde ant walde ȝeorne, ȝef Godes wil were, þet ha moste beon an of þe moni moderbern þet swa muchel drohen ant drehheden for Drihtin.

[So, meekest of the mild, she tended with other maidens out in the fields her fostermother's sheep; and heard on every side how Christ's chosen ones were being put to death for the true faith; and eagerly longed, if it were God's will, that she might be one of the many people who bore and suffered so much for God].[58]

Katherine is less passive; she does not wait for persecution but actively seeks it by setting out to challenge the emperor.[59] Juliana helpfully lists the tortures she is prepared to withstand.[60] The tyrants never understand that they are simply the virgins' instruments. The virgins stage their own spectacles and arrange the display of their own bodies.

The choice of the virgin identity, then, requires torture scenes. Katherine, Margaret, and Juliana choose a life of chastity, and then arrange to have themselves tortured. Their chosen virginal identity requires an unambiguous statement of their virginal bodies, and it is torture, or, more precisely, their behavior under torture, that can provide this. The virgin body is constituted by suffering and resisting torture. Torture reveals a body that is unfeminine, unashamed, impenetrable, miraculously self-healing. The Katherine Group legends provide an example of Butler's "performative gender," in which gender produces sex, the virginal identity produces an intact body. The torture scenes can be understood as a virginity test, simultaneously producing and revealing the virgin body. They take place in front of an audience because gender is a cultural construction that must be read. They are repeated because any gender, but perhaps particularly virginity, is unstable, requiring repeated enactment. I have referred throughout this paper to "virgins" as distinct from "women": this is perhaps an oversimplification. Katherine, Margaret, and Juliana occupy an unstable category of "virgins who were once women, and who could be women again if they aren't careful," whose virgin identity can only be finally confirmed after they are dead. Gender, in these legends, is a continuous process, not a fixed state. The legends offer a form of piety that does not require reveling in the body; instead, the body is shown to be negotiable and continually redefined.

Notes

1. "Seinte Margarete," Bella Millett and Jocelyn Wogan-Browne, eds. and trans., *Medieval English Prose for Women: Selections from the Katherine Group and* Ancrene Wisse, (Oxford: Clarendon Press, 1990), pp. 44–85: p. 74 [Middle English]/p. 75 [translation].

2. See the tabulation of tortures in Jocelyn Wogan-Browne, "The Virgin's Tale," in *Feminist Readings in Middle English Literature: The Wife of Bath and All Her Sect,* eds. Ruth Evans and Lesley Johnson, (London: Routledge, 1994), pp. 165–194; p. 176. I am confining my discussion to the three legends of the Katherine Group, of Saints Katherine, Margaret, and Juliana: I do not claim that my analysis is necessarily applicable to any virgin martyr legend. See notes 3 and 43 below for details of editions of the legends of Katherine and Juliana.

3. For instance, "Seinte Margarete," p.50/51: S.R.T.O. d'Ardenne, ed., *De Liflade ant te Passiun of Seinte Iuliene,* EETS OS 248, (London: Oxford University Press, 1961), p. 11 (emended text).

4. "Ancrene Wisse Parts 7 and 8," Millett and Wogan-Browne, *Medieval English Prose for Women,* pp.110–149; p. 138/139. I accept Millett's argument that recluses need not have been the primary audience of the Katherine Group but am borrowing Catherine Innes-Parker's useful distinction between the wider audience and the anchoritic readers of the surviving manuscripts. See Millett, "The Audience of the Saints' Lives of the Katherine Group," *Reading Medieval Studies* 16 (1990), 127–156; p. 132; and Innes-Parker, "Sexual Violence and the Female Reader: Symbolic 'Rape' in the Saints' Lives of the Katherine Group," *Women's Studies* 24 (1995), 205–217; p. 207.

5. Elizabeth Robertson, *Early English Devotional Prose and the Female Audience* (Knoxville: University of Tennessee Press, 1990), p. 97.

6. Caroline Walker Bynum, *Holy Feast and Holy Fast: The Religious Significance of Food to Medieval Women* (Berkeley: University of California Press, 1987), p. 246.

7. Karma Lochrie, *Margery Kempe and Translations of the Flesh* (Philadelphia: University of Pennsylvania Press, 1991), p. 4.

8. Robertson, *Early English Devotional Prose,* p. 193.

9. Lochrie, *Margery Kempe,* p. 4.

10. Judith Butler, *Gender Trouble: Feminism and the Subversion of Identity* (New York and London: Routledge, 1990), p. 8.

11. Butler, *Gender Trouble,* p. 33.

12. Butler, *Gender Trouble,* p. 6.

13. Henrietta L. Moore, *A Passion for Difference: Essays in Anthropology and Gender* (Cambridge: Polity Press, 1994), p. 13.

14. Butler, *Gender Trouble,* p. 17.

15. Butler, *Gender Trouble,* p. 7.

16. Miri Rubin, "The Person in The Form: Medieval Challenges to Bodily 'Order,'" in *Framing Medieval Bodies,* eds. Sarah Kay and Miri Rubin (Manchester: Manchester University Press, 1994), pp.100–122; p. 101.

17. Thomas Laqueur, *Making Sex: Body and Gender from the Greeks to Freud* (Cambridge, MA and London: Harvard University Press, 1990), p. 8.

18. See, among others, Peter Brown, *The Body and Society: Men, Women and Sexual Renunciation in Early Christianity* (New York: Columbia University Press, 1988); Jo Ann McNamara, "Sexual Equality and the Cult of Virginity in Early Christian Thought," *Feminist Studies* 3 (1976), 145–158; Elizabeth Castelli, "'I Will Make Mary Male': Pieties of the Body and Gender Transformation of Christian Women in Late Antiquity," in *Body Guards: The Cultural Politics of Gender Ambiguity,* eds. Julia Epstein and Christina Straub, (London and New York: Routledge, 1991), pp. 29–49.

19. Quoted in Wogan-Browne, "The Virgin's Tale," p. 166.

20. Castelli, "'I Will Make Mary Male,'" p. 33.

21. Wogan-Browne, "The Virgin's Tale," p. 166.

22. "Seinte Margarete," p. 52/53.

23. "Seinte Margarete," p. 52/53.

24. Elizabeth Robertson, "The Corporeality of Female Sanctity in the Life of Saint Margaret," in *Images of Sainthood in Medieval Europe,* eds. Renate Blumenfeld-Kosinski and Timea Szell (Ithaca: Cornell University Press, 1991), pp. 268–287; p. 281.

25. See Margaret Miles, *Carnal Knowing: Female Nakedness and Religious Meaning in the Christian West* (Boston: Beacon Press, 1989), p. 61.

26. "Seinte Margarete," p. 54/55. See Carol Clover, *Men, Women and Chainsaws: Gender in the Modern Horror Film* (Princeton: Princeton University Press, 1992), p. 191 for an account of looking as a dangerous or masochistic activity.

27. "Seinte Margarete," p. 52/53.

28. *Seinte Iuliene,* p. 19. All translations of *Seinte Iuliene* are my own.

29. Innes-Parker, "Sexual Violence and the Female Reader," p. 207.

30. For example, *Seinte Iuliene,* p. 25.

31. The legends thus reverse the romance technique of writing violence as desire; see Kathryn Gravdal, *Ravishing Maidens: Writing Rape in Medieval French Literature and Law* (Philadelphia: University of Pennsylvania Press, 1994), p. 11.

32. Thomas J. Heffernan, *Sacred Biography: Saints and their Biographers in the Middle Ages* (Oxford: Oxford University Press, 1988), p. 278.

33. Miles, *Carnal Knowing,* p. 24.

34. Gen. 2.25. I am grateful to the editors of this volume for suggesting this connection.

35. Gayle Margherita, *The Romance of Origins: Language and Sexual Difference in Middle English Literature* (Philadelphia: University of Pennsylvania Press, 1994), p. 44; Gravdal, *Ravishing Maidens,* p. 24.

36. Gravdal, *Ravishing Maidens,* p. 11.

37. *Seinte Iuliene,* pp. 25–27.

38. Gravdal, *Ravishing Maidens,* p. 24.

39. *Seinte Iuliene,* pp. 17–19.

40. *Seinte Iuliene,* p. 23.

41. Heffernan, *Sacred Biography,* p. 283.

42. *Seinte Iuliene,* p. 15. Watson and Savage's translation, however, understands this passage to mean that the bosom belongs to Juliana herself. Nicholas Watson and Anne Savage, eds., and trans., *Anchoritic Spirituality: Ancrene Wisse and Associated Works* (New York: Paulist Press, 1991), p. 308.

43. S.R.T.O. d'Ardenne and E.J. Dobson, eds., *Seinte Katerine,* EETS SS 7 (London: Oxford University Press, 1981), p. 110 (edited text). My translation.

44. *Seinte Katerine,* pp. 110, 114.

45. Gravdal, *Ravishing Maidens,* p. 105; "Seinte Margarete," p. 46/47.

46. *Seinte Iuliene,* pp. 25–27.

47. *Seinte Iuliene,* p. 27. Again, my translation differs in emphasis from Watson and Savage, for whom John is only *like* a virgin. Watson and Savage, eds., *Anchoritic Spirituality,* p. 311.

48. "Seinte Margarete," p. 52/53.
49. "Hali Meiðhad," Millett and Wogan-Browne, eds., *Middle English Prose for Women*, pp. 2–43; p. 18/19.
50. *Seinte Iuliene*, p. 71.
51. Clarissa Atkinson, "'Precious balsam in a fragile glass:' the ideology of virginity in the later Middle Ages," *Journal of Family History* 8 (1983), 131–143; p. 133.
52. Joyce E. Salisbury, *Church Fathers, Independent Virgins* (London:Verso, 1991), p. 30.
53. Wogan-Browne, "The Virgin's Tale," p. 187 n.16.
54. Augustine, *Concerning the City of God Against the Pagans* 16.26, intro. John O'Meara, trans. Henry Bettenson (London: Penguin, 1984), p. 591.
55. "Hali Meiðhad," pp. 8–10/9–11.
56. Esther Lastique and Helen Rodnite Lemay, "A Medieval Physician's Guide to Virginity," in *Sex in the Middle Ages: A Book of Essays*, ed. Joyce E. Salisbury (New York: Garland, 1991), pp. 56–82; p. 63.
57. Lastique and Lemay, "A Medieval Physician's Guide," p. 66.
58. "Seinte Margarete," p. 46/47.
59. *Seinte Katerine*, p. 12.
60. *Seinte Iuliene*, p. 11.

CHAPTER 5

THE PARADOX OF VIRGINITY WITHIN THE ANCHORITIC TRADITION: THE MASCULINE GAZE AND THE FEMININE BODY IN THE *WOHUNGE* GROUP

Susannah Mary Chewning

> *In the* Wohunge *Group, virgins are cast as lovers of Christ; within this construction, the gender of wooer and wooed shifts, showing a fluid sexual identity of readers and speakers.*

Virginity existed as a paradox for medieval religious women. It was encouraged as the ideal (for both sexes), and yet for women it was particularly problematic. Women were defined by their roles within medieval culture, and these were decidedly sexual roles: wife, mother, whore. If a woman chose not to participate in a sexually defined relationship with a man, she stood apart from her cultural obligation and pursued a different path. Thus religious women often existed on the margins of their society.

A further sense of the paradox of female virginity exists in the concept of the Christian virgin itself—one who is a virgin in the physical sense but who has experienced or hopes to experience a consummation of love with Christ: if she is the spouse of Christ, *sponsa Christi,* as the Church would call her, then she is only a virgin in the physical sense (a tenuous concept, of course) but more appropriately, and in her own heart and mind, a wife and therefore an active lover. One set of texts in which this idea is made most explicit is the group of anchoritic devotional texts known as the

Wohunge Group. These texts, including, for example, *Þe Wohunge of Ure Lauerd* and *On Lofsong of Ure Lefdi*, as well as their "sister" text, the *Ancrene Wisse*, identify the religious woman as a lover of Christ in a particularly erotic way. The authors use, for example, the familiar term *lefman* to refer both to themselves with respect to Christ and to Christ himself. In the *Wohunge*, for example, the speaker says:

> Iesu swete iesu
> þus tu fahy for me aȝaines
> Mine sawle fan. þu me deren-
> nedes wið like. & makedes of me
> Wrecche þi leofman & spuse.[1]

[Jesus, sweet Jesus, in this way you fought for me against the enemies of my soul. You vindicated me with your body, and made of me, a wretch, your lover and spouse].[2]

The audiences and the speakers of these texts were most definitely feminine,[3] while the authors are most likely to have been male,[4] thus calling into question the appropriation of a feminine voice by a masculine author within the genre of anchoritic mysticism. In fact, since there is no ultimate proof available of the authorship of these texts, the gender of the author becomes almost irrelevant: these poems and treatises, as well as the saints' lives and devotional works known as the Katherine Group,[5] are texts written for and read by religious women, and their provenance proves far less relevant in this context than does their influence.

One aspect of the "problem" of virginity within these texts is the exchange that appears to take place with respect to the object of the mystic's devotion. The speakers of these texts seem to speak with similarly erotic and devotional language about Christ, their bridegroom, and about Mary, their bride or mistress, thus shifting the gaze from a masculine Other to one that is, or seems to be, feminine. This further complicates the question of sexual identity for the speakers (and readers) of these texts: if the gender of the wooed can shift, then is the same true for the gender of the wooer? Does use of the gaze and consummation in a mystical union somehow masculinize the female mystic? This essay will pursue an examination of some of the central texts of English anchoritic mysticism, with special attention to *Þe Wohunge of Ure Lauerd*, with the intention of addressing these questions and their attention to the problematic position of the female virgin within the anchoritic community, problematic because of her tenuous and vulnerable position within medieval society itself, and also because of her use of the language of sexual union and eroticism in her description of the mystical union between the anchoress and the Divine. It is not intended as a review of the role of virginity within anchorism—such a role is obvious. It is more an exploration of the role of what John Bugge has called "virginity sexualized" within the lives and texts of these anchoritic women.

The medieval concept of virginity has been long discussed. John Bugge, in his book *Virginitas: An Essay in the History of a Medieval Ideal*, spells out in great detail the importance of virginity for both men and women in the Middle Ages. In a most interesting chapter, Bugge discusses what he terms "virginity sexualized," the erotic spirituality of the twelfth- and thirteenth-century monastic literature, particularly the texts known as the *Katherine* Group and the *Wohunge* Group. In his book, Bugge draws a clear line between what is described by the medieval writers as spiritual marriage and what may have transpired in earthly human marriages. He writes, "*libido,* the quintessential form of concupiscence in Augustine's view of sex, is exactly antithetical to the nature of pure love, since it is self-seeking, solipsistic, and oriented toward possession."[6] Bugge argues that the love of the anchoress or monk for Christ is passionate, but it is not libidinal, and therefore pure. However, when one reads the words of the speakers of these texts, the line between spiritual love and libidinal love begins to blur:

> aliht mine þeostri heorte.
> ʒif mi bur[7] brithnesse. & brihtte mine soule
> þet is suti. & make hire wurðe to þine swete
> wuninge. Ontend me wið blase. of þine leitinde
> luue. Let me beon þi leofmon. ler me for to
> louien þe liuiinde louerd

> [illuminate my darkened heart / give my dwelling brightness and brighten my soul / that is sooty and make her worthy of thy sweet / winning. Kindle me with the blaze of your radiant / love. Let me be your lover ; teach me to love thee living lord].[8]

The paradox of virginity and sexuality that seems to exist in these anchoritic texts is compounded when one addresses the treatment of the Virgin Mary by the anchoritic writers. Mary stands as a model for womanhood—how to behave as wives of Christ and how not to behave with their earthly bodies. Through Mary, religious women were taught that their earthly responsibility was not to marriage and motherhood. They had been chosen for a higher kind of marriage to Christ. In fact, much of what they did within their communities would be to deny and distance themselves from any similarity between themselves and earthly women.

Medieval medical writers and philosophers agreed with theologians of the time in their understanding of female physiology. Women were inferior to men both physically and spiritually—they were descended from Eve and could never be more than their bodies. Even chaste women were constantly reminded by the Church and their orders that they were fallen and that their female bodies were always to be seen as temptations to men. Friendships between the genders were always condemned and mistrusted. Relationships between men and women were immediately considered to be of a sexual nature, not because men were not in control of their lusts, but because a woman was always seen to be a source of temptation, a threat to the purity of men by her mere presence. In the *Ancrene Wisse,* a very thinly veiled metaphor is used to describe this notion: "Forþi was iha-ten o godes half Iþe alde lahe þat put were / eauere ihulet. & ȝif anj vnhulede þe put. & beast fel þer / in. he hit schulde ȝelde. þis is a swiðe dredliche word to / wepmon & | to wimmen þat swiðe sone scheawen ham to / hwase wile" [it was commanded in God's law that a pit always be covered, and if anyone uncovered a pit and a beast fell in, the one who had uncovered the pit had to pay for it (Exodus 21:33–34). This is a most fearsome saying for a woman who shows herself to the eyes of men].[9] Many women appear to have entered the cloister and the anchorhold for the purpose of protecting others from their temptation. Thus even a chaste woman was frequently identified by her innate sexual, seductive nature, and often, one can imagine, she would have been able to express feelings of love only in the language of eroticism—for except in the genre of courtly literature, sexuality was often the only means by which a woman could understand her own body. It is not surprising, then, that the language of love as it is expressed by the speakers of this text is a language of the erotic, of the body. In *On Ureisun of oure Louerde,* for example, the speaker says:

> hwi nam ich inþin earmes. In þin ear
> mes swa istrahte. & isprad on rode. and weneð ei to
> beon bi clupped bitwene þine blisfulle earmes. In heo
> uene bute he warpe. er her bitweone þine rewfulle ear
> mes on þe rode. Nai soþes. nai. Ne wene hit neuer no
> mon. þurh his lahe clupping. me mot come heh to þe þat
> þe wule bicluppe þe þear swilc. ase þu art þear louerd of
> leome. he mot cluppe þe ear her swilc ase þu makedest
> te her wreche. for us wreches.

[Oh that I were in thy arms, in thy arms so outstretched and outspread on the cross! And may any one ever hope to be embraced between thy blissful arms in heaven, unless he previously here has cast himself between thy piteous arms on the cross? Nay, of a truth! nay, let no man ever expect it.

Through this low embracing we may come to the exalted one. He who will embrace thee there, even such as thou art there, Lord of Light, must previously embrace thee here, even as poor as thou madest thyself for us wretches].[10]

This quotation exhibits the use of the words *warpe* and *cluppe,* both translated by Morris as *embrace.*[11] Anyone familiar with secular romance of the period will notice, however, that this word is often used with respect to an erotic embrace, sometimes in fact as a euphemism for the act of sexual union itself.[12]

The often violent measures to which medieval religious women would go to preserve their virginity (both, it would seem, to protect themselves from rape and to protect virtuous men from their feminine charms) has been thoughtfully outlined by Jane Tibbets Schulenberg in her article, "The Heroics of Virginity: Brides of Christ and Sacrificial Mutilation." She writes:

> Many convents, along with their nuns, suffered repeated devastation and violence from the Viking, Magyar or Saracen incursions. . . . How did [these religious women] cope with their very real and persistent fears, as well as the reality of rape and the loss of their virginity? How did they respond to the potential destruction and loss of their *raison d'être,* that is, their investment in *integritas,* in total virginity? . . . in facing this "fate worse than death," these brides of Christ had a great deal more to lose than did their contemporary male religious.[13]

Schulenberg makes a strong case for the need for these women to protect themselves and their chastity at great cost. In fact, most religious women of the period would have happily died (and Schulenberg gives a number of examples of those who did) rather than submit to rape. Suicide as a deterrent to rape was, in fact, the only sanctioned form of suicide for the medieval Church,[14] and since it was so often depicted in literature of the period (Chaucer's *Legend of Good Women* and *The Physician's Tale* are two excellent examples), it was probably a notion that most medieval women would have assumed to be a viable option. What was at stake for the medieval religious virgin, therefore, was tied closely to what was at stake for all medieval women: survival in the face of a repressive, often violent, often obliterating patriarchal culture.

Þe Wohunge of Ure Lauerd is a text that served a particular purpose in its original context. It was written sometime before 1250[15] for what was probably a community of anchoresses. The women whom we believe to have been the original audience for the text (and the other texts within both the Katherine and *Wohunge* groups) were educated to some degree, probably aristocratic, and definitely subject to a spiritual and devotional character.

Because of the background of these women, and perhaps because of the background of the authors of the works, literary patterns and images abound in these works that shed light both on the disposition of the original readers of the works and the genre of anchoritic mysticism itself.

A significant element within this genre is the heroic. In the early Middle Ages, heroism was very explicitly defined. Heroes exhibited certain characteristics and could not be seen as heroic without them. These characteristics (including generosity, kindness, bravery, honor, and courtliness) frame the nature of early medieval heroism. Within such works as those contained in the *Wohunge* Group, the nature of Christ is defined by just these same terms, with Christ described in similar terms of knighthood. Early in the *Wohunge* Christ is referred to as a prince, a king's son, one who is mild and generous. There are several more references in the anchoritic works to Christ's heroism, and also to his chivalry (*cnihteschipe*). For example, in *Ancrene Wisse,* the speaker explains:

> In scheld arn þre þinges. þe treo
> & te leðer. te litinge. Alswa was Iþis schild þe treo of
> þe rode. þe leðer of "licome" godes. þe litinge | of þe
> reade blod þat heowede hire se feire . . .
> After cnihtes deað mon henges ichir'che his scheld
> on his muneginge Alswa is tis scheld, þat is te crucifix in
> chirche iset iswuch stude. þer mon mei sondest seo hit.
> for to þenche þerbi o iesu cristes cnihteschipe. þat he dide o rode.

[In a shield there are three things, the wood, the leather, and the painting. So it was in this shield: the wood of the cross, the leather of God's body, the painting of the red blood that colored it so beautifully . . . after a brave knight's death, his shield is hung high in church in his memory. So is this shield, that is, the crucifix, set high in church on such a place where it is soonest seen, to bring to mind Jesus Christ's chivalry, which he performed on the cross].[16]

In the *Wohunge,* Christ's characteristics are also described heroically in the terms of romance.

Following the invocation early in the poem, the speaker lists the characteristics "þat eauer / muhen maken ani mon lu- / uewurði to oðer."[17] She argues that

> feirnesse &
> lufsum neb. flesch hwit under
> schrud makes moni mon beo
> luued te raðer. & te mare. Sum-

me gold & Gersum & ahte of
þis werlde makes luued & he-
ried. Sume fredom & largesce
þat leuer is menskli to ȝiuen
þen cwedli to wið halde. Summe
wit & wisdom & ȝapschipe of
werlde. Summe mahte & streng-
ðe to beo kid & kene ifiht his
riht for to halde. Summe no-
blesce. & hehnesse of burðe.
Summe þeaw. & hendeleic & laste-
lese lates. Summe menske & /
mildeschipe & debonairte of herte & dede.

[Beauty, a lovely face, a body white under clothing, make many men beloved
all the sooner and all the more; some are beloved and praised for gold and
riches and worldly possessions; some for liberality and largesse—those who
prefer giving generously to stingily keeping back; some for wit and wisdom
and worldly cleverness; some for power, and the strength to be renowned
and keen in battle to fight for his cause; some for nobility and highness of
birth; some for virtue and graciousness and perfect manners; some for honor
and gentleness and mildness in heart and deed].[18]

She then goes on to describe each of the characteristics of Christ as he fills
these requirements. Indeed, these are the characteristics of a romance hero,
a medieval epic hero. In fact, she argues in each case how much better
Christ is as a suitor than an earthly man:

Ah noble men & gentile & of
heh burðe ofte winnen luue
lihtliche cheape. for ofte mo
ni wummon letes hire mens-
ket þurh þe luue of wepmon
þat is of heh burðe. þenne swete
iesu up o hwat herre mon
mai I mi luue sette. hwer
mai I gentiller mon chese
þen þe þat art te kinges sune
þat tis world wealdes.

[Men of high birth, frequently win love at little cost, for often many a
woman loses her honor through the love of a man of high birth. Then, sweet
Jesus, upon what higher man can I set my love? Where can I choose a nobler man than you, who are the Son of the King who rules this world].[19]

What this seems to amount to is an accounting of all of the potential attractions of an earthly man, each being surpassed, in turn, by the attractions of Christ. This idea of ranking Christ up against the qualities of a human man is common in these works. For example, in a famous passage from *Ancrene Wisse*, the author writes: "Swa / muchel is bitwe-ne godes neohleachinge & mon-nes to / wummon. þat monnes nehlea-|chinge makes meiden wif. / & Godd makes of wif meiden" [there is so great a difference between God's coming to a woman and a man's, that a man's coming makes of a virgin a wife, and God makes of a wife a virgin].[20] Perhaps this is such a common situation in these texts because the women who are reading them have given up any chance of physical union with earthly men and must therefore substitute Christ as the image of their ideal suitor.

Another powerful metaphor in these works is the language of endearment and sexual love that is used by the speakers in the poems. There are a number of passages in the *Ancrene Wisse* that use the language of secular love to describe a spiritual union. For example, in the *Uriesun of oure Louerde*, the speaker begins with the invocation: "Ihesu swete. / ihesu mi leof . . . min bliþe breostes blisse. Ihesu teke þet tu art se softe. & se swote. ʒette to swa leoflic. swo leoflic and swa lufsum . . . Ihesu al feir . . . let me beo mi leofmon" [Jesus, sweet Jesus, my darling . . . blithe bliss of my breast! Jesus, teach me, thou that art so soft and so sweet, and yet too so dear and so lovely. . . . Jesus, all fair . . . let me be thy lover].[21] These words, particularly *leof, leoflic, lufsom,* and *feir,* are not recorded in any other Middle English texts in this context before 1250.[22] Until the authors of these poems begin to write about the expression of love between the anchoress and her Lord, these are terms used exclusively to describe secular, erotic love.

The use of this language can be interpreted in several ways. In one reading, the author of the poems is using terms that he associates with the kind of love experienced by women—sexual love, expressions of the erotic. This reading would argue that the author of the poem is appropriating a feminine voice in order to subjugate the feminine to the realm of the body and to deny her any expression of desire that exists outside of the body. It could be, in this scenario, that the true language of love used by the anchoresses in their description of their desire for Christ was unknowable to the author (as a male), so he uses instead a familiar language that other readers can identify as feminine. It may also have been that the author uses this language to try to convince the anchoresses who would surely read his texts that though they longed for a disembodied expression of love for Christ and a union with his spirit and power, they were only *allowed* to imagine such a union in terms of heterosexual love and metaphors of the body and thus feminine disempowerment.

Another reading of the author's use of courtly and erotic language to describe the union between the anchoress and Christ is to put it in terms of conquest and submission. In the words quoted above from *Ancrene Wisse*—"God's coming to a woman and a man's"—the language does not leave room for the possibility that the woman can be in pursuit of God (or a man). She is always to be taken; he comes to her. She is not in control of what happens to her body *or* soul. This is also true of romance. Rarely, if ever, are there courtly tales about women who "take" their lovers or who are even willing participants in the experience. Criseyde is tricked; Isolde is drugged; Guinevere is seduced. Few women in the romance tradition pursue their lovers. Instead, a great deal is made of the woman's reticence and her unwillingness to participate in the consummation until her lover has proven himself.[23]

The idea of the unwillingness of the lover to participate in union makes sense in terms of "male" mysticism as well. The mystic cannot choose to become united with God in a mystical union. As the author of *The Cloud of Unknowing* argues, you cannot expect or even hope for transcendence or perfection. He writes: "For parauenture, whan it likiþ vnto God, þoo / þat mowe not at þe first tyme haue it bot seldom & þat not wiþouten / grete trauayle, siþen after þei schulen haue it whan þei wile, as ofte / as hem likiþ."[24] It happens because God chooses you, not because you want it to happen or because you have earned it. Thus the role of the mystic (male or female) as mistress of Christ the knight makes perfect sense.[25] The mystic is chosen, wooed, and conquered by the power, attraction, and knightly qualities of Christ's love, not because "she" has set out to be Christ's lover but rather because he has selected "her." This brings to mind the notion of the "feminization" of the mystic and "her" complete submission to Christ as his *lefmon*. In male-authored (and male-centered) mystical works, the same metaphors of Christ as knight and mystic as mistress exist, so that it has been argued that the mystic is feminized during his or her experience of transcendence. His[26] identity is dissolved in the presence of Christ and he is no longer a subject but is instead a part of the larger subjectivity of Christ.[27] The author of *The Cloud of Unknowing* uses Mary Magdalene[28] as an example. He identifies her as the former prostitute and compares her unwavering contemplation of Christ to her sister Martha's equally unwavering activity in his honor. They become the ultimate models of contemplation and devotion. He writes:

> al þe tyme þat Martha maad hir besy
> aboute þe diʒtyng of his mete, Mary hir sister sat at his feet. & in
> heryng of his worde, sche beheeld not to þe besines of hir sister.
> . . . ne ʒit to þe preciouste of his blessid body, ne to þe swete voyce
> & þe wordes of his Manheed.[29]

Mary, in her contemplation of his masculine body and voice, is so over-whelmed that she enters "a hiȝe & wonderful cloude of / vnknowyng be-twix"[30] herself and her God. She becomes a model for all contemplatives, who "schuld conforme here leuyng after hirs."[31] Thus, in order for the male mystic to participate in this union of souls, his masculine subjectivity must be disintegrated. He must identify with a feminine model who is en-thralled by Christ's presence—both in his words and his body. This, of course, is the metaphor of heterosexual union and of the passivity and dis-solution of the feminine in the presence of the masculine subject translated into the language of contemplation. The mystic is feminine because "he" submits—his designation as feminine rests on the surrender of his subjec-tivity. He does not, however, exchange a female subjectivity for his male one. In fact, in medieval terms, the feminine has no subjectivity herself; she is defined only in terms of her relationship to a man: she is a virgin, a mother, a wife, a sister, a whore. She is never a female subject defined by her own presence; rather, she is defined by how she is acted upon by phal-lic power. Indeed, she has no voice of her own but instead must appropri-ate the language and voice of patriarchy if she is to communicate within patriarchal culture.

Thus the mystic is feminized in order to surrender his identity. The problem becomes, then, if there are women mystics who *also* surrender their subjectivity, then where do they *get* that subjectivity in the first place? How does a woman surrender what her culture denies her? Is it only a symbolic surrender, or is there a way in which the female speakers of these poems are able to obtain, or at least appropriate, a subjectivity through the process of their "wooing" of Christ? Indeed, if the title of the *Wohunge* refers to the speaker's wooing of Christ, then some kind of exchange of identity has already taken place, for it would not be possible, as I have al-ready mentioned, for a woman to woo a masculine subject. Thus it can be argued that the feminine speaker of this poem (and others like it) has been made masculine in her pursuit of union with Christ, and it will be her masculine subjectivity that she sheds during her moment of union.[32]

The "immasculation" of the speaker of the poem takes place on several levels. First, it occurs in the act of speaking itself. In her article, "Reading Ourselves: Toward a Feminist Theory of Reading," Patrocino Schweickart argues that women become "immasculated" as soon as they attempt to enter the Symbolic Order. Schweickart relies on Lévi-Strauss's theory "that woman functions as currency exchanged between men. The woman in the text converts the text into a woman, and the circulation of this text/woman becomes the central ritual that establishes the bond between the author and his male readers."[33] Schweickart then cites Judith Fetterly, who writes:

the cultural reality is not the emasculation of men by women, but the *immasculation* of women by men. As readers and teachers and scholars, women are taught to think as men, to identify with a male point of view, and to accept as normal and legitimate a male system of values, one of whose central principles is misogyny.[34]

Women *must* be immasculated, in fact, if they are to participate in language at all.[35] Otherwise they are silent (and many women, of course, do choose silence). This can be seen clearly in the lives of anchoresses. They have been taught since birth that their bodies are fallen and will tempt all men to sin. They have been encouraged to marry in order to have some access to cultural identity or, if marriage was not possible for them, they have been driven to a life of cloistered chastity. Even if these are women who entered the anchorhold by choice, out of a real sense of devotion, they have still in some way been encouraged to believe the misogynist values and ideals that were central to the medieval church. Few women in the Middle Ages were as immasculated as the anchoress, in fact, since most were educated within the Church and thus directly taught to "identify with a male point of view"—that being the teachings of the Church. But by her presence and her identification as a woman, the speaker of the *Wohunge* is not silent: at least she has been given access to a voice by her male author. Thus, while she has no doubt been immasculated through her education and her conformity to Church tradition, there is a chance that because of the existence of her text (as Schweickart argues), "other women will recognize themselves in her story, and join her in her struggle to transform the culture."[36] Thus while immasculation provides few readers with examples of female authors, perhaps the artifacts of women who seem to have transcended the process can lead to transformation in succeeding generations.

The immasculation of the feminine, for Schweickart, takes place during a woman's education within the patriarchal system. For the female mystic, this process took place on all levels of society, in her education, her family, her church, her lifestyle. Thus it was an accepted, perhaps expected, part of the process of "perfection" in the Middle Ages. In other words, women had to undergo some level of immasculation in order to participate in the Symbolic Order; thus they probably pursued the process, however unconsciously. Thus the process itself is clear in all levels of the anchoress' experience of contemplation and perfection. However, it seems likely that the process, while perhaps oppressive to a modern audience, was in some ways liberating to a medieval woman. As I mentioned earlier, there could be no mystical experience without a sense of one's own subjectivity. And medieval culture denied such subjectivity to its women. Thus, in order for a medieval woman to gain access to the possibility of transcendence,[37] she first had to gain access to subjectivity through education and through institutions such as convents and anchoritic communities. The process is a positive experience for such women, for as they acquire masculine characteristics through their educational experiences, they are endowed with access to transcendence. I would argue, then, that immasculation of several kinds is necessary for the female mystic, and she pursues it on many levels.

An important aspect of the immasculation of the feminine within the anchoritic tradition of mysticism is in the speakers' devotion to Mary. Certainly in the Middle Ages Mary was seen as an icon, as a role model, as one on whom a human woman patterned herself (that is, as perfect mother, perfect and silent Queen of Heaven). Mary herself is a mystic, of course. In the New Testament she is acted upon by the Holy Spirit quite literally and is impregnated with the infant Jesus. In another context, what takes place between Mary and the angel could be seen as rape—indeed it has been seen as such by some critics and poets.[38] But in the context of Christian, heterosexual union, this is seen as the silent and willing submission of the feminine to her masculine God. She does not participate in it; she does not enjoy it; she cannot prevent it. In fact, Catholic doctrine *depends* on the notion that Mary did not enjoy her experience of conception—tradition does not allow for a sexualized mother of God. In an interesting departure from this tradition, Aelred argues that the female recluse should relive the Annunciation and the conception of Christ—"joying in it" with Mary. He writes,

> O sweet lady, with what sweetness you were inebriated, with what a fire of love you were inflamed, when you felt in your mind and in your womb the presence of majesty. . . . All this was on your account, virgin, in order that you might diligently contemplate the Virgin whom you have resolved to imitate and the Virgin's Son to whom you are betrothed. . . . But now together with your most sweet Lady go up into the mountains and gaze upon the barren wife and the virgin as they embrace one another. . . . What are you doing, virgin! Run, I beg, run and take part in such joy, prostrate yourself at the feet of both, in the womb of the one embrace your Bridegroom, in the womb of the other do honor to his friend.[39]

The virgin recluse is encouraged to gaze upon the bodies of Mary and Anne—both mothers of holy people, and *enter their wombs* in order to embrace the beloved Christ while he is still within his mother's body, simultaneously sharing in Mary's maternity and in the glory of Christ as her bridegroom.

There is no doubt that Mary did serve as a model for many medieval women. She was constantly present—in sculpture or painting in every church, in their daily prayers, in the number of feast days attributed to her life. However, for the speaker of this poem, she is not seen as a model for feminine behavior. Instead, she is a focus of devotion and love, of the kind of devotion often used by male authors in their love lyrics to Mary.[40] Mary was not, strictly speaking, a woman, after all. She participated only symbolically in any of the defining activities of women. Marina Warner writes: "every facet of the Virgin had been systematically developed to diminish, not increase, her likeness to the female condition. Her freedom from sex, painful delivery, age, death and all sin exalted her *ipso facto* above ordinary women and showed them up as inferior."[41] Mary becomes not a woman (and thus a female wooer is not inappropriate in the medieval sense of *amour courtois*), not a model for those who were devoted to her worship. Instead she becomes the object of desire for the faithful of both genders, in much the same way that Christ does in mystical treatises. It is not common for mystical texts to contain references to "marriages of the Virgin," but as Marina Warner points out, it is common to find such references in drama and in love lyrics.[42] Thus if the female mystic must become "immasculated" in order to participate in a union with Christ, then by doing so she must also look to Mary, another spiritual bride/physical virgin, not only as a feminine role model but also as a desired Other.

Mary, then, and her presence within these texts becomes a paradox herself, in part because the references to her in the *Wohunge* Group often acknowledge her beauty and desirability but rarely her maternal qualities. In the *Wohunge,* Mary is mentioned only twice, both in reference to her maternity, but not as if that maternity is taken on in any way by the narrator. In a sense, Mary constitutes both a desired Other and a figure with which the mystic could identify, both through her abjection[43] and her maternity. In a most moving passage from the poem, the speaker says,

Bote lafdi for þe Ioie
þ*at* tu hefdes of his ariste þe þridde
dai þer efter. leue me vnderstonde
þi dol herteli to felen sum hwat
of þe sorhe þ*at* tu þa hefdes & hel-
pe þe to wepe.

[Lady, by the joy you had in his resurrection the third day after [his death], grant that I may understand your pain, and feel in my heart something of the sorrow that you had, and help you to weep].[44]

The references to Mary as a desired Other appear much more explicitly in several of the other works, however. In the *Ancrene Wisse* the anchoresses are instructed to pray a cycle of prayer based on the five joys of

Mary, beginning with the prayer: "Lady, sweet lady, sweetest of all ladies, most beloved lady, most lovable lady, O most beautiful of women [Canticles 1:8], lady St. Mary, precious lady, lady queen of heaven, lady queen of mercy; lady have mercy on me (Savage and Watson 63).[45] In the *Uriesun of Ure Lefdi,* the invocation begins: "Mines liues leome mi leoue lefdi. / To þe ich buwe and mine kneon ich beie. / And al min heorte blod to ðe ich offrie. / þu ert mire soule liht. and mine heorte blisse" [My life's light, my beloved lady! / To thee I bow and my knees I bend, / And all my heart's blood to thee I offer. / Thou art my soul's light, and my heart's bliss].[46] This is the same language used to describe Christ in other texts from the *Wohunge* Group. Later in the *Urieson* the speaker states:

> Mi leoue lif urom þine luue ne schal me no þing to-dealen.
> Vor oðe is al ilong mi lif and eke min heale.
> Vor þine luue I swinke and sike wel ilome.
> Vor þine luue ich ham ibrouht in to þeoudome.
> Vor þine luue ich uorsoc al þet me leof was.
> And ȝef ðe al mi suluen. looue lif Iþench þu þes.

[My dear love, from thy love shall nothing separate me, / For on thee depends my life, and my salvation also. / For thy love I toil and sigh very often, / For thy love I am brought into bondage, / For thy love I forsook all that was dear to me, / And gave thee all myself. Dear love, think thou of that].[47]

Still later in this poem is a more explicit use of the image of Mary as a desired Other: "Mi lif is þin mi luue is þin mine heorte blod is þin. / And ȝif ich der seggen mi leoue leafdi þu ert min" [My life is thine, my love is thine, my heart's blood is thine, / And if I dare say it, my dear lady, thou art mine].[48] Throughout the works of the *Wohunge* Group, there are references to the body: Christ's, the speaker's and Mary's. These are not always references or identifications with the maternity of Mary. In fact, in the female ascetic's pursuit of perfection, she must deny her own body and role as potential wife and mother—thus she identifies with Mary not as a model of motherhood, but rather as a partner, a "wife." In the same way that a male speaker can desire to be a bride of Christ, so, too, can a female speaker pursue Mary as a heavenly bride. A female ascetic, however, once she has taken the step from woman to anchoress, may feel autonomous and may deny her own body but in a sense makes it necessary for other women to be oppressed by theirs. Warner writes, "the little hard-won independence of nuns was gained at other women's cost, for belief in the inferiority of their state underpinned it."[49] Thus the oppression of women, the concept of the fallen state of the female body, is necessary for ascetic women. Without that standard, they have nothing to surpass, no goal to pursue, no need for disembodiment. And because of this "naturally" fallen state of the female body, the goal for the female ascetic is not perfection as a woman, which is never really possible, but rather the appropriation of masculine characteristics, a taking on of some qualities of manhood, and its consequent subjectivity.

Another way in which the female speaker is masculinized is through her visual ability—she looks at the body of Christ and really sees it. Using the terminology of Stephen Heath,[50] the speaker of the poem does not remain, as most women do, "absorbed on the side of the seen." She sees, as well, and her act of looking at Christ is another way that she appropriates masculinity or, here, the masculine gaze. She sees his "body under white clothing" and his great physical beauty. She says:

> al en-
> gles lif is to neb to bihalden.
> for þi leor is swa unimete lufsum
> & lusti on to loken. þat ȝif þe for-
> wariede þat wallen in helle mihten
> hit echeliche seon. al þat pinende
> pik. ne þat walde ham þunche bo-
> te a softe bekinde bað.

[to look into your face is life itself to the angels. For your face is so immeasurably lovely and alluring to look at that if the condemned who boil in hell could see it eternally, all the torturing pitch would seem to them no more than a gentle warm bath].[51]

Sarah Stanbury writes of the transgressive nature of the *Pearl*-maiden's gaze in that poem. She cites Kaja Silverman who argues that "the female subject's gaze is depicted [in film] as partial, flawed, unreliable, and self-entrapping . . . although her own look seldom hits the mark, woman is always on display before the male gaze."[52] An example of this notion of the feminine gaze as imperfect occurs again in *The Cloud of Unknowing*. After Mary is described as having been a perfect model for contemplation, the narrator describes her vision of Christ's body: "I hope þat sche was so deeply [affected] / in þe loue of his Godheed þat sche had bot riȝt lityl specyal / beholdyng unto the beute of his precious & his blessid body, in þe / which he sate ful louely, spekyng & prechyng beofre hir."[53] He imagines her sight to be limited, imperfect, in the presence of God. Women, Stanbury argues, suffer an "ocular castration" in traditional Western film and literature. However, in *Pearl*, the maiden "challenges . . . the authoritative strictures of [the masculine gaze] with a focused and steady look."[54] The speaker of the *Wohunge* looks, too. She sees Christ and she envisions her own body with his body—experiencing the pain of crucifixion and the joy of resurrection with him. Thus the *reader's* gaze (the female anchoritic reader) sees him too (sees them both) and symbolically becomes a masculine gaze of desire and compassion.

The use of the present tense on the part of the author of the poem makes this point even more strongly. The narrator has spoken in the past tense about Christ's suffering until the moment when she recounts the events of the crucifixion: "ha þe bunden swa / hetelifaste . . . dintende unrideli o rug & o schul / dres."[55] However, suddenly the verb tenses shift and the narration takes place in the present tense.

> A nu haue þai
> broht him þider. A nu raise
> þai up þe rode. Setis up þe warh
> treo. A nu nacnes mon mi lef
> A. nu driuen ha him up wið
> swepes & wið schurges . . .
> . . . A hu schal
> I nu liue for nu deies mi lef for
> me up o þe deore rode? Henfes
> dun his heaued & sendes his saw-
> le.

[Ah! now they have brought him there. Ah! now they raise up the cross, they set up the gallows. Ah! now someone strips my dear. Ah! now they drive him up with whips and with scourges. . . . Ah! how shall I live now? For now my love dies for me on the dear cross. He hangs down his head and sends out his soul].[56]

Then after a brief contemplation of his death and resurrection, there is another dramatic tense shift. The speaker first speaks of taking on Christ's suffering in the future tense: "My body will hang with your body, nailed on the cross, fastened, transfixed within four walls."[57] Then again suddenly, the verb tense shifts again to the present: "A. iesus swa swet hit is wið þe / to henge. forhwen þat iseo o þe / þat henges me biside. þe mu- / chele swetnesse of þe. rea / ues me fele of pine. [Ah Jesus, so sweet it is to hang with you. For when I look on you who hang beside me, your great sweetness snatches me strongly from pain].[58]

The narrator takes the speaker (and the reader) from past and future to present. Using, perhaps, the Augustinian sense of time as constant and recurring, the reader is brought from the realm of possibility (I will hang with you) to fulfillment (I do hang with you). The speaker gazes on the body of Christ as he is crucified; then she climbs up on the cross with him, and the gaze shifts from the speaker to the reader. Thus the feminine speaker's immasculation provides for the same effect in the female anchoritic reader. Stanbury warns that there is a danger when a feminine speaker takes on a masculine gaze. By appropriating a gaze, "she participates in a masquerade in which the positions she adopts oscillate between the seer and the seen, the appetitive male viewer and the object of his look. Playing the masquerade . . . she occupies an unstable and oscillating position in which she takes on the masculine gaze, adopting a 'phantasy of masculinization at cross-purposes with itself, restless in its transvestite clothes.'"[59] This is no doubt true, to some extent, in the immasculated anchoress. Like the *Pearl*-maiden, however, the speaker of the poem is not an actual woman but rather the product of a male author. Stanbury goes on to say (in the case of *Pearl*) "the Maiden's authoritative gaze and voice are registered within the program of the Dreamer's attempt to master her through a complex voyeuristic and fetishizing visual itinerary . . . [he] muffles her voice, screens her gaze, in essence absorbs her very presence within the drama of the . . . story."[60] This risk of muffling an authentic feminine voice through its appropriation in a male-authored text is central to an understanding of the *Wohunge* Group.

The medieval religious celibate woman existed on the margins of her culture both because of her existence as a woman within the Church and her choice not to be acted upon by masculine power. It may be said that some women actively sought the cloister or the anchorhold as a means to avoid the possibility of marriage and its potential oppression. However, even within the Church, women were still reminded constantly of the fallen condition of their bodies and souls—their abjection—and of their unsuitability for salvation. It is only through a direct connection to Christ—who was also abjected and marginalized by patriarchal culture in his persecution and death—that anchoresses and nuns had any access to the presence of the Divine. In the *Wohunge* Group, Christ takes on both the masculine and the feminine, the abject and the empowered and, through a transference of gender identity, allows the feminine speaker (and reader) to reach beyond her state as culturally defined, oppressed feminine object and attain a sense of transcendent subjectivity. In a significant passage from *On lofsong of ure louerde,* the descriptions of Christ fluctuate from line to line with images of his death interspersed with images of his immortal life: "clense & pe / asch mine sunfule soule þuruh þine fif wun / den iopened o rode. wiðneiles uor driuene / & seoruh fulliche fordutte. hel me uor-wunded / þuruh mine fif wittes wið deadliche sunnen" [cleanse and wash my sinful soul; through thy five wounds opened on the cross, pierced through with nails, and sorrowfully filled up, heal me sore wounded through my five wits with deadly sins].[61] This passage is a good representation of what occurs for the speaker(s) of the *Wohunge* Group during the mystical experience. They begin as sinful, fallen feminine bodies who are eventually brought to the glory of the resurrection through Christ's body and through the intellectual exchange that takes place during the moment of transcendence. Central to their understanding of the potential for their spiritual perfection is the knowledge and understanding of their physical and earthly abjection. Once they surrender to that notion of their own physical inadequacy and sin, they are enabled to reach beyond the body and participate in the wordless, bodiless experience of mysticism.

Notes

1. *Þe Wohunge of ure Lauerd,* ed. W. Meredith Thompson. EETS o.s. 241 (London: Early English Text Society, 1958), ll. 568–572. This edition of the Wooing Group includes Middle English transcriptions of *On Ureisun of oure Louerde, On Ureisun of God Almihti, On Lofsong of ure Louerde, On Lofsong of ure Lefdi, Þe Oreisun of Seinte Marie,* and *Þe Wohunge of ure Lauerd.* Citations for translations of this and other texts will follow references to the Middle English within the same note.
2. Ann Savage and Nicholas Watson, *Anchoritic Spirituality: Ancrene Wisse and Associated Works* (New York: Paulist Press, 1991), p. 256. I have used this text for translations of *Ancrene Wisse* and *Þe Wohunge of ure Lauerd.*
3. This notion is asserted by most contemporary critics of the texts, mainly because of the salutation "dear sisters" at the close of *Þe Wohunge.*
4. For further discussion of the authorship of these texts, see Bella Millet, "Women in No Man's Land: English Recluses and the Development of Vernacular Literature in the Twelfth and Thirteenth Centuries" in *Women and Literature in Britain, 1150 – 1500,* ed. Millet (Cambridge: Cambridge Univ. Press, 1993); Nicholas Watson, "The Methods and Objectives of Thirteenth-Century Anchoritic Devotion" in *The Medieval Mystical Tradition in England,* ed. Marion Glasscoe, Exeter Symposium IV (Cambridge: Brewer, 1987), pp. 132–153; and Anne Savage and Nicholas Watson, eds., *Anchoritic Spirituality: Ancrene Wisse and Associated Works.*
5. *Þe Wohunge of Ure Lauerd* is part of a group of poems called the Wooing or *Wohunge* Group. It has also been associated with the similarly constituted Katherine Group, based on its inclusion in the manuscript with the life of St. Katherine. Other works in these groups include the *Ureisun of God Almihti,* the *Oreisun of Seinte Marie, A Lofsong of Ure Lafdi, Hali Meiðhad, Sawles Warde,* and, in some of the manuscripts, the *Ancrene Wisse.*
6. John Bugge, *Virginitas: An Essay on the History of a Medieval Idea,* International Archives of the History of Ideas 17 (The Hague: Martinus Nijhoff, 1975), p. 89.

7. Thompson translates this word *bur* as "dwelling." According to the *Middle English Dictionary,* a more appropriate translation would be "a shelter for cattle, cow house" (3:878). Considering the gender of the speaker, the frequency of erotic language within the texts and the birthing context of "cow house," *bur* here could be interpreted as *womb,* an easy leap from "dwelling" and a very interesting image of feminine desire. As Elizabeth Robertson has pointed out, what women's bodies were believed to lack in the Middle Ages was heat, so when the speaker asks Christ to "illuminate her darkened heart" and "give her *dwelling* brightness," she could be asking for the needed heat that only a male body could supply.

8. *Wohunge,* ll. 15–20, my translation.

9. Frances Mack, *The English Text of the Ancrene Riwle* (Oxford: EETS, 1962), 145.4–12. Each page of this text is lined separately, thus my references refer to page and line numbers.

10. *On Ureisun of oure Louerde,* in *Þe Wohunge of Ure Lauerd,* ed. Thompson, pp. 49–57.

11. R. Morris, ed. and trans., *Old English Homilies and Homiletic Treatises,* EETS o.s. 34 (London: EETS, 1868), pp. 184–186. This text includes translations of most of the texts included in the Wooing Group: *On Ureisun of oure Louerde, On God Ureisun of Ure Lefdi, On Ureisun of God Almihti, On Lofsong of ure Lefdi, On Lofsong of Ure Louerde,* and *Þe Wohunge of Ure Lauerd.* Neither Thompson's edition or Savage and Watson's version includes translations of all these texts, so I have used Morris in these cases.

12. According to the *Middle English Dictionary,* the word *cluppe* was quite frequently understood as a euphemism for sexual intercourse (4:331).

13. Jane Tibbets Schulenberg, "The Heroics of Virginity: Brides of Christ and Sacrificial Mutilation," in *Women in the Middle Ages and the Renaissance: Literary and Historical Perspectives,* ed. Mary Beth Rose (Syracuse: Syracuse Univ. Press, 1986), pp. 29–72.

14. Schulenberg cites Jerome's *Commentary on Jonah* in which Jerome writes, "In persecutions it is not lawful to commit suicide except when one's chastity is jeopardized" (cited in Schulenberg, p. 34). However, by the twelfth and thirteenth centuries there was still some discussion among theologians of the time as to the validity of suicide to avoid rape. Schulenberg continues: "Self-mutilation, less extreme than suicide, was then a very practical methodology which would accomplish the desired end, that is, make the brides of Christ so hideously disfigured that no man would be tempted to sexually assault them" (Schulenberg, pp. 59–60). However, this puts the responsibility of the avoidance of rape back on the woman: she is so tempting and desirable that she must literally disfigure herself in order to prevent lustful men from acting upon her seductiveness—thus the focus of rape returns not to the lusts of men but to the inherent sexuality and weakness of women, making the crime of sexual assault less a crime and more a feminine trap that men must try to avoid.

15. A thorough discussion of the date of these texts is found in Savage and Watson, *Anchoritic Spirituality: Ancrene Wisse and Associated Works.*

16. Mack, 145.4–12; Savage and Watson, p. 192.

17. This line is translated, "that can ever make anyone worthy of another's love" (Savage and Watson, p. 248).

18. *Wohunge,* ll. 13–30; Savage and Watson, p. 248.

19. *Wohunge,* ll.160–170; Savage and Watson, pp. 248–250.

20. Mack, 146.5–8; Savage and Watson, p. 193.

21. *On Ureison of oure Lauerd,* in *Wohunge,* ll. 3–17; Morris, pp. 184–186.

22. None of these words appear in any sacred context until the texts of *Hali Meiðhad, St. Katherine,* and other members of the Katherine Group. In fact, in the cases of some of these words, they do not appear in the *Middle English Dictionary* until their appearance in these works.

23. Chaucer's *Book of the Duchess* is a good example of this notion of the knight's pursuit and the mistress' good-natured reticence.

24. *The Cloud of Unknowing,* ed. Phyllis Hodgson (Salzburg: Institut für Anglistik un Amerikanistik Universität, 1982), 71.27–30. Again, the lines in this text are numbered by the page rather than over the whole text, so references here refer to page and line numbers.

25. Bynum cites St. Francis of Assisi, who writes, "it is they who are the brides, the brothers and the mothers of our Lord Jesus Christ. A person is his bride when *his* faithful soul is united with Jesus Christ by the Holy Spirit; we are his brothers when we do the will of his Father who is in heaven [Matt. 12:50], and we are mothers to him when we carry him in our hearts and bodies by love with a pure and sincere consciousness, and give him birth by doing good deeds" (Caroline Walker Bynum, *Jesus as Mother: Studies in the Spirituality of the High Middle Ages* (Berkeley: University of California Press, 1982), p. 284.)

26. For the sake of argument at this point I would like to discuss the mystic as male.

27. This is a reference to the Pseudo-Dionysion notion of the Universal Soul: "Universal Soul (or Life) is generated from the energy overflowing from *Nous* as *Nous* from The One . . . the human souls . . . participate in the Universal Soul . . . rising higher, each soul has an image of the Universal Intellect. To approach Divine Intellect man must know his own soul when it is most like its source. When bodily things are shed, that which is left will be an image of Divine Intellect" (Hodgson, p. xlii).

28. Mary Magdalene is mis-identified as the prostitute to whom Christ says "Go and sin no more" in this passage. However, in identifying her as a prostitute he necessitates a sexualization of her devotion to Christ. This makes what he says about her behavior as a model for all contemplatives even more interesting.

29. *The Cloud of Unknowing,* 26.9–14.

30. *The Cloud of Unknowing,* 26.24–25.

31. *The Cloud of Unknowing,* 27.1–2.

32. Jo Ann McNamara makes this argument in her article, "Sexual Equality and the Cult of Virginity in Early Christian Thought," *Feminist Studies* 3–4 (Spring/Summer 1976):145–158. She writes,

> To be sure, the fathers [of the Church] did not forget that the category "man" included woman. But they had an ineradicable tendency to characterize certain psychological qualities as "masculine" and others as "feminine." And, it must be added, that their instinctive tendency was to equate "masculine" with the higher attributes. As a result of these predispositions of style, the sexual equality obtained by virgins was habitually expressed by viewing them as having become men. (152–153)

    This notion of the "virile" Christian woman has also been discussed thoroughly in Barbara Newman's book, *From Virile Woman to WomanChrist: Studies in Medieval Religion and Literature* (Philadelphia: University of Pennsylvania Press, 1995).

33. Patrocino Schweickart, "Reading Ourselves: Toward a Feminist Theory of Reading," *Gender and Reading: Essays on Readers, Texts, and Contexts,* ed. Patrocino Schweickart and Elizabeth A. Flynn (Baltimore: Johns Hopkins Univ. Press, 1986), p. 41.

34. Cited in Schweickart, pp. 41–42.

35. In order for a woman to speak, she much speak the language of patriarchy. Thus, for Kristeva, *immasculation* takes place for a woman as soon as she enters the Symbolic through speech. For Schweickart, that immasculation takes place when the female child enters the Symbolic through education and cultural conditioning. If a woman resists immasculation through education and language, then she cannot speak, and she is relegated (or relegates herself) to silence or, as Kristeva would argue, to madness.

36. Schweickart, p. 51.

37. This is not to deny the possibility of mystical experience to women who were less "immasculated," that is, women who were not anchoresses or nuns and simply claimed transcendent experiences with no institutional experience. These women may have existed; however, if they did, they did not produce texts. As I define mysticism, there must be a text—the process does not end with transcendence. All extant mystics are known for their experiences because of the texts they produced and which remain available to modern audiences.

38. Marina Warner cites Yeats's poem, "The Mother of God" as an example of this notion (*Alone of All her Sex: The Myth and the Cult of the Virgin Mary* (New York: Knopf, 1976), p. 34.

39. Aelred of Rievaulx, "A Rule of Life for a Recluse," in *The Works of Aelred of Rievaulx,* 2 vols., ed. and trans. Mary Paul Macpherson (Spencer, MA: Cistercian Publications, 1971), 1:81.

40. This is not to say that, through the experience, Mary and the female mystic share any kind of homoerotic bond. Instead, it may be said that there is

something about the nature of mysticism that requires a transference of sexuality or, perhaps, of gender itself.

41. Warner, p. 153.
42. Warner refers to several poems and plays in which Mary is seen as the heavenly spouse of the faithful. For example, she cites Gautier de Coincy—a Benedictine prior whose work is roughly contemporary with the *Wohunge*. His poem "Chansons de la Vierge" is translated: "Let us marry the Virgin Mary; no one can make a bad marriage with her. Believe you me, he who marries her could not make a better match" (Warner, p. 155).
43. For a more thorough discussion of this issue of the abjection of the mystic, please see my article, "Mysticism and the Anchoritic Community: 'a time . . . of veiled infinity" in *Medieval Women in Their Communities*, ed. Diane Watt (Cardiff: Univ. of Wales, 1997), pp. 116–137.
44. *Wohunge*, ll. 559–564; Savage and Watson, pp. 255–256.
45. Savage and Watson, p. 63. This quotation is given in translation because the manuscript from which I have made my transcriptions does not include the first chapter of the text.
46. Morris, pp. 190–191.2–5.
47. Morris, pp. 194–196.95–100.
48. Morris, pp. 198–199.
49. Warner, p. 78.
50. Cited in Sarah Stanbury's "Feminist Masterplots: The Gaze on the Body of *Pearl*'s Dead Girl," in *Feminist Approaches to the Body in Medieval Literature*, ed. Linda Lomperis and Sarah Stanbury (Philadelphia: University of Pennsylvania Press, 1993), p. 105.
51. *Wohunge*, ll. 37–44; Savage and Watson, p. 248.
52. Cited in Stanbury, p. 105.
53. *The Cloud of Unknowing*, 26.1–4.
54. Stanbury, p. 105.
55. *Wohunge*, ll. 467–471.
56. *Wohunge*, ll. 502–507 and 534–538; Savage and Watson, p. 255.
57. Savage and Watson, p. 256.
58. *Wohunge*, ll. 598–602; Savage and Watson, p. 256.
59. Stanbury, p. 105.
60. Stanbury, p. 107.
61. *On Lofsong of oure Lourede*, in *Þe Wohunge of ure Lauerd*, ed. Thompson, ll. 47–51; Morris, pp. 210–211.

CHAPTER 6

USEFUL VIRGINS IN MEDIEVAL HAGIOGRAPHY

Kathleen Coyne Kelly

> *The multiple examples of narratives in which intervention saves virginity show the essential value of virginity as a sign of the docility and utility of female bodies in hagiography.*

In the Golden Legend the martyrdoms of the saints are no more dwelt upon than are the trivial incidents of their lives; it is as though all human experience, measured against one supreme spiritual adventure, were of about the same importance.

—Willa Cather

Ultimately, to be a saint is to be a saint for others, to acquire the reputation of saint from others and to play the role of saint for others.

—Pierre Delooz

History, Fiction, Virginity

In Robertson Davies's novel, *Fifth Business,* the main character Dunstan Ramsay is a "saint-hunting, saint-identifying, and saint-describing" scholar. (He is proud to say that he has received an admiring letter from Hippolyte Delehaye, the leading expert on hagiography both inside and out of Davies's fictional world.) "There is a saint," Ramsay says, "for just about every human situation." The saint with whom Ramsay is most intrigued—he refers to her as "big game"—is Wilgefortis of Portugal, whom he describes as "a curious specimen whose intercession was sought by girls who wanted to get rid of disagreeable suitors."[1] Wilgefortis, daughter of the king of Portugal, took a vow of chastity, and then was betrothed to the king of Sicily against her wishes. She prayed to become ugly, and, miraculously, she grew a beard. The lover gave up his suit, and the girl's enraged father had her crucified.[2]

Wilgefortis's story, albeit more sensational than most, is one of several narratives of late antiquity and the Middle Ages in which divine intervention saves a virgin from compromising her vow of chastity. Such tales attest to the sacred and secular value and power of virginity in Christian society but also place hagiography on the cusp of fiction and history. In his critique of traditional historiography, Hayden White distinguishes between fiction and history by arguing that the forms ("systems of meanings production," or "modes of emplotment") are the same, but the content ("'real' rather than 'imaginary' events") is different.[3] Yet as his scare quotes demonstrate, "real" and "imaginary" are problematic adjectives, and this is particularly true with respect to hagiography. While White does not specifically discuss hagiography, this hybrid genre furnishes a fine test case for his theories, particularly when White argues that in the historical narrative, "experiences distilled into fiction as typifications are subjected to the test of their capacity to endow 'real' events with meaning." He adds: "it would take a *Kulturphilistinismus* of a very high order to deny to the results of this testing procedure the status of genuine knowledge." Indeed, hagiography functioned and still functions as "genuine knowledge" for many communities worldwide. Though the nature of that knowledge has changed over time, hagiography continues to be a productive mode of representation for its redactors and readers, figuring, as White would put it, "another order of reality."[4] While my chief interest in this essay is in virginity and how it functions as the sign of the "docility-utility" (Foucault's words) of female bodies in the hagiography of late antiquity and the Middle Ages, I also consider how the hagiographic blend of history, biography, panegyric, and allegory privileges meaning over event and the general and exemplary over the specific (even in narratives that are markedly detailed and localized) in order to produce "useful" virgins.[5]

Most obviously, the saint's life is "useful" in that it serves as a model, however idealized, for Christian behavior. But the saint and the saint's virgin body also came to represent the "body" of the Church metonymically, serving as the first line of defense, the lightening rod, the decoy, as it were, for the institution behind it. Ever since Christ said "this is my body," the way was cleared to construct parallels (both actual and hierarchical) between the individual body and the collective Church. In fact, the *female* virgin body, produced through a series of mystifications as closed, sealed, intact—both a wall and a door, as the Song of Songs puts it (8:9)—came to function as the most apt homology between the self and the institutionalized Church, even when that self was gendered male.

The body of the female virgin and the body of the Church came to be equated often enough in patristic texts with female virginity. Jerome avers that "no vessel of gold or silver was ever so dear to God as the temple of a virgin's body" [Neque enim aureum vas et argenteum tam carum Deo fuit, quam templum corporis virginalis]; Ambrose says that the virgin is a living *templum Dei.*[6] In commenting upon Song of Songs 4.12, Ambrose also says that "Christ says this [that is, "Hortus conclusus, soror mea, sponsa, Hortus conclusus, fons signatus"] to the Church which He wishes to be a virgin, without spot, without wrinkle. . . . And no one can doubt that the Church is a virgin" [Christus hoc dicit ad Ecclesiam, quam vult esse virginem, sine macula, sine ruga. . . . Nec potest dubitare quisquam quod Ecclesia virgo sit].[7] With such rhetorical equations in mind, historian Peter Brown calls the early virgins of the Church "human boundary-stones," whose presence marked a "privileged, sacred space."[8] A violation of a consecrated virgin could thus be construed as a violation of the Church, both literally and figuratively—and, as we shall see, rape is precisely the story that is suppressed in the hagiography of late antiquity. Inviolate virginity was produced as essential—and I use this word in both its traditional and current critical senses— to the construction and continuance of the early Christian Church.

Menaced Virgins

Virginity is most visible in what I call the tale of circumvented rape or near-rape, which invariably includes two parts: 1) the threat of rape, and 2) the prevention of rape, usually by miraculous means. In this type of tale, a pagan official or suitor either attempts to rape a consecrated virgin himself, or he sends her to the brothel to be raped. However, the rape is never committed, for a miracle prevents it. In the stories of circumvented rape, the consecrated virgin may lose her limbs or her life, but never her virginity. *Virginity* always outlasts the *virgin.* In every society, says Foucault, the body finds itself "in the grip of very strict powers, which imposed on it constraints, prohibitions or obligations."[9] The virgin body carried severe obligations indeed, as its very public, agonistic displays attest.

A few words about rape are in order at this point, for the subject of rape has recently received a good deal of scholarly attention, both as a historical phenomenon and a literary trope. One can hardly discuss rape in the Middle Ages without referring to Kathryn Gravdal's *Ravishing Maidens: Writing Rape in Medieval French Literature and Law.*[10] Gravdal's book has led me to call a rape a rape—no more circumlocutions such as "he forced his attentions on her" or "he attempted to seduce her." In the scores of saints' legends that I have read for this essay, it is very clear that rape is indeed the issue. However, so far as I have been able to determine, there are no extant saints' lives in which a virgin is actually raped by a Roman consul or in a brothel; I have never read a narrative that describes rape, or says that rape was committed, or even creates a "before and after" scenario, as in, for example, Richardson's *Clarissa* and Hardy's *Tess of the D'Urbervilles.* It is possible to argue that rape is "represented" in hagiography through a rhetoric of silence, if not displacement, but the fact remains that there is no direct narrative of rape in hagiography. As we shall see, the unrepresentability of rape is a correlative to the unrepresentability of virginity. The point at which the two converge in the saint's life is precisely and paradoxically the moment when the female body becomes most visible—subject to narrativization— while the actual circumstance or moment recedes into the background.

In the first half of this essay, I examine the evidence for near-rape and rape that exists outside of the traditional hagiography of late antiquity. I am defining "traditional" or "standard" hagiography as any narrative that *plots* the story of a saint or saints, as opposed to a summary of or reference to a story. For example, Augustine and others acknowledge that many avowed virgins were subjected to rape, but they provide only reports, not direct, consciously plotted narratives. In the second half, I examine the hagiographical legends themselves. Stories of near-rape exist in a number of different permutations (ranging from short anecdotes to substantial narratives in verse and prose) from late antiquity to the end of the Middle Ages. However, most tales of circumvented rape, and the most sensational of them, are clustered in the second through the fourth centuries, at a time when the Church was under particular assault both within the Roman Empire and at its ideological margins. The fourth century marks the institutionalization of a number of foundational saints' legends, which are then recycled and reshaped in the Middle Ages. I begin with the earliest known accounts of the legend of Agnes in order to emphasize its syncretic features and to identify the role narrative plays in its development. I then turn to the fully narrativized legend of Agnes as told by Jacobus de Voragine in the *Legenda Aurea,* and also discuss his version of the legends of three other menaced virgins of late antiquity—Agatha, Euphemia, and Lucy. The *Legenda Aurea,* most likely completed before 1267, gathers together tales from a range of sources, and includes over 130 saints' lives from the second to the thirteenth centuries. The *Legenda Aurea* becomes the major source for subsequent retellings, surviving in over eight hundred Latin manuscripts alone.[11] This compilation highlights the more prominent features of conventional hagiography, and it is the conventions of the genre, those elements that define it, which are my particular concern as I examine the ubiquitous motif of circumvented rape. As Simon Gaunt observes, "Hagiography creates the illusion of a united textual community, unchanging over time, for whom differences of gender (or class, for that matter) are entirely naturalized," but he does so in order to read against such effects in his study, *Gender and Genre*.[12] However, I am interested in reading *with* such effects, in reading the illusion itself, in order to explore how this illusion might function in and as Christian ideology. I argue that the menaced virgin in the near-rape narrative is more useful as a metonym, as an inviolate body that stands in for the Church, than as an actual, historical person. Hayden White argues that metonymy is "reductive"; it allows one to "simultaneously distinguish between two phenomena and reduce one *to the status of a manifestation of the other*" (emphasis mine).[13] The virgin indeed figures as a "manifestation" of the Church but does so most effectively when she is lifted out of her historical moment and textualized in the discourse of hagiography. Thus I am not so concerned with contextualizing the "facts" of a given saint's life, and how such facts were originally established (an almost impossible task), collected, and interpreted at various times, as I am concerned with interrogating the assumptions and conventions of hagiography in order to discover what the genre can reveal about the uses of the female virgin martyr in the early Church, and to examine how the trope of near-rape persists into the Middle Ages long after its immediate historical context is lost. While it would be a mistake to assume that the legends of Agatha, Agnes, and Lucy were read throughout the Middle Ages in the same way that they were read in late antiquity, it is clear that the story of the menaced virgin continued to resonate outside of the particular confines of the beleaguered Christian community of late antiquity. Jocelyn Wogan-Browne points out that most collections of saints' lives in medieval England were produced for women in religious houses (whose reading pleasure may have been as much vicarious as instructive), and notes that the figure of the virgin martyr was especially popular in the vernaculars of twelfth and thirteenth centuries. She argues:

> If [violence] is a literary convention necessary for the posing of obstacles for the heroine to overcome, it is a convention which a contemporary audience was able to accept as a true representation of the life of someone known to them.[14]

Medieval hagiographers often drew comparisons between their subjects and the virgin martyrs of antiquity. The trope of near-rape remained a productive, if not central, episode in subsequent retellings.

Real Women, Real Rape

Perhaps the earliest hagiographical tale of divine intervention can be found in the *Acts of Paul and Thecla* (c. 185 – 95 A.D.). Thecla of Iconium endured a number of trials because of her vow of chastity: first, her own mother condemns her to be burned because she would not marry, but a rainstorm miraculously extinguishes her bonfire. Then, when a certain Alexander attempts to rape her, she fights him off. Brought before the courts for her presumption, she is condemned to the beasts, but time after time they refuse to harm her. Thecla is humiliated by being publicly stripped, but the crowd is prevented from seeing her naked by a "cloud of fire" that surrounds her. Finally Thecla is left in peace, and she goes off to live as a hermit in a cave. When she is around ninety years old, a group of men appears, with rape evidently their intention. However, her prayers open a rift in the rocks and she vanishes within, never to be seen again.[15]

R. G. Collingwood said that the true historian "never asks himself [*sic*], 'Is this true or false?' . . . The question he asks himself is, 'What does this statement mean?' . . . He does not treat statements as statements but as evidence." Yet I *do* want to know if Thecla, when sentenced to the arena to be devoured by beasts, actually "asked of the governor that she might remain a virgin until she should fight the beasts." Was she really turned over to Queen Tryphaena for the safeguarding of her virginity until then?[16] I am perfectly willing to discount the miracles in the tale, but I want to know if there is a kernal of truth in her plea for protection. Yet even Tertullian and Jerome argued that the *Acts of Paul and Thecla* was spurious, though the cult of Thecla survived for centuries afterward. (The Vatican finally decanonized her in 1969.) Perhaps there was no "historical" Thecla, but did the textual "Thecla" have sisters now lost to history? Were consecrated virgins really threatened with rape, or actually raped? During the Great Persecutions, were Christian women who refused to sacrifice—thus making themselves candidates for execution (as decreed by the Edicts of Diocletian)—actually sent to the brothels to be raped? We can cite examples from twentieth-century history in which rape was made a part of a program of oppression: one of the hard lessons of Bosnia is the fact that Bosnian Serbs use rape routinely as a terrorist tactic. And consider the case of the hundreds of Korean women who recently initiated suits against the Japanese government for the actions of Japanese troops during World War II. Some 100,000 women were kidnapped, raped, and forced into prostitution in order to serve Japanese soldiers in occupied countries from Korea to Indonesia. Such women were known as *ianfu,* "comfort women."[17]

The documentation that we have for these contemporary events has no equivalent in late antiquity or the Middle Ages. When we look outside standard hagiographies for "evidence" of rape and near-rape, we must turn to such invested and interested writers as Lactantius, Eusebius, Jerome, Ambrose, and Augustine (many of whom, of course, also wrote standard hagiography). In his accounts of martyrs in the *Ecclesiastical History* (written ca. 300 and revised ca. 313 to 326) and *The Martyrs of Palestine*, Eusebius, who along with Lactantius chronicled the organized persecutions of Christians under the fourth-century emperors Diocletian and Maximian, suggests that rape (or the threat of rape) of a condemned consecrated virgin was all too routine in the days of the early Church. In the *Ecclesiastical History*, Eusebius reports that

> the women were not less manly than the men in behalf of the teaching of the Divine Word: as they endured conflicts with the men, and bore away equal prizes of virtue. And when they were dragged away for corrupt purposes, they surrendered their lives to death rather than their bodies to impurity.[18]

Eusebius tells of the many Christian women in Thebais who "were bound by one foot and raised aloft in the air by machines, and with their bodies altogether bare and uncovered, presented to all beholders this most shameful, cruel, and inhuman spectacle."[19] He also reports the story of a woman of Antioch and her two daughters, who drowned themselves rather than submit to "the things terrible to speak of that men would do to them—and the most unbearable of all terrible things, the threatened violation of their chastity."[20] In *The Martyrs of Palestine*, Eusebius recounts how one Ædesius attempted to intervene when a judge of Alexandria "consign[ed] women of greatest modesty and even religious virgins to procurers for shameful treatment."[21] Eusebius does shift from reportage to direct narrative in one instance: Potamiæna, says Eusebius in the *Ecclesiastical History*, was "famous . . . for the many things which she endured for the preservation of her chastity and virginity. For she was blooming in the perfection of her mind and her physical graces." The judge Aquila, frustrated in the face of her unwavering faith, after "having inflicted severe tortures upon her entire body, at last threatened to hand her over to the gladiators for bodily abuse."[22] At this point, instead of relating a stock story of divine intervention, Eusebius tells us that, "being asked for her decision [to renounce Christianity], she made a reply that was regarded as impious. Thereupon she received sentence immediately."[23] Potamiæna may have been saved from rape by her "impious" remarks (perhaps a condemnation of pagan worship),[24] but she was not saved from death: she was killed by having burning pitch poured over her body.

Throughout the *Ecclesiastical History* and *The Martyrs of Palestine*, Eusebius focuses not on miracles but on the strength and perseverance of the Christian martyrs, many of whom he himself saw tortured and put to death. Scholars today judge Eusebius to have been a reliable historian, especially given the standards of his day, yet he undeniably had an agenda—

which is not to say, of course, that there is such a thing as a historian without an agenda. For example, Eusebius says of Book VIII of his *History* that he will "introduce into this history in general only those events which may be useful to ourselves and afterwards to posterity . . . the sacred conflicts of the witnesses of the Divine Word."[25] Eusebius shapes the stuff of history to support a Christian teleology, and in the process, the virgin martyr is transformed into a social document, "useful" for those who would read such a "text." As I will argue in more detail, rape is not a "useful" narrative in a semiotic system in which the inviolate virgin functions as a metonym for the institution of the Church.

Ambrose, Jerome, and Augustine each embed stories about menaced virginity in their respective exhortations to chastity, yet they use the saint's life in the service of another project: to formulate doctrine on whether or not suicide in order to preserve virginity is justified. At the same time, these writers use the near-rape narrative to affirm that it is not the body that sins, but the will—and that spiritual virginity is not only more valuable than physical, but also impervious to corruption. For example, in *De Virginibus,* Ambrose tells the story of "a virgin at Antioch" who is consigned to the brothel but who is saved by a soldier who switches places with her. He declares:

> Christi virgo prostitui potest, adulterari non potest. Ubicunque virgo Dei est, templum Dei est: nec lupanaria infamant castitatem, sed castitas etiam loci abolet infamiam.

> [The Virgin of Christ can be exposed to shame, but she cannot be contaminated. Everywhere she is the Virgin of God, and the Temple of God: houses of ill-fame cannot injure chastity, but chastity does away with the ill-fame of the place.][26]

Though not unsympathetic, Ambrose is more interested in the story for its power to inspire: "Listen, ye holy virgins, to the miracles of the martyr, forget the name of the place" [Discite martyrum miracula, sanctæ virgines, dediscite locorum vocabula].[27] Offered up as a model to be emulated, the martyr counts far more than her historical moment. As Ambrose had said of Agnes, the virgin of Antioch—whose very name is forgotten, or at least thought not worth recording—represents a "new kind of martyrdom" [Novum martyrii genus]—that is, a new kind of *witnessing,* as in the original sense of *martnr,* a witnessing that works on and through the abstracted virginal body.[28]

In *De Civitate Dei,* Augustine acknowledges that Christian women, even *quasdem sanctimoniales* [certain consecrated virgins], were raped in the attack on Rome by the Goths. His announced subject: "whether the vi-olation of captured virgins, even those consecrated, defiled their virtuous character, though their will did not consent" [An stupris, quae etiam sacrarum forte virginum est passa captivitas, contaminari poterit virtus animi sine voluntatis assessu].[29] His audience is other Christians: "Nor are we here concerned so much to deliver a reply to those not of our kind as to bring comfort to our own people themselves" [Nec tantum hic cura-mus alienis responsionem reddere, quantum ipsis nostris consola-tionem].[30] This careful designation of audience strikes me as an instance of paradigm-building. While Augustine's comment may be intended to dismiss pagans as unworthy of hearing his message and to draw in the al-ready converted, it also reveals a conscious attempt to use these women as exempla only, as fodder for the fashioning of doctrine. Augustine goes on to argue that "no matter what anyone else does with the body or in the body that a person has no power to avoid without sin on his own part, no blame attaches to the one who suffers it" [Quidqiud alius de corpore vel in corpore fecerit quod sine peccato proprio non valeat evitari praeter culpam esse patiens] for "purity is a possession of the soul, [and not] lost when the body is violated" [Si autem animi bonum est, etiam oppresso corpore non amittitur].[31] This is apparently the only *consolatio* available for believing Christians.

As far as I can determine, there are no Roman—that is, non-Christian—sources that attest to the rape or attempted rape of the consecrated virgin during the persecutions of Christians in late antiquity. Not surprisingly, we must rely on the persecuted, not the persecutors, to tell this story. However, we do find evidence of laws against, or at least limiting, forced prostitution, which suggests that consignment to a brothel was not entirely a fiction in imperial Rome.[32] Let us also consider an intriguing remark that Ambrose makes in *De Virginibus* that leads us, albeit circumstantially, to an alleged cus-tom in certain state executions. He says that, at the time of her martyrdom, the virgin Agnes was "not yet of fit age for punishment but already ripe for victory" [Nondum idonea poenæ, et jam matura victoriæ].[33] According to Ambrose, Agnes was twelve years old when she died. In Roman society, a "fit age" for a woman was marked by the onset of the menses and/or the loss of virginity. Perhaps Ambrose had in mind the idea, or more likely the myth, that virgins could not or should not be executed by the Roman state. In the *Annals* (ca. 116 – 118 A.D.), Tacitus tells a story about the overam-bitious but doomed Sejanus, a prefect under Tiberius from 14 to 31 A.D. Tiberius ordered Sejanus' family to be killed, including his young daughter. Tacitus says carefully: "It is recorded by authors of the period that, as it was considered an unheard-of thing for capital punishment to be inflicted on a virgin, she was violated by the executioner" [Tradunt temporis eius auctores, quia triumvirali supplicio adfici virginem inauditum habebatur, a carnifice laqueum iuxta conpressam].³⁴ Suetonius also recorded this story in *The Lives of the Caesars* (120 A.D.); however, he is less careful and more sure about rape as a general practice: "Since ancient usage made it impious to strangle maidens, young girls were first violated by the executioner and then strangled" [Immaturae puellae, quia more traditio nefas esset virgines strangulari, vitiatae prius a carnifice, dein strangulatae].³⁵ This story was intended to illustrate the cruelty and depravity of Tiberius. To be sure, it is tenuous evidence for any sort of Roman "policy" on rape. However, it does suggest that rape as an instrument of humiliation and punishment had the status of an open secret (to borrow a phrase from D. A. Miller) in imperial Rome and its provinces.

Based on what little evidence we have for the historicity of near-rape and rape, we might construct the following scenario: in the cities of the Mediterranean in late antiquity, chastity came to be one of the more obvious practices and symbols of all that set Christians apart from pagans. The identity of the young woman and that of the Christian community that she represented depended upon her professed and visible virginity. If one were a pagan official, one might conclude that the best way to undermine a Christian woman's faith and demoralize her family and friends would be physical violence and sexual assault. Tertullian suggests as much in the *Apologeticum,* when he rhetorically addresses Roman officials: "Nam et proxime ad *lenonem* damnando Christianam *potius quam ad leonem* confessi estis labem pudicitiae apud nos atrociorem omni poena et omni morte reputari" (emphasis mine). The striking phrasing works just as well in English, as the following translation demonstrates: "Yes, but lately, when you condemned a Christian girl to the *pander rather than the panther,* you admitted that we count an injury to our chastity more awful than any penalty, any death" (emphasis mine).³⁶ In his *Peristephanon,* Prudentius steps into the mind of Agnes' tormenter (*trux tryannus*), having him declare that, while Agnes "scorns life as of little worth, still the purity of her maidenhood is dear to her. I am resolved to thrust her into a public brothel" [vita vilis spernitur, at pudor / carus dicatae virginitatis est. / hanc in lupanar trudere publicam].³⁷ As stylized as Tertullian's and Prudentius' representations are of the motif of the brothel, they carry the ring of psychological truth.

Fictional Women, Fictional Rape

The question of the historicity of the near-rape narrative is further complicated by the fact that hagiographical accounts of threatened but divinely protected chastity have their analogues, if not their partial origins, elsewhere. For example, in his *Controversiae* (first quarter of the first century), Seneca the Elder offers for debate the story of a virgin "captured by pirates and sold; she was bought by a pimp (*lenone*) and made a prostitute."[38] (Seneca does not say whether this story is true or not.) The Greek prose romance or novel, sometimes referred to as "chastity romance,"[39] furnishes ample evidence that the motif of the threat of rape and divine or magical intervention—or, in some cases, a creaking *deus ex machina*—circulated before the bulk of late antique hagiography was written down. Scholars have long noted that the earliest hagiography has much in common with the Greek novel of antiquity;[40] in fact, the plot lines are often very similar. In Xenophon's *An Ephesian Tale* (perhaps mid-second century A.D.), for example, the heroine Anthia is sold to a brothel, but she avoids rape by faking epilepsy; in Heliodorus' *Aethiopica* (perhaps third to fourth century A.D.), the heroine Chariclea is saved time and again from rape by a number of *deus ex* machinations. However, it must be said that comparing the dates of the Greek novel with the earliest hagiographical accounts of the menaced virgin presents a number of problems. Without a way to recover oral tradition and transmission, charting the flow of influence, from novel to hagiography or from hagiography to novel, is extremely difficult. These novels, long neglected by mainstream classicists, are just now beginning to receive serious attention. As we learn more about them, their readership, and their dissemination, we will surely learn more about the origins of the menaced virgin of late antique and medieval hagiography. Suffice it to say that the story of female chastity under assault seems to have been a perennial popular subject—and remains so today, as hundreds of Barbara Cartland novels attest.

In the Greek novels, highly entertaining and often self-consciously sensational fictions, the story of menaced virginity is easily consumed as just one more titillating tidbit. Indeed, the same can be said of the hagiographical tale—what differs (what is supposed to differ) is the context in which one reads the story. Yet what ties the two genres together are shared assumptions about the uses and significations of the virgin. The ideology that structured the virgin's tale in the Greek novel also shaped the parallel plot in the emerging literature of the Christian Church. In both contexts, the virgin functions as an originary figure, as an occasion for a number of very specific social structures and regimes. (In fact, as the story of Lucrece and countless tales of gods and their sexual interest in mortal women attest, the rape narrative also has the potential for inaugurating change in social relations.[41]) Sherry Ortner, in "The Virgin and the State," even hypothesizes a connection between the rise of the state and the ideological linkage of female virginity and chastity to the social honor of the group, such chastity being secured by the exertion of direct control over women's mobility to the point of lifetime seclusion, and/or through severe socialization of fear and shame concerning sex.[42]

Ortner defines the state as any development of a central locus of power and the attendant administration to support it. Not only would such a definition apply to the Greco-Roman state of the second through fourth centuries (in its various permutations), but also to the early Church (a syncretic institution shaped by Greco-Roman/Judaic/Middle Eastern values). It seems that virgins and their proper supervision and disbursement required a complicated bureaucratic infrastructure as well as heavily regulated customs and rituals in both the profane and the sacred spheres.

Both the Greco-Roman state and the early Church could count a wealth of virgins among their assets, though how they choose to deploy such assets differed radically, of course. In the secular realm of late antiquity, the virgin was not only an object of exchange between men but also served as a sign that the homosocial system was functioning properly. In the context of the early Church, however, the consecrated virgin came to figure very differently. As Peter Brown has shown in *The Body and Society,* as a treasure saved up, exempt from marriage (however humble or dynastic), the Christian virgin came to be seen as undermining the authority of the state, which hitherto had had sole power over virtuous bodies, their manners and their management. However, as the interests of the Church and the state gradually merged, or at least came to be reconciled, the avowed virgin secured a respected place in the larger culture, serving as an important and powerful symbol in both fiction and history.

Universalized Symbols

It may be helpful to borrow M. M. Bakhtin's distinction between centripetal and centrifugal forces in language and apply it to the heterogeneous genre that we call hagiography. It sometimes seems that hagiography is constituted of two contrary desires—the first a centripetal impulse to create and maintain a homogenized, authoritative discourse (by flattening difference and privileging universality), and the second a centrifugal impulse, to interrogate or critique the power of such a discourse (by registering difference and highlighting the particular). In fact, the *study* of hagiography is made up of similar conflicting centripetal and centrifugal desires. Such fluctuations and fashions suggest that Graham Pechey, in "Bakhtin, Marxism and Post-Structuralism," is correct when he asserts: "There are no monologic texts . . . only monological readings."[43] Authoritative discourse (formed by centripetal forces) and its opposite, internally persuasive discourse, do not necessarily represent innate qualities of discourse; they indicate functions or roles that discourse assumes in a social context. At certain points and in some places, when the centripetal forces of hagiography prevail, the universalized and dehistorized virgin is a more useful figure than the local version. I would argue that in the first centuries of the Church, when its founders and defenders were working most actively to establish and secure ecclesiastical authority, the tale of the menaced virgin was constructed in such a way as to remove the virgin martyr from history and re-place her in an idealized, transcendent narrative. Such a move, which aestheticizes and displaces real pain and suffering, expedited an untroubled, unproblematized identification between the virgin (and through her, every believing Christian) and the Church. Medieval redactors of hagiography, as they adapted legends in which the trope of near-rape appears for their own purposes and particular audiences, also inherited and preserved this identification of virgin and Church.

Let us turn to the legend of St. Agnes for an example. Our earliest extant version is Ambrose's account in his sermon, *De Virginibus* (377). Here, the trope of menaced virginity as I have described it is barely discernible. Ambrose gives us not a narrative of what "happened" to Agnes but an abstract panegyric that focuses on her bravery and eloquence in the face of her executioner. The closest he comes to suggesting that her virginity may have been threatened is found in the following passage:

> Quanto terrore egit carnifex ut timeretur, quantis blanditiis ut suaderet; quantorum vota ut sibi ad nuptia proveniret! . . . virgo permansit et martyrium obtinuit.

> [What threats the executioner used to make her fear him, what allurements to persuade her, how many desired that she would come to them in marriage! . . . She both remained a virgin and she obtained martyrdom.][44]

Similarly, no trace of threat can be found in two other early accounts; first, in the hymn, *Agnes beatae virginis,* dated later than Ambrose's sermon (and sometimes attributed to him) but written before the end of the fourth century, and second, in what is known as the inscription of St. Damasus (Pope 366–384), thought to have been composed in between Ambrose's sermon and the hymn.

As we have already seen, Prudentius provides us with a quite explicit reference to the threat of the brothel in the *Peristephanon* on the cusp of the fifth century. Prudentius gives us a fully plotted narrative, complete with dialogue and differing points of view. The miraculous is prominently featured. In his thorough and invaluable study of the origins of the Agnes legend, A. J. Denomy points out that we do not know if these early texts represent separate threads of the legend, or if they form part of a common genealogy.[45] It strikes me that Prudentius' embellishments must have come out of a very different rhetorical context than that in which Ambrose, Damasus, and the writer of Agnes's hymn are writing. It may be that Prudentius was influenced by a tradition represented by the Greek *Passio of Saint Agnes,* which also includes a reference to the threat of the brothel. Again, we are unable to identify clearly the trajectory of influence; that is, which text, the *Passio* or the *Peristephanon,* antedates the other. I would argue that it is likely that the conventions of the Greek novel influenced the writer of the *Passio* and/or Prudentius. Our next account, the Latin *Gesta sanctae Agnes,* is usually dated as fifth century or early sixth, with some seventh-century additions. Its sources are thought to be diverse, including Ambrose's and Prudentius' accounts, and, perhaps, the Greek *Passio.* The *Gesta* is the source for the legend of St. Agnes that we find in the *Legenda Aurea.*[46]

If one examines all of these versions of the legend, one might plausibly argue that the seeds of the near-rape narrative can be found in Ambrose's sermon. So Denomy suggests, though he concludes that the origins of this episode are pagan and classical. The number of miraculous details increases from redaction to redaction, which certainly gives the legend more coherence, if less veracity. Jody Enders recently observed that "the New Historicist tendency to revel in indeterminacy proves just as problematic as the Old Philologist tendency to try to resolve it," and trying to solve the problem of the origins of the near-rape episode in the legend of St. Agnes as well as in other, similar legends of late antiquity using Old Philology to make a New Historicist argument is tricky indeed.[47] And consider Donna Haraway's observation, though made in a different context:

> Technologies and scientific discourses can be partially understood as formalizations, i.e., as frozen moments, of the fluid social interactions constituting them, but they should also be viewed as instruments for enforcing meanings.[48]

The trope of near-rape is an excellent example of a "formalization" or "frozen moment"; not a matter of fact but of fiction, a result of a teleocentric Christian "technology." While the original impetus or inspiration (mainly irrecoverable, though available to speculation) for the narrative is lost, its effects remain beyond the particular historical moment of its creation.

Let me now turn to the legend of St. Agnes in the *Legenda Aurea,* which, despite Voragine's rhetorical arrangements and innovations, still serves as a fine example of a "formalization," and a formalization that served as a primary source for the bulk of vernacular saints' lives throughout the Middle Ages. The tale begins with a proprietary gaze: a prefect's son sees Agnes on her way home from school and falls in love with her. He offers marriage to Agnes, but she spurns him in no uncertain terms: "Go away, you spark that lights the fire of sin, you fuel of wickedness, you food of death! I am already pledged to another lover!" [Discede a me fomes peccati, nutrimentum facinoris, pabulum mortis, quia jam ab alio amatore praeventa sum, 113–114.] The boy then sinks into lovesickness, and his father seeks out Agnes to find out who her betrothed is. Once it is made clear to him that Agnes is talking about Christ, he orders her to sacrifice to the virgin goddess Vesta, or else she will be sent to a brothel. She refuses to sacrifice, and, when she is stripped, her hair miraculously grows long enough to cover her entire body [Ut melius capillis quam vestibus tegretur, 115]. (This detail is first found in the Gesta sanctae Agnes).[49] An angel throws a mantle of light around her once she enters the brothel, and this light is enough to deter anyone who approaches her. The prefect's son urges his companions to "take their pleasure" with her, but they are too terrified [Eos prius as ipsam invitavit, 115]. The prefect's son then "in a fury rushe[s] in to force himself upon Agnes" and is struck dead [Ad eam furens intrans cum eam vellet contingere, 115.] Though Agnes restores him to life, the prefect, too cowardly to set her free in the face of public opinion, turns her over to a deputy, who orders her to be burnt. The flames do not harm her. She is subjected to more tortures and finally dies with a dagger through her throat.

Consider a few more examples of what we might call centripetal narratives—that is, narratives that dramatize the miraculous and the global at the expense of the historical and local—in the Legenda Aurea. In the legend of Euphemia, the judge Priscus sends Euphemia to prison for refusing to sacrifice to the gods, and there tries to rape her. However, as Voragine says,

Sed illa viriliter reluctante manum ejus virtus divina contraxit. Tunc putans se incantatum praepositum domus suae ad ipsam direxit, ut multa promitteret, si eam faceret consentire. Sed ille carcerem clausum nec clavibus aperire potuit nec securibus frangere, donec a daemone arreptus clamans et se ipsum dilanians vix evasit.

[She resisted manfully, and the power of God paralyzed his hand. Priscus thought he was under some kind of spell. He sent his head steward to promise her all sorts of things if she would do his will, but the man was unable to open the jail door with keys or to break into it with an ax, and finally was seized by a demon, screamed, tore his own flesh, and barely escaped with his life.][50]

The Romans then try to behead her but are unsuccessful. Priscus consequently orders that the city's ruffians be rounded up in order to "enjoy her as long as they liked, until she dies exhausted" [Qui tamdiu eam illuderent, donec fatigata deficeret, 182]. But when Priscus' chancellor goes to Euphemia's cell, he is miraculously converted and refuses to give her over to the waiting crowd. After several attempts to torture her, all of which fail, Euphemia is finally stabbed to death by a follower of Priscus', who does so "in order to avenge the offence given to his master"—that is, the apparent frustration Priscus felt at his inability to break Euphemia [Inter quatuor magnos lapides sicut oliva constringeretur, 621]. It is significant that no torture, however ingenious, is able to have an effect on her physical body; for example, Euphemia was to be "crushed like an olive between great millstones," but the stones turn to harmless powder. That the virgin saint can be killed only by the (phallic) sword or knife is a motif repeated over and again in hagiographical legend.[51] It is very tempting to read this and other deaths as a displacement, as a rhetorical substitution for the act of rape itself. In a way, death is less complicated than rape, for it is a "discourse" that prevents any further traffic with the virgin/virgin body; it is an end to a narrative, an end to change and exchange. As the Church Fathers warned over and over again, so long as the virgin is in circulation, she is in danger. It is also possible that the depiction of the virgin's death functioned as a cathartic moment for its original audience, whose sense of what was at stake in the near-rape narrative would have been much greater than our own. Better the virgin lose her life and keep her virginity, for her reward in heaven would be that much more.

Stories of overt sexual humiliation and torture (another strategy of displacement and substitution) are frequently found in the near-rape narrative; for example, according to their legends, Agatha, Candida, and Febronia were first publicly stripped and then had their breasts removed as part of their torture.[52] The story of Agatha is particularly well known in the West. (Though Jerome includes Agatha in his martyrology, it is likely that her martyrdom is completely fictitious.) Depending on the version of the story, her breasts were cut off, ripped off, or, in the *Legenda Aurea,* twisted off. In each version, Agatha's breasts are miraculously restored. A detail that anticipates (and promises) the resurrection of the body at the Last Judgment, the restoration of Agatha's breasts also focuses the reader's attention on gender and how it matters—it is as if Agatha's sex must be initially asserted and foregrounded in order for it to be fully recuperated when she is later saved from rape through divine intervention.

In the *Legenda Aurea,* before Agatha is tortured, she is handed over to a brothel by the consul Quintianus. Voragine inserts some sound psychologizing at this point: Quintianus is

Beatam Agatham comprehendere nitebatur, ut quia erat ignobilis, compre-
hendendo nobilem timeretur, quia libidinosus, ejus pulchritudine frueretur,
quia avarus, ejus divitias raperet, quia ydololatra, Diis eam faceret immolare,
fecitque eam ad se adduci. (170)

[determined to get (Agatha) in his grasp. Being of low degree, he would gain
respect by lording it over a noble, her beauty would satisfy his libido, he
would steal her riches to feed his avarice, and, being a pagan, he would force
her to sacrifice to the gods. (154)]

Quintianus gives the prostitute Aphrodisia a month to debauch
Agatha—by what means Voragine doesn't say. Predictably, in the face of
Agatha's prayers and incessant weeping, Aphrodisia fails, declaring: "It
would be easier to split rocks or reduce iron to the softness of lead than to
move or recall that girl's mind from its Christian intention" (170) [Facilius
possunt saxa molliri et ferrum in plumbi mollitiem converti, quam ab in-
tentione christiana mens istius puellae converti seu revocari, 154]. The
"miracle" is not so much an example of divine intervention as it is of divine protection. However, whatever the form of the miracle, here, as in
other tales, only virginity is saved, not the body itself; after being rolled
naked over broken pots and live coals, Agatha dies in prison. Abstract virginity counts far more than the specific, fleshly body, according to a logic
in which the soul's eternity supercedes the body's chronicity. When particular bodies are effaced, only the abstract idea remains, transcending and
transmuting the historical moment into a universalizing, identificatory experience. The paradox inherent in the hagiographical narrative is that this
operation takes place when the virgin body is at its most visible and vulnerable to the gaze—that is, when the virgin is narrativized most explicitly and vividly as a female body.

Lucy, my next example of the menaced virgin, is unhappily betrothed.
She begins to give away her possessions, which alarms and angers her intended. After all, what she distributes to the poor was to be his. (We can
discern traces of an antique pagan *realpolitik* in this tale of an unauthorized
distribution of wealth.) He turns her over to the consul Paschasius, who in
turn summons procurers: "invite a crowd to take their pleasure with this
woman, and let them abuse her until she is dead" (31) [Invitate ad eam
omnem populum et tamdiu illudatur, donec mortua nuntietur, 29]. However, when they try to carry her off, she remains fixed to the ground. Even
a thousand men and a thousand oxen cannot move Lucy. Finally, as in the
story of Euphemia, "the consul's friends, seeing how distressed he was,
plunged a dagger into the martyr's throat" (32) [Videntes autem amici
Paschasii eum angustiari, in gutture ejus gladium immerserunt, 29]. Yes,

how distressed *he* was: just as Priscus was so disturbed by Euphemia's stead-fastness, so is Paschasius at his wit's end because he cannot harm the virgin Lucy. Once again, what cannot be violated by the act of rape is penetrated by a phallic weapon. In fact, that Lucy is stabbed in the throat (*guttur*) may well be significant, for in the gynecology of late antiquity, the throat was considered to be homologous to the neck of the uterus.[53] What cannot be narrated directly is merely suggested through a substitution of body parts. Moreover, that the throat is the site of the voice is surely significant. In this respect, death has a double valence, for while it protects Lucy from her would-be rapists, it also silences her so that she is no longer able to speak to and against her oppressors. It is also worth noting that hanging, not the sword, was "the privileged instrument of female death" in ancient Greece; in Rome, hanging was described as "a feminine death, unworthy of a man," whose only honorable death lay in the sword. In this and other hagiographical tales, it may be that death by the sword actually honors the female virgin martyr by recognizing her *arete* (that is, manliness, which is a quality of the spirit, not the body).[54]

These and other stories of near-rape chronicle the resistance to early Christianity within the cultures of the eastern rim of the Mediterranean but also capture a deep anxiety about how one defines and determines virginity itself. Perhaps more than other notions about human sexuality, virginity is perceived as a "natural" condition, an ideal that resides somewhere in the body and spirit. This belief underpins a number of fundamental assumptions about the ties that bind a society together. Female virginity in particular serves as an important counter in homosocial relations among men. As Patricia Klindienst Joplin provocatively puts it, "the virgin's hymen must not be ruptured except in some manner that reflects and ensures the health of the existing political hierarchy."[55] The Church, in fact, monopolizes the homosocial bond by monopolizing the hymen—by refusing to allow its goods on the market at all.[56] Perpetual virginity is valued precisely because the virgin remains perpetually *un*exchanged.

Gender and Genre

In *The Second Sex,* Simone de Beauvoir notes: "Most female heroines are oddities: adventuresses and originals notable less for the importance of their acts than for the singularity of their fates."[57] This is certainly true of the Christian heroines I have discussed in this chapter. Hagiography specializes in singular fates that take on symbolic, universal significance, as many a medieval hagiographer knows. The Abbot of Bonne-Esperance, for one, is well aware of this feature of the saint's life. In his life of the blessed Oda of Hainault (d. 1158; the Abbot was writing soon after), he describes how she cut off her own nose on the day of her wedding in order to preserve her chastity. Oda's story is unusual in that she is not martyred in attempting to save her virginity—she lives to become a nun and ultimately a prioress. This deviation from the conventions of the saints' life seems to disturb the Abbot's sense of order. He argues that Oda's act of self-mutilation, which had obviously been done out of love for God, is indeed a kind (*genus*) of martyrdom. "Oda is martyr and virgin, because virginity is not possible without martyrdom" [Martyr igitur & Virgo Oda est, quia virginitas esse non potest sine martyrio], he declares.[58] Almost a century later, Thomas Aquinas offers support for the Abbot's position in a *sic et non* disquisition on martyrdom. Under the heading of "Courage" in the *Summa Theologiæ*, he asks, "is death essential to the idea of martyrdom?" [utrum mors sit de ratione martyrii?].[59] Citing Jerome and Gregory, Aquinas first answers:

> Pro integritate carnis servanda aliquæ mulieres legunter laudabiliter vitam suam contempsisse . . . Sed quandoque ipsa integritas carnis aufertur, vel auferri intentatur, pro confessione fidei christianæ . . . Ergo videtur quod martyrium magis debeat dici si aliqua mulier pro fide Christi integritatem carnis perdat, quam si etiam vitam perderet corporalem.

> [We read that certain women held their lives in praiseworthy contempt in order to preserve their physical virginity . . . there are occasions on which persons are robbed of that physical virginity, or an attempt is made to rob them of it, because they confess the Christian faith. . . . So it appears that the term martyrdom should be used rather for a woman's loss of her physical virginity for belief in Christ, than for the further loss of her bodily life.][60]

In this regard, Aquinas specifically mentions Agnes and Lucy. Argued in this way, then, the answer is no: death is not necessary to martyrdom, for rape is a kind of martyrdom in itself. On the other hand, the answer is yes: "the perfect idea of martyrdom requires one to endure death for Christ's sake" [Et ideo ad perfectam rationem martyrii requiritur quod aliquis mortem sustineat propter Christum].[61] Yet this is a qualified yes, for Aquinas goes on to say that his authorities "speak of martyrdom figuratively" [loquuntur de martyrio per quamdam similitudinem].[62] However, since one cannot know if a woman lost her virginity (through rape) for love of Christ, or because she did not value her virginity enough, the question is moot. In short, for many ecclesiastics, as R. Howard Bloch has observed, "the only real virgin . . . is a dead virgin."[63] As I suggested earlier, death is the ultimate form of monologic discourse, the only real insurance against tampering with the borders and boundaries of the body—individual or ecclesiastical.

The Abbot of Bonne-Esperance transforms the stuff of Oda's life into a textual artifact, to be consumed by, and subsumed in, dominant ecclesiastical culture. Along with Aquinas, he asks us to focus not on the literal story but on the figurative. Moreover, I would say that the Abbot impels us to contemplate the genre itself. In fact, I would argue that genre and consecrated virgin follow a very similar trajectory in the hagiographic tale of near-rape. Allon White says that certain genres are

> sealed off from heteroglossia . . . immune from an intertextual interference. Nothing can intervene across their endless cycles of telling and retelling, production and consumption . . . [a genre is] a kind of discursive economy which cannot expand its base because it has not developed a division of linguistic labour to any significant extent.[64]

We can substitute *virgin* for *genre* with uncanny ease: *virgins* are "sealed off from heteroglossia . . . immune from an intertextual interference." And, as I said before, *virgin* is substituted for *church* with equal ease in the long history of Christianity. What Mary Douglas argues in *Purity and Danger* has special relevance here: "the body is a model which can stand for any bounded system. Its boundaries can represent any boundaries which are threatened or precarious . . . the powers and dangers credited to social structure [are] reproduced in small on the human body."[65] Ambrose seems to be as mindful of the implications of Douglas's point as any modern anthropologist would be.

Unrepresentable Rape and the Represented Church

At this juncture, I cannot resist the punning possibilities of the Abbot of Bonne-Esperance's name: he is indeed, like many another believing medieval Christian, in "good hope and expectation" that virginity is both a physical and mental condition that can somehow be recognized and measured, and therefore preserved. If rape is the aporia, the gap in the text, that early patristic and later medieval writers are determined to avoid, then the moment of divine intervention can be read as a moment of *anti*-aporia— an attempt to fix the textual/sexual body for all time.

Within the context of the Church, virginity, I have been arguing, is intended to function as the supreme expression of what Bakhtin calls monologic, or authoritative, discourse. Authoritative discourse is, Bakhtin says, "fully complete"; it

> has but a single meaning, the letter is fully sufficient to the sense and calcifies it . . . it demands our unconditional allegiance . . . authoritative dis-

course permits no play with the context framing it, no play with its borders, no gradual and flexible transitions.[66]

With Bakhtin's words in mind, let us return to the stories of Agatha and Lucy. It seems to me that Quintianus' lust for Agatha cannot be separated from the fact that he is both a) a representative of Roman authority, and b) a pagan. The fight over Agatha's body is thus located firmly in the public sphere—both *his* desire and *her* virginity are politicized. But Agatha's spiritual resolve is stronger than rock or iron. In other words, as Aphrodisia says, "that girl's mind"—as well as her other body parts—is admirably, transcendently monologic. Agatha's virginity shores up the Christian Church and guards against the riot of heteroglossia—Bakhtin's term for multi-voiced and many-intentioned discourse. It is important to note that, in the hagiographical paradigm, in which the details of a particular virgin's martyrdom drive the narrative, a virgin may be tortured—the Syriac hagiographies are particularly graphic in this regard[67]—but she *must* remain intact, sexually inviolate. To imagine her otherwise is too much of a threat to the system. The raped virgin is a paradox, an oxymoron that would cause the whole system of stable, fixed signs to collapse.[68] In this closed literary and hagiographic economy, rape must remain unrepresentable in order to insure that the virgin may continue to function as the first line of defense of the monologic.

The superordinary weight of Lucy's body, in metonymic relation to the religious body, has a special resonance when we pursue this line of thought. Impervious to persuasion, rhetorical or otherwise, Lucy's resolve is both spiritual and literal: she simply cannot be moved. (In these stories of frustrated fathers, suitors, and political appointees, "over my dead body" becomes a literal place indeed.) The metaphors that cluster around the notion of weight are the same that cluster around authoritative discourse. Violation simply cannot exist in the same space.

Authoritative Disorders

I have been arguing that the female virgin functions as a metonym for a monologic discourse that the early Church sought to erect around itself. Rape, the ultimate literal and figurative violation, is absent in the hagiographical narrative because neither the idea of the virgin nor the institution of the Church can tolerate such a violation. Actually, it would be more accurate to say that the virgin represents *a desire for* an absolute, unambiguous, transcendent discourse—a desire that is actually frustrated in and by the very act of attempting to create such a discourse. Consider, for example, how these tales of near-rape skew the narrative focus toward the virgin's body in a way that invites readers and listeners to situate themselves as voyeurs or victims (depending on their subject position). Indeed, a number of scholars have suggested that the stories in which a virgin is stripped, tortured, and/or sent out to be assaulted and defiled had a certain titillating appeal for medieval audiences—and has a similar appeal for modern readers, I should add. (By gathering together these stories, I am aware that I reproduce their titillating effects for yet another audience.) Elizabeth A. Castelli argues that, because the "practices and discourses of martyrdom" are "embedded in an androcentric framework . . . the sexual objectification of women is in some measure predictable and is tied not only to the historical experience of martyrdom but to its retelling."[69] It is in this paradox of vicarious, recurring violation that I would locate a breach in the figuration of the monologic, inviolate virgin. In other words, the very circulation, the constant repetition of the near-rape narrative—and the readerly enjoyment and consumption thereof—threatens and undermines a monologic discourse that hagiography tries to maintain/sustain as it works along its centripetal axis. As Tertullian and other patristic writers asserted over and over again—while violating their own admonitions to so argue— chastity is best maintained by a deliberate non-play of signifiers: by absence and silence. However, hagiography, in which the virgin is made subject to narration, which is inherently unstable and mutable, forces the virgin into play—and it is motion, not stasis, that puts her at risk.

In order to illustrate the point that the menaced virgin's tale often contains the seeds of its own deconstruction, let us return to the legend of Agnes. In defense of her chastity, Agnes uses language that depends upon an eroticized vision of love (recall: "Go away, you spark that lights the fire of sin, you fuel of wickedness, you food of death! I am already pledged to another lover!"). At one point, Agnes even declares to her distressed suitor: "The one I love is far nobler than you . . . his love is chastity itself, his touch holiness, union with him, virginity . . . Already his chaste embraces hold me close, he has united his body to mine" (102) [Illum amo, qui longe to nobilior est . . . cujus amor castitas est, tactus sanctitas, unio virginitas . . . Jam amplexibus ejus castis adstricta sum; jam corpus ejus corpori meo sociatum est, 114]. Agnes—so willing to speak and so willing to allow her words to be used against her—is produced by an appropriated discourse in which the language of carnal love is used to represent a purely spiritual ardor. Such words incite everyone who hears her, first to anger, then to lust, and finally to murder. (Agnes has a profane cousin in Iphigenia: both women sacrifice themselves on the altar of the monologic for a cause that insists on their compliance and complicity.) The struggle for her body/the Church's body is explicitly located in a discourse that never fully escapes or suppresses its original context. This language actually compromises Agnes's inviolate position because of its profane resonances. In its often-eroticized narratives of torture, threatened sexual assault, and murder, the story of the menaced virgin often reveals—or at least hints at—that which it seeks to suppress.The near-rape narrative is a bait-and-switch game that always leaves the audience fully aware of the bait that has been withheld.

To paraphrase Clifford Geertz, the saint's life is a story that Christians of late antiquity and the Middle Ages told themselves about themselves.[70] And they told it over and over again, following a script first written on Christ's body. One of the effects of this repetitive performance is to elide "real" experience, real suffering, real death in order to privilege both an Imaginary and an imaginary past. Moreover, hagiography, its miraculous content and repetitive formulae, its borrowings (obvious to us in hindsight, but perhaps just as obvious to much of its original readership, or at least to a portion of its educated readership), its resistance to documentation and authentication, and its overt ideological intentions, interrogates history in its most empirical, transparent form. Put another way, *Christianity* is capable of resisting history—that is, human-made history—in order to privilege an eschatology in which truth-value is registered on a different scale altogether.

Art historian Adrienne Auslander Munich says that "absolute virginity tells no story about itself but enables the story to be told."[71] "The story to be told" is not that of Euphemia, Agnes, Agatha, or Lucy, or Thecla—or of Iconium, Agape, Chionia, Hirena, or other menaced virgins—but of the ecclesiastical body that subsumes theirs. Hagiography, in telling the story of the menaced virgin martyr, is really telling the story of a Church that reserved to itself the right to recognize, sanction, and reward virginity.

Notes

1. Robertson Davies, *Fifth Business* (Hammondsworth: Penguin Books, 1993), p. 136.
2. *De. S. Liberata Alias Wilgeforte Virgine et Martyre,* Acta Sanctorum, V Iul.: 50–70 (July 20). Gregory the Great tells a similar story about a young widow named Galla who did not want to remarry, but who had, Gregory says, "a very passionate nature." Doctors warned her that she would grow a beard if she did not marry again—presumably if she did not engage in intercourse. She withdrew into a convent, undismayed by her beard, "since her body was not the object of her heavenly spouse's love." *Dialogues,* trans. Odo John Zimmerman (NewYork: Fathers of the Church 39, 1959), p. 206.
3. Hayden White, "The Question of Narrative in Contemporary Historical Theory," *The Content of the Form* (Baltimore and London: Johns Hopkins University Press, 1987), 26–57, p. 44.

4. White, "The Question of Narrative," p. 45.

5. Michel Foucault, *Discipline and Punish: The Birth of the Prison* (1975), trans. Alan Sheridan (New York: Vintage Books, 1977), p. 137.

6. Jerome, Epistola XII, "To Eustochium," in *Select Letters of St. Jerome,* ed. T. E. Page, E. Capps, and W. H. D. Rouse, trans. F. A. Wright (Cambridge, MA: Harvard University Press/Loeb Classsical Library, 1933), pp. 104–105. Ambrose, *De Virginibus* II, *PL* 16.225.

7. Ambrose, Epistola LXIII, "Letter to the Church at Vercelli," *Saint Ambrose: Letters,* trans. Sister Mary Melchior Berenka (New York: Fathers of the Church, 1954), pp. 333–334. Latin: PL 16.1250.

8. Peter Brown, *The Body and Society: Men, Women, and Sexual Renunciation in Early Christianity* (New York: Columbia University Press, 1988) p. 356. Later on, such canonists as Tancred (1078? – 1112) and Innocent IV (1200 – 1254) quite explicitly work out the metonymic relationship of the female virgin to the institutionalized Church in order to explain why it is necessary to monitor a woman's behavior and control her desires. See James A. Brundage, *Law, Sex, and Society in Medieval Europe* (Chicago and London: University of Chicago Press, 1987), pp. 350–351, 427.

9. Foucault, *Discipline,* p. 136.

10. Gravdal does mention in passing the topoi of forced prostitution and forced marriage in which divine intervention is featured. See *Ravishing Maidens: Writing Rape in Medieval French Literature and Law* (Philadelphia: University of Pennsylvania Press, 1991), pp. 22–24.

11. According to Sherry Reames in *The* Legenda Aurea: *A Reexamination of Its Paradoxical History* (Madison and London: University of Wisconsin P, 1985), p. 4. Reames approaches hagiography from a historian's point of view, and in doing so finds Voragine's text wanting. She is quick to point out that contrary to what many modern readers have thought of the text, it is not the sum of what medieval people thought about hagiography, or even "a splendid representative of its genre, or even a very adequate one," p. 7. Nevertheless, as an influential text in the Middle Ages, it is ideal for my purposes. I follow Reames on dating here.

12. Simon Gaunt, *Gender and Genre* (Cambridge: Cambridge University Press, 1996), p. 183.

13. Hayden White, *Metahistory: The Historical Imagination in Nineteenth-Century Europe* (Baltimore and London: Johns Hopkins University Press, 1973), pp. 34–35.

14. Jocelyn Wogan-Browne, "Saints' Lives and the Female Reader," *Forum for Modern Language Studies* 27.4 (1991): 314–332, p. 317. Wogan-Browne asks, "Did twelfth- and thirteenth-century girls *need* to develop wills capable of withstanding floggings, flesh-hooks and lighted tapers?" p. 316. She argues for a "potential relation between model virgin lives and the experience of the women who read them," for the possibility that many young women "might have to develop a will capable of withstanding . . . emotional and social pressures" p. 321. Wogan-Browne's point is vividly

supported by Jane Tibbets Schulenberg in her essay, "The Heroics of Virginity: Brides of Christ and Sacrificial Mutilation," discussed below. Many fine studies exist that historicize how and why the saints' legends in the Middle Ages were written and read. In addition to Wogan-Browne's and Shulenberg's work, see Sheila Delany's introduction to *A Legend of Holy Women: A Translation of Osbern Bokenham's* Legends of Holy Women (Notre Dame and London: University of Notre Dame Press, 1992). Delaney takes great pains to contextualize the first audience—the nuns of the Clare Priory in Suffolk, England—for Osbern Bokenham's *Legendys of Hooly Wummen* (after 1447), the first all-female hagiography. (This contains a number of stories about virgin martyrs who managed to keep their vow of chastity against all odds, from an unwelcome marriage proposal to rape.) Both Wogan-Browne and Brigette Cazelles (Introduction, *The Lady as Saint: A Collection of French Hagiographic Romances of the Thirteenth Century* [Philadelphia: University of Pennsylvania Press, 1991]), in their respective examinations of vernacular hagiography of the twelfth and thirteenth centuries, show that the story of the menaced virgin was very popular in England and France at this time, citing specific historical circumstances for this popularity.

15. *Acts of Paul and Thecla,* in *New Testament Apocrypha,* Vol. 2., ed. Wilhelm Schneemelcher (German); R. M. Wilson (English) (Westminster: John Knox Press, rev. ed. 1993), pp. 239–246. The story of the attempted rape at the end of Thecla's life is not preserved in all manuscripts; it can be found in *The Apocryphal New Testament,* ed. J. K. Elliott (Oxford: Oxford University Press, 1993), p. 372. Another early tale of circumvented rape can be found in the *Acts of Saint John* (second half, second century to first half, third century). Here, the pious Drusiana dies from shame when the obsessed (if not diabolically possessed) Andronicus threatens her with rape. Andronicus goes so far as to break into Drusiana's tomb in order to have intercourse with her dead body, but is prevented by an angel from doing so. *Acts of St. John,* in *New Testament Apocrypha,* Vol. 2, ed. Schneemelcher, pp. 194–201. Drusiana is later resurrected, and her would-be seducer reformed. She is the subject of a play by Hrotsvit, titled *Callimachus.*

16. *Acts of Paul and Thecla,* p. 278.

17. See George Hicks, *The Comfort Women: Japan's Brutal Regime of Enforced Prostitution in the Second World War* (New York: Norton, 1995). In their introduction to *Holy Women of the Syrian Orient* (Berkeley: University of California Press, 1987), a collection of translated saints' lives, Sebastian P. Brock and Susan Ashbrook Harvey say: "While historians have generally viewed the extent of . . . violence to be a literary exaggeration, our experience of torture in the twentieth century has taught us the extremes that can in fact be administered and suffered." They go on to say: "Still, in these martyr's stories a religious motive is present . . . The hagiographer's stylized portrayal of the martyr's interrogation, torture, and death represents these events as containing a greater significance than their physical occurrence

would indicate . . . literarily the violence is such that it moves all the participants beyond the realm of humanity," p. 17.

18. Eusebius, *Ecclesiastical History,* trans. Philip Schaff and Heny Wace, (1890; Nicene and Post-Nicene Fathers vol. 1, 2nd series, rpt. Peabody, MA: Hendrickson, 1994),VIII.XIX, p. 337. Eusebius adds: "Many others, unable even to listen to the threat of violation from the heathen rulers, endured every form of tortures, and rackings, and deadly punishment," p. 337. G. E. M. de Ste. Croix's "Aspects of the 'Great' Prosecution" (*Harvard Theological Review* XLVII.1 [January 1954]: 75–113) is still the definitive introduction to the Great Persecutions. For the historical background to the persecutions, as well as an assessment of Eusebius' works, see Timothy D. Barnes, *Constantine and Eusebius* (Cambridge, MA: Harvard University Press, 1991). Compare the *Acts of the Edessan Martyrs,* in which it is said that "priests and deacons were being tormented with bitter burdens, and Daughters of the Covenant were standing in bitter exposure, and Christians were all in afflictions and anguish," and that "chaste women [were] exposed and Daughters of the Covenant despised, or believers persecuted and women carried away captive." "Martyrdom of Shmona and Guria, Confessors of Edessa," in *Euphemia and the Goth, with the Acts of Martyrdom of the Confessors of Edessa,* ed. F. C. Burkitt (London: Williams and Norgate, 1913), pp. 90, 109.

19. Eusebius, *Ecclesiastical History* VIII.IX, p. 329.

20. Eusebius, *Ecclesiastical History* VIII.XII, p. 332; also told by Chrysostom in his homily, "Saints Bernice and Prosdoce," PG 50.629–40.

21. Eusebius, *Martyrs of Palestine* V, p. 347.

22. Eusebius, *Ecclesiastical History* VI.V, p. 253. Palladius tells the story of Potamiæna in his *Historia Lausiaca* (early fifth century). In the *Historia,* she is a slave whose master could not convince her to yield to his advances. The master accuses her of being a Christian, and, worse, critical of the Emperors and their policy of persecution. He bribes the judge to break her, or, failing that, to kill her so that she might not accuse him before the world. *Acta et temperantia Potamiænæ,* PG 34.1014. English translation by Robert T. Meyer, *Palladius: The Lausiac History* (Westminster, MD: The Newman Press and London: Longmans, 1965), pp. 34–35.

23. Eusebius, *Martyrs of Palestine* VI, p. 252.

24. As Timothy Barnes suggested in a letter to the author, January 3, 1996.

25. Eusebius, *Ecclesiastical History* VIII.II, p. 324.

26. Ambrose, *De Virginibus* II.IV, in *St. Ambrose: Select Works and Letters,* trans. H. de Romestin (Nicene and Post-Nicene Fathers 10, 2nd series, 1890; Peabody, MA: Hendrickson, rpt. 1994), p. 377. Latin: PL 16.225. Also in the *Legenda Aurea,* LXII.

27. Ambrose, *De Virginibus,* p. 377. Latin: PL 16.225.

28. Ambrose, *De Virginibus,* PL 16.201.

29. Augustine, *De Civitate Dei,* ed. and trans. George E. McCracken (Loeb Classical Library, Cambridge MA: Harvard University Press; London, William Heinemann, 1957), I.XVI.

30. Augustine, *De Civitate Dei*, I.XVI.

31. Augustine, *De Civitate Dei*, I.XVIII, I.XVI. See Jerome, "To Eustochium": "Perit ergo et mente virginitas. Istae sunt virgines malae, virgines carne, non spiritu" [Virginity therefore can be lost even by a thought. Those are the evil virgins, virgins in the flesh, but not in the spirit], pp. 62–63. Pope Leo (d. 461) takes up the nature of violated virginity in a letter to the Bishops of Africa about a number of consecrated virgins who had apparently been raped. The women were anxious about their continued status as virgins. Leo regrets that these women ("handmaids of the lord who lost their perfect virginity because they were violated by barbarians") can no longer compare themselves to "undefiled virgins." Pope Leo, Epistola XII, in *Correspondence*, trans. Edmund Hunt (New York: Fathers of the Church 34, 1957), pp. 54–55. Latin: PL 54.653.

32. Brundage, *Law*, p. 46.

33. Aldhelm, *De Virginibus*, trans. Callam, p. 364; PL 16.201.

34. Tacitus, *The Annals of Tacitus*, trans. John Jackson (Loeb 1937; rpt. 1951), VI.v.9, pp. 150–151.

35. Suetonius, *Suetonius: The Lives of the Caesars*, ed. J. C. Rolfe (Loeb Classical Library, NY: Macmillan; London, William Heinemann, 1924) Book III, *Tiberius*, 61, pp. 380–381.

36. Tertullian, in *Tertullian: Apology and De Spectaculis [and Minucius Felix]*, trans. T. R. Glover (Loeb Classical Library, Cambridge MA: Harvard University Press; London, William Heinemann, 1977), pp. 226–227.

37. Tertullian, *Works*, 2 vols., ed. H. J. Thomson (Harvard University Press, 1949–1953), pp. 338–339, ll. 23–25.

38. Seneca the Elder, *Controversiae*, ed. Michael Winterbottom (Loeb Classical Library, Cambridge MA: Harvard University Press; London, William Heinemann, 1975), 1.2, pp. 58–59.

39. See Gail Paterson Corrington, "The 'Divine Woman'? Propaganda and the Power of Celibacy in the New Testament Apocrypha: A Reconsideration," *Anglican Theological Review* 70 (1988): 207–220. Rpt. in *Studies in Early Christianity: A Collection of Scholarly Essays*, ed. Everett Ferguson (New York: Garland: 1993), pp. 169–182. Also see Tomas Hägg, *The Novel in Antiquity* (Swedish, 1980) (Berkeley and Los Angeles: University of California Press, 1983; rev. ed. 1991), 154ff., and "The *Parthenope Romance* Decapitated?" *Symbolae Osloenses* LIX (1984): 61–92.

40. The dates of these texts are taken from *Collected Ancient Greek Novels*, trans. B. P. Reardon (Berkeley and Los Angeles: University of California Press, 1989). In *The Novel in Antiquity*, Hägg notes that the legend of Thecla has much in common with the Greek novel, but he is cautious when it comes to ascribing influence, pp. 160–61. He speculates that "the same readership which provided a market for the Hellenistic novel was now devouring stories about apostles, martyrs, and saints," p. 161, and argues that "a new historical situation, with new demands, gave rise to a new literary form, which borrowed freely from predecessors and contemporaries," p. 161.

Hägg argues that chronology, the actual production and dissemination of the Greek novel as represented by Chariton and Xenophon, seems to taper off in the second century. These texts were followed by the so-called Sophistic novels (by Tatius, Longus, and Heliodorus); thus Hägg sees a break between the earlier Greek novel, which may have had an impact on Apocryphal Acts, but the Sophistic novel did not. Also see Kate Cooper, *The Virgin and the Bride: Idealized Womanhood in Late Antiquity* (Cambridge, MA: Harvard University Press, 1996), who describes the Apocryphal Acts as a "penumbral manifestation of the romance phenomenon," p. 44, and notes the "uncanny" resemblance between Leukippe and the Christian heroine, p. 30; and see Reardon, Introduction, *Collected Ancient Greek Novels,* pp. 3–9. Simon Goldhill's *Foucault's Virginity: Ancient Erotic Fiction and the History of Sexuality* (Cambridge: Cambridge University Press, 1995) is a particularly witty and insightful reading of the Greek novel.

41. See Ian Donaldson, *The Rapes of Lucretia: A Myth and its Transformations* (Oxford: Clarendon Press, 1982).

42. Sherry B. Ortner, "The Virgin and the State," *Feminist Studies* 4 (1978): 19–35, p. 23.

43. Graham Pechey, "Bakhtin, Marxism and Post-Structuralism," *Literature, Politics, and Theory,* ed. Francis Barker, Peter Hulme, Margaret Iversen, and Diana Loxley (London and New York: Methuen, 1986), p. 123.

44. Ambrose, *De Virginibus,* Chapter II, p. 364.

45. A. J. Denomy, *The Old French Lives of Saint Agnes and Other Vernacular Versions of the Middle Ages* (Cambridge, MA: Harvard University Press, 1938), p. 3. See also Anne-Marie Palmer, *Prudentius on the Martyrs* (Oxford: Clarendon, 1989), pp. 250–253. I am particularly indebted to Denomy's discussion of the origin of the legend of St. Agnes and of the various problems concerning dates and influences (pp. 3–32).

46. See Denomy, *Lives of Saint Agnes,* p. 154.

47. Jody Enders, "Medieval Snuff Drama," *Exemplaria* X.1 (Spring 1998), 171–206, p. 179.

48. Donna Haraway, "A Cyborg Manifesto: Science, Technology, and Socialist-Feminism in the Late Twentieth Century," in *Simians, Cyborgs, and Women: The Reinvention of Nature* (New York; Routledge), 149–181, p. 164.

49. See Eusebius, *Martyrs of Palestine* IX, for the story of the virgin Ennathas who is stripped and exhibited in the city of Caesarea. Trans. Philip Schaff and Henry Wace, and found between Book VIII and IX of the *Ecclesiastical History* (Nicene and Post-Nicene Fathers 1, 2nd ser. (1890; Peabody, MA: Hendrickson, rpt. 1994), pp. 350–351. See also *Holy Women of the Syrian Orient,* trans. with an introduction by Sebastian P. Brock and Susan Ashbrook Harvey (Berkeley and London: University of California Press, 1987), the legends of Anahid, p. 94; Elizabeth, p. 106; Mahya, p. 110; and Febronia, p. 165.

50. *The Golden Legend,* 2 vols., trans. William Granger Ryan (Princeton: Princeton University Press, 1993), p. 182. The Latin is from *Legenda Aurea,*

3rd ed., ed. T. Graesse (1890; Osnabrück: Zeller, photo rep. 1965), p. 621. Henceforth, page numbers will appear in the body of the text.

51. Elizabeth Petroff, in "Eloquence and Heroic Virginity in Hrotsvit's Verse Legends," argues that Hrotsvit's heroic virgins "must be killed with heroic weapons, the weapons of personal combat." *Hrotsvit of Gandersheim: Rara Avis in Saxonia?*, ed. Katharina M. Wilson (Ann Arbor: University of Michigan/MARC, 1987), 229–238, p. 236. Susan Ashbrook Harvey makes the point that "the deed must be done by human hands"; that is, not by some force of nature, such as fire or wild beasts. "Violence, Gender, and God: Male and Female Martyrs in the Early Church," paper presented at Amherst College (December, 1989).

52. For Candida and Febronia, see Brock and Harvey, pp. 181 and 168.

53. Ann Hanson and David Armstrong, "The Virgin's Voice and Neck: Aeschylus, *Agamemnon* 245 and Other Texts," *Bulletin of the Institute of Classical Studies* 33 (1986): 97–100. Hanson and Armstrong read allusions to an enlarged neck in Greek literary texts as a reference to loss of virginity. The neck in these texts functions as a homology to the neck of the uterus, which, according to Greek medical lore, widens for the first time after first intercourse. And since it was thought that one acquired a deeper voice when the neck was made wider, a change in voice was considered an index of chastity.

54. Eva Cantarella, "Dangling Virgins: Myth, Ritual and the Place of Women in Ancient Greece," *Poetics Today* 6.1–2 (1985): 91–101, p. 92. I quote Cantarella's paraphrase of Pacatus, p. 95.

55. Patricia Klindienst Joplin, "The Voice of the Shuttle is Ours," *Stanford Literature Review* 1 (1984): 25–53, p. 38.

56. I echo Luce Irigaray here, who, in discussing another topic altogether—the rich possibilities and circularities of lesbianism—asks, "*But what if the 'goods' refused to go to market at all?*" "When the Goods Get Together" (1977), trans. Claudia Reeder, rpt. in *New French Feminisms,* ed. Elaine Marks and Isabelle de Courtivron (New York: Schocken Books, 1981), 107–110, p. 110.

57. Simone de Beauvoir, *The Second Sex,* trans. and ed. H. M. Parshley (1952; New York: Random House/Vintage Books, 1989), p. 131.

58. *De Venerabili Oda, Acta Sanctorum,* April 2: 770–778 (April 20), 776. I owe this cite to Schulenberg, "Heroics," pp. 48–49.

59. Thomas Aquinas, *Summa Theologiæ* 2a2æ.124, 4, pp. 50–51.

60. Thomas Aquinas, *Summa Theologiæ* 2a2æ.124,4, pp. 50–51.

61. Thomas Aquinas, *Summa Theologiæ* 2a2æ.124, 4, p. 52–53.

62. Thomas Aquinas, *Summa Theologiæ* 2a2æ.124, 4, pp. 52–53.

63. R. Howard Bloch, *Medieval Misogyny and the Invention of Western Romantic Love* (Chicago: University of Chicago Press, 1991), p. 108.

64. Allon White, "Bakhtin, Sociolinguistics and Deconstruction," *The Theory of Reading,* ed. Frank Gloversmith (New York: Barnes and Noble; Sussex, England: Harvester Press, 1984), 123–146, p. 130.

65. Mary Douglas, *Purity and Danger* (1966; London and New York: Routledge, 1991), p. 115.

66. Mikhail Bakhtin, "Discourse in the Novel," in *The Dialogic Imagination,* trans. Caryl Emerson and Michael Holquist, ed. Michael Holquist (Austin: University of Texas Press, 1981), p. 343. The monologic, Bakhtin says, permits no "zone of contact," p. 345.

67. See, for example, the story of Febronia in *Holy Women of the Syrian Orient* (Brock and Harvey), 150–176. In this Syriac legend (late sixth- to early seventh-century; translated from a manuscript of the ninth century), Febronia is told by her older female companions that the tyrants "will grab you, seeing that you are young and beautiful, and they will upset you with their advances and words of seducement," p. 159. But they do much worse. She is stripped, whipped with rods, her intestines are burned with fire, her torso is raked with iron nails, her teeth pulled out, her breasts cut off (in spite of the crowd's pleading for mercy), and her chest burned with fire. Her right foot and her hands are cut off, and finally she is decapitated. In a fifth-century Persian legend in the Brock and Harvey collection, one Anahid has her breasts torn off by having string tied around them and pulled, p. 95.

68. See Joplin, "Voice," p. 42.

69. Elizabeth A. Castelli, "Visions and Voyeurism: Holy Women and the Politics of Sight in Early Christianity," *Center for Hermeneutical Studies,* New Series 2 (December 6, 1992): 1–27, p. 8.

70. Clifford Geertz, "Deep Play: Notes on the Balinese Cockfight," *The Interpretation of Cultures* (New York: Basic Books, 1973), 412–453, p. 448.

71. Adrienne Auslander Munich, "What Lily Knew: Virginity in the 1890s," *Virginal Sexuality and Textuality in Victorian Literature,* ed. Lloyd Davis (Albany: State University of New York Press, 1993), 143–157, p. 145.

CHAPTER 7

VIRGINITY AND SACRIFICE IN
CHAUCER'S "PHYSICIAN'S TALE"

Sandra Pierson Prior

> *"The Physician's Tale" has much to tell about the problems and inconsistencies that characterize the medieval Christian valorization of virginity; three ideas of virginity combine and conflict within the narrative.*

"The Physician's Tale" is one of Chaucer's most unpopular tales, and for good reason, since it is, by virtually any critical judgment, a badly told story: inconsistent in tone, inept in story line, incoherent in sentence, and devoid of *solaas*. Even Harry Bailly, our oft-fumbling but seldom completely inaccurate surrogate reader, is so upset by this tale of the virginal Virginia that he afterwards demands instant remedy: either "triacle / Or elles a draughte of moyste and corny ale" (314–315) or, better yet, "som myrthe or japes right anon" from the Pardoner (VI, 319).[1]

Despite its flaws—even in part because of them—the tale told by the Physician, one of only two stories in *The Canterbury Tales* with a virgin as its protagonist, has much to tell us about the problems and inconsistencies that characterize the medieval Christian valorization of virginity. Central to Chaucer's implicit critique of virginity is Virginia's allusion to the biblical tale of Jephtha and his daughter. By adding this seemingly inappropriate reference, Chaucer signals his rereading of the story of Virginia as a tale not so much about failed justice or preserved virginity as about a daughter sacrificed by her father.

Before examining the critical passage about Jephtha, I would like first to review the story of Virginius and Virginia, as Chaucer received it. In Livy and most of the other versions derived from Livy, the exemplum illustrates the failures of a corrupt justice system. Virginius, a Roman plebian, has a young daughter, patronymically named Virginia, who is engaged to Icilius, a young Roman of the same class. A corrupt magistrate, Apius, lusts for Virginia and plots to get possession of her. He arranges for a false suit against Virginia to be brought by his collaborator, and Virginius, with no hope for a fair hearing and therefore no possibility for exposing the falsehood and perjury, feels he has only two choices: turn his daughter over to the magistrate or kill her. Kill her he does, thus confirming that the virtuous plebians are helpless against the corrupt decemvirate and that society no longer has a rule of law to protect the innocent against evil.[2]

The tale of Virginius and Virginia enjoyed great popularity in the Middle Ages and has survived in several versions, of which the closest to Chaucer (and certainly either his only source or his principal one),[3] is Jean de Meun's, in the section of the *Roman de la Rose* in which Reason is explaining the relationship between Justice and Love.[4] Jean de Meun has kept some of Livy's concern with social order and the workings of justice, but he has shortened the story to a brief exemplum and in doing so has cut much of the dramatic dialogue in the court scene and dropped various details concerning Virginia, such as the fact that she is engaged to Icilius.

In *The Canterbury Tales,* Chaucer has also omitted mention of Icilius, and with him any suggestion that Virginia has a future as a married woman. In addition, "The Physician's Tale" leaves out much of the legal process and the exchange in court, which are recounted in detail in Livy and even picked up somewhat in Jean de Meun's much abbreviated version. In place of the climactic courtroom scene, which gives a public and social context to Livy's tale, Chaucer has added a melodramatic scene between Virginia and her father, which takes place in their home.

Further, to highlight the perfection of this virgin, Chaucer has made two important additions at the beginning of the story: a passage describing Nature's role in making Virginia; and, immediately following, another passage admonishing the audience to protect "lordes doghtres" (73) as valuable property. These important additions, when combined with Chaucer's other changes to Livy's story, work to draw our attention to Virginia and especially to her purity. Moreover, since Chaucer's version, unlike Jean de Meun's, is about the same length as Livy's,[5] the focus of Chaucer's tale has shifted markedly from a miscarriage of justice to a tragic sacrifice of a pure virgin, set within the private, domestic world of father and daughter.

"The Physician's Tale" begins by strenuously protesting the value of virginity, but it does not tell us why virginity is precious—no doubt because the views on virginity in the later Middle Ages draw on two quite different traditions: the pagan Roman one and the medieval Christian, monastic one. In the Roman tradition, the virginal daughter and the chaste wife are supremely valued because they are central to a patrilineal society, since only chaste women—virgins before marriage and monogamous afterwards—can guarantee that a man's sons are his biologically.[6] In fact, Livy's Virginius is horrified by Apius's attempt to acquire Virginia precisely because it will doom his daughter to concubinage or prostitution instead of the respectable marriage that was to have been her future.[7] For Livy, and for his pagan Roman society, perpetual virginity in women is as unthinkable, if not more so, as sexual promiscuity.[8]

Many of the assumptions and effects of this patriarchal view of virginity survived in Western European society and are still implicit in "The Physician's Tale," where, as in pagan societies, virginity is basically a physical fact and valuable not so much to the virgin herself as to the "owner" of that virginity—an ownership that in the story of Virginia is in dispute. However, "The Physician's Tale" does not embrace the other implicit assumption in Livy's tale, namely that virginity is only important because ultimately it will be lost (when the virgin marries and moves on to her destined role as a fruitful, chaste wife). Rather Chaucer's version seems to assume that Virginia will remain a virgin all her earthly life, and in this respect the tale's values are not those of a patriarchal culture but of the European monastic tradition, which idealizes a virgin of a very different kind.

Going back ultimately to gnostic beliefs and practices as well as to Pauline moral theology, virginity in the monastic tradition gained its fullest articulation with Ambrose, Augustine, and Jerome. The supreme Christian virtue, virginity—and now I mean perpetual, life-long virginity—represents perfection and rewards its exemplars the highest place in heaven and the greatest admiration in this.[9] As the Wife of Bath points out, a commitment to perpetual virginity asks for a superhuman (and therefore perhaps an antihuman) perfection, and, moreover, if embraced by all, that commitment would end the human race on earth (*Canterbury Tales* III 71–72, 105–112).[10]

In medieval adaptations of Virginia's story, it is inevitable that the stronger or at least more frequently and more explicitly articulated tradition of perpetual virginity should creep into what was originally a tale set in a pagan patriarchal society, which valued virginity for quite different reasons. The resulting clash between these two late medieval views on virginity accounts for some of the inconsistent and confusing attitudes in Chaucer's "Physician's Tale," which combines the patriarchal tradition that values virginity for the sake of marrying off the girl with the monastic attitude that exalts virginity for the sake of cloistering and perfecting the

Christian. However, the tale suffers the further burden of a third view, even less explicit than the pagan one but powerful in its effects: the sacrifical/cultic tradition that values virginity for the sake of killing and/or offering up a perfect victim.

The need for a perfect victim is imbedded in much of medieval Christianity's assumptions about purity and in certain of its inherited ancient myths. It is explicitly a concern in eucharistic theology, where Christ's sinlessness and perfection as a human render him a "pure" and "holy" and "spotless victim," worthy to atone for the sins of all humanity.[11] For medieval Christianity, virginity is the single most important aspect of purity in humans; virginity is what can make a human being worthy of being sacrificed to God. (For now let us assume we are speaking both figuratively—sacrifice in the sense of a person's giving herself or himself to God—and literally, as a victim immolated on an altar.) This aspect of Christianity's view on virginity probably owes something to the older, Greco-Roman tradition of Vestal Virgins, but it is important to note that the Vestal Virgins, like the marriageable ones still at home, were not expected to remain virgins for the rest of their lives, but only until the term of their service to the temple ended after thirty years.[12]

In "The Physician's Tale," it is the evocation of the story of Jephtha's daughter that points simultaneously to a virgin's place in a patriarchal culture and also to her potential role as a sacrificial victim. The reference is made by Virginia herself, who suddenly and strikingly has been given voice in the climactic scene of the tale. Having briefly pleaded for an alternative *remedye* (236), Virginia accepts her father's sentence of death with but one last request:

> "Thanne yif me leyser, fader myn," quod she,
> "My deeth for to compleyne a litel space;
> For, pardee, Jepte yaf his doghter grace
> For to compleyne, er he hir slow, allas!
> And, God it woot, no thyng was hir trespas,
> But for she ran hir fader first to see,
> To welcome hym with greet solempnitee." (238–244)

Virginia is referring to the story in Judges, in which Jephtha the Gileadite prays to God for victory and offers to sacrifice the first living thing he meets if and when he returns victorious.[13] Tragically and perhaps inevitably, the person who greets Jeptha is his only daughter (and only child), "who came forth, playing the tambourines and dancing" (Judges 11.34). Learning of her fate as sacrificial victim, Jephtha's daughter asks first to "mourn [her] virginity" (Judges 11.37)—that is, to mourn that she will die a virgin, without ever fulfilling her womanly role to marry and bear children. Her request granted, she departs for the hills with a small company of women for companions and remains there for two months before returning to die at her father's hands.

Given the assumption in "The Physician's Tale" that Virginia is to die in order to remain a virgin, the story of Jephtha seems a singularly inept allusion (and in fact several critics have taken it as proof that indeed the Physician's "studie was but litel on the Bible," as asserted in his portrait [GP I, 438]).[14] If Virginia were to invoke a biblical type, Susannah would seem the more appropriate predecessor.[15] Susannah's story, like Virginia's, involves lust, perjury, and a corrupt justice system, over which God's justice ultimately triumphs through the brilliant legal defense of the prophet Daniel. Unlike Susannah, however, Virginia has no divine judge in whom to place her trust. Further, Virginia and her father never seem to consider the possibility of fighting against a false lawsuit and a corrupt justice system. The question of justice—good or bad—has been implicitly laid aside by Virginius and is never mentioned by Virginia, who moves instead into the mode of sacrifice.

For one thing is clear about the supposedly inappropriate story of Jephtha's daughter: as a type of ritual sacrifice, more specifically of a sacrifice performed by a father on his daughter (the only such in all of Christian or Jewish sacred scriptures),[16] the story of Jephtha's daughter prefigures Virginia's death, in its actions, if not in its sentiments. In fact, Virginia's biblical allusion gives the fullest clue that "The Physician's Tale" actually records an unholy sacrifice. Once viewed as a story of child sacrifice, "The Physician's Tale" makes far more sense. The interpolations and digressions (such as the set piece on Nature's supreme power to create), the pathos and melodrama of the climactic scene, even the ugly violence of the ending—all these modifications to the received tale are appropriate in an account of pagan sacrifice.

Superficially, Virginius's sacrifice of his daughter could be seen as Christian, and has been interpreted so by several critics, who point to the figurative possibilities in the Jephtha story, especially as a type of the Crucifixion.[17] While there is no doubt that sacrifice is central to Christian teaching, there are vast differences between the Christian theology of sacrifice and the mode of sacrifice at work in "The Physician's Tale." Further, as Hoffman himself shows, it is a vexed question as to whether Jephtha's sacrifice constitutes a type of the Crucifixion or an unsanctioned sacrifice, with the weight of exegetical opinion definitely towards the latter. In fact, from patristic times the majority of commentators have strongly condemned Jephtha's vow as unholy,[18] since orthodox teaching in Judaism and Christianity insists that God does not demand human sacrifice and indeed is only offended by the offer of it.

Rather than trying to force this ugly story into a type of Christian sacrifice, we would do better to consider sacrifice in its largest context, which includes pagan, not just Christian, sacrifices. For whatever it may share with other rituals of human sacrifice, the sacrifice of Christ has certainly been cleansed of the most horrific aspects of killing a human being to appease a god, in part because Christ goes to his death willingly and in part because he *is* the god as well as the victim.

Nonetheless, Christ's Crucifixion and the story of Abraham and Isaac do share an important feature with the stories of Virginius and Jephtha: a father's sacrifice of his precious child. There is, however, a clear distinction between Christ and Isaac, on the one hand, and Virginia and Jephtha's daughter, on the other. While the latter are only children of fathers who have no sons (not apparently the case in any versions of Virginia's story except Chaucer's),[19] as girls they are necessarily less valuable in a patriarchal culture than a son would be. In contrast, Isaac is a far more valuable victim than a daughter, since he is the male child through whom Yahweh has promised Abraham's seed will descend and grow to a nation. And, of course, as the son of God, Christ is the perfect sacrifice, the supreme offering to the Christian god. Further, Virginius' and Jephtha's daughters really die, whereas Christ is resurrected and Isaac is spared at the last minute by divine intervention.[20]

The divine intervention in Isaac's case, with its last-minute substitution of a ram as victim, points to an important aspect of sacrifice. According to Maccoby in his illuminating study, *Sacred Executioner,* substitution is a central feature in rituals of sacrifice and in the myths that grew out of them. Maccoby cites the story of Cain and Abel, in which Cain is allotted a brother to kill instead of a son. By doubling Adam's sons, the story provides for the executioner, Cain, and the expendable victim, Abel—with Seth added as the heir to continue the line.[21] Maccoby explains that Abel's expendability is attested to by his name [*hevel*], which means "vapour," evidence that this sacrificed human is "a mere wraith, substituted for a more substantial and shocking reality."[22]

Isaac, however, is not so easily given up, since it is through him that Yahweh has promised to make a "great nation" (Genesis 17.20). Jephtha's daughter, on the other hand, is clearly not so valuable to the patriarchal community, while no one could be less "substantial" than the Virginia of "The Physician's Tale" (unless it is the Virginia in other versions). Until the climactic scene added by Chaucer, Virginia is a nonperson—only a girl, without voice, without character, without even her own name, apart from a patronymic. As the expendable, feminine form of her father, Virginia is cut off—circumcised, as it were, like the foreskins that replace baby boys as sacrifices to God.

The problem with seeing Virginia as an easily sacrificed extra is that "The Physician's Tale" goes to such lengths to stress her value. However, such an apparent contradiction is not really a problem, for sacrifice always involves the tricky business of juggling the need to sacrifice with our guilt and horror—the more precious the victim, the greater the guilt and reluctance; the more worthy the victim, the greater the satisfaction of the need (whether divine or human). It is also fairly common in human experience to praise what we give away, while knowing we are usually giving only what we can afford to lose.

In "The Physician's Tale" virginity is at the crux of both the victim's value and her expendability. As a virgin, physically intact and inviolate, kept within her father's home, innocent and whole and enclosed, Virginia is a part of Virginius and his household. Once she is decapitated and violated by her father, she is then broken off from him and easily thrown away. Were Virginia a son, or were she a married daughter with children, she would not only be less expendable, she would also be less obviously an extension of Virginius. As it is, however, Virginia is clearly a feminized version and therefore a doubling of Virginius, so that, in Maccoby's terms, the narrative provides both victim and executioner.

At the same time that virginity makes Virginius's daughter more expendable, it paradoxically also renders her more valuable. All the traditions implicit in the worldview of "The Physician's Tale" assume the value of virginity in a young unmarried woman, but as I have already pointed out, the reasons for such a valorization are quite different depending on their source. "The Physician's Tale" (like its Livy source) begins in a pagan culture, in a world where virgin daughters are valuable as potential wives, and as such they merit care and protection, just like any other precious goods or chattel. Moreover, what is being protected is the physical goods—the body, and specifically the hymen, although in this respect the pagan Roman tradition is somewhat less literal-minded than the Christian view.[23] When, however, "The Physician's Tale" moves into a ritualistic mode, virginity is prized because it renders the victim more worthy of sacrifice, especially in a medieval Christian understanding, which considers virginity and bodily integrity the defining features of purity and innocence.[24]

Yet even here, "The Physician's Tale" is not consonant with mainstream Christian teaching on virginity. Were Virginius to turn his daughter over to Apius, presumably only her body would be violated, not her spiritual innocence. As Augustine and Ambrose stress, when discussing specific cases like Lucretia's in which death was chosen over the dishonor that would follow rape, intention is all.[25] Thus, if a woman is raped, she incurs no sin and therefore no guilt. As Augustine puts it: "purity is a virtue of the soul . . . and since no one, however magnanimous and pure, has always the disposal of his own body, but can control only the consent and refusal of his will, what sane man can suppose that, if his body be seized and forcibly made use of to satisfy the lust of another, he thereby loses his purity?"[26] In other words, the physical loss of a maidenhead would not be a violation against chastity or purity, as long as the loss was against the woman's will and was unaccompanied by desire or pleasure.

Virginius, on the other hand, clearly equates virginity with the material presence of a hymen. "The Physician's Tale" thus adduces the value medieval Christianity accorded virginity without acknowledging the orthodox teaching on the nature of purity. This selective approach to Christian attitudes is especially characteristic of the climactic scene, where Virginia uses terms appropriate to late medieval piety in her plea for "mercy":

> "O *mercy,* deer fader!" quod this mayde,
> And with that word she both hir armes layde
> Aboute his nekke, as she was wont to do.
> The teeris bruste out of hir eyen two,
> And seyde, "Goode fader, shal I dye?
> Is ther no *grace,* is ther no *remedye?*"
> (213–236; my italics)

Virginia's words, sounding much like the childish pleas of Isaac in the Brome *Sacrifice of Isaac,* build a mood of pathos and melodrama.[27] At the same time, the Christian overtones, implicit in words like "mercy" and "grace," strike a jarring note. In particular, the word "grace" cannot fail to evoke a Christian worldview, in which human grace works as a reflection or emanation of God's perfect and always abundant grace. The Christian answer to Virginia's question is, of course, yes, there is *grace*—if not in this world, at least in the rewards of the next. However, Virginius gives an unequivocally unChristian reply to his daughter's loaded question: "No, certes doghter myn" (237).

The Christian sensibility in "The Physican's Tale" is invoked only for its usefulness in creating pathos. By making us hear and see for the first time an actual human child, with a voice, Chaucer's additions to the received story of Virginia heighten the drama and involve us in the sacrifice. We, like Virginius, are moved but unmoving. We weep for the loss, which, however, bears all the necessity and inevitability of divinely sanctioned ritual. Virginia's plea for a *remedye* is not just denied verbally at the moment, but has been framed by Virginius's determination, which sets the scene for the killing of his daughter. Returning home from court, Virginius calls for his daughter:

And with a face deed as asshen colde
Upon hir humble face he gan biholde,
With fadres pitee stikynge thurgh his herte,
Al wolde he from his purpos nat converte. (209–212)

This "purpos" is then articulated in a relatively lengthy speech (18 lines in a tale of only 286), in which Virginius explicates the necessity for his daughter's death while simultaneously bewailing his own pain. The focus on necessity, when combined with the formal announcement of the necessary deed, emphasizes the performative, ritualistic, and divinely sanctioned aspects of Virginius's sacrifice of his daughter.

The scene of sacrifice in "The Physician's Tale" adds one more ingredient to this combination of melodrama with ritual necessity: feelings of sensual desire and pleasure, which help build the excitement. Joining love to his violent attack, Virginius tells his victim:

Take thou thy deeth, for this is my sentence.
For love, and nat for hate, thou most be deed;
My pitous hand moot smyten of thy heed." (224–226)

Virginius's words to his daughter here sound suspiciously like January's apology to May in "The Merchant's Tale," articulating his regret on their wedding night that he will have to "trepace" and "greetly offende" May with sexual violation (*Canterbury Tales* IV, 1828–1830). Certainly the decapitation of Virginia is as violent and as violating as any rape or sexual assault would ever be—and, as at least R. Howard Bloch has seen, Virginia does, in fact, lose her maiden('s) head.[28] While these tones of mounting excitement accompanying a forced physical violation do not fit with the Augustinian view of virginity, they are fully consonant with the mode of sacrifice, which is characterized by the emotional intensity common in ritualistic performances.

What finally confirms the sacrificial aspects of Virginia's death is the violence surrounding it. According to René Girard, violence informs and inspires all sacrifice, which Girard claims in turn is at the center of or behind all sacred ritual. Ritualistic sacrifice is a community's means of controlling and limiting the violent tendencies common to all. In Girard's words: "Sacrifice too can be defined solely in terms of the sacred, without reference to any particular divinity; that is, it can be defined in terms of maleficent violence polarized by the victim and metamorphosed by his death (or expulsion from the community, which amounts to the same thing) into beneficent violence."[29] Part of Girard's argument is that in so-called "civilized societies," judicial systems (and systematic legalized punishment) replace the ritualistic sacrifice characteristic of more primitive cultures.[30]

While I am not comfortable with the seeming development from "primitive" to "civilized"—and indeed Girard himself is partly pointing to the violence imbedded in what we consider advanced and civilized ways of regulating criminal behavior—nonetheless, I find it remarkable that Chaucer too apparently saw the connection between justice systems, violence, and sacrifice. Chaucer even seems to confirm that ultimately violence is controlled by sacrifice, although at first all Virginius' sacrifice of his daughter seems to do is unleash a storm of punishment and revenge.

When Virginius displays the head of his daughter in a ritualistic act of presentation, Apius angrily reacts by ordering that Virginius be seized and hanged (258–259). This violent response is aborted by the sudden appearance of the Roman people:

> But right anon a thousand peple in thraste
> To save the knyght for routhe and for pitee,
> For knowen was the false iniquitee. (260–262)

This horde of people (who, in Chaucer's version, have no previous existence)[31] restores justice after a series of swift judgments and punishments: Apius is thrown in prison and condemned to hang, but kills himself first; Claudius is pardoned through the efforts of Virginius, who "of his pitee / So preyde for him" (272–273); and "the remenant were anhanged moore and lesse / That were consentant of this cursednesse" (274–275).

Many readers find Virginius' pity for Claudius sorely misplaced—granting to a "false cherl" (164) what was denied to his own daughter. From mainstream Christian thinking, as well as from any reasoned understanding of justice, we are bound to see a discrepancy in the ways in which both justice and mercy are exercised in "The Physician's Tale." However, in a world where sacrifice is still the way of dealing with violence, the "grace" shown to Claudius makes sense, as does the necessary killing of the victim Virginia. Until the threat embodied in Apius is dealt with through sacrifice, no pardon, "no grace," "no remedye" is possible, for this society is too filled with violence, too much at the mercy of evil. Once the sacrifice has been performed, then and only then is a return to an ordered society possible.

The Physician, however, continues to inhabit a world ruled by malevolent, terrifying powers. Moving back from the lately introduced and quickly dismissed public arena of Rome, the Physician brings his audience into the irrational microcosm of a frightened Everyman, threatened by the arbitrary action of a vengeful god:

> Heere may men seen how synne hath his merite.
> Beth war, for no man woot whom God wol smyte

In no degree, ne in which manere wyse;
The worm of conscience may agryse
Of wikked lyf, though it so pryvee be
That no man woot therof but God and he.
For be he lewed man, or ellis lered,
He noot how soone that he shal been afered.
Therfore I rede yow this conseil take:
Forsaketh synne, er synne yow forsake. (277–286)

These lines are hard to read, hard both because editors and readers have trouble with the syntax and meaning, and also because the mindset behind the words is ugly and irrational. In particular, the description of the "worm of conscience" seems confused, mostly, I believe, because the causal chain itself is confused. It is nearly impossible to figure out who is doing what to whom, and why conscience is frightened instead of frightening—if, in fact, Skeat is correct that we should read *agryse* as the passive construction of a transitive verb (but without the verb *to be*).[32]

The Physician provides no process of responsibility, just guilt and fear, no rational Christian conscience informed by late medieval penitential practices, but a mindset belonging to a culture of violence. This tale has certainly not shown the "merite" of sin: Claudius, as guilty as anyone except possibly Apius, has been spared, as has Virginius (in my view the guiltiest of all, since infanticide is the worst kind of murder), while Virginia, the powerless and innocent, has been killed. Sin, at least in the orthodox Christian views of it, can hardly be an issue here.[33] What we have seen instead is that evil, if not sin, demands recompense and the atonement of sacrifice.

While the Physician's concluding comments thus fit with the tale's sacrificial motif, they seem to work against the traditional use of Virginia's story as a critique of social justice—or lack thereof. For Livy and Jean de Meun, the story of Virginia is the story of a society that breaks down because it no longer functions according to reason and justice. But as Chaucer has the Physician retell the story, Virginia's death demonstrates the necessity to meet corruption with the ritualized violence of sacrifice.

Implicit in this necessity for sacrifice is the value of virgins as spotless and inviolate victims, with an emphasis upon bodily wholeness in general and an intact hymen in particular. While this literal sense of virginity has been disputed by Augustine and his followers and is usually suppressed in treatises on virginity, it would seem, in fact, to underlie their more figurative, moral discussions of innocence and purity. Likewise, in medieval Christian writings sacrifice tends to be translated into a spiritual offering, the giving up of worldly needs and desires, and yet the doctrine of atonement provides evidence that sacrifice as the ritual murder of humans is central to Christian faith. By recasting Virginia's story in the light of sacrifice, Chaucer points to the violence in both pagan and Christian sacrifices and at the same time raises questions about why his culture valued virginity in particular and innocence and purity in general.

Notes

1. Unless otherwise noted, all quotations and citations for Chaucer are to *The Riverside Chaucer,* gen. ed. Larry D. Benson (Boston: Houghton Mifflin, 1987). I have also relied heavily on the notes and textual apparatus of the *Variorum* edition: *The Physician's Tale,* ed. Helen Storm Corsa, vol. 2, part 17 in A *Variorum* Edition of the *Works of Geoffrey Chaucer* (Norman: University of Oklahoma Press, 1987); I will not, however, quote text from this edition. The link between "The Physician's Tale" and "The Pardoner's Tale" has a complex textual history, although the oldest and most authoritative manuscripts all have some version of it (and Ellesmere and Hengwrt have about the same version), the one I quote here being from Ellesmere since that is the base text for the *Riverside Chaucer.* For a comprehensive summary of the variants and the textual history of the Physician-Pardoner link, see Corsa's discussion in her introduction to the *Variorum* edition (pp. 45–53).

2. For Livy's version, see Edgar Finley Shannon, "The Physician's Tale," in *Sources and Analogues of Chaucer's Canterbury Tales,* ed. W. F. Bryan and Germaine Dempster (Chicago: University of Chicago Press, 1941), pp. 398–408; and Livy, *History,* vol. 5, *Ab urbe condita,* trans. B. O. Foster (Cambridge: Harvard University Press, 1953), book 3, chaps. 44–58. See also Corsa's detailed comparison of Chaucer's version with Livy's and with other medieval adaptations: Corsa, *Variorum,* pp. 4–10.

3. Livy's version circulated widely in the Middle Ages and was frequently translated: by Jean de Meun in *Le Roman de la Rose,* by Boccaccio in *De mulieribus claris,* and by Gower in *Confessio Amantis.* See Corsa, pp. 4–10; see also Shannon, pp. 398–408.

4. Jean de Meun, *The Romance of the Rose,* trans. Charles Dahlberg (Hanover, NH: University Press of New England, 1983), p. 114, ll. 5589–5658. See also Shannon's excerpted text from the *Roman de la Rose,* which is in the original Old French, pp. 400–401.

5. As Shannon prints it, the central narrative of Livy's story of Virginius occupies slightly fewer than 200 lines of prose, as compared to the 286 lines devoted to "The Physician's Tale" proper (not counting the Host's commentary that follows), but, of course, Livy's Latin prose gets far more words to a line than Chaucer's iambic pentameter. Still, roughly speaking, the two versions seem to be about the same length, whereas Reason's retelling in the *Romance of the Rose* is a typical medieval exemplum, short and to the illustrative point.

6. We can assume the Roman tradition is operative since the tale proclaims Livy as its source in the opening line. For an excellent discussion of the pagan Roman views on virginity, see Peter Brown, *The Body and Society* (New York: Columbia University Press, 1988), pp. 5–32.

7. Livy, Bk. 3, chap. 47; Shannon, p. 405.

8. On imperial Roman society's pressure on girls to marry and bear children, see Brown, pp. 6–8; on Roman views regarding promiscuity and loss of virginity, see Brown, pp. 28–31.

9. John Bugge, *Virginitas: An Essay in the History of a Medieval Ideal* (The Hague: Martinus Nihjoff, 1975), esp. pp. 30–32. Bugge's study is a useful bibliographic source for major church writings. For primary sources, see esp. Ambrose, *Three Books of St. Ambrose, Bishop of Milan, concerning Virgins, to Marcellina, His Sister* in *Ambrose: Select Works and Letters,* ed. Philip Schaff and Henry Wace, trans. H. de Romeslin (Peabody, MA: Hendrickson, 1994), pp. 363–387. As Bugge explains, this view of virginity developed as a monastic ideal (although Bugge traces it back even further—to gnosticism); see esp. pp. 13–14 and chapter 2, "Virginity and the Monastic Economy of Perfection" (pp. 30–58). See also a fuller discussion in Peter Brown, whose study traces the development of the Christian valorization of virginity and celibacy from the beginnings of Christianity through Augustine and into the early Middle Ages.

10. This awareness is hardly original with the Wife of Bath. See, for example, Novatian, *In Praise of Purity,* trans. Russell J. DeSimone, *The Fathers of the Church* (Washington, DC: The Catholic University of America Press, 1974), chap. 7, p. 170. See also R. Howard Bloch, "Chaucer's Maiden's Head: 'The Physician's Tale' and the Poetics of Virginity," *Representations* 28 (1989): 113–134. Bloch, citing the passage in Novatian, claims that the "patristics are, of course, highly aware that if everyone practiced chastity, the human race would perish" (p. 120).

11. In the Canon of the Mass, coming immediately after the consecration, in which the bread and wine have become Christ's body and blood, the actual words refer to the sacrificial offering as "Hostiam puram. Hostiam sanctam. Hostiam immaculatam" [Pure victim. Holy victim. Spotless victim] (*Sarum Missal,* Edited from *Three Early Manuscripts,* ed. J. Wickham Legg [London: Oxford University Press, 1916; rpt. 1969], p. 223; trans. mine).

12. Mary Beard, "The Sexual Status of Vestal Virgins," *Journal of Roman Studies* 70 (1980):14, n. 21; Hans J. Drijvers, "Virginity" in The *Encyclopedia of Religion,* ed. Mircea Eliade (New York: Macmillan, 1987), vol. 15, p. 280. Cf. Peter Brown, who refers to the Vestal Virgins as "not marrying until they were thirty" (p. 9), but since Brown cites Beard and Drijvers as sources, I assume that the implication that the Vestal Virgins ended service at thirty was simply an inadvertent mistake on Brown's part. Brown points out that there was great pressure on girls to begin childbearing early in order to prevent a dangerous decrease in the population (pp. 6–7), and that "the Vestal Virgins stood out as glaring anomalies" (p. 9).

13. Angela Jane Weisl drew my attention to the fact that the text, in both the Hebrew and the Vulgate versions, does not specify that the victim Jephtha expects to meet on his return will necessarily be "human." The Vulgate has *quicumque* [whoever/whatever], but both the Hebrew and Latin texts also make it clear that Jephtha expects this "whatever" to come out of the doors of his house ["foribus domus meae" in the Vulgate]. For my purposes, it is more important that, as I discuss below, Christian tradition assumed that Jephtha was vowing a human sacrifice and moreover believed his to be an unholy vow. On the vow in particular, but also for an insightful discussion of Jephtha's sacrifice in general, see Phyllis Trible, "The Daughter of Jephthah: An Inhuman Sacrifice," in *Texts of Terror: Literary-Feminist Readings of Biblical Narratives* (Philadelphia: Fortress, 1984). I am grateful to Moshe Gold for pointing me to Trible's essay and especially for translating and explicating the Hebrew text for me. For a recent discussion of child sacrifice in general, and "The Physician's Tale" and Jephtha's daughter in particular, see Barbara Newman, "Crueel Corage": Child Sacrifice and the Maternal Martyr in Hagiography and Romance," in *From Virile Woman to WomanChrist* (Philadelphia: University of Pennsylvania Press, 1995), pp. 76–107.

14. See, for example, Richard L. Hoffman, "Jephtha's Daughter and Chaucer's Virginia," *Chaucer Review* 2 (1967): 24–25.

15. I am grateful to Robert M. Stein for suggesting the relevance of Susannah's story. An immensely popular biblical tale from the Book of Daniel (chap. 13), the story of Susannah and the Elders appears frequently in early Christian and medieval art. (Chapter 13, like chapter 14, which contains the story of Bel and the dragon, is barely canonical—modern Catholic Bibles usually list these last two chapters as an "Appendix" to Daniel, while most non-Catholic Bibles exclude them altogether.) The relevance of Susannah's story to the virtue of virginity is attested to in Augustine's *Of Holy Virginity,* trans. C. I. Cornish, in *Nicene and Post-Nicene Fathers,* ed. Philip Schaff (Peabody, MA: Hendrickson, 1994), 3:417–438. Here Augustine cites Susannah's victory as evidence of the Holy Spirit's defense of women against false witnesses (article 20, p. 423). Note, however, that the reference to Susannah is in the context of Augustine's argument that the defense of purity is not a condemnation of marriage—a more moderate and reasoned view of marriage, sexuality, and virginity than is reflected in "The Physician's Tale" or in many of the late medieval discussions of virginity.

16. See Hyam Maccoby, *The Sacred Executioner: Human Sacrifice and the Legacy of Guilt* (London: Thames and Hudson, 1982), p. 189 (note 1 to p. 27), where he cites the story of Jephtha's daughter as "one of the examples of possible human sacrifice in early strata of the Bible."

17. Hoffman, p. 29. See also Anne Lancashire, "Chaucer and the Sacrifice of Isaac," *Chaucer Review* 9 (1975): 320–326.

18. Hoffman, p. 26; Hoffman cites Ambrose in particular. See also C. David Benson's note in the *Riverside Chaucer,* p. 903.

19. Corsa, p. 90; Corsa summarizes the major critical assessments of this addition, which does not appear in all the manuscripts, some having "And neuer had he mo in al his life," which could just mean he never had any more daughters (as Livy has it).

20. Trible points out that the sacrifice of Isaac is far more detailed and therefore more suspenseful than Jephtha's—for "that suspense [in Isaac's story] is bearable because Isaac is spared" (p. 105). The actual moment of sacrifice of Jephtha's daughter is, in contrast, barely narrated. All we get is the brief statement that Jephtha "did to her as he had vowed" (Judges 11.39). As Trible says, "truly the deed is unspeakable" (p. 114, note 42).

21. Maccoby, p. 17

22. Maccoby, p. 24.

23. See Peter Brown's discussion of the ancient Roman views on sexuality and virginity (pp. 5–23). Brown claims that the chief objection to allowing young girls to enjoy premarital affairs is the assumption that they would then continue loose sexual behavior after marriage (p. 29).

24. Bugge, pp. 1, 45, and *passim.*

25. The discussion of spiritual chastity (as opposed to literal bodily integrity) occupies much of the Fathers' and early Christian writings, as both Bugge and Brown make clear. For the clearest and most explicit discussion, especially in light of Lucretia's suicide, see Augustine, *The City of God,* trans. Marcus Dods (New York: Modern Library, 1950), Book I, 10:18–19, pp. 22–25.

26. *City of God,* Book I, 10:18; p. 22.

27. The Brome *Sacrifice of Isaac* is anthologized in several collections, for example, *Medieval Drama,* ed. David Bevington (Boston: Houghton Mifflin, 1975), pp. 308–321. See also Lancashire, pp. 323–324.

28. The title of Bloch's article, cited above (n. 10) is "Chaucer's Maiden's Head: 'The Physician's Tale' and the Poetics of Virginity."

29. *Violence and Sacrifice,* trans. Patrick Gregory (Baltimore: Johns Hopkins University Press, 1977), p. 258.

30. Girard, pp. 197–198. I think I can see that Livy's story of Virginius exemplifies the failure of a justice system and the consequent reversion of society to violence and sacrifice.

31. On the much reduced role of the populace in Chaucer's version, see Sheila Delaney, "Politics and the Paralysis of Poetic Imagination in The Physician's Tale," *Studies in the Age of Chaucer* 3 (1981): 47–60. Delaney argues that Chaucer's most important changes from the version in Livy are the ones that reduce the original tale's social commentary.

32. In other words, the lines in question (280–281a) are probably best translated as "the worm of conscience may be atremble from its wicked life." Skeat argues for the passive reading by explaining that "when *agryse* is used with of it is commonly passive, not intransitive" (Walter W. Skeat, *The Complete Works of Geoffrey Chaucer,* vol. 5, [Oxford: Clarendon Press, and New York: Macmillan, 1894], p. 264, note to line 280). Skeat and Corsa point to

Innocent III's *De contemptu mundi* as Chaucer's ultimate source for the lines. The Latin text has "vermis conscientae tripiliciter lacerabit" [the worm of conscience will tear apart in a threefold manner]; in this case, the implied object of the Latin active verb *lacero* is clearly the human subject. See Corsa, p. 135, note to 280, for the Latin text and translation, as well as for a full discussion of the problems [for early scribes as well as modern editors] created by these lines and the word *agryse*.

33. Virtually no one has anything good to say about the ending to "The Physician's Tale," but for one of the strongest condemnations, see Jeanne T. Mathewson, "For Love and Not for Hate: The Value of Virginity in Chaucer's Physician's Tale," *Annuale Mediaevale* 14 (1973): 35–42.

CHAPTER 8

BLOOD AND ROSARIES: VIRGINITY, VIOLENCE, AND DESIRE IN CHAUCER'S "PRIORESS'S TALE"

Kathleen M. Hobbs

> *Mary's inviolate body allowed the Church to perceive itself as a wellspring of absolute truth; in the "Tale," Mary provides a direct opposition to the Jewish community that proves ironic in the connection between women and Jews in medieval society.*

In the year 381, at the Second Council of Constantinople, the Church established the perpetual virginity of Mary as doctrine, and hence the doctrine that Christ was born "of a virgin." This doctrine established an absolute barrier between Christian and Jewish systems of belief. As Marina Warner observes,[1] the emphasis on the Incarnation through a specifically virgin birth is a dogma established by the Church Fathers, despite its having no particular basis in scripture;

> The pressure to prove Jesus' Davidic descent and consequent authenticity as the Messiah outweighed the urgency of arguments for the virgin birth at the time Matthew and Luke wrote and for the audience they addressed. Paul too, in his Epistle to the Romans, the earliest writing in the New Testament, expresses the same scale of values, when he asserts that Christ is the son of God on a metaphysical plane, through his resurrection from the dead, but "made of the seed of David according to the flesh" (Romans 1:3–4). Nor does Paul's choice of words in Galatians stand as a bulwark to the doctrine of the virgin birth since Jesus is "born of a woman" not "of a virgin" (Galatians 4:4).[2]

New Testament writings, contrary to the decrees of the Church Fathers, stress Jesus' high noble lineage as it is traced through Joseph, and thus preserve the historical connection between Christian and Jewish systems of belief. The virgin birth, which would of course, invalidate any association of Jesus with Joseph's lineage, ultimately works to undermine the basis for Jesus' claim to divinity, as well as to sever all historical ties between Judaism and Christianity.

The idea of virgin birth, then, was not always essential to the establishment of Christ's divinity nor so central to Christian belief. But the Church's insistence on the "truth" of the Incarnation allowed it to divorce itself entirely from the continuum of history and thereby effectively to deny the origins of Christianity as an outgrowth of Judaism. The rituals of Christian devotion, especially those addressing the Virgin Mary, gave vehement display to this central doctrinal difference between Christianity and Judaism. For example, in the hymn "Gaude Maria" are the lines:

> Gaude, Maria virgo, cunctas hereses sola interemisti;
> Quae Gabrielis archangeli dictis credidisti.
> Dum Virgo Deum et hominem genuisti,
> Et post partum Virgo inviolata permansisti.
> (Versus:) Gabrielem archangelum scimus divinitus te esse affatum;
> Uterum tuum de Spirito Sancto credimus imprae gnatum;
> Erubescat Judae us infelix, qui dicit Christum Joseph semine esse natum.[3]

> [Rejoice, Mary virgin, who alone have slain all heresies;
> Who believed the words of the archangel Gabriel.
> While a virgin you gave birth to God and man,
> And after giving birth, you remained an inviolate virgin.
> (Versus:) We know the archangel Gabriel prophecied to you with divine inspiration; We believe your womb was filled by the Holy Spirit;
> Let the unfortunate Jew blush, who says that Christ is born from the seed of Joseph.][4]

The hymn emphasizes Christian unity with respect to the virgin birth and juxtaposes that unity clearly with the singularity of the unbelieving Jew. But a failure to recognize the Incarnation does not seem to end with Christians simply casting shame upon the Jew. That Mary is also established here as the slayer of all heresies carries the implicit threat that physical violence, in addition to shame, is the penalty for failing to accept Christian doctrine.

According to Carleton Brown, the "Gaude Maria" is the hymn most usually sung by the little clergeon as he travels through the ghetto in the analogous versions of "The Prioress's Tale." Florence Ridley makes use of Brown's findings to assert that Chaucer consciously chose the milder "O alma redemptoris" over the more typical "Gaude Maria" as a way of softening the traditional tale's anti-Semitism, with which Chaucer was uncomfortable.[5] Ridley's assertion stands in opposition to Robert Worth Frank's argument that Chaucer's choice of hymn is indicative of the pervasive anti-Semitism of fourteenth-century England, with which Chaucer could not help but engage. Philip Alexander represents the middle ground in this debate, arguing that the anti-Semitism of Chaucer's tale is bad, though it could have been much worse.[6] But no matter what position one takes in the debate, one must admit that what Chaucer's actual feelings toward Jews may have been is ultimately impossible to determine. What is possible to determine, however, is that in "The Prioress's Tale" Chaucer engages with an array of anti-Semitic notions at work in many of the hymns of Marian devotion.

Like the blushing Jew on whose shame Christian ideas about Christian virtue are built, the virtue of the ever-virginal Mary provides the foundation upon which the inherent sinfulness of all women rests. Ecclesiastical treatises conventionally described women as daughters of Eve, and as such they were always deemed already sinful, libidinous, filthy, spiritually inferior. Women were always seen as already guilty of all the sins of embodiment and inextricably bound to the flesh. Though Mary's purity was said to provide a way for women to avoid the corruption brought about by Eve, the rhetoric of woman's responsibility for original sin worked too much in the ecclesiastical establishment's favor for it to be put to rest. Not only did it help to maintain general systems of patriarchal authority, but it also proved invaluable in quelling heretical movements (like that of the Lollards in fourteenth-century England) in which women claimed equal access to the divine. And despite being closer to Mary in their pledge to perpetual chastity, nuns were denied much of a distinction from other women (that is, wives and widows) in canon law. Like other women, the nun was a target of pollution fears and cordoned off from men by an elaborate system of prohibitions and taboos focusing on her unclean nature. Canon law fed off of these beliefs, prohibiting nuns from touching the regalia of the Mass, burning incense, or approaching the altar,[7] thereby limiting women physically from symbolic contact with divinity.

Only heretics used the idea that God recruited the assistance of a woman in order to manifest Himself in the flesh as support for a claim against the inherent and greater sinfulness of women, or that like men, women could be priests or otherwise serve as their equals within the Church. The Catholic Church placed its emphasis on Mary's marked difference from women and used the Incarnation as a means by which simultaneously to praise and condemn them. Mary, the Church Fathers proclaimed, delivered her child without pain or blood, without the destruction of her "bodily integrity"; and so satisfied was she to bear the son of God that she remained forever clean of all desire.[8] Even in death, she left behind no corpse, nothing to remind the world that she might ever have lived within a physical, female body.[9] The Marian ideal was used by the Church as the standard against which the purity of all women was measured, but to which it was impossible for women to measure up as the Immaculate Conception allowed only one woman to escape the stain of Eve's sin.

But it is specifically Eve's sin that marks the body as female in the first place. Mary, it seems, could not really have a (specifically female) body if she were as pure as the Church Fathers would have her. She could neither menstruate (that is, show the mark of Eve's sin)[10] nor lose her "bodily integrity" (that is, take part in Eve's curse to bear her children in pain). The rejection of a standard sexual physiology for Mary again reaches back to the devotional writings and decrees of the fourth century. Most notably, the canons of Laodicea forbade women to enter the sanctuary for fear that their menstruation might pollute it.[11] And just as the Church Fathers determined the perpetual virginity of Mary without regard to the contradiction of that decree with Scripture, so they held on to the association of menstruation with pollution despite the events recounted throughout the Gospels where women are allowed to touch Christ himself.[12] The elimination of the pain and blood of childbearing from Mary's experience is yet another way of positioning her as entirely opposite to Eve but also yet another factor in "the equation of the supernatural and the unnatural."[13] Whereas Eve was cursed to bear children, Mary is blessed with romanticized, less physical motherhood, exclusive of the post-Lapsarian process of actual birth.

In addition to severing the historical ties between Judaism and Christianity, the establishment of Mary's perpetual virginity allowed Christianity to exalt itself as a fixed and timeless institution, thereby allowing it to declare itself the well-spring of absolute truth. For Christianity to acknowledge its place within the continuum of history would imply the destruction of its status as an absolute. Thus, the Church was required continually to re-create the fiction of its position as the source of absolute truth while simultaneously acknowledging its position within history as a development out of Judaism in order to support the revelatory nature of that truth. The Church projected the frustration with its necessary position in history in countless ways, but perhaps most notably it projected such frustration outwardly toward its source of being in the form of anti-Semitism.

Recent scholarship has dealt quite thoroughly with issues of anti-Semitism as well as gender in relation to "The Prioress's Tale." Surprisingly, however, there seems to have been little commentary thus far on the overlapping of these issues. Thomas Hahn perhaps comes closest to an examination of this overlap in "The Prioress's Tale" in a discussion connecting women and Jews, but only insofar as he sees them both to have developed a strategy of "(dis)simulation" in "adapting to those roles designed for them by social and psychic drives of the dominant Christian culture."[14] Daniel Pigg makes passing reference to the significance of the connection between women and Jews, noting that the Prioress "defines her own struggle against evil," but also locating the anti-Semitism of the tale as "only a peripheral concern."[15] What these critics seem to ignore, however, is that clerical anti-Semitism and clerical antifeminism are both manifestations of an institutional hatred and fear of an identifiable other, and thus are equivalent in that respect. It will be my argument in this essay that the anti-Semitism of "The Prioress's Tale" doubles for the antifeminism consistently and openly leveled at women—even (or perhaps especially) at women of the Prioress's standing—by the Church. Far from excusing the anti-Semitism of the tale, I mean to stress in this argument that Chaucer deliberately but strategically deploys common anti-Semitic themes and tropes in order to expose and satirize the naive assumptions and hypocrisies of the Church of his day. Likewise, in the General Prologue he deploys common romance tropes in his portrait of the Prioress ostensibly to praise, but ultimately to undermine, typical representations of and assumptions about ecclesiastical women.

In "Criticism, Anti-Semitism and the Prioress's Tale,"[16] Louise Fradenburg adopts the Kristevan notion of abjection to articulate her position that "The Prioress's Tale" is about Christian anxiety and fear of the Jewish community. Fradenburg sets forth a largely historical reading of "The Prioress's Tale" in which she argues that the tale's narrative crisis, the murder of the little Christian boy, is ultimately about what the medieval Christian community was metaphorically doing to itself, with the act of mutilation rendered literal and projected onto a community of Jews as a means of scapegoating these actions:

> In short, the violence done to children of "Cristen blood" by "Cristen folk" is being attributed to the Jewish scapegoat, just as, in the doctrine of the New Law versus the Old, the repressive authoritarianism of Christianity is being attributed to Judaism so that new icons of belief—Mary,

for example, who is herself a libidinal threat to "monotheism" and a champion of the abject—can be instituted with all the fervor of what Bataille calls "affective effervescence."[17]

Though Fradenburg begins to introduce some discussion of gender here, her emphasis remains firmly on the anti-Semitism of "The Prioress's Tale." However, in bringing together the notions of projection and abjection, she complicates wider-ranging problems of separatism and community found in "The Prioress's Tale," including gender.

In a rather general discussion of treatments of gender in Chaucer, Alcuin Blamires notes that "while Chaucer's most visible cross-interpretations in the sphere of gender were no doubt partly calculated to engage an antifeminist-conscious public in playful banter, they were also designed to unsettle complacent opinion about failings and traits deemed to be characteristic of each sex."[18] It is precisely this calculated engagement with and undermining of popularly received opinions about "others" that I think is so important to an understanding of the complex irony of "The Prioress's Tale" and her portrait in the General Prologue.

Though a psychoanalytic reading of "The Prioress's Tale" is central to the argument of this essay, and though the idea of projection certainly has its root in psychoanalysis, I think it is important to note that a Christian projection of frustrations onto the Jewish community is reflected by historical material, as well. In addition to the tale's generic familiarity to fourteenth-century English audiences and the genre's typical engagement with some of the more outrageous and chilling aspects of medieval anti-Semitism, the Prioress's Marian devotion seems also typical and carries with it the same anti-Semitic implications. As Frank points out in his article on "The Prioress's Tale," "Mary . . . is the confuser of heretics, and this . . . brings her into direct opposition to the Jewish people,"[19] insofar as the Jewish rejection of the Incarnation as an affront to God's dignity marks the central doctrinal difference between Christians and Jews.

The Virgin Mary who, in Fradenburg's words, is "a libidinal threat to 'monotheism' and a champion of the abject," is a figure with whom the Prioress closely identifies but with whom she cannot merge. The Prioress ends the prologue to her tale with the following prayer to the Virgin:

> My konnyng is so wayk, O blisful Queene,
> For to declare thy grete worthynesse
> That I ne may the weighte nat susteene;
> But as a child of twelf month oold, or lesse,
> That kan unnethes any word expresse,

Right so fare I, and therefore I yow preye,
Gydeth my song that I shal of yow seye. (481–487)[20]

The Prioress portrays herself here as childlike and weak, and in need of divine intervention in order to speak. Of course, the Prioress is evidently not a child, and she is quite obviously capable of speech. But she sees her speech, coming as it does from the body that binds her to sin, as inadequate for prayer, and so she prays for the voice of the Virgin—who, dissected by centuries of Church decrees denying her birth pangs, a ruptured hymen, and sexual desire, has been effectively disembodied—to take over for the purposes of her prayer. Thus we see the Prioress in the impossible state of all monastic women: holy enough to identify herself with the mother of God but too sinful in her mortality to reach the heavenly ideal that Mary represents. Just as the Church simultaneously required and denied its relationship to Judaism, so the Church simultaneously exalted and debased its monastic women, and womanhood in general.

Chaucer's Prioress plays out the unique predicament of the medieval monastic woman, as she must acknowledge her status as a daughter of Eve, doing penance for an inherited and inescapable sin, while she must simultaneously strive to meet the impossible requirements of the Marian ideal. Such a predicament forces the ecclesiastical woman to wallow in her inescapably bodied femininity while trying desperately to meet the standards of a monolithic dogma that requires her disembodiment. Thus, the Mary/Eve (madonna/whore) dichotomy is magnified in the Prioress who, as a high-ranking ecclesiastical woman, stands in a simultaneously debased (feminine) and exalted (masculine) position. In her tale, she simultaneously affirms and denies her gender, identifying with both the Virgin Mary and the little clergeon, playing at both embodiment and disembodiment. In other words, she comes to represent the abject state of women in the medieval Church, playing out Julia Kristeva's definition of abject as "The shame of compromise, of being in the middle of treachery. The fascinated start that leads me toward and separates me from them."[21]

Drawing attention to their respective standings as "other" in relationship to the Church, Chaucer describes the Prioress and in turn has her describe the community of Jews in fetishized and stereotypical terms, with generalizations about their respective natures applied to them equally. Chaucer draws obviously on medieval anti-Semitic traditions in the Prioress's description of the Jews. Of course, Jews had not been present in England since their expulsion in 1290, and so Chaucer and his audience had likely encountered few if any Jews in their lifetime.[22] While some critics have used this probability as a means of excusing the anti-Semitism of "The Prioress's Tale," I would argue that Chaucer at this point engages us in a moment of high irony. While it is true that most English people at this time had likely never come into contact with a Jew, most were likely to have "seen" Jews in the dramatic productions, religious and secular, that gained in popularity throughout the fourteenth century in England.[23] In these productions, Jews played the singular role of villain; they were always represented as evil, and were "graphically portrayed . . . as abducting Christian children, crucifying them, and extracting their blood for Passover rituals."[24] Likewise, the Prioress describes the Jews in the opening lines of her tale in singular terms, engaged in activities that unite them in a singular purpose:

> Ther was in Asye, in a greet citee,
> Amonges Cristene folk a Jewerye,
> Sustened by a lord of that contree
> For foule usure and lucre of vileynye,
> Hateful to Crist and to his compaignye. (488–492)

She draws a gender-free portrait of the "Jewerye," marking differences between them only by their association with one of the twin professions of usury and profiteering.[25] Similarly, the "homycide" who is hired to kill the little clergeon, in his greed that leads to murder comes to stand synecdocically for his community, pointing out the Christian alignment of all Jews with Judas,[26] rendering them always already sinful, filthy, spiritually inferior. Thus, the Prioress uses religious affiliation rather than gender as a scapegoat for the disruption of a harmonious Christian settlement.

Though the Prioress describes the community of Jews exclusively in stereotypical and negative terms, Chaucer describes the Prioress in the General Prologue in stereotypical but ambiguous terms.

> But of to speken of hire conscience,
> She was so charitable and so pitous
> She wolde wepe, if that she saugh a mous
> Kaught in a trappe, if it were deed or bledde.
> Of smale houndes hadde she that she fedde
> With rosted flessh, or milk and wastel-breed.
> But soore wepte she if oon of hem were deed,
> Or if men smoot it with a yerde smerte;
> And al was conscience and tendre herte. (142–150)

The Prioress's sensitivities are high and refined, but her feelings are directed toward helpless little beasts rather than helpless human beings.[27] The implicit critique here works to foreshadow the Prioress's intense horror at the fate of the little clergeon and to render all the more horrific and ironic her apparent relish in the hanging and dismemberment of the Jews at the end of her tale (628–634).

The narrator's fetishization of the Prioress in the General Prologue is also found in the hyperbole applied to the description of her femininity, all of her qualities being preceded by "semely," "so," "sikerly," or "ful" (127–141). The hyperfemininity that the narrator attributes to the Prioress suggests that for her, sex denied results in an emphatic reaffirmation of gender. Even if we read the narrator's description of the Prioress in the General Prologue as so much literary convention, the idea still remains that gender takes the place of sex in the construction of characters that culture (or literary convention) demands must be designated male or female.[28] In this case, it seems hardly unconventional that any noble woman, even an ecclesiastical woman, would be described in terms of her beauty and womanly conduct in order to indicate the degree of her virtue. The tropes Chaucer deploys here firmly bind together ideas of feminine beauty and feminine virtue.[29] The Prioress's portrait, combined with the highly ambiguous inscription *Amor vincit omnia* that dangles from her rosary, establishes her as a participant "in the heterosexual contract or matrix, for to be celibate and unfeminine would make her a sexual suspect rather than simply a contradiction."[30] In other words, she is firmly caught in the middle of the madonna/whore dichotomy, completely abject.

The Prioress's portrait draws on conventional descriptions of romance heroines whose goal is not spiritual transcendence, but marriage and its consummation. Descriptions of romance heroines usually point up their desirability in the eyes of hopeful male suitors. But as R. Howard Bloch points out,[31] many of the literary conventions of love and eroticism found in the medieval romance are based on an ascetic model that requires a denial of the flesh as necessary to the elevation of the spirit. Though the romance heroine may be described as pure, chaste, or virtuous, the early Christian models on which these later conventions are based only undermine the possibilities of those distinctions. Ultimately, what Bloch gives his readers is a catalogue of sources proclaiming the impossibilities of a simultaneously chaste and female existence.[32] He highlights especially the teachings of the Church Fathers, many of whom assert that a woman or a young girl is not only responsible for the preservation of her "bodily integrity" and the containment of her own desire but that in addition she is responsible for the desires of men when they look upon her, and when desired, she necessarily loses her virginity.

Thus Cyprian:

> But if you . . . enkindle the fire of hope, so that,
> Without perhaps losing your own soul, you nevertheless ruin
> others . . . who behold you, you cannot be excused on the ground
> that your mind is chaste and pure. Your shameless apparel and your
> immodest attire belie you, and you can no longer be numbered
> among maidens and virgins of Christ, you who so live as to
> become the object of sensual love.[33]

The requirements for female chastity are ideals as impossible and as unattainable as the Marian ideal.

The only women that the Prioress has included in her tale are the Virgin Mary and the mother of the clergeon, a widow. Both are mothers completely devoted to their children; both are removed from marriage, and thus virginal in the eyes of the Church. While Mary has the distinction of an official declaration of her perpetual virginity,[34] the widow, devoted to her son and to his Christian education and upbringing (509–512), is forgiven her fall into marriage. As Howard Bloch explains: "Though Jerome asserts . . . that 'God cannot raise a virgin once she has fallen', it is clear, according to the Christological model of salvation history, that redemption implies a return to the state of virginity, to the vita angelica—an eschatological abolition of sexuality."[35] Neither of these women are characters with whom the Prioress could identify. Neither presents any of problematic elements of femininity that constitute and trouble the Prioress in her portrait. The female characters whom the Prioress includes in her tale are completely divorced from femininity and sexuality altogether.

The only character with whom the Prioress might identify would be the little clergeon, who represents the unattainable ideal of virginity that is nevertheless required of monastic women. Only through a reversal of her gender in her own fictional creation can the Prioress achieve such an ideal. Though it may be true that "Chaucerians have long recognized that the Prioress identifies with the little clergeon of the tale,"[36] it does not seem to be the case that critics have treated this identification as an indication of the Prioress giving voice to a desire to "become male," after the teachings of Jerome; rather, her identification with the clergeon is an indication of her childlike innocence. Because the boy is martyred at the age of seven, the Prioress's identification with him is more than just a reversal of her gender. It is a process of desexualization as well. Not only does she make herself masculine, but she makes herself prepubescent and masculine. Gender (and sex, as well) is hardly relevant to a child of seven. Only to the Church Fathers would the gender of such young children be relevant. Taking the writings of Tertullian as a case in point: "a virgin ceases to be a virgin from the time it becomes possible for her to not be one."[37] In other words, as soon as a girl is desired by a man, she is no longer a virgin. So even at the age of seven, a female child would be in danger of being seen and desired. A male child, on the other hand, seems to be immune to the direction or reception of desire, according to the Church Fathers, and thus the preservation of his chastity is doubly insured.

But this series of connections leads to yet another point where Chaucer seems to toy with naive assumptions. For in addition to the vast amount of didactic literature stressing virginity as the essential requirement for the salvation of women, numerous and equally popular clerical treatises condemning homosexual practices between male clerics had been circulated and widely read within monastic communities for centuries.[38] Thus Chaucer draws us into yet another moment of high irony when his Prioress finds her safe haven from eternal damnation behind a childish male mask. In order to preserve her virginity, the Prioress must continually deny her gender, but at the same time her position as "bride of Christ" requires that her gender be continually reaffirmed. So although the narrator of the General Prologue portrays her as hyperbolically feminine (and therefore hyperbolically sinful), in her tale she translates herself into a perfect representative of eternal virginity—an illiterate, blindly devoted Christian schoolboy.

After the little clergeon is killed by the Jews in the ghetto and thrown into their privy, the Prioress asserts the philosophical significance of his death.

> O martir, sowded to virginitee,
> Now maystow syngen, folwynge evere in oon
> The white Lamb celestial—quod she—
> Of which the grete evaungelist, Seint John,
> In Pathmos wroot, which seith that they that goon
> Biforn this Lamb and synge a song al newe,
> That nevere, flesshly, women they ne knewe. (579–585)

In this passage, the Prioress reaffirms the biblical assertion of the inherent sinfulness of women and the virtues of dying before having known the desire that women inflict. The little clergeon, dead at the age of seven, had not yet reached an age where desire or desirability would have been an issue. Only in matters of faith had he matured. Thus the little clergeon seems destined for eternal life as one of Christ's 144,000 singing virgins.

It is probably safe to assume, however, that the scatological disposal of the boy's body has hardly left him *sine macula,* as those virgins in Apocalypse 14 are said to be. Such ironic humor appears to escape the Prioress, however, whose point here seems to be a deeply earnest belief that despite the little boy's body being covered in filth, his spirit is impervious to stain. The Prioress, however, may also speak for herself. Her obsession with cleanliness, with remaining quite literally *sine macula* is obvious in her portrait:

> At mete wel ytaught was she with alle;
> She leet no morsel from hir lippes falle,
> Ne wette hir fyngres in hir sauce depe;
> Wel koude she carie a morsel and wel kepe
> That no drope ne fille upon hir brest. (127–131)

On the above points, I follow Stephen Spector, who argues further that the Prioress portrays the Jews not only as the representatives of spiritual stain in their alignment with Judas but also as a source of physical defilement in their disposal of the clergeon's body. Hence "they symbolize the most offensive possible contrary to the immaculate Eglentyne. The non-specific anti-Jewishness of the tale and its analogues is thus translated into the Prioress' revulsion at the qualities that constitute her own negation."[39] The quality that most forcefully constitutes the Prioress's negation, however, is her own bodily existence. This, too, is a quality projected onto the community of Jews, the ghetto itself sprawling like a great body "free and open at eyther ende" (494), into whose "Hell-mouth"[40] the little clergeon enters. He is killed and subsequently disposed of "where thise Jewes purgen hir entraille" (573).[41] The scatological imagery here serves to project all the sins of embodiment onto the Jews who, after murdering the little clergeon, attempt to mark him with the foulest reminder of bodily existence.[42]

On a less graphic and more historical level, the Prioress also identifies herself with the young martyr in matters of education. Monastic women before the twelfth century were usually given the opportunity to be learned. But after the twelfth century, monastic women—even women as highly placed as the Prioress—were often restricted from Latin learning.[43] Moreover, as Julia Bolton Holloway asserts, "The vernacular languages . . . were associated with nature, with sexuality and the world of motherhood and childhood."[44] Thus the desire for Latin learning corresponds to a desire to transcend the corporeality and cupidity with which women are charged. The little clergeon's desire to learn the "O alma redemptoris" is motivated by his desire to worship the Virgin Mary in a way that would better demonstrate the ardor and absolute purity of his love for her, in a way that would be impossible in the vernacular prayers taught to him by his mother. Additionally, it seems important that the clergeon offer praise to the Virgin in words he does not understand. The clergeon's repetition of a Latin song does not signify knowledge; rather, it signifies only dutiful repetition. And in this case, language does not get in the way of worship as the words to the "O alma redemptoris" evoke only their immediate referent without interference from the problematic ambiguities of language.

At first the little boy "where as he saugh th'ymage/Of Cristes mooder, hadde he in usage,/As hym was taught, to knele adoun and seye/His Ave Marie, as he goth by the weye" (505–508). But after he has memorized all of the Latin hymn, under pain of punishment for neglecting his primer and without knowing the meaning of the words: "Twies a day it passed thurgh his throte,/To scoleward and homward whan he wente;/On Cristes mooder set was his entente" (548–550). The consequences of this learning constitute the vehicle for the crisis of the narrative, but they also underscore the notion that this is a tale about the violence that Christianity inflicted upon itself through its strict codes of behavior and hierarchy. Remarking specifically on the clergeon's fear of being beaten, Fradenburg observes that "The tale's association of violence with the school reminds us . . . of the extent to which the control of knowledge in the service of belief was backed up, in the Middle Ages, by force."[45]

But additionally this scene presents an interesting reversal of a detail in English history. In the limited areas where synagogues were allowed to stand in pre-1290 England, there was some concern that Christians passing by them might overhear the activities of the worshippers within, resulting in "more alarming contamination."[46] The nervousness felt by churchmen regarding Christian/Jewish contact is firmly in evidence given situations like that in Hereford in 1286 where the bishop excommunicated a group of Christians who attended a Jewish wedding. Christian codes of behavior and hierarchy thus resulted not only in physical violence but in spiritual violence as well.

Although the Jews are accused and viciously punished for the death of the clergeon in "The Prioress's Tale," he does not truly die until the grain placed on his tongue by the Virgin Mary is removed by the monk (663–672). Until this point, he continues to sing and to worship in an exuberant and macabre display of spiritual endurance and strength over the body's frailty. The death of the little clergeon is a cathartic moment for all of the elements that have been building in intensity from the beginning of the tale. It is the moment in which the exercise of violence and the celebration of martyrdom are placed side by side. Jews and Christians alike play the double role of persecutor and persecuted,[47] and it becomes evident that physical suffering and devotion are quite interchangeable in the Prioress's system of worship.[48]

In terms of viewing "The Prioress's Tale" as a narrative reflecting the abject state of women within the ecclesiastical hierarchy, this scene's celebration of murder in all of its varieties is doubly rich. In addition to waste, sewage, and the putrefying corpse, Kristeva lists blood among the tabooed bodily materials that signify the abject:

> Blood, indicating the impure, takes on the "animal" seme of the . . . opposition [between vegetable and animal] and inherits the propensity for murder of which man must cleanse himself. But blood, as a vital element, also refers to women, fertility, and the assurance of fecundation. It thus becomes a fascinating semantic crossroads, the propitious place for abjection where death and femininity, murder and procreation, cessation of life and vitality all come together.[49]

The "crossroads" that Kristeva outlines in regard to the signification of blood is especially interesting in connection with the Prioress's Marian aspirations, since the connection of blood with fecundity and procreation is simultaneously celebrated and denied in relation to Mary. Mary is simultaneously virginal and procreative. Likewise, the clergeon's blood indicates simultaneously his (bodily) death and his (spiritual) life; and he is, at this point in the tale, simultaneously dead and alive. The Prioress is denied procreativity because she must be virginal, but denied virginity because she is (potentially) procreative. She is a bodied woman vested in an institution that demands women's disembodiment.

At the tale's denouement, however, the multivalent contradictions of life and death, embodiment and disembodiment, are quickly dispersed. After the grain is removed from the clergeon's tongue, "he yaf up the goost ful softely./And whan this abbot hadde this wonder seyn,/His salte teeris trikled doun as reyn,/And gruf he fil al plat upon the grounde,/And stille he lay as he had ben ybounde" (672–676). The lines that follow detail the Marian devotion of the monks and the burial of the clergeon's body "in a tombe of marbul stones cleere" (681). The Prioress makes no mention of the fate of the clergeon's soul after its release from his body; rather, she pays attention only to the corpse. Once the clergeon's soul is released, the Prioress concentrates her focus not only on the dead body of the little clergeon but also on the prostrate body of the monk, lying as if he had "ben ybounde." Like the monk, Christianity remains fixed in a kind of figurative death, even after such a miracle as the one the Prioress recounts—bound, static, fearful of change, and perhaps ready to take part in enacting similar violence upon a similar scapegoat when the threat of change, or even miracle, again presents itself.

The Prioress, in her position as narrator of a Christian tale on a Christian pilgrimage, couches her frustration with an institution that effectively denies salvation to women in terms of the tension between Christian and Jew. This narrative strategy allows "The Prioress's Tale" to undermine the patriarchal and monolithic structure of the Christian Church at the same time that it contributes to the myth of Christian unity and reaffirms its claim to absolute truth. As both woman and Jew function as equivalent others in the eyes of the Church, the outward story of "The Prioress's Tale" is able to tell her inward story, and she is able to vent her frustration with the Church without overtly upsetting its order or shaking its foundations, preserving her own security within her estate while at the same time criticizing the impossibility of her position within it.[50]

Notes

1. Marina Warner, *Alone of All Her Sex: The Myth and the Cult of the Virgin Mary* (1976; repr. New York: Vintage Books, 1983), chaps. 1 and 3.
2. Warner, *Alone,* p. 20.
3. Carleton Brown, "Prioress's Tale," in *Sources and Analogues of Chaucer's* Canterbury Tales, ed. W. F. Bryan and Germaine Dempster (1941; repr. New York: Humanities Press, 1958), pp. 447–485. See esp. p. 448, n. 1
4. My translation.
5. Florence Ridley, *The Prioress and the Critics* (Berkeley: University of California Press, 1965), p. 26.
6. Philip S. Alexander, "Madame Eglentyne, Geoffrey Chaucer and the Problem of Medieval Anti-Semitism," *Bulletin of the John Rylands University Library of Manchester* 74 (1992), 118 and n. 22.
7. Shulamith Shahar, *The Fourth Estate: A History of Women in the Middle Ages,* trans. Chaya Galai (London: Methuen, 1983), pp. 27–28.
8. Warner, *Alone,* pp. 64–66.
9. Warner finds the cults of Marian worship anomalous among the various cults of the saints extant during the Middle Ages: "The cult of the saints in the early Christian Church concentrated on their martyrdom, its site, and their relics. But in Mary's case there were no contemporary records at all of her death, and . . . no tradition of her martyrdom existed. Most perplexing of all, there was no knowledge of her grave—no body to venerate, no relics to touch" (*Alone,* p. 82).
10. See Joshua Trachtenberg, *The Devil and the Jews: The Medieval Conception of the Jew and Its Relation to Modern Anti-Semitism* (Philadelphia: The Jewish Publication Society of America, 1983), p. 50, for a discussion of the Christian intimation that, among the Jews, men as well as women experienced menstruation.
11. Shahar, *Fourth Estate,* p. 27.
12. See, for example, Luke 7.36–50 and Matthew 26.6–13.
13. Warner, *Alone,* p. 63.
14. Thomas Hahn, "The Performance of Gender in the Prioress," *Chaucer Yearbook* 1 (1992), 118.
15. Daniel F. Pigg, "Refiguring Martyrdom: Chaucer's Prioress and Her Tale," *Chaucer Review* 29 (1994), 69 and 66, respectively.

16. Louise O. Fradenburg, "Criticism, Anti-Semitism, and the Prioress's Tale," *Exemplaria* 2 (1990), 105. Fradenburg's article has been invaluable to my thinking on "The Prioress's Tale." Though my concern is with gender in addition to anti-Semitism in relation to the tale, her work has provided a number of useful models for this paper.

17. Fradenburg, "Criticism, Anti-Semitism," p. 105.

18. Alcuin Blamires, "Questions of Gender in Chaucer, from Anelida to Troilus," *Leeds Studies in English* n.s. 25 (1994), 86–87.

19. Robert Worth Frank, Jr., "Miracles of the Virgin, Medieval Anti-Semitism, and the 'Prioress's Tale'" in *The Wisdom of Poetry: Essays in Early English Literature in Honor of Morton W. Bloomfield,* ed. Larry D. Benson and Siegfried Wenzel (Kalamazoo, MI: Medieval Institute Publications, 1982), p. 183.

20. Quotations from "The Prioress's Tale" and the General Prologue refer to Larry D. Benson, ed., *The Riverside Chaucer* (Boston: Houghton Mifflin, 1987).

21. Julia Kristeva, *Powers of Horror: An Essay on Abjection,* trans. Leon S. Roudiez (New York: Columbia University Press, 1982), p. 2.

22. Frank, "Miracles," p. 187. An opposing argument is offered by Alexander, "Madame Eglentyne," pp. 118–119.

23. Elisa Narin van Court makes the argument that the expulsion and/or absence of Jews within Christian societies did not preclude a Christian preoccupation with Jewish presence ("The Siege of Jerusalem and Augustinian Historians: Writing About Jews in Fourteenth-Century England," *Chaucer Review* 29 [1995], p. 228).

24. Hyam Maccoby, *Judas Iscariot and the Myth of Jewish Evil* (New York: The Free Press, 1992), p. 109. Chapter 7 ("Judas and the Growth of Anti-Semitism," pp. 101–126) provides a concise discussion of the influence of clerical anti-Semitism on the representations of Jews in religious and secular drama, literature, and art through the Middle Ages to the twentieth century.

25. John Archer, "The Structure of Anti-Semitism in the Prioress's Tale," *Chaucer Review* 19 (1984), pp. 49–50. Archer offers the argument that Jews were forced into the position of moneylenders by increasingly powerful guilds that systematically excluded them from trade and industry. Thus Christian society forced them to fit an image that it had already determined for them. See also Jeremy Cohen, *The Friars and the Jews: The Evolution of Medieval Anti-Judaism* (Ithaca: Cornell University Press, 1982), p. 51. Cohen locates this trend more specifically as a phenomenon beginning in the twelfth century and in connection with the appearance of the ritual-murder charge. Such accusations resulted in increased threats of physical violence toward Jewish communities, forcing them into greater dependence upon the protection of (Christian) kings and princes.

26. On this point, Maccoby offers the interesting argument that the authors of the Gospels intentionally minimized Roman involvement in Christ's crucifixion in order to promote Christianity as nonthreatening to Roman

power. Thus the Jews are presented as the primary enemies of Jesus, and Judas' betrayal is made to seem more drastic but also quite simple: "he has gone over to the Jews. His name then, which continually echoes Ioudaioi, acquires the meaning 'Jew.' Judas now encapsulates the aura of treachery and hostility emanating from the Jews that has been shown surrounding Jesus throughout. Judas's treachery is now not only seen as the culmination of a lifetime of meanness, but as the fulfillment of the potentialities of his name" (*Judas Iscariot,* p. 80).

27. Critics like Edward Condren have read these lines as an indication of the Prioress's frustrated "maternal instincts." See Condren, "The Prioress: A Legend of Spirit, a Life of Flesh,*" Chaucer Review* 23 (1989), p. 194.

28. On the sex/gender split and the cultural demands that each subject be constituted as one of two genders, see Judith Butler, *Gender Trouble: Feminism and the Subversion of Identity* (New York: Routledge Press, 1990), pp. 1–34. See also Carolyn Dinshaw, *Chaucer's Sexual Poetics* (Madison: University of Wisconsin Press, 1989) for a discussion of Chaucer's use of figurative and abstract gender formulations; and Hahn, "Performance," esp. pp. 119–121.

29. Contrary to my reading of the Prioress's portrait as yet another manifestation of Chaucer's conscious ironizing of the assumptions and conventions of his culture, Allen Koretsky follows D. W. Robertson, Jr. in his reading of the Prioress as an allegorical figure embodying "innocence." See Koretsky, "Dangerous Innocence: Chaucer's Prioress and Her Tale" in *Jewish Presences in English Literature,* ed. Derek Cohen and Deborah Heller (Montreal: McGill-Queen's University Press, 1990), pp. 10–24; and more generally on reading allegorically, see Robertson, *A Preface to Chaucer: Studies in Medieval Perspectives* (Princeton: Princeton University Press, 1962), pp. 286–390.

30. Hahn, "Performance," p. 114.

31. R. Howard Bloch, *Medieval Misogyny and the Invention of Western Romantic Love* (Chicago: University of Chicago Press, 1991), pp. 93–112.

32. A similar catalogue is offered by Jane Tibbetts Schulenburg, "The Heroics of Virginity: Brides of Christ and Sacrificial Mutilation" in *Women in the Middle Ages and Renaissance: Literary and Historical Perspectives,* ed. Mary Beth Rose (Syracuse: Syracuse University Press, 1986), pp. 29–72. Schulenburg's arguments are not incompatible with Bloch's, though they are much more firmly anchored historically than are his. She offers an especially interesting argument on the particular vulnerability of nuns to rape during times of war. The clerical response to this vulnerability, she argues, may be seen in the wide circulation of exempla highlighting the virtues of suicide and self-mutilation for women in order to avoid the loss of treasured virginity (and therefore her place at the right hand of God) through sexual assault.

33. Bloch, *Medieval Misogyny,* p. 99; Cyprian, "The Dress of Virgins," ed. Roy J. Deferrari, p. 39.

34. Warner, *Alone,* pp. 65–66.

35. Bloch, *Medieval Misogyny,* p. 97.

36. Judith Ferster, "'Your Praise is Performed by Men and Children': Language and Gender in the Prioress's Prologue and Tale," *Exemplaria* 2 (1990), p. 151.

37. Tertullian, "On the Veiling of Virgins" in *The Ante-Nicene Fathers: Translations of the Writings of the Fathers Down to A.D. 325,* vol. IV, ed. Alexander Roberts and James Donaldson (1885; repr. Grand Rapids: William B. Eerdmans Publishing Company, 1979), p. 34.

38. See, for example, Alain de Lille, *The Complaint of Nature* [De planctu naturae], trans. Douglas M. Moffat (Hamden: Archon Books, 1972). See also Peter Damian, *Book of Gomorrah* [Liber Gomorrhianus]: *An Eleventh-Century Treatise Against Clerical Homosexual Practices,* trans. Pierre J. Payer (Waterloo: Wilfred Laurier University Press, 1982). Peter Damian's work especially stresses the sinfulness of pederastic homosexual relations, most explicitly in Book VI.

39. Stephen Spector, "Empathy and Enmity in the Prioress's Tale" in *The Olde Daunce: Love, Friendship, Sex and Marriage in the Medieval World,* ed. Robert R. Edwards and Stephen Spector (Albany: State University of New York Press, 1991), p. 222.

40. Archer, "Structure," p. 50.

41. See Wolfgang E. H. Rudat, "Gender-Crossing in the Prioress's Tale: Chaucer's Satire on Theological Anti-Semitism?" *Cithara* 33 (1994), 11–17. See esp. p. 14 for a bizarre reading of this scene. Rudat is convinced that Chaucer's description of the Prioress's size in the General Prologue indicates that she is or has been pregnant, and thus he reads the clergeon being stuffed into the Jews' privy as a "birth reversal."

42. Brown, "The Prioress's Tale," p. 450 and pp. 454–455.

43. Helen Jewell, *Women in Medieval England* (Manchester: Manchester University Press, 1996), pp. 154–185; Shahar, *Fourth Estate,* pp. 50–51.

44. Julia Bolton Holloway, "Crosses and Boxes: Latin and Vernacular" in *Equally in God's Image: Women in the Middle Ages,* ed. Julia Bolton Holloway, Constance S. Wright, and Joan Bechtold, (New York: Peter Lang, 1990), p. 60.

45. Fradenburg, "Criticism, Anti-Semitism," p. 105.

46. Jewell, *Women,* p. 168.

47. Steven F. Kruger, "The Bodies of Jews in the Late Middle Ages" in *The Idea of Medieval Literature: New Essays on Chaucer and Medieval Culture,* ed. James M. Dean and Christian K. Zacher (Newark: University of Delaware Press, 1992), pp. 306–307.

48. Condren, "The Prioress," p. 205.

49. Kristeva, *Powers,* p. 96.

50. An earlier version of this paper was delivered at the fifth annual Texas Medieval Association conference at Trinity University, San Antonio, Texas in September 1995.

CHAPTER 9

LIKE A VIRGIN:
MARY AND HER DOUBTERS
IN THE N-TOWN CYCLE

Cindy L. Carlson

> *The deep connection between Mary's virginal body and the social body of medieval society is demonstrated in the "Trial" play; the visibility of Mary's pregnancy and the invisibility of her virginity present a challenge to the conception of the female body.*

The miraculous conception, painless birth, and continuously maintained virginity of Mary is often dramatized on the English medieval stage as a matter of doubt that receives glorious resolution. Joseph expresses his doubts as to whether he is a cuckold, the midwife ascertains Mary's continued virginity, detractors accuse her of infidelity. This paper will explore the connections between Mary's virginal body and the social body of which she is an anomalous part, with special reference to the trials of Mary in the N-town cycle. Mary's continuing virginity through conception and childbirth and her undergoing these events without sexual intercourse and its accompanying defloration both threaten the cohesion of the society she lives in and provide a model for that society to recover its purity and wholeness. Verifications of the virginity of Mary, complaints about its loss, scandal contrived by detractors all become tests for doubters. Accepting this miracle becomes a sign of inclusion in the portion of forgiven and redeemed humanity, rejection a sign of faction and doom.

Reference to Mary Douglas's *Purity and Danger* has become a usual point
of departure for explorations of the connection between the physical body
and the social body.[1] There she demonstrates that the body's boundaries are
inextricably linked with anxieties about a society's own systems of organization, with its social integrity. Theresa Coletti relies on Douglas as she
makes the point that Mary's body's "integrity and impermeability identify
that body as holy; with holiness understood as chaste marriage and physical purity; its putative signs of sexual pollution—disturbances in the margins—open it up to the 'dirt' that accompanies marital disorder—domestic
strife, public shame, potential punishment."[2] In this essay, I will explore how
the social body, with its potential for dirt, creates anxieties of containment
and exclusion in which the social body displaces doubts and transgressions
to the boundaries of the body or beyond the boundaries into the category
of the abject, those beings finally rejected as utterly impure contaminants of
the body. Mary's contested and discussed virginity, dramatized in the cycles,
becomes an example of that social enterprise in which what was internal to
the body becomes externalized and impure.[3] Because the visibility of her
pregnancy and motherhood, when combined with the invisibility of her
virginity, presents such a challenge to the constitution of the chaste female
body, characters in the cycle plays want to discredit Mary's chastity, discover
her unchastity, and degrade her with insults. Without belief and repentance,
these characters who act with "common sense" expectations combined
with some level of low malice attack Mary's integrity and, by implication,
the integrity of the social body as well. The plays' vindication of Mary
through her own humility and acceptance of judgment serves as a social
model, not only for women but also for men and especially men exercising
princely or judicial power as they come to re-create themselves as virtuous
believers and enactors of God's will.

Mary bears God but always knows herself as a humble part of God's
plan. So, too, the ruler must recall humility in his exercise of a power that
is incommensurable with that of God. While the plays all conclude with
harmony and belief apparently reestablished, they also enact a process in
which the interior doubts of the individual believer become exteriorized—
whether in the withered hand of an impiously doubtful midwife or in the
rejections and abjection of unbelieving Jews. Doubts about the integrity of
church courts or the integrity of rulers are exteriorized as the characters of
scandal-mongers and worldly advisors. Meanwhile, the judge retains his authority, the emperor his majesty by exercising their respective roles with a
humility that is the analogue of Mary's chastity, always present though not
always patently apparent to the skeptical or commonsensical observer and
subject. This move to exteriorize internal doubt to the margins of the social body—the humbly born midwives and scandal mongers, the "foreign"

Jews or Romans—protects the body from realizing its own doubts, its own vulnerable openings to questioning. The social body becomes like the Virgin's body: sacred, untouched, and apparently untouchable.

Touching the virginal body in order to test for the existence of its virginity could, of course, occur. However, while medical texts may contain tests for virginity, few records of midwives testing for virginity remain from the medieval period; those that do exist arise from "notorious cases" like that of Joan of Arc.[4] On the medieval English stage, Mary regularly becomes such a notorious case. In the Chester "Nativity," when Joseph arrives home after a long absence, upon seeing his wife, he immediately draws the conclusion that old men should never marry young women because the man's age will render him unable to satisfy his young, desirous wife with the all-too-foreseeable result that the foolish husband will find himself cuckolded. Joseph is certain that the child that Mary so visibly carries in her "great bellye" cannot be his because he has been too "ould and could" to make love for the past thirty years.[5] With this cuckold anxiety out of the fabliaux tradition, Joseph's complaints seem to promise, and create the possibility, that what Joseph knows, his whole world will know, so he determines that the best plan is to abandon Mary. If she is to be notorious, let her be notorious without him. Only angelic reassurances in his dream reconcile Joseph to remaining with Mary and shielding her from the potential enmity of other men.

For the birth of God's son, Joseph acquires midwives and promises to pay them though Mary assures her husband that midwives are welcome but unnecessary. In fact, a little quiet on stage suffices for the painless delivery. At Mary's announcement of this astonishing state of affairs, a star appears and Joseph is fully reconciled to the Angel's message: "Nowe leeve I the angells worde is trewe/ that thow art a cleane maye."[6] The painless delivery also provides sufficient proof of virginity to one midwife, Tebell. She has never until this night seen a painless delivery, so she takes Mary as a "cleane mayden" because she has given birth in "blys."[7]

Her more cynical colleague, Salome, rejects Tebell's judgment as impossible and declares that she will examine Mary and "know yt [the existence of virginity] if I cann."[8] Joseph's expectable doubts and his expectable hiring of midwives have turned a private doubt into a more public occasion. What Joseph and one midwife accept on angelic assurance and appearances of bliss during childbirth, the suggestively named Salome must examine. At her attempt to touch Mary in her "sexu secreto" as indicated by the stage directions, Salome declares that her hands dried up and lost their feeling.[9] Salome has taken her cue from the medical texts that recommend that a midwife may examine a woman by sight and by touch as to the existence of virginity, but has reckoned without the divine plan that has rendered the medical texts and their common learning otiose. Indeed, when feeling has been restored to her hands, and with it her professional capacity to examine other women, Salome declares that her experience has validated the angel's message and has established her belief in Mary's virginity. The miracle of Jesus' conception and birth and a continual virginity that has been doubted, nearly tested, then considered proven, and all three steps on the path of belief have tried the limits of belief and respectability, not to mention representability. The test for virginity has turned into a test of the doubting midwife's hand as it withers. To test Mary's virginity is to risk a reversal or a discovery of scandal that injures the would-be tester. What has been made visible is the doubt, the lack, of the unbeliever rather than the virginal status of the new mother. Indeed, the test turns out to damage the physical integrity of the doubter, not the immaculate doubted. Doubt about the secret sex of the Virgin has turned into an examination of a midwife's hand and, in the process, has moved a doubt at the center to a doubt at the margins of the social body. Proper belief and its open acknowledgment restore Salome's own body and her acceptability to the scene being played on stage as she is reincorporated as a believer.

Within the same play, Octavianus is tempted by his own people to accept their acclamations of his divinity. Octavianus will eventually conclude that he cannot claim the limitless power appropriate only to a divine being when he compares his birth with that of Jesus. As Jesus is accepted as God's son by the extraordinary circumstances of his death and the virginity of his mother, so Octavianus notes his own birth circumstances, those shared by all other humans, as a primary reason to refuse the wrongly offered "divinity." When Octavianus first strides on to the stage preceded by his nuntius, he sees his power as virtually limitless. He is the "prince moste of 'powere' and able to destroy, at will, any rival leaders of whatever rank.[10] He claims to rule the whole world at his "owne will" and has doubled the size of Rome's empire so that all other realms are tributary to her.[11] In fact, his power is so mighty that in addition to an English exposition he explains its extent in (very "corrupt") French, the language of the medieval English court system.[12] He closes the French portion of his speech by declaring his uniqueness as a ruler by the "clare et sanke mater."[13]

The oath by the Virgin should be taken seriously, for his further assertions of greatness and his resolution to count all the heads of his empire and to make an account of all the pennies that they shall pay in the census seem expressions of limitless power until two of his senators come to him with the senate's universal approbation of honoring Octavianus as God. Secundus Senator recommends the offer as a kind of "meede" that is a just reward for all of Octavianus' accomplishments.[14] Octavianus' response is surprisingly meek for one so powerful: he declares himself but flesh, blood and bone, born of a woman like any other human. As he was born, so is he aging in a natural process that will end with death. He has much more in common with other men than his earlier speeches that claimed absolute power had admitted. Because Octavianus realizes that he does not exist outside of time, without beginning or ending, he therefore declares that he is not a god, for "Hit were unkynde," considering that he does not fulfill the requirements of divine existence.[15] Octavianus must admit that despite his unusual temporal (and temporary) power, he is not unique because he has been conceived and born in the usual fashion and is now subject to time and its decay in the way common and natural to all humankind.

From the ruler's perspective of his own power limited by its very physicality and its attendant decay, the play moves to the ruled. Mary, upon seeing the number of people caught up in the census and taxation imposed by Octavianus, wonders that men may show such various feelings—surely the coming of God's son should naturally unite them in bliss of the contemplation of the great fact of his advent. The angel reassures her that this unity will be forthcoming as they see the fulfillment of God's promise to Abraham and Christ's aid to needy believers. Only the Jews are to be shut out from his unity; they pass out of "kinde" at Christ's coming.[16] In the apparently natural unity created by belief in Christ, a unity more universal and enduring than that asserted by Octavianus, a disturbing, unnatural remnant, the Jews remain as outcasts, not renewed by God's grace because they will not believe what even the great Roman emperor believes through the prophecies of the sybil. That belief unites (most of) humankind in one body. That belief shows the emperor the limit of his own worldly power. Believers become like the Virgin in accepting the overwhelming power of God and, to the extent that they act on that belief, usher in an era of human integrity and wholeness, recovered out of human separation and diversity.

The Roman Empire is the attempt to create peace and union that is doomed to fail, maintained as it is by the threat of force. The military might of the Roman empire demonstrates not strength but fragility, for this social body is always subject to invasion, betrayal, and corruption. The empire of all believers is created through the gracious belief in an invisible truth, whether of Mary's virginity, Jesus' divinity, or the triune God. Furthermore, this grace has no time limit as does the empire, a purely human creation and limited as all human works are.

In all this harmony and holy fellowship underwritten by the Virgin's belief, who is herself an embodiment of that belief, a disturbing remnant of humanity hold on to past experience and identity. In the angel's announcement of a world of recovered integrity, the Jews mourn and maintain their separate status and their final division from the newly natural unity of humankind. Without minimizing the anti-Semitism of this passage, I would add that, for an audience who perhaps has never seen a member of a Jewish community, the Jews serve as an image of those who separate themselves from the body of humanity, adhering to an older covenant that made them God's chosen, uniquely His own people. Mary, the seemingly fallen woman, one who might be expected in ordinary circumstances to mourn her own abjection, has now to be understood as the miraculous, ever-virginal source of the new (near) unity of humankind in the world, as well as the mother of the God who will unite his believers in heaven. The two midwives are made believers, but the spectacular convert is Octavianus, and with him the potential conversion of the Roman Empire and the subsequent transformation of the uneasy Pax Romana into an eternal peace for all believers. That transformation receives a fitting image in the church that Octavianus causes to be built, St. Marye, dedicated to the Virgin, she who is the altar of God. This church remains standing even at the time of the play's presentation, in contrast to the pagan temple that collapses once the sybil has prophesied that a virgin will conceive a child. Men know that the church still exists and know its name, whereas the pagan temple has become a thing neglected and feared as a part of a "feendes phantasye."[17] The pagan past is a dead past, abandoned in favor of the living church.

In similar fashion, Expositor adduces a second miracle, the rotting of Salome's impious hand as a negative example of the "fowle sinne of unbelief."[18] Belief leads to a living church and a vividly recognized bodiliness of belief in the body of the Virgin, the body of the church building, and the social body of all believers. Unbelief, while presented as expectable, results in the corrupting of the body of Salome and the mourning of the Jews at their exclusion from the Christian body; they have become the offending hand that has been cut off. Salome quickly learns her lesson and has her hand restored by the infant Jesus. Thus she is ultimately stronger than the Jews who are unable to give up their unbelief. The self-declared greatest of emperors can be humble himself while a lowly midwife and the abjected Jews resist. The thus feminized Jews can be no part of the body of Christian believers while the hypermasculine Roman emperor and the men of this empire can establish a new church.[19] In this play, the experiences of the Virgin turn out to be models for (mostly) male believers on the creation of the social, believing body of the church, a body modeled after her own. The disturbing, exotic element remains at the margins of the body—the hand, the Jews—and remains as a threat to bodily integrity.

Yet, without this disturbing remnant, does the social body have integrity? Is the Virgin virginal if not questioned? Stallybrass and White remark that in social organization, "the 'top' attempts to reject and eliminate the 'bottom' for reasons of prestige and status, only to discover, not only that it is in some way frequently dependent on that low-Other . . . but that the top *includes* that low symbolically, as a primary eroticized constituent of its own fantasy life."[20] The body of all believers constitutes itself by casting out of the body the nonbelievers and placing them at the margins, never becoming part of the body yet remaining as a threat, a challenge, a site for fantasy. The hand of the doubter withers as it seeks to question the Virgin's "secret sex," and its shriveled incapacity is a fearful and thrilling demonstration of the very virginity it meant to test. This testing of received belief in the virginity of the Virgin does not threaten the Christian body of believers, for the questioners and doubters in this play are already on the margins of the social body. In fact, this play further relegates any genuine challenge to belief to those social margins to which believers have already relegated those of low or abject status: women, Jews, pagan Romans.[21]

This same process of abjecting the doubter occurs in the various plays that dramatize Joseph's doubts about Mary's virginity and fidelity. These plays turn Joseph into the comic, elderly, incapacitated man only too likely to be cuckolded by his young, nubile wife. Both York and Towneley include plays that show Joseph troubled by his obviously pregnant wife who claims that the child she bears belongs to God and her husband. The York cycle relies heavily on an "official" interpretation of its own drama in the"Doctour of the Annunciation" and of Symeon in "The Purification," yet Joseph, in "Joseph's Trouble About Mary," is allowed plenty of stage time to lament that he, an old man, ever allowed himself to be talked into the comic (to others) and inappropriate marriage to a young woman. An angel sets Joseph straight as to the circumstances of his marriage and the behavior of his wife in his absence and plainly forbids Joseph to abandon his wife as he had planned. In Towneley, Joseph's long speech lamenting his cuckolding also requires an angel to explain the facts of divine conception and to command Joseph to continue living with his still virginal wife. From these sorts of play, Flanigan, using the Wakefield "Joseph's Trouble About Mary," argues that

> although the play does hold out Mary and Joseph as models for conjugal conduct, and in this way serves to reinforce the prevailing social structure, the universalizing claims on which such modes are based are partially and periodically undercut by the very conditions that enable Mary and Joseph to function as models. Thus the play simultaneously affirms and undercuts the inherited social and theological order.[22]

The audience's trouble about Mary, and Joseph, is seen to rest in the way this chaste marriage signally does not resemble the marriages of those in the audience.[23] Yet the marriage and Mary are surely not news to this audience; they are unlikely to be in suspense as to the father of the child or Joseph's conduct in cleaving to his wife. So James may find that the plays that explore Joseph's doubts offer a nearly "blasphemous" view of the continuing virginity of Mary but that the same "blasphemy" allows that "opposites of social wholeness and social differentiation could be both affirmed, and brought into creative tension one with the other."[24] If the blasphemous exists in these plays, it is marginalized into the comic figure of the old man worrying about cuckoldry even as the drama puts into play the examination of the body of Christians in the town's audience and in the wider Christian society. Without the "blasphemy," there may be no holiness to protect from unbelief. The play can reassure the audience as it invites the audience to consider themselves to be members of the integral body of Christian believers, never doubted but in jest, never doubted without the resolution of doubt. The very unworthiness of Joseph's doubts, even if they might be seen as "typical" rather than stereotypical, reduces the danger of such doubts.

The Towneley "Annunciation" follows a similar pattern with a Joseph who worries about a young wife's sexual energy. He rejects the story of the angelic visitation as a tale of an unnatural, perhaps impossible, sexual congress in favor of a more likely story that would involve the pregnant Mary with a young man. The angel's explanations, coupled with Mary's own meekness reassure Joseph and reconcile him to the facts of his marriage. In the "Salutation" play, Mary explains that God will throw "myghty men" from their thrones and exalt the meek.[25] This reversal and the attendant unity of all believers is presented as unnatural but possible through grace. And the model of the miraculous is Mary, exalted virgin and meek, even though vindicated, wife. Because she unites and explores these opposing qualities, she and Joseph can maintain a union that only Joseph wanted to escape. To the extent that he is like the Virgin and has his doubts resolved by a heavenly messenger, to the extent that he gives up a belief in what he might expect would naturally be true, he can be happy with Mary. He must even take the child who is not his as his own, surely a reversal from the majesty of the righteously angered husband, painfully touched in his sexual capabilities and dominion. Joseph's wand may have flowered, but he is like a patriarch without being one; he is like the Virgin without being more than a virgin. In retrospect, Joseph's righteous anger takes on the aspect of a tantrum of a child shut out from the great secret shared by Mary and the angel.

In York, the same secret is shared by Mary's maids, too. Joseph, as in the other plays centering on his worries about having been cuckolded, bemoans his marriage to a "yonge wenche" when his old bones are as "heuy als lede."[26] He complains that he did not know what it meant when his rod flowered, so that he was suddenly married before he had time to consider what the whole process had been about. Joseph's flowering rod images a virility that Joseph expressly disclaims in practice and in theory; this virility of Joseph's, which would have been quite troublesome in a chaste marriage, has also, like the doubt of and resistance to the virginal birth and its implications, been moved to the exterior away from Joseph's body into a wooden rod that may flower without threatening a virginal marriage. And that virtual virility provides a fitting image for how the Christian "family" has been formed through belief rather than through birth. The believer is part of and partakes of the spiritual body of belief.

Where Joseph is agitated, the two maids partake of Mary's calm, calling her to arise from her book and greet her husband, assuring Joseph that he should reject his own weak fears. While Joseph initially rejects angelic reassurance, begging the angel "A, I am full werie, lefe, late me slepe," he recovers his strength along with his belief and offers to carry the family's possessions to Bethlehem.[27] Manliness has been restored to the newly courageous Joseph, apparently taking away his former exhaustion. This restoration of the believer's body and the reestablishment of marital harmony through that same belief, common in the plays of Joseph's doubts, may add to a discourse of marital harmony that comes from what Schnell calls the "discourse on marriage":

> The discourse on marriage thus presents a more differentiated image of women that the discourse on woman. In contrast to the black-and-white world of the latter (Eve/Mary; evil women/good women; women create a hell/heaven on earth) the perspective of the discourse on marriage is pragmatic and realistic: women, like men, possess good and bad qualities. Therefore both sexes have to be understanding and forgiving.[28]

If texts about women tend toward the extravagant praise of a few women at the expense of the reviled many, texts about marriage for married couples are far more capable of seeing two faulty human beings trying to sustain a marriage by some degree of mutual forbearance. The comedy of the Joseph plays may come from a combination of the two sorts of discourse. Mary is idealized so that Joseph's humanity can seem quite comic in contrast. Yet that contrast may comfort the faulty believer who may be able to surpass Joseph, or imagine that it might be possible to do so, in purity and steadfastness of belief. When Joseph presents himself as excluded even before he weds his new wife, he has yet to adjust to his humble status as a redeemed version of the old man fooled by a young wife. Yet, in this understanding reached by Mary and her Lord, Joseph may yet be included, not as a cuckold but as the father of Jesus, a fatherhood that he has only to accept in spite of its disturbing otherness. By acceptance, Joseph himself removes the sting of the cruel comedy in which he has cast himself. The comedy becomes one of inclusion for the humble, and perhaps humbled, husband. Belief, in these plays, cures the feelings of doubts and rejections, but through a maneuver that casts unbelief as a form of choice, even perverse choice. If the unbeliever rejects the Virgin, then it is seen as just that the unbeliever be rejected through exile, relegation, and mockery. The choice to rejoin the body of believers is presented as a choice thoroughly under the control of the nonbeliever who receives helpful visions and signs and who could, if necessary, borrow from the book that the industrious Virgin reads.

The N-town pageants that concern Mary are, like those of the Chester cycle, political as well as spiritual and direct their political attention to the men who run the world's institutions. In these plays, Joseph and Mary go to trial because they have apparently violated their vows to retain their virginity even as they fulfill their duty to marry.[29] With this "trial" pageant, N-town opens up the issue of integrity to a whole society, particularly those in power or those who invoke the power of its institutions.[30] Once again, the witness of Mary's pregnant body seems to be unimpeachable, for the sexual act must naturally have preceded Mary's all-too-visible pregnancy. To resolve this contradiction between what Joseph and Mary represent as the truth of their lives and vows and what Mary's body seems to "say," the judge in the "Trial of Mary and Joseph" must put aside a too easy reliance on what is expectable and examine, too, what other bodies may reveal about their natures. The "truth" potion that should have revealed, as the Detractors thought, that Mary and Joseph have lied about their continence, reveals instead that the accusers have a malicious intent to destroy the social unity of the world of true believers.

In order to appreciate the social impact of the trial of Joseph and Mary, we need to reconsider the eleventh pageant, "The Parliament of Heaven," in which the four initially discordant daughters of God, Misericordia, Pax, Justicia, and Veritas, puzzle out their conflicting claims in reconciling mankind's merited punishment for sin and God's promise to redeem mankind. The two requirements of mercy and justice seem to be in hopeless conflict because God's reliability, his truth, depends on fulfilling these irreconcilable promises. The birth of Christ allows mutually exclusive vows to be fulfilled, to the great joy of the newly reconciled daughters of God. This pattern of reconciliation bears on the virginity of Mary because it appears to recall the "so-called 'juridical' theory of atonement" which, Bugge argues, threw "the weight of emphasis on Christ's humanity" and so upon his sexuality.[31] Christ in this theory becomes the most desirable husband for the believer; in fact, he can become a "rival with other men for the affections of holy women."[32] Mary and Joseph's marriage rests purely on its spiritual union and yet remains vulnerable, as other more common marriages, to human jealousy over a rival, even a holy one. N-town sets up the play of Joseph's doubts with a theory of redemption that makes the humane and human Christ a potential lover for Mary. At the moment of conception, Mary exclaims that she feels in her body the perfect formation of the infant Christ, both "Parfyte God and parfyt man."[33] Indeed her physical reactions go even further as she declares: "I cannote telle what joy, what blysse, /Now I fele in my body."[34] The physical response to the conception in Mary's sinless body shows a kind of untainted sensual joy available only to those whose lover is Christ, the reconciler of opposites. That joy of union is available, too, to the member of the body of believers, created through the joy of Mary in the body with Christ in her body.

Immediately after the tender farewells of Mary and Joseph, Joseph arrives home and finds the all-too-pregnant Mary. Like other Josephs in other pageants, he rejects her story of an angel and accuses Mary of consorting, instead, with "sum boy" who "clothyd was clene and gay."[35] In this most legal of plays, Joseph considers his legal options before deciding to abandon Mary: he could report his erring wife so that, as an adulteress, she might be stoned. He does not want to exact vengeance, but he does not want to live as a dishonored husband, either. At their prayers, including Mary's that she does not want to be the one to reveal the secret of her son's conception as a matter of "privite" between the mother and father of the child, God sends down a messenger angel to calm the fears of the worried Joseph. After prayer has reconciled husband and wife, this same information is requested by Joseph and shared by Mary as the triangle of the virginal union of Mary with Joseph and her physical as well as spiritual union with God in the conception of Christ here find harmony on the model of the four daughters of God. The human husband has replaced doubts with knowledge, and this enlightenment does not dismay Joseph as finding out about a human lover would, for appearances to the contrary, Mary has not violated her marriage vows to him. Mary is the wife in whom irreconcilable conditions meet: she is faithful to her husband and pregnant by another's means, she is obedient and exalted, she is virginal and without concupiscence and yet has experienced physical bliss in abundance. In this union spiritual marriage is held out as an ideal that may seem to denigrate the more usual consummated marriages of other men and women.[36] Yet Schnell's work that indicates that women can be seen in a number of ways in "discourses of marriage," so that its versions of wives and husbands, more various than a simple hierarchy common to what he calls "discourses of woman," might complicate the picture for our understanding of a medieval audience perhaps enjoying a pious couple, perfect in the wife and less so in the husband, finding reconciliation through mutual forbearance.[37] A comedic husband whose blustering here seems harmless might resonate with an audience, even as the role relegates religious, as well as marital, doubt to the ribald, jealous-old-man tales of cuckolds who deserve their cheating wives.

This same variety of aspect in the presentation of Mary as the embodiment of all Christian believers is present, too, in "The Trial of Mary and Joseph." With reference to the image of Mary, we should keep in mind what Victor and Edith Turner have usefully called the "entire semantic field, an area of multivocality" of religious images during the Middle Ages.[38] While the Turners are speaking about cult images associated with pilgrimage sites, we can see a similar "multivocality" in the character of Mary in the N-town series of pageants devoted to her honor. Indeed, the N-town pageants have traditionally been seen as especially concerned with Mary and her worship, meriting a separate publication of the Marian plays. But in order to honor Mary, her honor must be called into question so that it may be defended. In this regard, N-town goes farther than York, Chester, or Wakefield because the resolving of Joseph's trouble about Mary in N-town does not settle the matter of the Virgin's integrity in this cycle. From private doubts and a near comic tone as Joseph behaves as the stereotypical old man cuckolded, N-town moves to public denunciation, trial, and truth serums. An angel speaks to Joseph; the results of the legal trial by ordeal "speak" to the audience "summoned" to the trial and to the judges who must resolve the issue.

Putting Mary and Joseph on trial for breaking their vows of chastity poses several problems for the N-town pageant, not least of which is the danger of bringing into disrepute exactly what the pageant seems to want to exalt, the continuing virginity of the Virgin. To borrow Bloch's formulations of the problem with virginity: virginity transcends the corporeal, which is itself linked to the feminine, allowing a certain equality only to those women who are not feminine and have come to be masculine in their escape of the corporeal.[39] If, then, virginity escapes corporeality, it becomes an absolute without material existence.[40] If this abstract virginity is spoken, it suffers the sort of exposure that destroys the universality of the abstraction in the particular words of its exposure.[41] But if the establishment of an ideal Virgin and the corresponding ideal of the integrity of the social, believing body requires delineation through the defining and the rejection of those elements that question the ideal, then a virginity not questioned could hardly be said to exist at all. "The Trial of Mary and Joseph" picks its way through these issues by creating a stage audience of lawyers and judges, all male, whose own obedience and humility come to stand in for Mary's virginity. This connection with Mary's virtues connects them, too, as objects of denunciation, for just as Mary is accused in scandalous language of unchastity, the integrity of judges is just as basely accused. Finally, the comic lowness of the accusers places this scandalous doubt in the mouths of the unworthy, proved to be so during the trial by ordeal.

Because all the characters on stage, with the exception of Mary, are men, there will be no question of examining or revealing the Virgin's body in this pageant. The issue of virginity has been transferred to an issue of fidelity to an oath of chastity—this is a trial about words first of all. The virtuous do not speak in order to demonstrate fidelity to their oaths of chastity because that oath is protected by an oath of truth-telling within the court. And that second oath is "proved" true by swallowing a potion, by a taking in rather than a speaking out. Both Joseph and Mary subject themselves to this judicial ordeal in an effort to let another version of their bodies "speak," especially necessary when Mary's pregnancy seems to communicate a worrisomely corporeal message of fallibility, of the body triumphing over any effort to transcend its desires and capabilities. Because the bystanders on stage are men who will recuperate their own exercise of power by becoming like the Virgin, physical and spiritual chastity become models for a less problematic humility, able to be demonstrated without the close physical examination that virginity would seem both to require and to refuse. The threatened annihilation of the Virgin and Joseph and their disquieting chastity is moved to the background as the Virgin becomes an image for the judge's embodied virtue.

The judge will need his humble capacity to await the revelation of the truth because the court appears to be in a fury of wild accusations of summoners against the audience, witnesses against the accused, and the judge. In his first appearance, Den names both men and women he could call into court, but the move into court is actually initiated by two detractors, Reysesclaundyr and Bakbytere, who have a relationship that allows each to call the other "brother." In this world of language, they delight in calling into question what seems and what is, and they begin with the Virgin who is "Calede Mayd Mary" and who "semyed so holy" that "Men seyd" she was fed by an angel.[42] Against this holy seeming and pious report, Primus Detractor points out Mary's pregnancy that has left her with a belly as swollen as "thinne or myne."[43] This curious comparison incites the detractors to more energetic slander, but it might give the audience pause. The men's swollen bellies suggest that their own bodies have indulged in some grotesque excess; with their own bodies speaking against their own probity, these detractors relegate themselves to the margins of acceptability and believability. Their inflated bellies model their inflated scandal-mongering. Mary's own apparent vow-breaking frees them to break their own bounds in their vituperative treatment of her reputation. If Mary is pregnant, then it must mean, says Secundus Detractor, that Joseph did not take her in marriage until he had tried her sexually. Primus Detractor disagrees only in order to say something more vile: Mary has done worse than consummate her marriage despite her vows of virginity because she has taken a young lover. That restatement intensifies the loathing of both detractors, for now they feel free to imagine Mary as a delectable "mursel" and to rue the way old men naturally allow themselves to be cuckolded when they marry a "fresche wench."[44] In the world of male language, Mary cannot be spoken about without having her virginity explored and threatened with rupture. Secundus Doctor Legis warns the detractors to control their language, but even before Mary and Joseph appear in court, they are a source of reported shame to Episcopus, ecclesiastical judge and Mary's cousin.

As Mary is a source of potential shame and scandal among men, so is she a source of silence and humility. The potion meant to give her pain for swearing a false oath does not harm her but burns Primus Detractor, who slanders the court by alleging that Mary survived the ordeal because the judge switched bottles in order to protect a member of his family. Not only does the ordeal show that Mary is fair and clean, but it also motivates the men in court to ask forgiveness of Mary for their "cursyd langage" and "schame unswond."[45] That language has been a "trespace" and a "defamacyon" to Mary and has resulted in "hynderawns" and "maculacion."[46]

Within this circle of male lawyers, judge, detractors, and spouse, there are no other women. The potion taken as a judicial ordeal meant to reveal the truth takes over women's functions of examining the female body for signs of sexual experience.[47] The virginal body cannot be too closely examined from a doubtful perspective without damage to the doubter. Mary's court experience is initiated through doubt and scandal; her body remains beyond examination yet subject to ordeal. N-town creates an ordeal of potion-drinking, a far cry from archaic ordeals that involved the grasping of hot iron and examination of the palm for damage. The pageant avoids a physical examination by ordeal, and the ordeal itself avoids any rupture of the body; indeed the ordeal heals the ruptured social body in the court.

In fact, three people imbibe: Joseph, Mary, and Primus Detractor. Once Joseph has proven his own chastity and freedom from sexual desire by drinking the potion, the most immediate question to Mary concerns her possible adultery. Joseph's innocence now incites Primus Doctor Legis to fury as he call Mary a "bolde bysmare" for denying that sexual contact has led to her pregnancy.[48] The level of masculine abuse rises immediately when it seems that Mary has not only disavowed her oath of virginity and so offended God, but has done so outside of marriage and so offended Joseph, and apparently the male spectators as well, now aligned with the detractors in intemperate speculation that both enjoys and condemns the sinfulness of women.[49]

When Mary drinks the potion and calls God to witness her purity, she shifts the emphasis; after drinking, she prays:

> God as I nevyr knew of mannys maculacion
> But evyr haue liyved in trew virginite,
> Send me this day thi holy consolacyon
> That all this fayr peple my clennes may se.[50]

The spotting of virginity here seems to arise from men, both their language and their gestures, and yet a group of "fayr" people should be able to see Mary's virginity, her cleanness as a freedom from spotting. The beauty of fairness in the people and cleanness in Mary unites them in a visibility of acceptance and belief. Because virginity distances itself from the pleasures of the body, both in action and in prospect, physical integrity may not be the whole issue.[51] If the issue is a will toward purity, then that decision is available to all and may be modeled in pure and controlled speech. At the end of any accusation of Mary, the accuser, whether detractor, speculative midwife, or doubting husband, falls silent and gives up certain desires for dominance. In her study of celibate marriage, Elliot points out that "spiritual marriage repeatedly coincided with or facilitated a collapse in the husband's authority and enabled a relative suspension of gender hierarchy."[52] We can see a suspension in certain other hierarchies as well in the paradox of the chaste wife and mother who imposes silence. Judges are confounded, midwives are less than wise women, detractors feel the sting of their own words.

Other hierarchies remain: doubters who are of sufficiently high status may be readmitted to full belief without intervening physical harm or exile. Jews, curious women, foolish husbands, base scandal-mongers all are reduced by punishment or mockery. The socializing body of Mary may contain all believers, but these believers have a social order inscribed upon them. The doubters who define the hierarchy through their exile or relegation to the lowest rungs confirm the virginity of Mary, the integrity of believers, and the status of judges and emperors.

Notes

1. Mary Douglas, *Purity and Danger: An Analysis of the Concepts of Pollution and Taboo* (New York: Ark, 1984).
2. Theresa Colletti, "Purity and Danger: The Paradox of Mary's Body and the En-gendering of the Infancy Narrative in the English Mystery Cycles," in

Feminist Approaches to the Body in Medieval Literature, ed. Linda Lomperis and Sarah Sainsbury. (Philadelphia: University of Pennsylvania Press, 1993), p. 70. Colletti goes on to connect the questioning of the Virgin's body with the medieval domestic world of couples living in harmony or in conflict, and their impact on the social world of village and ecclesiastical court. She argues that the Virgin's body, in its very corporeality, can destabilize gender expectations and so the social expectations built upon notions of the gendered body. My own project is rather different because I argue that the Virgin's body, as a site for exploration and discussion, shapes what might be acceptable beliefs or behaviors within the social body and what must be excluded from the social body as abject. As such, I do not examine Mary and the relationship that female believers might have to her virginal body but the relationship that powerful men might have with the social body, using the Virgin's body as an image of the ideal social body.

3. This social act is by no means a monolithic, unquestionable act. As Jonathan Gil Harris argues in a work concerned with the body in early modern England, "containment does not necessarily entail a confident, monolithic power turning all subversion to account; more often than not, the production and containment of an *external,* infiltrating threat involves an anxious negotiation—and repudiation—of genuinely disruptive problems generated *within* the body politic, as a result of which the locus of social conflict is symbolically (if not actually) displaced from inside the body to its boundaries and vulnerable apertures." See *Foreign Bodies and the Body Politic: Discourses of Social Pathology in Early Modern England,* Cambridge Studies in Renaissance Literature and Culture 25 (Cambridge: Cambridge University Press, 1998), p. 13.

4. Esther Lastique and Helen Rodnite Lemay, "A Medieval Physician's Guide to Virginity," *Sex in the Middle Ages: A Book of Essays,* ed. Joyce E. Salisbury (New York: Garland Publishing, Inc, 1991), p. 58.

5. *The Chester Mystery Cycle,* eds. R. M. Lumiansky and David Mills, The Early English Text Society, SS 3 (London: Oxford University Press, 1974), 6, lines 131, 134–135.

6. *Chester Mystery Cycle,* 6, lines 511–512.

7. *Chester Mystery Cycle,* 6, lines 530–531.

8. *Chester Mystery Cycle,* 6, line 538.

9. *Chester Mystery Cycle,* 6, lines 542–543.

10. *Chester Mystery Cycle,* 6, line 185.

11. *Chester Mystery Cycle,* 6, lines 196, 201–208.

12. R. M. Lumiansky and David Mills, *The Chester Mystery Cycle: Commentary and Glossary,* The Early English Text Society, SS 9 (London: Oxford University Press, 1986), p. 85.

13. *Chester Mystery Cycle,* 6, line 217.

14. *Chester Mystery Cycle,* 6, line 311.

15. *Chester Mystery Cycle,* 6, line 336.

16. *Chester Mystery Cycle,* 6, line 448.

17. *Chester Mystery Cycle,* 6, line 635.

18. *Chester Mystery Cycle,* 6, line 721.

19. Julia Kristeva, *Powers of Horror: An Essay in Abjection* trans. Leon S. Roudiez (New York: Columbia University Press, 1982). She says the "corpse . . . takes on the abjections of waste in the biblical text. A dying body, lifeless, completely turned into dejection, blurred between the inanimate and the inorganic, a transitional swarming, inseparable lining of a human nature whose life is undistinguishable from the symbolic—the corpse represents fundamental pollution. A body without soul, a non-body, disquieting matter, is to be excluded from God's *territory* as it is from his *speech*" (109, emphasis in the original). The particular horror of the withered hand of the midwife and the withered human remnant of the Jews arises from the sense that the corpse is irremediably attached to living, vital believing flesh and humanity. The text may abject the Jews but cannot quite deny them territory or speech, at least not speech about them.

20. Peter Stallybrass and Allon White, *The Politics and Poetics of Transgression* (Ithaca: Cornell University Press, 1986), p. 5.

21. Stallybrass and White, *Transgression,* p. 19: This process resembles that noted in carnival and "its nostalgia; its uncritical populism (carnival often violently abuses and demonizes *weaker,* not stronger, social groups—women, ethnic and religious minorities, those who 'don't belong'—in a process of *displaced abjection*); its failure to do away with the official dominant culture, its licensed complicity)."

22. C. Clifford Flanigan, "Liminality, Carnival, and Social Structure: The Case of Late Medieval Biblical Drama," in *Victor Turner and the Construction of Cultural Criticism: Between Literature and Anthropology,* ed. Kathleen M. Ashley (Bloomington: Indiana University Press, 1990), p. 61.

23. See, for a thorough treatment of the notion of chaste marriage, Dyan Elliot, *Spiritual Marriage: Sexual Abstinence in Medieval Wedlock* (Princeton: Princeton University Press, 1993).

24. Mervyn James, "Ritual, Drama and Social Body in the Late Medieval English Town," *Past and Present* 98 (1983), p. 27, 4.

25. Towneley "Salutation" in *English Nativity Plays,* ed. Samuel B. Hemingway (New York: Russell & Russell, 1964), lines 67–68.

26. *The York Plays,* ed. Richard Beadle (London: Edward Arnold, 1982), 13, lines 12, 15.

27. *York,* 13, line 247.

28. Rudiger Schnell, "The Discourse on Marriage in the Middle Ages," *Speculum* 73 (1998) 3: 778.

29. See my own "The Trials of the Virgin in the N-town Cycle," *Comparative Drama* 29 (1995), 348–362, where I discuss the marriage and subsequent trial of Mary and Joseph with reference to contemporary English practice.

30. See Peter Brown's *Society and the Holy in Late Antiquity* (Berkeley and Los Angeles: University of California Press, 1982), p. 309, where he points out the connection between the body of the accused and the ritual of the or-

deal that draws together the social body of the people who administer and witness the results of the ordeal. This work clearly reflects that of Mary Douglas, whose *Purity and Danger* also makes the connection between the human body and the social body.

31. John Bugge, *Virginitas: An Essay in the History of a Medieval Ideal,* International Archives of the History of Ideas, Series Minor, 17 (The Hague: Martinus Nijhoff, 1975), p. 81.

32. Bugge, *Virginitas,* p. 83.

33. *The N-town Play, Cotton MS Vespasian D. 8,* ed. Stephen Spector, The Early English Text Society SS 11 (Oxford: Oxford University Press, 1991), 11, line 294.

34. *N-town,* 11, lines 305–306.

35. *N-town,* 12, lines 74–75.

36. Bugge, *Virginitas,* 85 et seq.

37. Schnell, "The Discourse on Marriage," p.781 et seq.

38. Victor Turner and Edith Turner, *Images and Pilgrimage in Christian Culture: Anthropological Perspectives* (New York: Columbia University Press, 1978), p. 145.

39. R. Howard Bloch, *Medieval Misogyny and the Invention of Western Romantic Love* (Chicago: University of Chicago Press, 1991) p. 106–107.

40. Bloch, *Medieval Misogyny,* p. 109.

41. Bloch, *Medieval Misogyny,* p. 109.

42. *N-town,* 14, lines 75–77.

43. *N-town,* 14, line 81.

44. *N-town,* 14, line 87.

45. *N-town,* 14, lines 348, 371.

46. *N-town,* 14, lines 374–375, 377.

47. See James A. Brundage, *Law, Sex, and Christian Society in Medieval Europe* (Chicago: University of Chicago Press, 1987), pp. 412, 545. Brundage briefly notes that while practices and volume of particular cases might vary widely among the many ecclesiastical courts, most church court business in many jurisdictions concerned sexual and marital matters and those courts could rely on the physical examination of women by women in order to discern traces of sexual activity.

48. *N-town,* 14, line 298.

49. We might refer again to Kristeva's *Powers of Horror,* where she writes of the history of religion and its "cathexis of maternal function—mother, woman, reproduction. But the biblical test . . . performs the tremendous forcing that consists in subordinating maternal power . . . to symbolic order as pure logical order . . . (p. 91). The Virgin, then, with her closed maternal body lacking blood and pain, can be threatened with abject status but never becomes abject. As a closed body that images social cohesion in the N-town trial, the social body can be at least potentially rescued from its tendency to break down, to collapse on itself through the use of ab-

jecting language. And this denatured body of the Virgin can then be a model for male imitation, once it is rescued from abjection.

50. *N-town,* 14, lines 334–337. Here Mary seems to call for a new kind of speech, at least in so far as the speech concerns her.

51. See Pierre J. Payer, *The Bridling of Desire: Views of Sex in the Later Middle Ages* (Toronto: University of Toronto Press, 1993), p. 164.

52. Elliot, *Spiritual Marriage,* p. 298.

PART III

CONSTRUCTING WIDOWHOOD

CHAPTER 10

BETWEEN THE LIVING AND THE DEAD:
WIDOWS AS HEROINES OF MEDIEVAL ROMANCES

Rebecca Hayward

The two prevailing stereotypes of widows are examined in light of the romance hero-
ine, who when also a widow, becomes a problematic figure, caught between the neces-
sity of possession and ideals of chastity.

In medieval literature, a misogynistic stereotype of the widow developed
out of the satirical tradition of writing about women.[1] The best-known
example is the story of the Widow of Ephesus, who switched very rapidly
from being a devoted widow grieving at her husband's tomb to a seduc-
tive woman who was prepared to desecrate her husband's body for the sake
of her new lover. This story from Petronius' *Satyricon* was very popular in
the Middle Ages and was transmitted in such diverse texts as John of Salisbury's *Policraticus*, the *Romulus vulgaris* and the elegiac version of *Romulus*
that was widely circulated, Marie de France's *Fables*, and the *Seven Sages of
Rome* story collection.[2] Other manifestations of the misogynistic stereotype of the widow are to be found in Jehan le Fèvre's *Les Lamentations de
Matheolus*, Gautier le Leu's *La Veuve*, William Dunbar's *Tretis of the Twa
Mariit Wemen and the Wedo* and Boccaccio's *Corbaccio*.[3]

The key feature of the misogynistic stereotype of the widow was that
the widow was associated with inconstancy, because it was assumed that
once her husband had died, she would begin to lust for another husband
or lover immediately. This was based on the deeply rooted misogynistic
understanding of the nature of female sexuality as lustful and fickle.

Married women could be kept under restraint by their husbands, but widows were free to do as they liked, and thus their actions revealed wider truths about women's natures, according to satirical authors. In part, the cultural tensions revealed by the misogynistic stereotype of the widow were caused by the conflict between the Christian ideology of chaste widowhood, which coincided with masculine fantasies of exclusive possession of a woman, and social pragmatism, which ensured that remarriage was a common phenomenon.

In the romance genre, women are often represented in an idealized way as beautiful and virtuous. Romance narration is frequently structured around the heterosexual love relation, and readers are encouraged to anticipate the success of the hero's quest for an idealized woman. Since such a result often provides closure for the narrative, digressions from this goal are essential to sustain the plot. A romance heroine who is also a widow is a problematic figure, as an ideal widow remains celibate, whereas an ideal romance heroine yields to love for the hero. The conflict between these two ideals for women means that there is a risk that a romance widow heroine may be associated with the misogynistic stereotype of the widow. In such a case, the misogynistic stereotype functions as a contrasting discourse to that of romance convention. If such a counterdiscourse becomes too powerful, it will threaten the stability of the idealized romance elements in the narrative and thus the generic boundaries of the text.

To negotiate the representation of a widow who remarries or loves again in a romance text, narrators use other characters to mediate between the widow's switch of roles and rhetoric to structure the process in a way that is less open to misogynistic interpretation. The threat of scandal in this representation can be used to give an erotic charge to the widow's characterization, as there are problems that must be overcome before the quest for love can be fulfilled. However, narrators do not protect heroines or female characters completely from misogynistic imputations. First, I will compare the portrayal of Jocasta in the *Roman de Thèbes* with that of Laudine in Chrétien de Troyes's *Yvain*. Both are widows who remarry rapidly, accepting the killers of their first husbands as their new spouses.[4] In the second half of this chapter, I will discuss the potential associations of Criseida in Boccaccio's *Filostrato* and Criseyde in Chaucer's *Troilus and Criseyde* with the misogynistic stereotype of the widow.[5]

In the mid-twelfth-century *Roman de Thèbes,* a text that shows the early development of the romance genre, Jocasta is not a heroine. Her story is a brief introduction to the main narrative, which tells of the struggle between her two sons, Ethiocles and Polynices, with Oedipus for the throne of Thebes. There is a marked contrast between her behavior in the opening segment, which is characterized as foolish and inconstant, and her impeccable conduct throughout the rest of the story.

At first, when Jocasta hears of the death of her husband Laius, she is fully associated with the role of the grieving widow. However, she is also conscious of her role as ruler of the lands. Without a husband, she is unprotected, as are her people and the lands. From the beginning of her characterization, we see that there is a tension between her private desire to mourn Laius and her public role as queen of Thebes:

Or sui ge veuve sanz seignor,
si n'ai enfant qui gart m'anor.
Se besoingne me sort ou guerre,
ne pourrai pas tenir ma terre.[6]

[Now I am a widow without a lord, I have no child to safeguard my kingdom. If there is any danger or warfare, I will not be able to hold my lands.]

The widow's lands are inextricably linked with her body. Whoever is granted possession of her body will have the lands also, and thus will displace her former husband in two ways. The lands and the responsibility for protecting them should go to Jocasta's adult son on the death of his father, but Oedipus' exile has disrupted the patrilineal order of inheritance. This distortion of order is later ironically refigured by the unnatural sexual bond between Jocasta and Oedipus.

The threat which Jocasta perceives to herself and the kingdom is represented by "Pyn," the Sphinx who terrorizes travelers and kills those who cannot answer its riddle. Oedipus manages to answer the riddle and kill Pyn. The people take him back to the palace and ask the queen to retain him in her household. She agrees but reaffirms her role as a grieving widow:

Bien veul qu'il soit de ma mesnie,
mes ce sachiez: ne sui pas lie,
car l'autrier fu mis sires morz,
dont est granz donmages et torz.[7]

[I wish that he should be part of my household, but know this well: I am not at all happy, because my lord died recently, and from this is great injury and wrong.]

During the meal that follows, Jocasta, mellowed by food and wine, begins to desire Oedipus. This emotion is scandalous because she is unaffected by the news that Oedipus has killed her husband. They do not know that they are mother and son. There is no equivalent to this episode in Statius' *Thebaid*,[8] the model for the *Roman,* which opens with Oedipus having already blinded himself. In the Sophocles version of the Oedipus myth, *King Oedipus*[9] (not a direct source because Greek was not known in twelfth-century France), neither Oedipus nor Jocasta is aware when they marry that Oedipus is Laius' killer.

For such a shift to take place in the widow's emotions, romance narrators frequently use the devices of go-betweens and elaborate rhetoric to soften the imputation that the widow is lusting after another man so soon after the death of her husband. The narrator of the *Roman de Thèbes* uses simplified versions of these techniques. Oedipus manages to deflect Jocasta's concern to know the name of her husband's killer, which is part of her role as a grieving widow, by telling her that he knows who it was but will tell her only if she promises not to be angry with the killer. The possibility that she might forgive the man who killed Laius once she finds out that it is Oedipus opens the way for Jocasta's role to change from that of the grieving widow to that of the widow keen to remarry, who offers him her body and her lands. In ideal circumstances, her fertility would provide a link between these two gifts, and they would produce children to inherit the lands. As it is, their sons are fated to struggle in bloodshed until they are engulfed in the destruction that their quarrel unleashes.

Jocasta's role begins to change when she takes the hand offered to her by Oedipus after his confession. At this point, the narrator associates her with the inconstancy of women: "car fame est tost menee avant,/qu'en em puet fere son talent."[10] [Because a woman is soon led on, so that someone does with her all his desire.] The willingness of the widow to change roles is associated with the fickleness of the living community toward a dead man. At first members of the community grieve, but eventually they return to normal pursuits. This is heightened in the case of a man who was a protector; he must be replaced in the interests of all. Instead of an individual mediator to smooth the path of Jocasta's transition from grieving widow to woman in love, her barons ask her to marry him, as his dispatch of Pyn has found favor with the people, and they wish for a defender. They do not know that he killed Laius. This means that Jocasta can marry Oedipus ostensibly for the common good rather than out of lust. The motif of the displacement of her first husband by her second is stressed: "Le deul du roi est oubliez,/cil qui mort l'a est coronnez."[11] [The mourning for the king was forgotten, the one who killed him was crowned.]

In this instance, we have seen that a widow who was a character in a text influenced by romance conventions, although not a heroine, was associated with the misogynistic stereotype of the inconstancy of women because of her willingness to marry her husband's murderer. Her marriage is a tragic mistake because its incestuous nature leads eventually to the destruction of the city. But the narrator implies that despite Jocasta's unusual situation, her behavior is similar to that of other women. A more positive image of the remarriage of widows is given in the poem when Parthenopeus, who is dying, sends a message to his mother instructing her to remarry.[12] There is no negative comment by the narrator in this case. It is the incestuous situation, the fact that Oedipus has murdered her husband and the speed of her change of heart that associates Jocasta with misogynistic stereotypes. Since the purpose of her marriage is to advance the narrative rather than to provide its central structure, as it would if she were a heroine in a love plot, the narrator has no interest in presenting her desire for him in a positive light. Her transition from grieving widow to loving wife, eased as it is only slightly by Oedipus' eloquence and the intervention of the barons, remains scandalous, with destructive consequences for herself, her family, and her city.

Chrétien de Troyes uses a similar motif in his representation of Laudine in *Yvain* as a woman who rapidly marries her husband's killer.[13] Yet several factors combine to deflect Laudine's association with the misogynistic stereotype of the widow. The tone of the romance is lighter, Laudine is a romance heroine, and her marriage to Yvain and its consequences provide an overarching structure to the plot. The intermediary figure, Lunete, is well developed and engages in elaborate rhetorical discourse to aid Laudine's transition. Above all, there is no incest motif, and while the course of Laudine and Yvain's marriage does not run smoothly, their differences are eventually resolved in a kind of harmony. All these factors mean that Laudine's quick change of roles has a different impact on the narrative to that of Jocasta's in the *Roman de Thèbes*.

The opening of *Yvain,* dated to approximately 1177 by D. D. R. Owen,[14] structures the hero's adventures in a way that is similar to the beginning of the *Roman de Thèbes*. Yvain does not set out to win Laudine or her lands, but rather to look for excitement and fulfill a vow he has made to his cousin, Calogrenant, to avenge the latter's defeat by Esclados the Red, Laudine's husband. Yvain's killing of Esclados in combat is similar to Oedipus' hasty attack on Laius at the crossroads, as both acts are carried out with no regard for the consequences.

Yvain finds himself in Laudine's castle, invisible because of the ring Lunete has given him. The contradictions inherent in representing a widow as the heroine of a romance are fully developed here. Laudine fulfills her role as a grieving widow, yet by doing so she becomes an erotic love object to Yvain. We see that the desirability of the widow derives from her apparent unobtainability. All the signs displayed by the widow, black clothing, weeping, and tearing her hair and clothes, which on the

surface place her beyond sexual interest as they symbolize love for one
who has died, on a deeper level become charged with an erotic meaning. It is possible that the widow will love again. Mourning is a sign of
her husband's absence; his role is once again open for a successor. The
widow's grief provides an obstacle, but all that must be overcome are the
widow's own feelings and a consideration of what is socially appropriate,
aspects that are covered by the devices of mediators and rhetoric. The
need for a protector makes the widow's marriage seem more suitable. As
in Jocasta's case, Laudine's conflict is heightened by the fact that Yvain
killed her husband.

Initially, Laudine's grief is extreme, and Lunete suggests that she is near
death:

> Ma dame an fet un duel si fort,
> Et ses janz anviron li crïent,
> Que por po de duel ne s'ocïent . . .

[My lady is in such a state of grief along with her people lamenting around
her that they're almost killing themselves with sorrow.][15]

Her behavior is associated with the Christian ideal of the chaste widow.
She expects to remain in this state indefinitely: "Don ja ne cuide avoir con-
fort" [for that she thinks she will never be consoled].[16] Laudine's behavior
assists the passage of Esclados's soul, as the religious rites are carried out on
his body. We are told that his "cheitive ame" [unfortunate soul][17] desires
final absolution. Laudine's prayers will reduce the time that Esclados's soul
must spend in Purgatory, so her faithfulness as a widow can affect his
progress through the afterlife.

Throughout Laudine's grief, the religious rites and the funeral, where
the widow stands isolated as Yvain looks on from a window, Yvain remains
invisible. His secret gaze renders him powerful in that his privileged position enables him to admire Laudine's beauty and be drawn by what he perceives as the erotic atmosphere of her inaccessible widowhood, but
impotent because of the precariousness of his own position. He cannot reveal himself without risking being put to death, as Laudine's double role as
the grieving widow and the lady of the lands ensures that she has the
power of judgment and can punish her husband's killer if she finds him.
There is an analogy here with our position as readers. We are powerful, in
that we have access to all that goes on in the narrative, and powerless, as
we see from a hidden vantage point and cannot intervene in the narrative
to obtain our desire directly.[18]

Yvain's desire for Laudine is scandalous. It seems also to be foolish, given the circumstances. He acknowledges this to himself, but then concludes that he is despairing too hastily:

> D' "ore androit" ai je dit que sages;
> Que fame a plus de mil corages.
> Celui corage, qu'ele a ore,
> Espoir changera ele ancore,—
> Ainz le changera sanz "espoir" . . .

[I was right to say "at this moment," because a woman has more than a thousand fancies. Perhaps she will change again from her present frame of mind: or rather she will change it, with no "perhaps" . . .][19]

Because Yvain associates women with fickleness and instability, he believes that a grieving widow will not retain this role forever. This raises the question of Laudine's sincerity, both during her mourning and throughout her transition to participation in love once more.

A. C. Spearing observes that the narrative is shaped by Yvain's gaze, which makes Laudine's mourning seem theatrical. Along with Jean Frappier and Tony Hunt, he cites Ovid's comment that women at their husbands' funerals are conscious that mourning becomes them, and are searching for new husbands,[20] a motif associated in the Middle Ages with the misogynistic widow stereotype. Laudine does not fit into this category of the flirtatious widow, for when she performs her emotions through her gestures, she believes herself to be unobserved except by her own household. However, when she debates with herself whether to follow Lunete's advice and love Yvain, we see little of her inner subjective identity. It is a formal rhetorical problem rather than a naturalistic exploration of her own feelings. She moves from the role of grieving widow to that of prospective wealthy wife who longs for Yvain, and the narrator's concern is to present this shift in a relatively graceful and charming way, so that the sympathy of the audience will not be totally alienated. Her character is not presented in any deeper way.

The central problem of this section of the text is how this shift of Laudine's roles may be arranged without her being associated too strongly with the misogynistic stereotype of the widow. One of the notable features of that stereotype is that the widow is motivated by lust. Lunete becomes the mediator who arranges matters so that the seemingly irrevocable conflict between Laudine's role as a chaste widow and her potential desire for a husband and protector can be reconciled. Lunete did not set out to make Yvain fall in love with Laudine, but she did provide him with the ring of

invisibility and the seat at the window to observe the funeral, the two devices that shaped his gaze and thus his desire.[21]

To effect the shift in Laudine's emotions, Lunete uses rhetoric. She plays
on Laudine's repeated assertions that Esclados was the best knight in the
world, and argues that such a knight can only be replaced by the man who
defeated him. Lunete also points out that remarriage will be socially useful. Laudine needs a knight to defend the spring, and they know that King
Arthur and his court are approaching.[22] Laudine resists these arguments at
first, but is eventually persuaded by them. She debates with herself the
grounds on which she could forgive this knight for killing her husband,
and eventually decides that if he was acting in self-defense and meant no
wrong to her, she will forgive him.[23] In her thinking, she has separated
what is due to her husband from what is due to herself. The reader has already been encouraged to be caught up in Yvain's erotic fantasy, that a
beautiful woman whose husband he has killed will suddenly offer him herself and her wealth. A reader who is swept along by this does not need to
examine the reasons for Laudine's change of heart too closely but does
need to continue to respect Laudine, and not to consider her as the de-
graded figure of the misogynistic stereotype of the widow.[24]

When Laudine announces her intention to make Yvain "seignor de ma
terre et de moi" [lord of my land and my person],[25] we see the association
between her gift of her body and of her lands. We have been told that she
was the original heiress of the lands before her marriage to Esclados. She
stipulates that no one must be able to reproach her for marrying her husband's killer. This is paralleled by the stratagems used by the narrator to en-
sure that readers will not wish to criticize Laudine for this either. Lunete
points out that the barons are eager to find someone to defend the spring,
so they will be happy for her to remarry.[26] The scene from the *Roman de
Thèbes* in which the people of Thebes ask Jocasta to do for the common
good what she already desired personally is expanded here. Through marriage, and his new identity as the Knight of the Spring, Yvain completes
the displacement of Esclados. However, through Yvain's own carelessness,
he must endure a long exile before he can resume his life with Laudine.

Chrétien's narrator limits carefully the possibility of associating Laudine
with the misogynistic stereotype of the widow. But he does not suppress
totally the scandal attendant upon her marriage to Yvain. In a verbal echo
of the *Roman de Thèbes* that stresses the transition of the widow's loyalties
from the dead to the living, the narrator says after the wedding:

Mes ore est mes sire Yvains sire,
Et li morz est toz obliëz.

Cil, qui l'ocist, est mariëz
An sa fame, et ansanble gisent,
Et les janz aimment plus et prisent
Le vif, qu'onques le mort ne firent.

[Now, though, my lord Yvain is master, and the dead man is completely forgotten. His slayer is married to his wife, and they sleep together, whilst the people love and esteem the living man more than they ever did the dead.][27]

Despite Yvain's carelessness, his marriage to Laudine is not doomed in the way that Jocasta's marriage to Oedipus was through incest. The narrative goal of the union of the heterosexual couple is achieved once in the middle and again at the end of the romance. The narrator has successfully negotiated Laudine's transition from the role of a chaste widow to that of a remarrying one without associating her too strongly with the misogynistic satirical image of the lustful widow. Because of the greater degree of romance narrative investment in the union of Laudine and Yvain, in comparison with that of Oedipus and Jocasta in the *Roman de Thèbes,* the scandalous nature of Laudine's rapid marriage to her husband's killer is diminished, although it is not suppressed entirely.

Historically, widows enjoyed a greater degree of control over property and independence in their actions than married women in medieval England, France, and Italy.[28] Widows remarried frequently, and this was often encouraged by society, particularly if the widow was young and had minor children.[29] The scandal that lingers in these texts, like other manifestations of the misogynistic vidual stereotype, is an indication of the discomfort felt by male authors that the remarriage of widows was socially acceptable, as it conflicted both with the Christian image of the chaste widow to which theologians and preachers clung, and with masculine fantasies about the purity of a woman who had had marital relations with only one man. It is probable that such misgivings surfaced primarily in bawdy jokes and literary motifs like these rather than as overt criticism from members of the community, given the respectability of many remarrying widows.

In the representation of the Criseyde figure as a widow in the fourteenth century, we find a different narrative pattern from that of Jocasta and Laudine. There are many similarities in the portrayal of widowhood between Criseida in Boccaccio's *Filostrato,* written around 1335, and Criseyde in Chaucer's *Troilus and Criseyde,* dated to approximately 1385. The two narrators use similar images of the heroines as widows, yet the conclusions they draw from them are quite different. Boccaccio's Criseida is freely associated with the misogynistic stereotype of the widow, albeit in a somewhat modified romance form, in which the widow was understood to be a suitable partner for a lover to direct his attentions towards, because of her experienced nature and independence, yet at the same time unlikely to be constant because of her youth, levity, and previous experience. Chaucer's narrator resists any suggestion that Criseyde falls into this category, but to do this he must overlook the ending of the story. Criseyde is willing to adapt herself to a role that will suit those around her. The narrator employs romance conventions to protect Criseyde's representation from facile misogyny as long as her actions contribute to the fulfillment of the hero's desire, and thus the romance goal of union between hero and heroine, but as soon as her actions disappoint the hero it becomes difficult for the narrator to relate her fate without relying on misogynistic stereotypes. This situation highlights the limitations of representing women according to idealized or misogynistic images.

Boccaccio's Criseida is based on Briseida, a character from the antique novels about Troy, who is an unmarried woman rather than a widow. Briseida was associated with the inconstancy of women.[30] When Boccaccio came to amplify the story of Troiolo's love affair, he made Criseida into a beautiful widow, no doubt with the theme of female inconstancy in mind. The *Filostrato* begins as a romance dedicated to the narrator's lady, "Filomena," and he tells her that any good quality of Criseida's belongs to her as well, but by the end Criseida is so strongly associated with the misogynistic stereotype that the romance convention of the dedication is undermined. Laura Kellogg provides a convincing explanation for this, reading the *Filostrato* as an ironic work that exploits the disjunction between its frame and its narration to imply that the narrator learns nothing from his material.[31]

To understand why Boccaccio changed the marital status of Troiolo's lover, an examination of a passage from the *Filocolo,* a prose work written by him at around the same time as the *Filostrato,* is helpful. In a debate about whether a lover is more likely to obtain satisfaction from a maiden, a married woman, or a widow, widows are characterized as the most suitable candidates for intrigues, because they are sexually experienced and independent of a husband's control.[32] This attempts to resolve the contradictions of a widow who engages in a love affair but does not solve the problems of chastity and constancy, which in part lead to Criseida's association with the misogynistic stereotype of the widow.

Criseida's father, Calcas, leaves the besieged city of Troy to join the Greeks, as he has received divine warning that the Trojans will lose the war. Criseida's loyalty is to Troy, and she is given permission by Hector to stay. She carries out the role of the chaste and faithful widow. There is no mention of her husband, and of course she had not been married in previous versions of the story. This changes the pattern of representation from the rapid remarriage of Jocasta and Laudine, with the faintly lingering sense of scandal when their former husbands are mentioned in the text. The fact that Criseida's husband is never discussed contributes to the impression that she is free to love again, but at the cost of mystifying her past. We feel that we do not really understand her as a person apart from Troiolo's interest in her and whether she will return it. Her childlessness indicates that she has few ties in her life.

The eroticism of the young, beautiful, and chaste widow is apparent in this characterization of Criseida. She is dressed in black with a white veil when Troiolo first sees her, a mourning symbol that, as with Laudine, on the surface emphasizes her attachment to her husband and yet underscores the fact of his absence. She is at once socially unobtainable because of her adherence to the role of chaste widow and a tantalizing erotic possibility, all the more so because the barriers of her emotions must be dismantled before she can be won by a lover.

The ambivalence of the representation of the widow as a sexually experienced woman is revealed by Pandaro when he hears upon whom Troiolo's heart is fixed. On the one hand, he believes Criseida to be chaste: "che ella è più che altra donna onesta, / e più d'amore ha le cose dispette" [she is more chaste than other ladies and has scorned the things of love more].[33] However, Pandaro's second impression of vidual sexuality is that it must be simmering powerfully beneath the chaste surface: "La mia cugina è vedova e disia, / e se 'l negasse non gliel crederia." [My cousin is a widow and has desires, and if she should deny it, I would not believe her.][34] This means that when Pandaro approaches the delicate task of ascertaining whether Criseida will accept Troiolo as a lover, he regards it not so much as corrupting her chastity as allowing her to reveal and express the vidual sexuality that he believes to exist. It is this statement more than anything else that associates the character with the misogynistic widow stereotype by removing the possibility of personal choice. Pandaro claims that because she is a widow, she will love Troiolo. As with Lunete's role in *Yvain,* the presence of Pandaro as a mediator lessens the imputation that the widow has instigated the affair out of lust.

When Pandaro broaches the subject with Criseida, she admits a certain attraction to Troiolo but tells him firmly that an affair would not be appropriate, partly because she is still grieving for her husband:

> . . . ma poi che 'l mio sposo
> tolto mi fu, sempre la voglia mia
> da amor fu lontana, ed ho doglioso
> il core ancor della sua morte ria,

ed avrò mentre che sarò in vita,
tornandomi a memoria sua partita.

[but since my husband was taken from me, my desire has been ever far from
love, and I have still a sorrowful heart for his grievous death and shall have
while I live, calling to memory his departure.][35]

At this point, Criseida reconfirms her reputation as a chaste widow as she
turns down temptation for love of her husband and faithfulness to him.
Boccaccio juxtaposes "morte" [death] and "vita" [life] to show that the
heroine believes that her husband's death determines her future.

Once Criseida has had time to reflect, it turns out that Pandaro's understanding that all widows carry around hidden desire, however much
they resist the suggestion initially, is correct in her case:

> Io son giovane, bella, vaga e lieta,
> vedova, ricca, nobile ed amata,
> sanza figliuoli ed in vita quieta,
> perchè esser non deggio innamorata?

[I am young, beautiful, lovely and gay, a widow, rich, noble, and beloved,
without children and leading a quiet life. Why should I not be in love?][36]

As she returns to consideration of the world, "vita" becomes a noun that
she can affirm again. This is a statement of independent identity, and the
rhetorical question invites us as readers to endorse her appeal.

Despite Criseida's misgivings about the unreliability of love and the inconstancy of men, she begins to conceive of herself as a subject who desires what is to come rather than one who mourns for what is past. Shortly
after this scene, the narrator tells us that she undergoes a sudden transformation, and it is clear to us, if not immediately to Troiolo, that she is in the
grip of passion. The balance of the narrative is concerned with the implications of this change of heart for Troiolo and Pandaro, not Criseida herself. However, both Pandaro and Criseida demonstrate their awareness that
Criseida is risking her reputation as a chaste widow by loving Troiolo.

The scandalous nature of Troiolo and Criseida's illicit love for one another is submerged in the happy consummation. The romance reader is expected to desire their union and take pleasure in its description. Any sense
that Criseida as a previously chaste widow is an inappropriate love object
is diverted into a further erotic charge as the aura of secrecy and transgression merely adds to Troiolo's delight. However, once the consummation has been achieved, the plot begins to move towards the misogynistic

conclusion that when women are subjected to the vagaries of time and circumstance, they become untrustworthy.

Criseida discovers that she is to be exchanged for Antenor and sent to
the Greek camp. She considers herself to be widowed even more intensely
than upon the death of her husband:

> Or vedova sarò io daddovero,
> poi che da te dipartir mi conviene,
> cuor del mio corpo, e 'l vestimento nero
> ver testimonio fia delle mie pene.

[Now I shall in truth be a widow, since I am obliged to part from you, heart
of my body, and the black attire will be a true testimony of my sufferings.][37]

As readers, we may interpret this as evidence of her passion for Troiolo.
However, her willingness to transfer her feelings for him onto the symbols
she is supposedly wearing for someone else becomes a misogynistic warning signal. Although she now longs to be true to Troiolo, beyond the desire she once felt to remain celibate for the sake of her husband, the fact
that she was persuadable once means, according to this understanding of
widows, that it will happen more easily the next time. The link between
widowhood and mutability of purpose has been established. Boccaccio,
having elaborated the original story well beyond his sources, then rede-
ploys the ending of the earlier versions. Criseida forms a connection with
Diomede in the Greek camp, and never returns to Troy.

Once Criseida has arrived in the Greek camp, Diomede takes the opportunity to speak to her of love, and she presents herself to him as a chaste
widow, concealing the affair with Troiolo:

> Amor io non conobbi, poi morio
> colui al qual lealmente il servai,
> sì come a marito e signor mio,
> nè Greco nè Troian mai non curai
> in cotal atto, nè m'è in disio
> curarne alcun, nè mi sarà giammai.

[I have not known love since the man died to whom I gave it loyally as my
husband and lord. Nor did I ever care for any other, Greek or Trojan, in such
fashion; nor do I desire to care for any, nor ever shall.][38]

Once this would have been a true statement. Now it is palpably false, but
it shows that she wishes to appear in a good light. This statement height-
ens the association of deceit with the figure of the widow and prepares us

for the narrator's misogynistic conclusion that: "Giovane donna, e mobile e vogliosa / è negli amanti molti" [A young woman is both fickle and desirous of many lovers].[39]

The narrator's ability to associate the heroine with the supposed fickleness and mutability of women shows that the scandal of Criseida's willingness to be attached to more than one man emerges more strongly once the relationship she is engaged in is no longer in harmony with the desire of the hero. When this happens, it becomes acceptable for the narrator to stereotype her behavior and criticize her for qualities that previously enhanced the hero's pleasure, and this ironically undermines the romance convention of his appeal to his own lady.

Troilus and Criseyde is influenced by several genres, and is not a romance, although it is heavily influenced by romance convention. Barry Windeatt says that "Chaucer's poem achieves a specially mixed and combinative use of different genres," including epic, romance, history and tragedy.[40] Gayle Margherita comments further on the instability of the genre, arguing that the progression of the romance depends on the excision of the narrator's historical understanding, as he is already aware of the ending that will destroy the romance elements.[41] The importance of romance conventions is seen in the first half, in the drive toward the consummation of Troilus and Criseyde's love. Yet when the narrator unwillingly associates his heroine with misogynistic stereotypes after she fails to return to the hero, this contributes to the disintegration of the romance elements within the text.

Chaucer's narrator adopts the events of the *Filostrato* and develops some of the same images of Criseyde as a widow. However, the context of these images has been changed by the development of the characterization of Criseyde herself and also of the narrative persona. It is much more difficult to associate Criseyde with the facile misogyny applied to Criseida's behavior, when she is portrayed as a person who considers her roles carefully and performs them to the best of her ability, according to the circumstances she finds herself in. The narrator is aware of this and does not include two blatant instances of misogyny in the *Filostrato*, Pandaro's comment on the nature of vidual sexuality and the narrator's conclusion that a young woman is likely to be fickle. He acknowledges that Criseyde's choice of roles is constrained by social conventions and does his best to represent her in a way that does not depend on the polarized images of the chaste widow and the lustful one.[42] This succeeds as long as Criseyde's desire harmonizes with that of Troilus, just as the *Filostrato* narrator was more positive about Criseida while she was Troiolo's lover. But once Criseyde's analysis of her options leads her to abandon any thought of attempting to return to Troy and Troilus, the narrator distances himself from her fate, referring frequently to his unspecified sources and minimizing direct representation of her.

When the narrator introduces Criseyde, he emphasizes her isolation and lack of protection as aspects of the role of the chaste widow.[43] In the temple scene, the possible contradictions in the image of Criseyde as a beautiful, young, chaste widow begin to emerge. The two stanzas which describe Criseyde's appearance contain several rapid juxtapositions. Criseyde at first seems to blend in among the other well-dressed people, costumed as a widow, but her beauty is so striking that she is the object of everyone's attention. Her humble clothes serve only to accentuate her beauty. Despite this, she shows her modesty, remaining in the background. It is a striking detail that she does this confidently:

> Among thise othere folk was Criseyda,
> In widewes habit blak; but natheles,
> Right as oure firste lettre is now an A,
> In beaute first so stood she, makeles.
> Hire goodly lokyng gladed al the prees.
> Nas nevere yet seyn thyng to ben preysed derre,
> Nor under cloude blak so bright a sterre

> As was Criseyde, as folk seyde everichone
> That hir beholden in hir blake wede.
> And yet she stood ful lowe and stille allone,
> Byhynden other folk, in litel brede,
> And neigh the dore, ay undre shames drede,
> Simple of atir and debonaire of chere,
> With ful assured lokyng and manere.[44]

In a public setting, Criseyde presents herself as a chaste widow, dressed in black. Yet her beauty means that she cannot be marginalized. The incongruity between the desirability of her body, agreed upon by the narrator, the community, and Troilus, and her role as a widow, which is to remain chaste and modest, makes the contradiction of having a romance heroine who is also a widow more acute than in the equivalent description of Criseida. Sheila Delany has noted the pun on "makeles," meaning that she is both "matchless" and "without a mate."[45] This forms a connection between her beauty and the absence of her husband.

Criseyde throws herself into any role that she is expected by those around her to perform, and does it thoroughly. This does not mean that she is insincere but that she reveals the expectations that are placed upon female characters. In this situation, she presents herself as a very correct chaste widow, a role that offers her a social identity. As we saw with Laudine and Criseida, mourning emphasizes the fact that the widow's husband is not there and that she is potentially available. Criseyde's occupancy of the role of chaste widow cannot escape a similar implication, particularly because of her beauty, a conventional attribute for a romance heroine and one shared with Laudine and Criseida.

In a conversation with Criseyde in which Pandarus tries to interest her in loving Troilus, Pandarus asks her to remove her "barbe," a symbol of widowhood, in order to dance. She reacts indignantly, saying that what he suggests is not suitable for a chaste widow, and that she should stay retired, pray, and read saints' lives.[46] However, we know that this is what she should do, not what she does; prior to their conversation, she and her ladies have been listening to a maiden read "the geste / Of the siege of Thebes."[47] This interest in nonhagiographical literature suggests that her adherence to the role of the chaste widow is more of a desire to fulfill social expectations than a deep inner conviction of the ideals it represents. Here is an example of the religious anachronism of the text, in which pagan characters reflect on Christian ideology. Later, Pandarus tells her to cast aside her widow's clothes, asking why she wishes to "disfigure" herself when she has such an opportunity to love Troilus.[48] He does not acknowledge that any of the possible social roles available to her will disfigure her because she is unable to represent herself on her own terms.

Criseyde's transition to participation in the love affair is more painful and complex than Criseida's. There is no suggestion that Chaucer's heroine's sexuality is simmering and likely to overwhelm her simply because she is a widow. Criseyde has no equivalent statement to that of Criseida, who refuses to have anything to do with Troiolo because of her love for her husband. From the beginning, Criseyde is willing to entertain the thought of loving Troilus. However, she is more conscious than Criseida is of the possible dangers of risking her identity as a chaste widow. She behaves for a long time as if she expects their affair to remain unconsummated. The reader is encouraged to desire their union, and thus to overlook the hypocrisy of an ostensibly chaste widow having a lover in secret. In misogynistic satire, widows are castigated for just such deceitfulness. The fact that Criseyde remains a credible romance heroine during her relationship with Troilus is a sign that romance conventions are used to control her representation at this point.

In the misogynistic stereotype, widows are often ridiculed for being too independent and exercising their choice of a new husband or sexual partners badly. Criseida gives a joyful summary of her own independence as a widow, citing this as a reason for involvement with Troiolo. For Criseyde, her statement of independence, "I am myn owene womman, wel at ese— / I thank it God—as after myn estat,"[49] is also an acknowledgement that as a widow she is well placed for love, but it is followed by concern for what perils may result. She worries about the changing fortunes that love entails, the likelihood of male infidelity, and the danger in which her reputation may be placed. Although Criseida has similar thoughts, we do not see Chaucer's heroine's doubts resolved suddenly by passion. The devices of Antigone's song and Criseyde's dream of the eagle who takes out her heart and exchanges it for his own, neither of which exists in Boccaccio's text, make the process of change more subtle and interiorized.

When the consummation takes place, there is no mention of Criseyde's widowed status. Pandarus' elaborate schemes place Troilus in Criseyde's bed, and once she relinquishes her protestations, it is clear that she is happy with the situation. Criseyde has made the transition to the role of the romance heroine who satisfies the hero's desire with apparently minimal damage to her reputation for chastity. Troilus first desired her when she presented herself as a chaste widow[50] but expected to be able to replace her husband without any fear of being replaced himself. Criseyde was prepared to exchange the first role for the second, and this very adaptability implies mutability, the consequences of which are shown after the consummation.

When Criseyde hears that she must leave Troy she is distraught and emphasizes her intention to embody the role of chaste widow again, for a different man. Although there is no equivalent to the line "Or vedova sarò io daddovero," she says when she is grieving alone:

> And, Troilus, my clothes everychon
> Shul blake ben in tokenyng, herte swete,
> That I am as out of this world agon,
> That wont was yow to setten in quiete;
> And of myn ordre, ay til deth me mete,
> The observance evere, in youre absence,
> Shal sorwe ben, compleynt, and abstinence.[51]

Criseyde adopts the religious observance of widowhood, saying that she will mourn Troilus' absence until her death, which she anticipates will happen soon. She does her best to embody Troilus' ideal of female constancy through vidual imagery. With Boccaccio's Criseida, this was a misogynistic signal that she would not be able to keep her promise. Criseyde's representation of herself as a widow once more hovers between romance convention that she will be faithful to her lover and the implication that however sincere she is in her desire to remain true to him, recycling the imagery of chaste widowhood to describe her feelings for him is a lapse of good taste, given that she relinquished that role for his sake. It shows once more Criseyde's willingness to fulfill her current role to the best of her ability.

When Criseyde goes to the Greek camp, like Criseida she is asked by Diomede if she has a lover among the Trojans. She replies that she has never loved anyone except her husband, until his death, swearing an oath by Pallas,[52] which is ironic as it was in Pallas's temple that Troilus first fell in love with her. This deceitful use of her self-presentation as a widow associates her with the misogynistic stereotype of the widow. Yet her pretense of being a chaste widow was not made to seem dishonest earlier when it was Troilus who benefited from the deception. Our attention is distracted from this point by the narrator's emphasis on her break with Troilus.

Throughout the progress of Criseyde's love affair with Troilus, the narrator portrays her as a widow who is the heroine of a romance but who escapes misogynistic stereotyping. Although she does give up her status as a chaste widow while continuing to assume that image in public, she is not criticized for it by the narrator, as she does it to fulfill Troilus' desire, which is the narrative goal of the first three books of the poem. Once she fails to return to Troilus from the Greek camp, this cover for her actions is lost. The narrator is reluctant to admit that she has fulfilled misogynistic expectations. He begs the reader to excuse her slip[53] and asks women not to be angry with him for retelling the story, as he would rather write about faithful women,[54] thus distancing himself from his heroine.

The narrator's attempts to divert our attention from the association of Criseyde with the misogynistic stereotype reveal his entrapment within the system of polarized images for representing women. He has no way of portraying women that does not rely on the categories of chastity or lustfulness, and he is aware that Criseyde's character goes beyond these simplistic stereotypes. This is part of the breakdown of romance elements within the text. If Criseyde cannot be an unambiguous romance heroine, then the text cannot be a romance. The only refuge for the narrator from these perplexing issues about the representation of women is in his praise of the Virgin Mary: "For love of mayde and moder thyn benigne."[55] She is the only woman who can evade polarized imagery by being both chaste and fertile.

Barry Windeatt has remarked that it is unusual for a romance heroine to be a widow.[56] From these examples, we can see that it is difficult to harmonize the idealization that a widow will remain chaste with the demands upon a romance heroine to carry out her part in a love affair or marriage for the satisfaction of the hero and implicitly the narrator and reader as well. The result of this conflict is that a romance heroine or character who is also a widow runs the risk of being represented according to the misogynistic stereotype of the lustful widow. Narrators are often concerned to deflect this, so as not to destabilize the romance conventions in their texts. The narrator of the *Roman de Thèbes,* who was not presenting Jocasta as a heroine, used the unusual circumstances and unfortunate consequences of her remarriage to associate her with the inconstancy of women. Chrétien de Troyes's narrator in *Yvain* employed a similar motif, the speedy remarriage of the widow to her husband's killer, like that of *Roman de Thèbes*, but went to far greater lengths to protect the heroine from misogynistic imputations, using rhetoric and mediators, because of the importance of her marriage for the structure of the romance plot. The narrator of Boccaccio's *Filostrato* used Criseida's widowhood to make her a more likely candidate for a love affair, but the corollary to this was that she would not be faithful to Troiolo, which led the narrator to a misogynistic conclusion that undermined his use of romance conventions. Adopting the plot of the *Filostrato*, the Chaucerian narrator of *Troilus and Criseyde* did his best to avoid associating the heroine with misogynistic stereotypes, but when forced to confront the similarity of her actions to the stereotype of the lustfulness of women, he distanced himself from the heroine, which revealed the masculine bias of the traditionally polarized representation of women and contributed to the generic instability of his text. All these instances show the way in which scandal is associated with the widow who becomes involved with another man, as part of the cultural tensions of the portrayal of widowhood. Depending on the implications of the widow's marriage or new relationship for the text, this scandal is either suppressed or allowed to surface. The treatment of the widow's shift of loyalties from a dead husband to a living man is an indication of the status of romance conventions within the text.

Notes

1. I would like to thank Professor Jill Mann for discussing this material with me and giving valuable feedback for the preparation of this chapter, and also to thank Associate Professor Stephanie Hollis, Lucy Lewis, and the editors of this volume for reading drafts and making helpful suggestions. Part of this article was presented at the Australasian Universities' Language and Literature Association's Twenty-ninth Congress in Sydney in February 1997.

2. Petronius, *Satyricon Reliquiae*, ed. Konrad Mueller (Stuttgart and Leipzig: Teubner, 1995), pp. 117–120; John of Salisbury, *Policraticus* 8.11, ed. Clemens C. J. Webb, 2 vols. (Oxford: Clarendon, 1909), 2:301–304. For the *Romulus vulgaris*, see *Der lateinische Äsop des Romulus* 3.9, ed. Georg Thiele (Heidelburg: Winter, 1910), pp. 192–197, and for the elegiac version of Romulus see *Les fabulistes latins*, ed. Léopold Hervieux, 5 vols. (Paris: 1893–1899, repr. New York: Burt Franklin, 1964), 2:340–341. Marie de France, *Fables* 25, ed. Karl Warnke (Halle: Niemeyer, 1898), pp. 85–87, and *Fables* 16, eds. A. Ewert and R. C. Johnston (Oxford: Blackwell, 1966), pp. 20–21. For the *Seven Sages* tradition, see *Deux rédactions du Roman des Sept Sages de Rome*, ed. Gaston Paris (Paris: Firmin Didot, 1876), pp. 35–40, 150–155; *Le Roman des Sept Sages*, ed. Jean Misrahi

(Paris: Droz, 1933), pp. 99–105; *The Seven Sages in English Verse,* ed. Thomas Wright, Percy Society Publications (London: Richards, 1845), pp. 85–89; *The Seven Sages of Rome,* ed. Killis Campbell (Boston: Ginn, 1907), pp. 96–103; and *The Seven Sages of Rome,* ed. Karl Brunner, EETS os 191 (London: Milford, 1933), pp. 118–127.

3. Jehan le Fèvre, *Les Lamentations de Matheolus et le Livre de Leesce,* ed. A.-G. van Hamel, 2 vols. vol. 1 (Paris: Bouillon, 1892,1905).This edition also includes the text of the *Liber lamentationum Matheoluli.* Gautier le Leu, *La Veuve,* in *Le Jongleur Gautier le Leu,* ed. Charles H. Livingston (Cambridge, MA: Harvard University Press, 1951), pp. 165–183, William Dunbar, *The Tretis of the Twa Mariit Wemen and the Wedo,* in *William Dunbar: Selected Poems,* ed. Priscilla Bawcutt (London and New York: Longman, 1996), pp. 33–57; Giovanni Boccaccio, *Corbaccio,* ed. Pier Giorgio Ricci (Turin: Einaudi, 1977).

4. *Le Roman de Thèbes,* ed. Guy Raynaud de Lage (Paris: Champion, 1966), *Yvain: Le Chevalier au Lion,* ed. Wendelin Foerster, introduction, notes, and glossary by T. B. W. Reid (Manchester: Manchester University Press, 1942, repr. 1984), translations taken from *Yvain (The Knight with the Lion)* in *Chrétien de Troyes: Arthurian Romances,* trans. D. D. R. Owen (London: Dent, 1987), pp. 281–373.The resemblance between these two texts is noted by Reid in Foerster and Reid, *Yvain,* pp. xiii, 200, Jean Frappier, *Étude sur Yvain ou le Chevalier au Lion de Chrétien de Troyes* (Paris: Société d'édition d'enseignement supérieur, 1969), p. 77, and by Tony Hunt, *Yvain (Le Chevalier au Lion)* (London: Grant and Cutler, 1986), pp. 46, 53.

5. Giovanni Boccaccio, *Il Filostrato,* ed. Vincenzo Pernicone, trans. Robert P. Roberts and Anna Bruni Seldis (New York and London: Garland, 1986); Geoffrey Chaucer, *Troilus and Criseyde,* in *The Riverside Chaucer,* ed. Larry D. Benson (Oxford: Oxford University Press, 1987).

6. *Le Roman de Thèbes,* 259–262.Translations are my own, guided by the modern French translation by Aimé Petit, *Le Roman de Thèbes* (Paris: Champion, 1991) and the English translation by John Smartt Coley, *Le Roman de Thèbes (The Story of Thebes)* (New York and London: Garland, 1986). Coley translates *Le Roman de Thèbes,* ed. Léopold Constans, 2 vols. (Paris: Firmin Didot, 1890).

7. *Le Roman de Thèbes,* 395–398.

8. *Thebaid,* in *Statius,* ed. and trans. J. H. Mozley, 2 vols. (London: Heinemann and Cambridge, MA: Harvard University Press, 1928, repr. 1967).

9. Sophocles, *King Oedipus,* in *The Theban Plays,* trans. E. F. Watling (Harmondsworth: Penguin, 1947), pp. 25–73.

10. *Le Roman de Thèbes,* 441–442.

11. *Le Roman de Thèbes,* 485–486.

12. *Le Roman de Thèbes,* 8793–8804.

13. Wendelin Foerster, *Kristian von Troyes Yvain (Der Löwenritter)* (Halle: Niemeyer, 1902) suggests that Laudine should be seen as a type of the easily comforted widow, like the Widow of Ephesus (p. xxxi). However, Frap-

pier stresses the dissimilarity between the characterization of Laudine and that of the Widow of Ephesus (*Étude sur Yvain,* p. 150). Hunt notes the Widow of Ephesus story as part of the context within which Chrétien de Troyes was working (*Yvain,* p. 53).

14. Owen, *Arthurian Romances,* p. x.
15. Chrétien de Troyes, *Yvain,* 984–86.
16. Chrétien de Troyes, *Yvain,* 1164.
17. Chrétien de Troyes, *Yvain,* 1172.
18. A. C. Spearing, *The Medieval Poet as Voyeur* (Cambridge: Cambridge University Press, 1993), p. 76.
19. Chrétien de Troyes, *Yvain,* 1435–1439.
20. Spearing, *Medieval Poet,* pp. 77–78, Frappier, *Étude sur Yvain,* p. 75, Hunt, *Yvain,* p. 81. "Funere saepe viri vir quaeritur; ire solutis / Crinibus et fletus non tenuisse decet." [Often a husband is sought for at a husband's funeral; it is becoming to go with disheveled hair, and to mourn without restraint.] *Ars amatoria,* in *Ovid, The Art of Love and Other Poems,* ed. and trans. J. H. Mozley, rev. ed. G. P. Goold (Cambridge, MA: Harvard University Press and London: Heinemann, 1929, 2nd ed. repr. 1985), 3, 431–432.
21. Grace M. Armstrong, "Women of Power: Chrétien de Troyes' Female Clerks," in *Women in French Literature,* ed. Michel Guggenheim (Saratoga, CA: Anma Libri, 1988), pp. 29–46, draws an analogy between Lunete's role as a stage manager and the role of the narrator (p. 42).
22. Chrétien de Troyes, *Yvain,* 1614–1625, 1694–1709.
23. Chrétien de Troyes, *Yvain,* 1759–1772.
24. Fanni Bogdanow, in "The Tradition of the Troubadours and the Treatment of the Love Theme in Chrétien de Troyes' *Chevalier au Lion,*" in *Arthurian Literature II,* ed. Richard Barber (Cambridge: Brewer, 1982), pp. 76–91, suggests that there is an element of parody in Laudine's characterization as a participant in love, in part because she is able to forget her first husband (p. 90). She also argues that Yvain is a less than perfect lover (pp. 86–87).
25. Chrétien de Troyes, *Yvain,* 1806.
26. Chrétien de Troyes, *Yvain,* 1845–1868.
27. Chrétien de Troyes, *Yvain,* 2164–2169. Reid in Foerster and Reid, *Yvain,* p. 200, and Hunt, *Yvain,* p. 46, note the similarity between this passage and *Le Roman de Thèbes* 485–486. However, they quote from Constans, *Le Roman de Thèbes,* which in this instance relies on the manuscripts of the "long" version of the text, in contrast to the "short" version edited by de Lage. The "long" version includes another line, which increases the resemblance of these passages: "Li dueus del rei est oblïez, / Cil qui mort l'a est coronez / Et la reïne a moillier prent . . ." (vol. 1, 447–449).
28. For widows' control of property and independence, see Rowena E. Archer, "Rich Old Ladies: The Problem of Late Medieval Dowagers," in *Property and Politics,* ed. Tony Pollard (Gloucester: Sutton, 1984), pp. 15–35; Ann J. Kettle, "'My Wife Shall Have It': Marriage and Property in the Wills and Testaments of Later Mediaeval England," in *Marriage and Property,* ed. Elizabeth Craik

(Aberdeen: Aberdeen University Press, 1984), pp. 89–103; Kay E. Lacey, "Women and Work in Fourteenth and Fifteenth Century London," in *Women and Work in Pre-Industrial England,* eds. Lindsey Charles and Lorna Duffin (London: Croom Helm, 1985), pp. 24–82 (pp. 26–46); Joseph Biancalana, "Widows at Common Law: The Development of Common Law Dower," *Irish Jurist* n.s. 23 (1988), 255–329; Caroline M. Barron, "The 'Golden Age' of Women in Medieval London," *Reading Medieval Studies* 15 (1989), 35–58; Judith M. Bennett, "Widows in the Medieval English Countryside," in *Upon My Husband's Death,* ed. Louise Mirrer (Ann Arbor: University of Michigan Press, 1992), pp. 69–114.

29. For the remarriage of widows, see Joel T. Rosenthal, "Aristocratic Widows in Fifteenth-century England," in *Women and the Structure of Society,* eds. Barbara J. Harris and Jo Ann K. McNamara (Durham: Duke University Press, 1984), pp. 36–47; Christiane Klapisch-Zuber, "The 'Cruel Mother': Maternity, Widowhood and Dowry in Florence in the Fourteenth and Fifteenth Centuries," in *Women, Family and Ritual in Renaissance Italy,* trans. Lydia Cochrane (Chicago and London: Chicago University Press, 1985), pp. 117–31. Klapisch-Zuber points out that the remarriage of widows in Florence could be a financial disadvantage to their minor children. For case studies of remarrying widows, see Jennifer C. Ward, "Elizabeth de Burgh, Lady of Clare (d. 1360)," in *Medieval London Widows,* eds. Caroline M. Barron and Anne F. Sutton (London: Hambledon, 1994), pp. 29–45; and Carole Rawcliffe, "Margaret Stodeye, Lady Philipot (d. 1431)," in *Medieval London Widows,* pp. 85–98.

30. Benoît de Sainte-Maure, *Le Roman de Troie,* ed. Léopold Constans, 6 vols. (Paris: Firmin Didot, 1906), vol. 2, 13111, 13438–13446; Guido delle Colonne, *Guido de Columnis, Historia destructionis Troiae,* ed. Nathaniel Griffin (Cambridge, MA: Medieval Academy of America, 1936), 19, 159–73.

31. Laura Kellogg, "Boccaccio's Criseida and her Narrator, Filostrato," *Critical Matrix* 6 (1991), 46–75 (pp. 46–48).

32. Giovanni Boccaccio, *Il Filocolo,* ed. Salvatore Battaglia (Bari: Laterza, 1938), 4, q. 9; Ernest H. Wilkins, "The Enamorment of Boccaccio," *Modern Philology* 11 (1913), pp. 39–55 (p. 48 n. 1), points out the relevance of the *Filocolo* passage to Criseida's situation, as do Karl Young, "Aspects of the Story of Troilus and Criseyde," *University of Wisconsin Studies in Language and Literature* 2 (1918), 367–394 (p. 381), and Giulia Natali, "A Lyrical Version: Boccaccio's *Filostrato,*" in *The European Tragedy of Troilus,* ed. Piero Boitani (Oxford: Clarendon, 1989), pp. 49–73 (pp. 66–67).

33. Boccaccio, *Il Filostrato,* 2, 23.

34. Boccaccio, *Il Filostrato,* 2, 27.

35. Boccaccio, *Il Filostrato,* 2, 49.

36. Boccaccio, *Il Filostrato,* 2, 69.

37. Boccaccio, *Il Filostrato,* 4, 90. Kellogg, "Boccaccio's Criseida," p. 69, connects Criseida's image of herself as Troiolo's widow with her description of

herself and Troiolo during the consummation scene as "Le nuove spose" [newly married], *Il Filostrato* 3, 31.

38. Boccaccio, *Il Filostrato*, 6, 29.

39. Boccaccio, *Il Filostrato*, 8, 30.

40. Barry Windeatt, *Troilus and Criseyde* (Oxford: Clarendon, 1992), pp. 138–140.

41. Gayle Margherita, "Historicity, Femininity and Chaucer's Troilus," *Exemplaria* 6 (1994), 243–269 (p. 250).

42. Margaret Hallissy, in *Clean Maids, True Wives, Steadfast Widows* (Westport, CT: Greenwood, 1993), pp. 145–153, discusses the characterization of Chaucer's Criseyde in relation to the stereotypes of the lusty and the chaste widow, and also as a *persona miserabilis*, a technical term applied to widows in canon law. She does not compare this representation with that of Boccaccio's Criseida as a widow in detail, or consider the role of the narrator.

43. "For bothe a widewe was she and allone / Of any frend to whom she dorste hir mone," Chaucer, *Troilus and Criseyde*, 1, 97–98. The narrator neglects to mention that Criseyde does have her uncle Pandarus in Troy.

44. Chaucer, *Troilus and Criseyde*, 1, 169–182.

45. Sheila Delany, "Techniques of Alienation in *Troilus and Criseyde*," in *Chaucer's Troilus and Criseyde: "Subgit to alle Poesye,"* ed. R. A. Shoaf (Binghamton, NY: Pegasus, 1992), pp. 29–46 (p. 41).

46. Chaucer, *Troilus and Criseyde*, II, 110–119.

47. Chaucer, *Troilus and Criseyde*, II, 83–84.

48. Chaucer, *Troilus and Criseyde*, II, 221–224.

49. Chaucer, *Troilus and Criseyde*, II, 750–751.

50. Diane Vanner Steinburg, "'We Do Usen Here No Wommen For To Selle': Embodiment of Social Practices in *Troilus and Criseyde*," *Chaucer Review* 29 (1995), 259–273 (p. 268), believes that Troilus interprets Criseyde's black clothing as a symbol of loyalty, an important quality in his own character.

51. Chaucer, *Troilus and Criseyde*, IV, 778–784.

52. Chaucer, *Troilus and Criseyde*, V, 975–978.

53. Chaucer, *Troilus and Criseyde*, V, 1093–1099.

54. Chaucer, *Troilus and Criseyde*, V, 1772–1778.

55. Chaucer, *Troilus and Criseyde*, V, 1869.

56. Windeatt, *Troilus and Criseyde*, p. 150.

CHAPTER 11

THE WIDOW'S TEARS:
THE PEDAGOGY OF GRIEF IN
MEDIEVAL FRANCE AND THE
IMAGE OF THE GRIEVING WIDOW

Leslie Abend Callahan

> *Because widows, in medieval French literature, did not encode one specific meaning, their display of grief was a polyvalent sign as well; this grief reveals tensions between secular concerns and religious duty.*

Throughout the Middle Ages, the image of the grieving widow was, to say the least, ambiguous. Located between the polar opposites of the heroic Judith, model of virtuous widowhood,[1] and the descendents of Petronius' Widow of Ephesus, prototype of the "easily consoled widow,"[2] the cultural representations of widows in circulation during the Middle Ages were often contradictory, communicating "mixed messages."[3] One aspect of the representation of the medieval widow's behavior—her display of grief upon the death of her husband, and particularly her tears—bears further examination. Such display is discussed in religious writings on widowhood by the Fathers of the Church, is represented in tales and in romance, and is treated in medieval French sermons and conduct books. I suggest that the tears of the widow constitute a polyvalent sign that performs a multitude of functions; a sign that changes through the centuries and that differs according to the class and age of the widow; a sign that reveals tensions between the religious duties of the widow and her secular concerns. By considering the gaps between the grieving widow's image and the behaviors prescribed for her, it becomes apparent that the function of the discourse on tears can be interpreted as an attempt to control the conduct of women, even on the part of women writers themselves.

Writings on the expression of grief for the widow are inscribed within a tradition of commentary on the demonstration of grief in general. Elsewhere I have termed the set of models for the appropriate expression of grief, as well as negative examples of inappropriate mourning, the "pedagogy of grief."[4] This didactic tradition articulates a conflict that is to remain more or less constant in Christian thought: is it not selfish, even "unchristian" to mourn for someone who has entered into eternal life?

In the writings of the Church Fathers we find that the shedding of tears is acceptable if moderate and directed toward the salvation of the soul of the dead individual. Where the widow is concerned, tears and mourning for a dead husband constitute an important component of the duties of a devoted wife. As Margaret Hallissey observes, the widow's function is "to act as chief mourner (Job 27:15), to 'raise the dirge' for her husband (Ps. 78:64), and to act as a living memorial."[5]

In his study of remarriage in classical canon law, James A. Brundage demonstrates that the patristic commentaries on the remarriage of widows continued, throughout the Middle Ages, to influence attitudes toward women who had lost their husbands.[6] In two such early medieval texts in Latin, Ambrose of Milan's treatise "Concerning Widows," and Jerome's "Letter to Furia," the widow's tears are considered to have a positive effect. Far from condemning the display of grief, Ambrose praises the widow's tears: "Sed tristes videtur ducere dies, et lacrymis tempus exigere. Hoc beatior, quod perpetua sibi gaudia exiguis fletibus emit, parvisque momentis tempora acquirit aeterna." [But she seems to spend sad days, and to pass her time in tears. And she is the more blessed in this, for by a little weeping she purchases for herself everlasting joys, and at the cost of a few moments, gains eternity.][7]

The Bishop of Milan continues:

> Habet igitur vidua bonam commendationis materiam, ut, dum virum fuget, fleat saeculum: ac in promptu sint lacrymae redemptrices, dum impenduntur mortuis, viventibus profuturae. Paratus est moesbitudini animae fletus oculorum: misericordiam conciliat, laborem minuit, dolorem ablevat, servat pudorum; nec jam misera sibi videtur, quae consolationem in lacrymis habet, in quibus sunt charitatis stipendia et pietatis officia.

> [The widow has, then, this excellent recommendation, that while she mourns her husband she also weeps for the world, and the redeeming tears

are ready, which shed for the dead will benefit the living. The weeping of the eyes is fitted to the sadness of the mind, it arouses pity, lessens labour, relieves grief, and preserves modesty, and she no longer seems to herself so wretched, finding comfort in tears which are the pay of love and the proofs of pious memory.][8]

For Ambrose, then, the widow who gives vent to her grief by "a little weeping" doesn't merely bemoan her loss but also commemorates the lost one. Tears provide a release for emotion and constitute a sign of devotion to the deceased spouse. In addition, as Ambrose explains, the display of grief can serve to protect the widow from unwanted suitors:

> . . . atque ipse lugubris habitus, pompa funebris, fletus assiduus, et moestae fronti inarantibus rugis impressa tristitia, petulantium premit oculos, restinguit libidines, procaces avertit aspectus. Bonus custos pudoris, pietatis dolor: non obrepit culpa, si cura non desit.

> [. . . the very mourning attire, the funeral solemnities, the constant weeping, and grief impressed on the sad brow in deep wrinkles, restrains wanton eyes, checks lust, turns away forward looks. The sorrow of regretful affection is a good guardian of chastity . . .][9]

Although the widow's weeping is described as being "constant," the function of the tears outweighs any possible transgression in the duration or extent of the widow's mourning: her chastity is the primary concern for Ambrose as for many other early Christian writers. As the best means of approaching the highest ideal, that of virginity, chaste widowhood was the optimum choice for women who had lost their husbands.[10]

Like Ambrose's treatise, Jerome's "Letter to Furia" is largely concerned with helping its intended reader resist pressures to remarry. Whereas in Judaic and Roman custom women were encouraged, even required to remarry, in the early Christian centuries, they were urged to remain unmarried. According to Joyce E. Salisbury, "Widows who lived chaste lives were thought to have a special power of prayer, and people gave charity to widows in exchange for their prayers."[11] If they were unable to support themselves, widows could take advantage of the possibility of entering into "chaste" marriages of convenience in which they abstained from sexual activity.[12] When, in the "Letter," Jerome discusses the display of grief in general and weeping in particular, it is within the context of a critique of remarriage and the ills it causes the widow's children from her first marriage: "Inflammata libidine obliviscitur uteri sui, et inter parvulos suas miserias nescientes lugens dudum nova nupta conponitur." [Inflamed by lustfulness she forgets her own offspring, and in the midst of the little ones who know nothing of their sad fate the lately weeping widow arrays herself afresh as a bride.][13] The weeping is not a transgression; it is the cessation of the tears that is a problem.

The display of grief and specifically the shedding of tears by widows is not then, in and of itself, considered transgressive by these two Fathers of the Church who seem to have been more interested in providing positive examples for acceptable conduct—and in praising the virtues of generosity, modesty, and, above all, chastity—than in advocating the control of what was later to be perceived as "excessive" behavior. I would suggest, however, that even if these writings were not intended as a corrective to "negative" modes of behavior, by praising and recommending "moderate" behavior they reassert the control of a male-dominated society over women's lives, coercing them into compliance with norms of behavior advocated by the Church Fathers, as well as protecting the father's interests and those of the children of the first husband.[14] The sentiment against remarriage remained strong and was often in direct conflict with the social and cultural demands placed upon women as well as with the practical realities of their lives.

One less moderate voice can be heard, however. Whereas Ambrose and Jerome stress the efficacy of the widow's tears and valorize them as proof of her fidelity, John Chrysostom interprets such tears as a way of attracting attention. He exclaims:

> I have heard that many women, forsooth, attract lovers by their mournful cries, gaining for themselves the reputation of loving their husbands because of the vehemence of their wailings. Oh, what devilish scheming! Oh, what diabolic trickery![15]

Critical attitudes concerning the behavior of the widow find expression in the negative role model of the "easily consoled widow" whose specter, as even Jerome's comments cited above suggest, hovers in the background. One such type, the Widow of Ephesus, is ubiquitous in medieval French texts as well as among folklore sources.[16] The outcome of these stories is generally the same: the widow whose raw grief is represented as being beyond control participates, after her husband's death, in a sexual encounter with a stranger, often on her recently dead husband's grave. The implication is that her violent expression of emotion is false—and that the widow's display of grief is negated or erased by her subsequent actions. I do not intend to concentrate on this motif, which has been studied in great detail by Norris Lacy and by Heather Arden,[17] but to focus on the way in which the widow's grief is represented and described in selected texts from the eleventh and twelfth centuries.

In what might be considered a counterexample, the sincerity of the widow's grief is called into question because her demonstration of mourning is too restrained. In the account of the second of the miracles brought about by Sainte Foy, as recounted in the early eleventh century by Bernard of Angers, one Raymond is shipwrecked and believed by all, including his wife, to have perished. When his servant tells his wife of his death, she "feigned grief for a while, but did not turn it into a matter of heavy weeping or long sighs as is the custom of good women."[18] For Bernard of Angers, the proof that the widow's grief is "feigned" or false is that it was not unrestrained. Here, as for Ambrose and Jerome, weeping was not in itself a wholly negative reaction but could function as a sign of a "good woman" by signaling a wife's devotion to her deceased husband.

Another widow, that in the anonymous fabliau, *Cele Qui se Fist Foutre Sur La Fosse de Son Mari* displays all the signs of grief: she weeps uncontrollably; she faints repeatedly, and she rends her clothes:

> Qant la dame vit devié
> Son seignor, qui l'ot tant amee,
> Sovant s'est chaitive clamee;
> De grant duel demener se poine.
> Mout i enploie bien sa poine:
> Ses poinz detort et rontses dras,
> Et si se pasme a chascun pas.
> Et qant ce vint a l'anterrer,
> Lors oïssiez fame crier
> Et dementer et grant duel faire,
> Que nus ne lo porroit retraire.

> [When the woman sees, lifeless,
> her seigneur who had so loved her,
> she repeatedly expressed her unhappiness
> She demonstrates her pain, making good use of it:
> wringing her hands and rending her garments,
> fainting with each step
> and when it comes time to bury him
> then you will hear the woman cry and rave
> and to be in such a state of grief.
> that no one can restrain her.][19]

Yet, despite the apparently heartfelt emotion, she embarks upon a sexual escapade shortly after her husband is laid to rest. As the widow grieves on her husband's grave, a knight comes riding by and makes a bet with his companions that he will be able to seduce her. He succeeds. It is not her

tears that are criticized here, but her changeability: "Ensi la dame se con-
forte / Qui or demenoit si grant dol" [Thus the woman took comfort,
who earlier had exhibited such grief.][20]

In Gautier Le Leu's fabliau "La Veuve," the widow's grief is equally
dramatic:

> . . . sa molliers le siut aprés.
> Cil qui a li montent plus pres,
> le tienent par bras et par mains
> des paumes battre, c'est del mains,
> car ele crie a haute vois:
> "C'est mervelle conment je vois!
> Bele dame Sainte Marie,
> con sui dolante et esmarie!
> Ce poise moi que je tant dure;
> molt est ceste vie aspre et dure.
> Ne place Deu que je tant voie
> que je repair par ceste voie,
> si soie avuec mon segnor mise
> cui j'avoie ma foi promise."
> Ensi va acontant ses fables
> qui ne sont mie veritables.

[The grieving wife brings up the rear; her closest relatives, for fear she'll beat
her palms, or do worse harm, restrain the woman, hand and arm, because
she cries out, woebegone: "It's a wonder I can still go on! Oh Holy Mary,
Lady Fair, I'm torn by sorrow and despair! I'm sorry I must go on living—
life's so cruel and unforgiving—and if it please the Lord today that I should
not come back this way, then let me by my lord be laid, to whom my marriage vows were made." She goes on, keeping up the act by telling tales quite
free of fact.][21]

As in the case of the previous widow, neither the reader nor the spectators
within the story know that the woman's grief is false. Here it is the narrator who interjects, informing us that the widow is deliberately performing
acts of mourning and that her hypocrisy is about to be exposed. The acts
in and of themselves, however, are not inappropriate, and while, for later
writers, they may push the boundaries of acceptable behavior, they are
very much within the norms of the manifestation of a widow's grief.

Finally, Marie de France's[22] version of the widow who finds comfort in
the arms of another, "De la femme ki fist pendre sun mari" [The Woman
Who Had Her Husband Hanged] is direct and to the point: The book explains how this all occurred: "De un homme cunte li escriz / Que mort
esteit e' enfuïz. / Sa femme demeine grant dolur / sur sa tumbe e nuit e

jur . . ." [A man had died and was interred. / His wife mourned him most woefully / Over his grave both night and day.][23] In the telling of her grief, we have no hint that the emotion is not genuine.

Heather Arden suggests that "the motif of the grieving but easily consoled widow" represents "an archetypal embodiment of deeply rooted male attitudes toward women and female sexuality."[24] Indeed, it is this aspect, the sexual voracity of the widow, that is emphasized in these texts. Her sexual appetite, the appetite that the Church Fathers had earlier attempted to suppress by advocating chastity, is transgressive, not her tears, although the tears make her appear a hypocrite.

Laudine in Chrétien de Troyes's *Yvain* is, according to Arden, another example of the "easily consoled widow." Arden qualifies Laudine's grief as being "indescribable"—a common topos for the literary expression of grief during the Middle Ages. Arden continues, "Yet within a day she will have accepted the idea of marrying another man . . ."[25] It might be useful to consider the description for what it was—a set piece of the expression of grief on the death of a loved one. The romance reads:

> De si bele crestïene
> ne fu onques plez ne parole;
> mes de duel feire estoit si fole
> qu'a po qu'ele ne s'ocioit
> a la foiee, si crioit
> si haut com ele pooit plus,
> elle recheoit pasmee jus;
> et quant ele estoit relevee,
> ausi come fame desvee,
> se commançoit a dessirier
> et ses chevols a detranchier;
> ses mains detuert et ront ses dras,
> si se repasme a chascun pas,
> ne riens ne la puet conforter,
> que son seignor en voit porter
> devant li, en la biere, mort,
> don ja ne cuide avoir confort . . .

[Of so fair a Christian lady, no one has ever heard tell. But she was so distraught with grief that she was, at that moment, on the verge of suicide. She cried out at the top of her voice, then fell in a swoon. When she had been set back on her feet, she began, like a madwoman to tear at herself and pull her hair, clawing her hands and ripping her clothing and fainting at every step. Nothing could comfort her when she saw her lord carried dead before her on the bier. Believing that she could never be consoled, she was screaming in anguish . . .][26]

A comparison of the account of Laudine's behavior with that of the grief-stricken Enide, who makes no attempt to moderate or hide her grief upon seeing her husband Erec riding toward her, wounded and seemingly lifeless and falling off his horse—uncovers few significant differences:

> Lors comança li diax si forz,
> qant Enyde cheü le vit:
> molt li poise quant ele vit,
> et cort vers lui si come cele
> qui sa dolor mie ne cele.
> An haut s'escrie et tort ses poinz;
> de robe ne li remest poinz
> devant le piz a dessirier;
> ses chevox prist a arachier
> et sa tandre face desire.

[When Enide saw that he had fallen, her heavy sorrow began. Deeply despondent at the sight of him, she rushed toward him, not concealing her pain. She cried out at the top of her voice, wringing her hands and tearing away every thread of the dress at her breast. She began to pull her hair and claw her delicate face.][27]

As do the various "sexualized" widows described in the tale literature, Enide performs traditional gestures of grief: she wrings her hands, rips her clothes, tears her hair, and begins to rend the flesh of her cheeks. The two characters, both created by Chrétien de Troyes, behave in a very similar manner: the difference between the manifestations of grief of the "variable" Laudine[28] and those of the faithful Enide lies in the reception and perception of the reader: it is not the grief that is out of bounds but the actions that follow. Furthermore, I would suggest that Laudine's ultimate capitulation is not of the same sort as that of the widows in the fabliaux discussed above who give in to their sexual urges in a socially unsanctioned manner. Within the male-dominated world of Arthurian knighthood, women were objectified, in this case, viewed as prizes: the original "trophy wives" were the women of Arthurian romance. Laudine had, in fact, been "won" by Yvain who became, in the scheme of things, the protector of her fountain and, by extension, her protector. In his study of widows from the later Middle Ages, Joel Rosenthal demonstrates that remarriage was perhaps the most effective mode of "reintegration" of widows into society after the death of a husband.[29] Widows who eschewed remarriage, especially during the later Middle Ages, could wield considerable power and could assert their independence from men's economic control and control over their bodies. As Barbara Hanawalt asserts, "Widows were an object of concern in medieval society. On the one hand, they could be vulnerable, but, on the other, they were potentially independent, powerful individuals."[30] Laudine marries Yvain because not to do so would leave her without a protector, and, paradoxically, would demonstrate that perhaps she did not need one. The fact that Yvain did not at first prove to be a very effective protector and that Laudine developed a certain autonomy and functioned as a women alone lends Chrétien's work its subtlety and complexity and perhaps points to a shift in the values of the society in which his work was produced.[31]

If we consider Laudine's and Enide's reactions as set pieces of grief, we must also consider that men's grief was also described as being violent and extreme. For example, in the twelfth-century chanson de geste, *Raoul de Cambrai,* Raoul falls on the field of battle, struck down by Bernier, his one-time companion turned enemy. Raoul's uncle, Guerri, finds the body:

> Et vos G[ueri] sor un grant destrier bai;
> Son neveu trueve, s'en fu en grant esmai—
> il le regrete si con je vos dirai:
> "Biax nies," dist il, "por vos grant dolor ai."

[He finds his nephew, and was overcome with dismay—he mourns him as follows:"Nephew," he said, "I feel great grief for you."][32]

We witness the uncle's grief over the body of his nephew in its verbal expression, as well as in his actions:"G[ueris] se pasme sor le piz del baron," [Guerri falls in a faint on the noble baron's breast.][33] At another point in the text he sheds tears and rests his head in his hands in a conventional grief gesture:"et G[ueris] pleure, sa main a sa maisele. / R[aoul] en porte, dont li diex renovele." [and Guerri weeps, supporting his cheek on his hand. He carries Raoul's body away, and his grief for him breaks out anew.][34]

Another example of male grief is found in Marie de France's *Chaitivel,* the story of a woman loved by and loving four men who undertake to participate in a tournament to force her to decide among them. Three of them are killed and one is severely wounded. Here we have a rare example of a public, communal expression of grief:

> Mut esteïent pur eus dolent:
> Nel firent pas a escïent.
> La noise levat et li criz,
> Unques tels doels ne fu oïz!
> . . . Pur la dolur des chevaliers

> I aveit iteus deul milliers
> Ki lur ventaille deslacierent,
> Chevoiz et barbes detrahierent . . .

[Those who had mortally wounded them threw their shields to the ground, grief-stricken on their account, as they had not intended to kill them. A great outcry and clamour arose; such sorrow had never before been heard. The inhabitants of the city came out on to the field with no fear of the other fighters. In their grief over the knights a full two thousand men unfastened their visors and tore at their hair and their beards, united in their sorrow . . .][35]

The scene of general grief described here is overwhelmingly male. The grief of other men on the field of tournament is especially strong: they undo their helmets, tear at their beards and their hair, and exhibit traditional mourning gestures, similar to those exhibited by Enide and the other widows discussed here, and yet far from being stigmatized, their shared grief, stemming from combat at arms, is idealized.

One final example is particularly fitting here, because it represents the lamentation of a male over the death of his wife. In Philippe de Rémi's romance *La Manekine,* we see the king of Hungary mourn his wife:

> Pour li s'est mainte gens lassee
> De plours; meïsmement li rois
> Se pasma sur li mainte fois,
> Ne nus ne le puet conforter.
> Quant devant li en voit porter
> La roïne en la biere morte,
> Mout se plaint, mout se desconforte.
> Ains plus grans deuls ne fu veüs
> Que cil qui pour li fu meüs.[36]

[Many people spent all their tears over her. So, too, the did king swoon on her body many times. None could comfort him. When he saw her carried before him, dead in her coffin, he lamented greatly and was deeply distressed. Never had such great mourning been seen as that which he manifested for her.]

In the twelfth century (and early thirteenth),[37] then, the expression of grief is neither transgressive nor gender-specific. The tears and other gestures of mourning are neutral, or even positive signs, signaling the devotion of the widow toward her dead husband. The tears are, however, outward markers of a change of status of a woman, and an indication that she is "available," thus back in circulation. She thus courts temptation, and when she does not resist, she is vilified, her grief discounted, her tears read as a sign of hypocrisy.

What was a widow to do, then? Was she to retire from the world in perpetual mourning, refusing to remarry, donning sackcloth and ashes as did Judith, the timeless model for the virtuous widow? In the later Middle Ages, we find widely conflicting attitudes toward widowhood and remarriage. Most young widows, especially those with children, could not afford not to remarry. It became increasingly difficult for a widow to make a claim on her husband's estate, and even if she had been provided with a dower, her husband's family was not obliged to honor his commitments.

As in the Early Christian period, the widow's grief can be placed within a larger context of writings on the expression of grief in general, such as the sermon, "Consolation on the Death of Friends," delivered by Jean Gerson in 1403:

> Je ne veul pas dire . . . que on ne puisse bien plourer raisonnablement et plaindre la mort de ses amis et parens; condicion de humaine nature cecy requiert et contraint a faire, et n'est a la fois ni constant ni virtueulx qui s'en puisse du tout abstenir pour compassion naturelle que l'on ha; mais cecy s'entent des larmes et tristesses immoderees et excessives qu'aulcunes prennent sans reconfort

> [I do not mean to say . . . that one cannot weep reasonably and mourn the deaths of one's friends and relatives, for human nature requires and compels us to do so, and it is neither loyal nor virtuous to completely repress the natural compassion that one possesses, but I refer to immoderate and excessive sadness for which one can find no comfort.][38]

Advice for the widow was available in many forms, among them sermons and conduct books. One sermon directed toward widows was preached (in Latin) by Simon Cupersi, an Augustinian friar living in Bayeux in the early years of the fifteenth century. In it, Cupersi addresses general questions of conduct: widows must prudently manage their households (preferably with the help of sons and / or nephews); they must set an example for their family and must regularly attend mass and religious services. They must not be overly talkative. And regarding grief, Cupersi admonishes widows to put their trust in God and to seek consolation in faith. If they wallow in their "*tristitia*" and tears, and are visibly melancholic, they become vulnerable, a target for wicked men and for the devil who may wish to take advantage of their state and do them harm.[39] The tears that for Ambrose and Jerome had functioned as a sign of inaccessibility and wifely devotion have become an invitation to ill-intentioned suitors.

We also find advice directed at widows in conduct literature. In chapters CXIII and CXIIII of his *Livre* the Chevalier de la Tour Landry provides his daughters with examples of widows who did not remarry, demonstrating loyalty to their first husbands and concern for the children of their first marriages.[40] About one hundred years later, the Goodman of Paris instructs his wife to be "curieuse et songneuse" [solicitous and careful] regarding her husband's person. Referring to himself and to any subsequent husbands she may have, he explains that because of the difficulties a widow encounters in finding a second husband, when that second husband dies, she remains "toute esgaree et deconseillie long temps; et par plus grant raison quant elle pert le second" [completely distraught and disconsolate, and with better reason when she loses the second husband].[41] What is implied here, and this certainly has something to do with class, the Goodman's wife being of a somewhat lower station than the Chevalier's daughter, is that remaining unmarried is no longer the ideal solution, the spiritual origins of the earlier period giving way to an acknowledgment of the practical realities of the everyday lives of middle-class widows and even noblewomen, many of whom were young and had young children.

Among the most convincing writings regarding the widow's grief and the dangers of an excess of tears comes from two women who lived during the fifteenth century, two who had themselves experienced widowhood: Christine de Pizan and Anne de Beaujeu.

Christine de Pizan returns again and again in her writing to her own experience of widowhood.[42] She was one individual who experienced tremendous difficulties in gaining access to funds and spent much time tied up in litigation toward that end. In the first twenty of her *Cent Balades,* in the first nine *Rondeaux,* and in the *Livre du Chemin de Long Estude,* Christine represents herself as a woman in perpetual mourning.[43] Yet, in her treatise, the *Livre des Trois Vertus,* where she devotes three chapters to appropriate conduct for widows, she advocates restraint.[44] As in much of the writing concerning widows, the greater part of these three chapters is taken up with practical matters: all widows, princesses or not, should be familiar with their late husband's financial and property dealings; they must know how to claim what is rightly theirs and how to look out for the welfare of their children; they must learn how to govern (for princesses) or manage whatever lands or property they possess as well as those in their employ. The princess must be aware of the social etiquette required of her. She may not marry without her friends' approval, and must follow a strict code of conduct regulating her public and private interactions with men.

But what about grief? Christine is sympathetic to the emotional state of the widow and opens the first of three chapters on widowhood in a tone of gentle sympathy:

. . . se il avient que la sage princepce demeure veuve, n'est pas doubte qu'elle paindra et pleurera sa partie si que bonne foy le donne; se tendra closement meismement un temps aprés le service et obseques, a petite clarté de jour, a piteux et adoulé habit et attour selon l'onneste usage. Si n'obliera pas l'ame de son seigneur, ains en priera et fera prier tres devotement par grant soing en messes, services, aumosnes, offerendes et oblacions, et moult la fera recommander a toute gent de devocion. Et ne durera pas pou de temps ceste memoire ne ses biensfais, mais tant qu'elle vivra.

[The good princess becoming a widow will grieve and cry for her spouse, as good faith dictates. After the burial service she will follow custom's requirements and withdraw for a time in dim light, in piteous and mournful costume and headdress. Ever mindful of her lord's soul, she will pray and will have prayers said devoutly in masses. She will organize services, alms offerings, and oblations, and will recommend his memory to all devout people, requesting their prayers. Such remembrances and good deeds will not be limited to a brief period but will continue as long as she lives.][45]

The ritual aspect is stressed here, as is the need to follow traditional mourning customs. Yet there is a balance—Christine also knows that the activities of life must continue and that the widow's grief must remain within bounds:

. . . que nonobstant sa tres grant perte et son grant dueil et regraiz de la mort de son seigneur et de la bonne loiale amour qu'elle lui portoit, il convient estre pacient de tout ce qu'il plaist a Nostre Seigneur estre fait . . .

[. . . in spite of her great loss, her mourning, her sorrow over her lord's death, and the admirable, loyal love she bore him, still she must be patient in accepting all it pleases Our Lord to do . . .][46]

She continues in this more spiritual vein:

. . . tous sommes néz pour aler celle voye quant lui plaira. Si pourroit bien pechier et courroucier Nostre Seigneur de tant estre adoulee, et par si long espace. Si convient que elle prengne autre maniere de vie, ou grever pourroit son ame et sa santé, si n'en seroit pas de mieulx a ses nobles enfans, qui encores ont tous mestier d'elle.

[. . . All of us are born to walk that same way whenever He so decides. So it is sinful and displeasing to God for mourners to grieve overmuch and for too long a time. Therefore, she must adopt that manner of life which will avoid damage to both her soul and to her health. Furthermore, she must turn from deep grief to her noble children, who still have need for her.][47]

The statement that widows must not grieve excessively, coupled with the expression of concern for the welfare of the overly grieving widow's children that we saw earlier in the writings of the Church Fathers, can be interpreted in two ways: Christine has either internalized the teachings of the Church Fathers, or she is speaking from within the subject position of "the widow," drawing on her own experience and wishing to share her own life lessons with her reader.

In her chapter addressed to "widows young and old" who do not belong to the noble classes, Christine passes even more quickly over the grief reaction, saying "nous, meues par pitie de vous cheues en l'estat de veuvete par Mort, qui despoillees vous a de voz mariz, qui qu'ils fussent" [we pity each one of you in the state of widowhood because death has deprived you of your husbands, whoever they have been]. She then moves on to a discussion of practical matters such as the trials and tribulations that await them.[48] It is somewhat ironic that Christine, who on so many occasions eloquently rehearses her own experience of grief, advocates moderation in the *Trois Vertus.* One is led to wonder if she was not perhaps influenced by the cry for restraint voiced by Jean Gerson (cited above), her close ally in the debate over the *Roman de la Rose.*[49]

In her *Enseignements,* Anne de France, Duchess of Bourbon, offers her daughter, Suzanne de Bourbon, similar advice on how to behave if her husband were to die and she should remain "vefve ou seulle et chargee d'enfants" [widowed or alone and burdened with children].[50] Anne guides her daughter toward a middle ground, counseling her to be patient and to comport herself wisely—to act neither like "ces folles, qui effraiées se tempestent et crient" [foolish women who rant and rave] nor like those who act, after only a month's time has passed, "sans qu'il leur souviengne plus de leur bon mary qui est mort . . . qui est moult deshonnest a femmes de bien" [as though they no longer recall their dead husband . . . which is very unworthy of good women].[51] She continues, advocating moderation:

Au regard du dueil, le plus grant n'est pas le plus loué. Car . . . en toutes choses on doit tenir le moien, voire ès choses esquelles on puist, courroucer Dieu par excès; mais de prières, jeusnes, et aulmosnes, femmes vefves n'en peuvent trop faire: car dévotion doist estre la principalle occupation des femmes vefves.

[Concerning grief, the greatest is not the most praiseworthy, for in all things one must act with moderation, considering that in such matters, one may anger God by excess. But as for prayer, fasting, and almsgiving, widows can never do too much; for devotion must be the widow's principal occupation.][52]

Like Christine before her, Anne goes on to address the practical concerns about running a household, not trusting servants, etc.[53]

In the writing of these two more "modern" widows, one a nonaristocrat who nevertheless moved within the world of the court, the other a titled noblewoman, we have the first indications that the free expression of grief has become a more negative sign. What factors might explain this shift? First of all, one must ask if there really is a shift, or if there is simply a distinction between fictionalized representations—the tears of the widows in the twelfth-century texts described above are pure sign, whereas the tears discussed by Christine de Pizan and Anne de France are "real" tears.[54] This might explain the paradox I alluded to earlier—that Christine as self-represented mourner as both subject and object of her writing, has difficulty controlling her textual tears, whereas Christine as speaking subject in the *Trois Vertus* divorces herself from her original position and provides advice from a new authorial stance. The case of Anne de France is less complicated than that of Christine, because she has not previously constructed herself as a grieving widow but is writing much more in the tradition of the Chevalier de la Tour Landry, illustrating proper behavior for her aristocratic young daughter.

Ironically, the writings of both women with their practical aim as the education of women, continue to serve the same function as the writings of the Church Fathers: to teach them to live in accordance with the values of the society of which they are a part. These values, specifically the attitudes toward the widow's tears and her manifestations of grief, change through time, but one constant remains—the systems from which the values emerged are largely constructed and controlled by men. The textual tears of the twelfth-century widows, coupled with their sexual transgressions, can in some sense, be read as a sign of resistance,[55] while the moderate tears that Christine advocates can be read as a gesture of compliance.

Notes

1. For more on representations of the figure of Judith in the Middle Ages, see my essay, "Ambiguity and Appropriation: The Story of Judith in Medieval Narrative and Iconographic Tradition," in *Telling Tales: Medieval Narratives and the Folk Tradition,* ed. Francesca Canade Sautman, Diana Conchado and Giuseppe Carlo DiScipio (New York: St. Martin's Press, 1998), pp. 79–99.

2. Among the fine studies on the motif of the Widow of Ephesus in the medieval French tradition, see Norris J. Lacy, "La Femme au Tombeau: Anonymous Fabliau of the Thirteenth Century," diss. Indiana University, 1967, and Heather Arden, "Grief, Widowhood, and Women's Sexuality in Medieval French Literature," in *Upon My Husband's Death: Widows in the*

Literature and Histories of Medieval Europe, ed. Louise Mirrer (Ann Arbor: University of Michigan Press, 1992), pp. 305–319.

3. For a fuller discussion of the dichotomy between the representation of the chaste and the sexually voracious widow, see chapter 9, "'Wel at ese': Widowhood," in Margaret Hallissey's *Clean Maids, True Wives, Steadfast Widows: Chaucer's Women and Medieval Codes of Conduct* (Westport, CT: Greenwood Press, 1993), pp. 135–161.

4. I deal with this question in great detail in chapter 3 of my "Signs of Sorrow: The Expression of Grief and The Representation of Mourning in Fifteenth-Century French Culture," diss., City University of New York Graduate School, 1996.

5. Hallissey, *Clean Maids,* p. 136.

6. James A. Brundage, "The Merry Widow's Serious Sister: Remarriage in Classical Canon Law," in *Matrons and Marginal Women in Medieval Society,* ed. Robert R. Edwards and Vickie Ziegler (Woodbridge, Suffolk, UK: Boydell Press, 1995), pp. 33–48.

7. Ambrose of Milan, "De viduis," PL 16: 258. Translated as "The Treatise of St. Ambrose, Bishop of Milan, Concerning Widows," in *Select Library of Nicene and Post-Nicene Fathers,* 2nd series, vol. 10 (Wheaton, IL: Christian Classics Ethereal Library, 1961), p. 397.

8. PL 16: 258; trans. "Treatise Concerning Widows," p. 397.

9. PL 16:263; trans. "Treatise Concerning Widows," pp. 399–340.

10. This is also the opinion of St. John Chrysostom, as expressed in his treatise "Against Remarriage." Nevertheless, this particular Father of the Church had quite a different attitude towards the widow's tears, as shall become clear below. For the treatise, see *"On Virginity" and "Against Remarriage,"* trans. Sally Rieger Shore (Lewiston, NY: The Edwin Mellen Press, 1983), pp. 129–157; the introductory notes to the bilingual Greek/French edition of this text also merit consultation. See also *"A une jeune veuve"* and *"Sur le mariage unique,"* ed. Bernard Grillet, Sources Chrétiennes, no. 138 (Paris: Editions du Cerf, 1968).

11. Joyce E. Salisbury, *Church Fathers, Independent Virgins* (London: Verso, 1991), p. 29.

12. Jo Ann McNamara, "Wives and Widows in Early Christian Thought," *International Journal of Women's Studies* 2.6 (1979), p. 588.

13. Jerome, *Select Letters of Saint Jerome,* trans. F. A. Wright (Cambridge, MA: Harvard University Press, 1933), pp. 256–257.

14. Although a considerable amount of scholarship has been produced concerning the legal status of widows, most concentrates on English widows in the later Middle Ages. Nevertheless, despite specific details dictated by time and location, the concerns expressed remain remarkably consistent. See Barbara Hanawalt, "Remarriage as an Option for Urban and Rural Widows in Late Medieval England," in *Wife and Widow in Medieval England,* ed. Sue Sheridan Walker (Ann Arbor: University of Michigan Press, 1993), pp. 141–163; Caroline M. Barron, Introduction, *Medieval London Widows, 1300*

− *1500,* ed. Caroline M. Barron and Anne F. Sutton (London: Hambledon Press, 1994), pp. xiii–xxxiv; Chapter 8, "Widows," in Hernietta Leyser, *Medieval Women: A Social History of Women in England 450 − 1500* (New York: St. Martin's Press, 1995), pp. 168–186; Joel T. Rosenthal, "Fifteenth-Century Widows and Widowhood: Bereavement, Reintegration, and Life Choices," *Wife and Widow in Medieval England,* pp. 33–58. One study on the status of widows in medieval France is Harry A. Miskimin, "Widows Not So Merry: Women and the Courts in Late Medieval France," in *Upon My Husband's Death: Widows in Literature and Histories of Medieval Europe,* ed. Louise Mirrer (Ann Arbor: University of Michigan Press, 1992), pp. 207–219. It is interesting to note the inclusion of the word "merry" in two of the above-cited titles. Perhaps our own cultural constructions of what constitutes "appropriate" behavior for widows need to be considered as well.

15. John Chrysostom, *Homilae in Ioannem* No. 62. English translation by Sister Thomas Aquinas Goggin, in *Commentary on Saint John the Apostle and Evangelist. Homilies 44–88* (Washington, D.C.: The Catholic University of America Press, 1960), p. 177.

16. According to Frederic C. Tubach's *Index exemplorum: A Handbook of Medieval Religious Tales* (Helsinki: Suomalainen Tiedeakatemia, 1969), the pattern of the story, found in the *Sermones vulgares* of Jacques de Vitry, is as follows: "A widow, matron of Ephesus, mourning at the tomb of her recently deceased husband, is consoled by the sentinel at the gallows," p. 397. See also motifs K2213.1 and T231.2, Stith Thompson, *Motif-Index of Folk Literature A Classification of Narrative Elements in Folktales, Ballads, Myths, Fables, Medieval Romances, Exampla, Fabliaux, Jest-Books and Local Legends* (Bloomington: Indiana University Press, 1932).

17. See note 2 above.

18. *The Book of Sainte Foy,* trans. Pamela Sheingorn (Philadelphia: University of Pennsylvania Press, 1995), pp. 115–116.

19. *Nouveau recueil complet des fabliaux,* ed. Willem Noomen and Nico van den Boogard, vol. 3 (Assen: Van Gorcum, 1983), p. 400. Translation mine.

20. *Nouveau recueil complet des fabliaux,* vol. 3, p. 400.

21. In *Gallic Salt: Eighteen Fabliaux Translated from Old French,* ed. and trans. Robert Harrison (Berkeley: University of California Press, 1974), pp. 343–345.

22. Although "La Veuve" begins with the detailed description of the widow's violent grief, the misogynist message of the piece goes way beyond that grief and focuses (somewhat obsessively) on the widow's sexual transgressions. In her version of the story, Marie de France adds elements that make it something other than a "fabliau." See Hans R. Runte, "'Alfred's Book,' Marie de France and the Matron of Ephesus," *Romance Philology* 36.4 (1983), pp. 556–564.

23. Marie de France, *Fables,* ed. and trans. Harriet Spiegel (Toronto: University of Toronto Press, 1987), pp. 92–93.

24. Arden, "Grief, Widowhood, and Women's Spirituality, " p. 306.

25. Arden, "Grief, Widowhood, and Women's Spirituality," p. 314.

26. Chrétien de Troyes, *Le Chevalier au Lion (Yvain)*, ed. Mario Roques (Paris: H. Champion, 1982), pp. 35–36. Translation from *The Knight with the Lion* in *The Complete Romances of Chrétien de Troyes*, trans. David Staines (Bloomington and Indianapolis: Indiana University Press, 1990), p. 279.

27. Chrétien de Troyes, *Erec et Enide*, ed. Carleton W. Carroll (New York: Garland, 1987); trans. David Staines, *The Complete Romances*, pp. 57–58.

28. The term is Arden's.

29. Rosenthal's study deals with the fifteenth century, but this aspect of his argument is also true for the earlier period.

30. Barbara Hanawalt, "Remarriage as an Option," p. 141.

31. In her chapter "The question of women in *Yvain* and *Le Chevalier de la Charrete*," in *Women Readers and the Ideology of Gender in Old French Verse Romance* (Cambridge: Cambridge University Press, 1992), Roberta L. Krueger fully contextualizes the episode within its sociocultural setting and provides a cogent and compelling reading of Laudine's actions.

32. *Raoul de Cambrai*, ed. and trans. Sarah Kay (Oxford: Clarendon Press, 1992), pp. 194–195.

33. Sarah Kay, *Raoul de Cambrai*, pp. 194–195.

34. Sarah Kay, *Raoul de Cambrai*, pp. 212–213.

35. Marie de France, *Lais*, ed. Jean Rynchner (Paris: H. Champion, 1983), p. 147. Translation from *The Lais of Marie de France*, trans. Glyn S. Burgess and Keith Busby (Harmondsworth, Middlesex: Penguin Books, 1986), p. 107.

36. Philippe de Rémi, Sire de Beaumanoir, *Oeuvres poétiques*, vol. 1 (Paris: Firmin Didot, 1884), p. 8. Translation mine.

37. Another example of male grief from the thirteenth century, although somewhat more complex, is the case of Saint Louis. See William Chester Jordan, "The Case of Saint Louis," *Viator* 19 (1988), pp. 209–217.

38. Jean Gerson, *Oeuvres complètes*, ed. Monseigneur Glorieux (Paris: Desclee, 1960), 7.1, p. 325. Translation mine.

39. Bayeux, MS 48, fol. 33r–34v.

40. *Le Livre du Chevalier de la Tour Landry pour l'enseignement de ses filles*, ed. Anatole Montaiglon (Paris: P. Jannet, 1854), pp. 220–224.

41. *Le Ménagier de Paris*, ed. Georgine E. Brereton and Janet M. Ferrier (Oxford: Clarendon Pres, 1981), p. 99.

42. The question of the sincerity of Christine's grief has been widely debated and was the subject of a paper entitled "The Widow's Voice: Self-Consciousness and the Construction of Subjectivity in Christine de Pizan" presented by the author at the 1995 Modern Language Convention in Chicago. Among scholars who have taken up the question of Christine's widowhood are: Barbara Altmann, "Les poèmes de veuvage de Christine de Pizan," *Scintilla* 1 (1984), pp. 24–47; Kevin Brownlee, "Widowhood, Sexuality and Gender in Christine de Pizan," *Romanic Review* 86.2 (1995), pp. 339–353; Liliane Dulac, "Un mythe didactique chez Christine de Pizan: Sémiramis ou la Veuve héroïque," in *Mélanges de Philologie Romane offerts à Charles Camproux*, Vol. I (Montpellier: CEO, 1978), pp. 315–343; Charity

Cannon Willard, "A Fifteenth-Century View of Women's Role in Medieval Society: Christine de Pizan's *Livre des Trois Vertus,*" in *The Role of Women in the Middle Ages: Papers of the Sixth Annual Conference of the Center for Medieval and Early Renaissance Studies,* SUNY at Binghamton, May 6–7, 1972, ed. Rosemarie Thee Morwedge (Albany: SUNY Press, 1975), pp. 90–120.

43. The *Cent Balades* and the *Rondeaux* are found in the three-volume edition, *Oeuvres poétiques de Christine de Pizan,* ed. Maurice Roy (Paris: Firmin Didot, 1886). The *Livre du Chemin de Long Estude* was edited by Robert Püschel (Berlin: R. Damköhler, 1881).

44. Christine de Pizan, *Le Livre des Trois Vertus,* ed. Charity Cannon Willard and Eric Hicks (Paris: H. Champion, 1989), trans. Charity Cannon Willard as *A Medieval Woman's Mirror of Honor: The Treasury of the City of Ladies* (Tenafly, NJ: Bard Hall Press, 1989). The three chapters in question are: Book I, chapters 22 and 23, and Book III, chapter 4.

45. *Livre des Trois Vertus,* p. 83; *A Medieval Woman's Mirror,* p. 119. Christine also speaks of tears in a more general context in the *Cité des Dames;* see Maureen Cheney Curnow, "The *Livre de la Cité des Dames* de Christine de Pisan: A Critical Edition," diss. Vanderbilt University, 1975, pp. 657–659.

46. *Livre des Trois Vertus,* p. 83; *A Medieval Woman's Mirror,* p. 119–120.

47. *Livre des Trois Vertus,* p. 83; *A Medieval Woman's Mirror,* p. 120.

48. *Livre des Trois Vertus,* p. 188; *A Medieval Woman's Mirror,* p. 197.

49. For another case of Christine being inspired by Gerson, see Charity Cannon Willard's discussion of Christine's use of the human body as analogy for the organization of society, *Christine de Pizan: Her Life and Works* (New York: Persea, 1984), pp. 177–178. It is interesting to speculate, however, whether the influence went in only one direction, or whether Christine may have exerted some influence on Gerson's thought.

50. Anne de Beaujeu, *Les Enseignements d'Anne de France, Duchesse de Bourbonnais et d'Auvergne à sa fille Susanne de Bourbon,* ed. A.-M. Chazaud (Moulins: C. Desrosiers, 1878), p. 114. Translation mine.

51. *Les Enseignements,* p. 115.

52. *Les Enseignements,* pp. 115–116.

53. Charity Cannon Willard discusses Christine's influence on the younger writer in her essay, in "Anne de France, Reader of Christine de Pizan," in *The Reception of Christine de Pizan from the Fifteenth Through the Nineteenth Centuries: Visitors to The City,* ed. Glenda McLeod (Lewiston, NY: Mellen, 1991), pp. 59–70.

54. This distinction may also help to explain the critiques leveled against the grieving Saint Louis by Jean de Joinville as discussed by William Chester Jordan in the article cited above (see note 37). For a discussion of the representation of grief in chronicles of the later middle ages, see chapter 6 of my "Signs of Sorrow."

55. On the construction of the female body as a site of resistance, see E. Jane Burns, *Bodytalk: When Women Speak in Old French Literature* (Philadelphia: University of Pennsylvania Press, 1993).

CONTRIBUTORS

LESLIE ABEND CALLAHAN recently completed a post-doctoral fellowship at the University of Pennsylvania. She has also been a Visiting Assistant Professor of French at Vassar College and has taught at SUNY-New Paltz and Marist College.

CINDY L. CARLSON is an assistant professor in the English Department of Metropolitan State College. Her writings on the legal material of the trials of Joseph and Mary in the N-town cycle have been published previously as have been her writings on the legal problems of marriage in Shakespeare's *Measure for Measure*.

SUSANNAH MARY CHEWNING recently completed her doctorate at Drew University in Madison, New Jersey. She is teaching at Kean College and Montclair State College. She is currently editing a volume on women's spirituality and sexuality in medieval literature.

REBECCA HAYWARD received her doctorate from Gonville and Caius College, Cambridge University, and received an M. Phil. in Medieval Literature in 1994. She holds an M. A. in English from the University of Canterbury. She is now a tutor in the English Department at the University of Auckland, New Zealand.

KATHLEEN M. HOBBS is a doctoral candidate in the Program in Comparative Literature and adjunct faculty member in the Department of English at Rutgers University, New Brunswick, New Jersey. She is currently at work on her dissertation, *Romance and the Formation of Ethnic Identity in England and Wales, ca. 1050 to ca. 1200*.

KATHLEEN COYNE KELLY is Associate Professor of English at Northeastern University. She has published in *Allegorica, Arthuriana, Assays, Parergon,* and

Studies in Philology. With Marina Leslie she has edited a volume of essays, *Menacing Virgins: Representing Virginity in the Middle Ages and Renaissance* (University of Delaware Press, 1999) and is currently completing a book, *Hymenologies: Testing Virginity in the Middle Ages.*

MONIKA OTTER is Associate Professor of English and Comparative Literature at Dartmouth College. She is the author of *Inventiones: Fiction and Referentiality in Twelfth-Century English Historical Writing* (University of North Carolina Press, 1996) and several articles on medieval Latin literature.

SANDRA PIERSON PRIOR is affiliated with Columbia University, where she directs the Composition program and teaches medieval literature. She is the author of two books on the Pearl Poet (*The Pearl Poet Revisited* and *The Fayre Formez of the Pearl Poet*), an essay on Marie de France's *Eliduc,* and articles on Chaucer. Her other scholarly interests include medieval drama, typology, and the apocalyptic tradition. Her essay for this volume, "Virginity and Sacrifice in Chaucer's 'Physician's Tale'," is part of a larger study on the sacrificial role of women in medieval narrative.

ANNA ROBERTS is Assistant Professor of French at Miami University, Ohio. She has published numerous articles on medieval and early modern French literature and political writings and is the editor of *Violence Against Women in Medieval Texts* (University Press of Florida, 1998). She is currently working on a study of women's friendships in Old French texts.

SARAH SALIH holds a B. A. in English and Related Literature and an M. A. in Medieval Studies from the University of York. She recently completeted her doctoral thesis, "Medieval Virginities in Text and Practice" supervised by David Lawton and Cath Sharrock, at the University of East Anglia, where she is also teaching.

ANGELA JANE WEISL is an assistant professor of English and Women's Studies at Seton Hall University. She is the author of *Conquering the Reign of Femeny: Gender and Genre in Chaucer's Romance* (D. S. Brewer, 1995) as well as several articles on medieval subjects.

INDEX